D1447089

Jews in Poland-Lithuania
in the Eighteenth Century

Jews in Poland-Lithuania in the Eighteenth Century

A Genealogy of Modernity

Gershon David Hundert

UNIVERSITY OF CALIFORNIA PRESS

Berkeley / Los Angeles

The publisher gratefully acknowledges the generous contribution to
this book by the Jewish Studies Endowment Fund of the University
of California Press Associates, which is supported by a major gift from
the S. Mark Taper Foundation.

University of California Press
Berkeley and Los Angeles, California

Library of Congress Cataloging-in-Publication Data

Hundert, Gershon David.
   Jews in Poland-Lithuania in the eighteenth century : a genealogy
of modernity / Gershon David Hundert.
      p.   cm.
   Includes bibliographical references and index.
   ISBN 0-520-23844-3 (alk. paper).
      1. Jews—Poland—History—18th century.   2. Jews—Poland—
Economic conditions—18th century.   3. Jews—Poland—Social
conditions—18th century.   4. Poland—Ethnic relations.   5. Jews—
Lithuania—History—18th century.   6. Jews—Lithuania—Economic
conditions—18th century.   7. Jews—Lithuania—Social conditions—
18th century.   8. Lithuania—Ethnic relations.   9. Mysticism—
Judaism—History—18th century.   10. Hasidism—Europe, Eastern—
History—18th century.   I. Title.
DS135.P6 H85   2004
943.8'004924—dc21   2003003880
                                                              CIP

Manufactured in the United States of America

13   12   11   10   09   08   07   06   05   04
10   9   8   7   6   5   4   3   2   1

In memory of Charles Hundert (1917–2001)

The story is told of one who lit a candle and it was extinguished; he lit another and it too was extinguished. He said, How long! I am weary and I despair of this candle; I shall await the light of the sun.

So it was with Israel. They were enslaved in Egypt and Moses arose and redeemed them, but they were enslaved again . . . in Babylonia . . . in Greece . . . and in the evil Edom. Israel said . . . we are weary of being enslaved and redeemed and enslaved again. From now on we will not look for light from flesh and blood . . . rather we shall await the light of the Holy One Blessed Be He.

Midrash Tehillim

דש וויר פוילן נון מעהר מיט דעם ריקן אן זעהן
דש איזט אייני מדינה זאגי איך   וויא תשעה באב
איין יום טוב איזט פר ניכטש איזט דארין גזארגט אלש
פיר דען אברגלויבן אונד פיר קארן בראנדטוויין. נון מעהר
אויך פרפאשט פערדי דאהער מאן זא גשווינד אלש
מעגליך דורך פאסירן מוז.

Moses Mendelssohn to his wife, Fromet, July 1777

Contents

Maps

Tables

Preface

More than once during the very long period of preparation of this book, I have felt like a pirate, raiding the work of colleagues and predecessors. This is a hybrid work that combines close and careful analysis of certain issues in the service of a very broad synthetic argument about the Jewish experience in recent times. Consequently, the book is based in part on my own research and substantially on work done by scholars mainly in Poland, Israel, and North America. I have tried to acknowledge all of these debts in the notes. If I have failed to credit a source, I ask forgiveness.

A recent tendency in the historical profession has focused attention on marginal and oppressed groups, for example, homosexuals, women, and Jews. This tendency to look at the edges of "mainstream" culture is often in the service of contemporary argument for a more inclusive and accepting society. I both reject and accept this trend in this book. On the one hand, I have tried to focus attention on the *majority* of Jews and their situation in East Central Europe in the eighteenth century; even the clarification of marginality requires a firm understanding of the center. On the other hand, Jews in Poland-Lithuania were themselves marginal both in terms of their relative numerical significance and in terms of political power. I have learned from my colleagues who study colonized groups how the historiography of the colonized encodes the dominance of the elite. I have tried to write about Jews without using the language of dominance and subjugation as if their situation were defined by their place in the state.

I have also tried to avoid essentializing the eastern European Jewish community. In order to make my broader argument, however, I have had

xv

to commit two "sins": not only do I speak of eastern European Jewry collectively and corporately, but my thesis proceeds from the more recent to the more distant past. I began my work in an effort to explain why, in my view, the mentality of eastern European Jewry, even as they moved in the nineteenth and early twentieth centuries to many destinations, continued to include, at its very core, a positive evaluation of Jewishness. For all of the myriad changes in belief and practice, ideology and worldview, this positive view of themselves as Jews persisted, and its roots can be found in the eighteenth century among the ancestors of the majority of Jews in the world today. Seeing matters at this stratospheric and, at least for me, breathtaking level of generalization will undoubtedly be troublesome to some readers, whose minds will move immediately to the exceptions. To these readers I offer the more limited findings in the various chapters of the book, which I hope they will find valuable, even if detached from my framing hypothesis.

Use of the word "genealogy" in the title is intended to be an allusion to Nietzsche, who used the term to affirm multiplicity and diversity. It is my attempt to free the term "modernity" from its ossified or coagulated set of associations in Jewish historiography, its being linked to particular criteria such as Enlightenment, Emancipation, urbanization, and the like, and thus to let "modernity" float freely, signifying only a vast set of possibilities during the past two hundred years or so.

A Note on Place-Names and Transliteration

The thorny issue of how to designate the names of places has not been easy to resolve consistently. The simplest solution would have been to use exclusively the contemporary name of the town or region with the exception of places like Kiev, Kraków, and Warsaw that have well-known and commonly used designations in English. There are, though, serious problems with this solution. Since this book is concerned primarily with the period before the partitions of Poland, I have designated places named in the text by their eighteenth-century names. The first time a place is mentioned, the contemporary name of the place is given in parentheses together, if appropriate, with other names. As a reference authority for contemporary place-names, I have relied on *Merriam-Webster's Geographical Dictionary,* 3d ed. (2001). All the variants on place-names are found in the index. Modern place-names are used on the maps for the convenience of the reader.

I have used a highly simplified system of transliteration from Hebrew that is intended simply as a guide to pronunciation. The reader who knows Hebrew will be able to deduce what word is meant, while the reader who does not will be able to know how the word is pronounced. There are no dashes between articles and the words they modify. Only proper names are capitalized.

Abbreviations

ADO	Administracja dóbr opatowskich
AGAD	Archiwum Główne Akt Dawnych, Warsaw
AGZ	*Akta grodzkie i ziemskie z czasów Rzeczypospolitej polskiej z archiwum tak zwanego Bernardyńskiego we Lwowie.* Edited by O. Pietruski, K. Liske, and A. Prochaska. 24 vols. Lwów, 1868–1931.
AP	Archiwum Państwowe, Kraków
BZIH	*Biuletyn Żydowskiego Instytutu Historycznego*
CAHJP	Central Archive for the History of the Jewish People, Jerusalem
KH	*Kwartalnik Historyczny*
KHKM	*Kwartalnik Historii Kultury Materialnej*
MDSC	*Materiały do dziejów Sejmu Czteroletniego.* 6 vols. Wrocław, 1955–69.
MGWJ	*Monatsschrift für Geschichte und Wissenschaft des Judentums*
PML	*Pinkas hamedinah, o pinkas va'ad hakehilot harashiyot bimedinat Lita.* Edited by Simon Dubnow. Berlin, 1925.
PVAA	*Pinkas va'ad arba aratsot: Likkutei takkanot ketavim vereshumot.* Edited by Israel Halper[i]n. 1945. 2d ed., vol. 1, rev. and ed. Israel Bartal. Jerusalem, 1990.
TB	Babylonian Talmud
TJ	Jerusalem Talmud

VL   *Volumina legum: Przedruk zbioru praw staraniem XX.*
pijarów w Warszawie, od roku 1732 do roku [1793] wydanego.
10 vols. Warsaw, 1980.

Introduction

I write to advocate a revision of the understanding of modernity in Jewish history. Treatments of the modern history of Jews in Europe have tended to minimize or even omit the community in Poland-Lithuania in the eighteenth century because the defining criteria of modernity cannot be found there. Most often, these defining criteria of modernity in Jewish history are understood to be the progressive integration of Jews into society at large and the exchange of particularistic Jewish values, in varying degrees, for a more universal worldview. Whatever the criteria, the largest concentration of Jews in the world is omitted from the discussion. Since historians have always been part of the very process they describe, they tend to seek out the origins of modernity along the same continuum of westernization in which they find themselves, rather than seeking it in the considerably different experience of eastern European Jews. I contend that the criteria for dividing Jewish history into periods should be drawn from the Jewish experience itself—in particular, from the experience of the majority of the Jewish people.

The contention that modern Jewish history should be seen in its own right is not new. Almost seventy years ago, Benzion Dinur (1884–1973), the founder of Zionist historiography, pointed out that historians have most often invoked criteria drawn from outside the realm of Jewish historical action to define the modern period in Jewish history. By action, he meant something akin to what contemporary students of postcolonial history refer to as "agency." Dinur rejected both the Jewish Enlightenment (Haskalah) and Emancipation as beginning points of modernity, because neither development reflected "the real historical content" of the

life of Jews in the modern period, and nor could either be identified with
the realm of Jewish "historical activity." For Dinur, modern Jewish history began with the ʿaliyah ("going up" to the Holy Land) of Judah Hassid of Szydłowiec (ca. 1660–1700) and his several hundred Shabbatean
followers in 1700. By this act of emigration in preparation for the return
of Shabbetai Tsevi (d. 1676), whom they believed to be the Messiah, these
Jews became agents of their own history. "There is no other event that is
so interpenetrated with the historical paths of the people of Israel in modern times in all their variety," Dinur writes. "This period . . . which culminated with international recognition of Jewish independence in the land
of Israel . . . necessarily begins with the first ʿaliyah, which saw itself as a
harbinger of redemption."[1]

Dinur's analysis is obviously open to criticism as a Whiggish choice dic-
tated by his understanding of Jewish history as leading inevitably to the
establishment of the State of Israel in 1948.[2] On the other hand, the very
enterprise of Jewish historiography is predicated on the assumption that
Jews have *made* their own history and have not merely been carried along
like so much flotsam and jetsam on the currents of wider trends. Gershom
Scholem (1897–1981), the towering figure of twentieth-century Jewish
studies and architect of the study of Jewish mysticism, suggested that the
Shabbatean messianic movement of 1665–66 marked a break in Jewish history. He argued that a new period emerged at that time in which growing numbers of people, intoxicated by the belief that the Messiah had come,
freed themselves in varying degrees from the regimens of traditional Jewish society.[3] Be this as it may, surely the so-called freeing of the individual had more to do with Renaissance values and subsequent developments
in European thought than it did with "the mystical messiah."

Whatever criteria have been used, the historical literature implies that
for a century or more after it had reached western Europe, the majority
of Jews, living in the largest Jewish community,[4] eluded modernity. This

1. Benzion Dinur, "Hazemanim hahadashim betoledot yisraʾel: Avhanatam mahutam udemutam," reprinted in id., *Bemifneh hadorot* (Jerusalem, 1972), 29. The article first appeared
in *Zion* 2 (1937).
2. Gershon Hundert, "Reflections on the 'Whig' Interpretation of Jewish History: *Maʿas-
sei banim siman leʾavot*," in *Truth and Compassion: Essays on Judaism and Religion in Memory
of Rabbi Solomon Frank*, ed. Howard Joseph et al. (Waterloo, Ont., 1983), 111–19.
3. Gershom Scholem, "Redemption through Sin," in id., *The Messianic Idea in Judaism
and Other Essays on Jewish Spirituality* (New York, 1971), 78–141 (first published in 1937).
4. The issue here is not size per se; obviously there are vanguards in history. My concern is the exclusive focus on that "vanguard" in a way that omits the pattern of development of the majority of Jews in Europe.

is the approach I seek to revise. I believe that there are grave distortions in the way scholars have described modernity in Jewish history. Historians have placed too much emphasis on change and ideology, too much emphasis on religious behavior and belief as indicators of change; too much emphasis on regions where few Jews lived and not enough on the areas where most Jews lived. History is not a train that progressively moved across Europe from west to east bringing the same developments to different countries, each in its turn. Such thinking involves the twin fallacies, in historical contexts, of teleology and linearity. Jews in Europe responded to the developments associated with modernity—the rise of the bourgeoisie, technological change, the Enlightenment—along a continuum from total identification to utter rejection, all of which are part of modern Jewish history. The responses of many Jews in East Central Europe to the Hasidic movement, for example, are an important part of the same story. There is no single goal toward which human history moves, and there is no consistent direction in which humanity has developed.

Consequently, I propose to empty the term "modernity" of all but its chronological content and to define it merely as roughly the past two centuries. Anyone inhabiting that time period is thus, by definition, "modern." In this way, we free ourselves from the restrictive dichotomy (and coercive discourse) of "tradition and change" and can confront the more complex, and more human, reality of the coexistence of a multitude of behaviors and outlooks that were constantly in a state of flux. This book looks at the question: "Who were the Jews when they encountered modernity?" I suggest that the various aspects of the Jewish experience highlighted here formed a particular *mentalité* and self-evaluation at the core of Jewish identity.

To understand the developments among Jews of recent centuries properly, one must investigate the experiences of the majority of Jews in their own contexts. Because the ancestors of about 80 percent of world Jewry lived in the Commonwealth of Poland-Lithuania in the eighteenth century, it is they who must be placed at the center of any understanding of the Jewish experience. The lives and values of such a great number were not marginal and should not be subordinated to some extraneous "progressive" model of modernity. By close reading of the past, I hope to identify a magmatic level of Jewish experience, that is, the elemental continuities that persist from the early modern period almost to the present. I contend that the conventional aspects of modernity have been grafted, often imperfectly, onto those elemental continuities through adaptation, appropriation, and negotiation. The task is to reread the historical record with an eye to understanding what in the actual experience and life of eastern European Jewry has led to this subterranean stratum that continues to underlie the modern Jewish sensibility.

I am going to argue that a combination of elements in the experience of eighteenth-century eastern European Jews, including the concentration of large numbers, a continuing attitude of superiority to their neighbors, the secure place of and indispensable role played by Jews in the economy of the region, and the general absence of what I call the "beckoning bourgeoisie," strengthened and deepened a positive sense of Jewish identity. This became the central ingredient of the *mentalité* of East European Jews and constituted a kind of social-psychological translation of the concept of chosenness. My suggestion is that, in subsequent centuries, despite ideological, geographical, economic, political, and even linguistic and cultural change, and for all the exceptions that might be cited, the vast majority of eastern European Jews and their descendants carried this core, even if transvalued, sense of chosenness with them. This book is an attempt to explain how this *mentalité* was formed.

A number of obstacles, or existential problems, impede the recovery and representation of the experience of Jews in early modern Poland-Lithuania and obscure efforts to see the period clearly. These impediments arise along the asymmetrical and uneven cusp between the expectations and desires of the reader and those of the historian. Although they cannot be overcome entirely, it may be helpful to explicate these problems briefly before turning to the eighteenth century.

There is, first, the Jewish reader's desire to see his or her ancestors in a favorable light, coupled with a reluctance to accept impiousness in the generations of the past and a natural tendency to romanticize, even sanctify, the historical record. A second, more difficult problem is the Holocaust. Our knowledge of where history leads acts as a distorting prism, impeding our vision of what came before. It is important to avoid the fallacy of seeing all of eastern European Jewish history as leading inexorably to the Nazi genocide. The earlier periods should be viewed unshadowed by future events. While it is true that the story ends in virtual annihilation, many centuries of life and vitality preceded those terrible events. The third problem is the tendency of many contemporary Jews to equate the terms "Pole" and "antisemite." A former prime minister of the State of Israel echoed the opinion of many when he summed up this view by declaring that "Poles get antisemitism with their mothers' milk." The bitterness underlying such a statement arose from the personal experiences of many Polish Jews in the 1930s. Whatever the perceived accuracy of this view is for the period between the world wars, if extended back in time to the eighteenth century, this attitude constitutes a profound distortion of the historical record and conceals a much more complicated and varied picture.

Throughout this book, I have assiduously tried to avoid placing a definite article before the word "Jews" when Jews are the subject of a sentence. Certainly, *the* Jews were treated collectively in legislation, and prejudice was directed against an undifferentiated group, and, what's more, Jews in Poland and Lithuania shared a common language and culture. Jews, however, did not act *collectively* to gain control of domestic commerce, for example. One may say that *the* Jews of the Polish Commonwealth spoke Yiddish, but one may not say that *the* Jews controlled international trade in Poland in the late eighteenth century. Polish Jews, in such cases, cannot be seen as a monolithic community without endangering truth. I cannot stress enough the heterogeneous character of this very large community of Jews. On the other hand, the central hypothesis of this book concerns just such a generalization. I am endeavoring to explain the roots of what I characterize as an eastern European Jewish mentality. If I plead guilty to essentializing eastern European Jews in this way, it is because I believe my argument provides a useful framework for distinguishing the eastern European Jewish experience from other Jewish stories.

The earliest known portrait of a Polish Jew depicts a woman. In Żwaniec (Zhvanets) in 1781, the king himself ordered his court painter, Krzysztof Radziwiłłowski, to paint a portrait of Chajke, the daughter of Abramek of Lwów.[5] The dignity, pride and wealth of the subject of the

5. The painting, listed in the catalogue of Poniatowski's collection as *Portrait de la juive Czayka,* is in the collections of the National Museum in Warsaw (Inv. 129541). A companion painting of a younger, unmarried woman, listed in the same catalogue as *Portrait de la juive Elia,* is housed in the Palace Museum at Wilanów (National Museum Inv. 129165). I found the inscription: "Roku 1781 dnia 14 listopada z rozkazu Najjaśniejszego Pana Króla J Mości zwiedzającego brzegi Dniestru w Żwanca przedstawiona Chajka córka Kupca Abramka Lwowskim zwanego tym portretem odmalowana przez urodzonego Krzysztofa Radziwiłłowskiego" on the back of both paintings! However, in both cases the inscriptions are copies of the originals. The younger woman has been identified by some as possibly the daughter of Chajka. For another interpretation, see E. Podhorizer-Sandel, "Judaica w Muzeum Narodowym w Warszawie," *BZIH 78* (1971): 55–56. Scholarly opinion as to which painting depicts Chajke and which Elia, or Ella, has been divided. Both the original catalogue and the scholar Marek Rostworowski identify the older woman, whose portrait is reproduced here, as Chajke. I agree with them. Tadeusz Mańkowski, *Galeria Stanisława Augusta* (Lwów, 1932), 347; Marek Rostworowski, *Żydzi w Polsce: Obraz i słowo* (Warsaw, 1993), 126–27; Michał Walicki, "Nowoodnalezione obrazy z galerii Stanisława Augusta," *Biuletyn Historii Sztuki i Kultury* 9 (1947): 299–305; Jan K. Ostrowski, "Krzysztof Radziwiłłowski, malarz kamieniecki," in *Arx Felicitatis: Księga ku czci Profesora Andrzeja Rottermunda w szesdziesiąta rocznice urodzin od przyaciol kolegów i współpracowników* (Warsaw, 2001), 283–87.

portrait on the one hand and the circumstances of the commissioning of the painting on the other, reflect both the security and the dependence of Polish Jewry. Chajke's evident self-respect and self-confidence embody the central motif of my book and that is why she graces its cover.

Ibrahim ibn Jakub, a tenth-century Spanish Jew who traveled to Prague, provided an early report of Poland to his monarch. He may have gathered his information from Jewish merchants in Prague without personally visiting Polish lands. There is evidence of Jewish communities in Poland by the early eleventh century, but we do not know whether these were permanent settlements.[6] The presence of Jews in the western parts of the country in the twelfth and thirteenth centuries is attested by hordes of silver coins with Hebrew inscriptions that date from those years. Among the earliest documentary evidence is the first charter or privilege to Jews in Poland issued by Bolesław the Pious in 1264. It contained no restrictions on Jewish rights of residence or economic activity and established the principle of Jewish juridical and communal autonomy. Indeed, the legal status of Jews improved continuously during the ensuing centuries. Precisely when Jews first came to Poland is unknown. A few Jews may have come from Khazaria, Byzantium, and from Kievan Rus (the medieval Russian kingdom, with its capital at Kiev) in the early Middle Ages, but the overwhelming majority came from the west, from Ashkenaz (German and Bohemian lands west of Poland). The expulsion of Jews from the Iberian Peninsula had no significant impact in Poland. Only a tiny number of Spanish exiles came to Poland, mainly via the Ottoman Empire or Italy.[7]

Migration of Jews to Poland continued during the fourteenth, fifteenth, and sixteenth centuries. By the sixteenth century, there were some 50,000 Jews in Poland. Their situation surprised a visiting papal diplomat, who reported in 1565:

6. Franciszek Kupfer and Tadeusz Lewicki, *Źródła hebrajskie do dziejów słowian i niektórych innych ludów środkowej i wschodniej Europy* (Warsaw, 1956); Israel Ta-Shama, "On the History of the Jews in Twelfth- and Thirteenth-Century Poland," *POLIN* 10 (1997): 287–317. There is no evidence to support the theory that the ancestors of Polish Jewry were Jews who came from the Crimean Jewish kingdom of Khazaria. The best-known advocate of this theory was Arthur Koestler, whose book *The Thirteenth Tribe* (New York, 1976) was heavily influenced by Abraham Poliak's *Khazaria: Toledot mamlakhah yehudit* (Tel Aviv, 1951).

7. Jan Zamoyski, one of the most interesting and powerful noblemen of his day (1542–1605), decreed that he would only allow Sephardic Jews in a new city he was building (Zamość), and a dozen or so Sephardic families settled there. Jacob Shatzky, "Sefardim in Zamoshch," *Yivo bleter* 35 (1951): 93–120; Janina Morgensztern, "Notes on the Sephardim in Zamość, 1588–1650," *BZIH* 38 (1961): 69–82.

In these principalities one still comes upon masses of Jews who are not disdained as much as in some other lands. They do not live here under pitiful conditions and do not engage in lowly pursuits. . . . But rather, they possess land, engage in commerce, and devote themselves to study, especially medicine and astrology. . . . They possess considerable wealth and they are not only among the respectable citizens, but occasionally even dominate them. They wear no special marks to distinguish them from Christians and are even permitted to wear the sword and to go about armed. In general, they enjoy equal rights.[8]

A contemporary Jewish assessment of the community's happy situation in Poland is gleaned from a gloss on a rabbinic tale by Samuel Eliezer ben Yehuda Halevi Edels, known as MaHaRShA (Moreinu *HaRav Sh*muel *Edels*) (1555–1631).[9] In the original story, Jews wandered in the sea searching for a place to settle; in Edels's adaptation, they wandered in the heart of the "sea of exile" *(be'imkei metsulot yam hagalut)*. In both stories, they found a great, flat, fertile plain and settled there, for they thought they had found dry land and forgot they were in exile *(sevurim hem deyabashta hava ve-leika galuta)*. (It turned out, the tale warns, that the field was the back of a great beast. When fires were kindled in the hearths, the flames awakened the beast. It reared up and threw them off.) An echo of this sense of rootedness and comfort is caught in the words of the eighteenth-century mystic Pinhas of Korzec (Korets) (1726–1791), who said that "in Poland exile is less bitter than anywhere else."[10]

Polish Jews and their neighbors felt that the Jewish community was a rooted and permanent one. Jewish legends of origin reveal a positive outlook and a conviction of the antiquity of their residence in the country. A pun on the Hebrew name for Poland, Polin, is revealing. A group of exiled Jews is said to have crossed the Polish border and to have heard a divine voice saying to them, *"Poh lin,"* that is, "Dwell here."[11] Other tra-

---

8. Antonio Maria Gratiani, bishop of Amelia (Italy), *La Vie du cardinal Jean-François Commendon,* trans. Fléchier (Paris, 1614), 190, as quoted in Tadeusz Czacki, *Rozprawa o Żydach i Karaitach,* ed. Kazimierz Józef Turowski (Kraków, 1860), 51.

9. Benzion Dinur, "Darkah hahistorit shel yahadut Polin," in id., *Dorot vereshumot* (Jerusalem, 1978), 199, also cites the story.

10. As quoted from Cincinnati Hebrew Union College MS 62 by Abraham Joshua Heschel, *The Circle of the Baal Shem Tov: Studies in Hasidism,* ed. Samuel H. Dresner (Chicago, 1985), 40. And see also M. J. Rosman, "A Minority Views the Majority: Jewish Attitudes towards the Polish-Lithuanian Commonwealth and Interaction with Poles," in *From Shtetl to Socialism: Studies from POLIN,* edited by Antony Polonsky (Washington, D.C., 1993), 39–49.

11. S. Y. Agnon, in his retelling of the story, treats *poh lin* as a prayer: "Why was it called *Polin*? Because the Jewish people said before the Holy One, Blessed be He: 'Master of the Universe, if the hour of our redemption has not yet arrived, dwell here [*poh lin*] through this night of exile with us, until You bring us up to the Land of Israel.'" S. Y. Agnon,

ditions played on a different version of the Hebrew name of the country, parsing it as *"poh lan Yah,"* that is, "Here dwells the Lord".

As early as the fifteenth century, a leading rabbi, Moses ben Isaac Mintz, could say that Poland was "from of old a refuge for the exiled children of Israel."[12] In the same century, the Polish chronicler Jan Długosz recorded the legend of Esterke, the Jewish mistress of Kazimierz Wielki (Casimir the Great), king of Poland (1333–1370). Długosz reports that Esterke used her influence over the monarch to persuade him to invite Jews to settle in Poland and to grant them extensive rights and privileges. Kazimierz had four children by Esterke, Długosz adds: two boys and two girls, and they raised the sons as Christians, the daughters as Jews.[13]

Długosz wished to cast aspersions both on the king and on the legitimacy of the Jews' privileges, but whatever the historicity of the details of the story—to this day the burial place of Esterke can be found in several Polish towns—it tells us a good deal about fifteenth-century attitudes to Jews in Poland. The tale also conveys some other messages, among them that Jews had resided in Poland for a long time; that Jews were perceived as a fixed and continuing part of the social landscape of Poland; that Jews had extensive rights and privileges; and that the Polish crown protected Jews. The detail that the girls were raised as Jews is particularly telling. Such a thought would have been outlandish if not unthinkable in western Europe of the fifteenth century. Despite the fact that Długosz condemns King Kazimierz for this ("id quoque abhominabile et execrandum, quod filias ex eadem Iudea Hester susceptas in ritum Iudaicum transferri asseritur permisisse") and wrote his chronicle under the influence of a patron who bore great animus toward the king, the assertion remains a noteworthy one.

Thus, both Polish Jews and their Christian neighbors shared the sense

---

"Kedumot," as quoted by H. Bar-Itzhak, *Jewish Poland: Legends of Origin. Ethnopoetics and Legendary Chronicles* (Detroit, 2001), 33, with minor changes.

12. For an earlier and similar expression, see B. D. Weinryb, *The Jews of Poland: A Social and Economic History of the Jewish Community in Poland from 1100 to 1800* (Philadelphia, 1973), 30.

13. Jan Długosz [Ioannis Dlugossi], *Annales seu cronicae incliti regni Poloniae*, vol. 9 (Warsaw, 1978), 284–85. See Salo Wittmayer Baron, *A Social and Religious History of the Jews*, vol. 10 (New York, 1965), 44, and the literature cited there. See also Gershon Hundert, "Some Basic Characteristics of the Jewish Experience in Poland," in *From Shtetl to Socialism*, ed. Polonsky, 19–25. On the impact of the Esterke traditions on Polish and Jewish literature in more recent centuries, see Chone Shmeruk, "Hamaga'im bein hasifrut hapolanit levein sifrut yidish al pi sippur Esterkeh veKazimir hagadol melekh Polin," in id., *Sifrut Yidish bePolin* (Jerusalem, 1981), 206–80. Cf. Bar-Itzhak, *Jewish Poland*, 113–32.

that Jews were permanently settled in the land. The legendary etymologies of the terms "Polin" and "Polanyah" reveal an understanding by Jews of their residence as divinely ordained. It is very striking indeed that this huge Jewry, resident in Polish lands for so many centuries, produced no messiahs. There were messiahs from Spain, from Italy, from Yemen, and from elsewhere, but none from Poland.[14] The great movement of spiritual awakening that arose in Poland-Lithuania at the end of the eighteenth century did not have a messianic character. The emphasis was on personal, not national, redemption.

Another "myth of origin" recorded in the eighteenth century conveys the sense of cultural and moral superiority characteristic of eastern European Jews. The gap between Jew and Christian was not only a matter of cultural difference. On the side of Jews, it was also a consequence of their conviction of cultural superiority. The multiple references in the Jewish literature of the time to "our long and bitter exile," for example, had a binary connotation. They not only lamented Jewish suffering and oppression but also provided a certain oblique comfort in the conviction of superiority to other nations. An eighteenth-century preacher berated his listeners one Sabbath using the following interpretation:

"These are the people of the Lord, yet they had to leave His land" [Ezek. 36:20, cf. BT Yoma 86a]. The explanation of the passage is similar to the response of one of the noblemen of Poland to the Jews who were "goring" each other before him: "Why are you here? When you were exiled from your land, your enemies drove you far away, not to nearby regions." This was because in those days, the residents of Poland were immoral in their ways, and the noblemen saw that the Jews were restrained. And so the nobles brought Jews to this country to learn from their deeds. "Now [continued the nobleman to the Jews] since your ways are more immoral than those of the Gentiles here in your pursuit of honors and in your squabbling, why are you here?" Thus it is written: It was said to them, is this the people of God famous for their goodness? And so we should read, "They had to leave the land to which they were exiled." They did not stay there to teach the Gentiles their ways, since now they are worse than them. And what are you doing here?[15]

---

14. Gerson D. Cohen, "Messianic Postures of Ashkenazim and Sephardim," in *Studies of the Leo Baeck Institute,* ed. M. Kreutzberger (New York, 1967), 115–56. See Gershon Hundert, "No Messiahs in Paradise," *Viewpoints: The Canadian Jewish Quarterly* 2, no. 2 (Fall 1980): 28–33, for a more extensive, though unannotated, discussion of this point. For a cogent critique of Cohen, see Elisheva Carlebach, *Between History and Hope: Jewish Messianism in Ashkenaz and Sepharad* (Third Annual Lecture of the Victor J. Selmanowitz Chair of Jewish History, May 17, 1998) (New York, 1998).

15. Hayyim Hayke ben Aharon, *Tseror hahayyim* (Lublin, 1908), 19.

In other words, what makes even temporary settlement during the Exile possible is the people of Israel setting an example, by reason of its good qualities, for the nation among which it lives. Now, says the preacher, when Jews are even worse than their neighbors, the Polish nobleman may well ask, "What are you doing here?" Implicit in the preacher's message is the unquestionable moral superiority of Jews. The rhetoric of absurd exaggeration in an effort to rebuke his people has him putting into the mouth of a Polish nobleman the unimaginable idea that Jews were even more immoral than the native Poles.[16]

Polish Jewry was Ashkenazic in every respect. The migrants brought their culture with them: their language—Yiddish; their spiritual values; their liturgical and legal (halakhic) traditions; their autonomous institutions; their political strategies and behavior. We turn first to spiritual values. The sixteenth-century Polish rabbi Solomon Luria, known as Ma-HaRShaL (*Moreinu HaRav Shlomoh Luria*), claimed descent from the medieval German Jewish Pietists known as *Hassidei Ashkenaz*. For Luria, this was not merely a question of biology. For Polish Jewry, the writings of the Pietists became *the* models of the loftiest spiritual values. Indeed, the *mentalité* of Polish Jewry—its worldview and outlook—was fundamentally shaped by the teachings of *Hassidei Ashkenaz*.[17] Israel Ta-Shma has argued that groups of *Hassidei Ashkenaz* actually moved to Poland in the thirteenth century.[18] Whether, and to what extent, they were actually present in Poland, their influence is undeniable. The teachings of the Pietists can be seen as embracing four distinct attitudes. Above all, the Pietists stressed personal humility. A *hassid* ex-

16. I should like to draw attention in passing to the historical construction here that has precisely the nobility bringing Jews to Poland, and not, as might intuitively be expected, the monarch.

17. These *hassidim* should not be confused with the eighteenth-century movement of religious revival known as Hasidism. See Hayyim Hillel Ben-Sasson, "Shorshei hamahshavah shel hokhmei Polin," in id., *Hagut vehanhagah* (Jerusalem, 1959), 11–17; Jacob Elbaum, *Teshuvat halev vekabalat yisurim: Iyunim beshitot hateshuvah shel hokhmei Ashkenaz uPolin, 1348–1648* (Jerusalem, 1992). Haym Soloveitchik, "Piety, Pietism and German Pietism: *Sefer Hasidim I* and the Influence of *Hasidei Ashkenaz*," *Jewish Quarterly Review* 92, nos. 3–4 (2002): 488–90, seeks to qualify the idea expressed here. On *Hasidei Ashkenaz*, there are a considerable number of studies: see, e.g., Yosef Dan, *Torat hasod shel hassiduth Ashkenaz* (Jerusalem, 1968); Ivan Marcus, *Piety and Society: The Jewish Pietists of Medieval Germany* (Leiden, 1981); id., ed., *Dat vehevrah bemishnatam shel hassidei Ashkenaz* (Jerusalem, 1986). And see n. 24 below.

18. Israel M. Ta-Shma, "Letoledot hayehudim bePolin bame'ot ha12-ha13," *Zion* 53 (1988): 347–69; id., "Yedi'ot hadashot letoledot hayehudim bePolin bame'ot ha12-ha13," *Zion* 54 (1989): 208; id., "On the History of the Jews in Twelfth–Thirteenth Century Poland," *POLIN* 10 (1997): 287–317.

pected to be insulted and expected of himself that he would suppress the urge to respond. This humility of the Pietists, secondly, was linked to a negative valuation of *hana'ah,* of physical, this-worldly pleasure in the hope of an increased reward in the next world. Moreover, they stressed *retson haBore* ("the desire of the Creator") or *din shamayim* ("the law of Heaven"), that is, the necessity for a Pietist to go beyond the simple requirements of the halakha. Finally, the Pietists' focus was largely interior, and they were preoccupied with attaining purity of soul. Their constant concern was *yirat shamayim,* the fear of God, understood to be the fear that one was not sufficiently constant or intense in one's love of God.

With such a spiritual and interior focus as an important religious ideal, it is not surprising that Polish-Lithuanian Jews appear to us as passive in the face of history and to have abdicated from collective, national, political action as opposed to reaction. It is well to remember, however, that townspeople in general in the Commonwealth were virtually powerless to initiate political action.[19] The *wielding* of power was confined to the nobility. This is not to say that Polish Jews did not know how to defend themselves by "lobbying" centers of power. In fact, they were quite adept at it. The prowess of Jewish lobbyists at the Polish parliament, or Sejm, was legendary. Such endeavors, however, were reactive and defensive. On the other hand, we might well regard such political behavior as rooted in realism. And because a sense of "at-homeness" characterized Polish Jewry, it did not need to resort to the fantasy of messianism as a means of altering reality.

The eight or nine decades of material prosperity and relative security experienced by Polish Jews prior to 1648 witnessed the appearance of a virtual galaxy of sparkling intellectual figures. The list of prominent halakhists, commentators, and preachers from this period includes Solomon Luria (ca. 1510–1574), Moses Isserles (ca. 1525–1572), Ephraim Lęczyce (Luntshits, 1550–1619), Meir Lublin (1558–1616), and Joel Sirkes (1561–1640), who among others produced enduring contributions to the canon of high culture. Great academies were established in Lublin and Kraków, in Brześć Litewski (Brest Litovsk; Brisk) and Lwów (L'viv), in Ostróg (Ostrog), and in other towns. These attracted students from all over Poland and from territories further west. Most of the scholars mentioned were drawn from the same thin stratum at the top of Jewish society and,

19. See Jacob Goldberg, "Posłowie miasta Lwowa na sejmy wobec Żydów lwowskich w XVII–XVIII wieku," *Rocznik Naukowo-Dydaktyczny WSP w Krakowie* 203 (1999): 85–94.

as Haim Hillel Ben-Sasson has shown, reflected the values of the cultural and economic elite.[20]

While the rabbinic members of the elite were teaching and writing, they often also were involved in trading, and to a limited extent, banking. This same group dominated the elaborately organized and oligarchic communal governments, so that the authority deriving from their learning was accompanied by a measure of political power. The courts over which they presided resolved disputes according to halakha or by arbitration. Taxes, direct and indirect, were assessed and collected. Weights and measures in the marketplace were monitored; the water supply was assured; hygiene was maintained in the streets; the equivalent of a police force and fire brigade protected inhabitants. The welfare of the poor was provided for and a "hospital," along with midwives, and a doctor were paid for by the community. With a view to protecting collective interests, all relations with the government and with individual Christians were supervised, including loans, partnerships, and other business dealings. The community imposed sumptuary laws regulating, among other things, how many people could be invited to a festive occasion and how much jewellery women could wear. The right to live in a town and the right to marry required the assent of communal officials.[21] Communities sent representatives to regional and, if they were of sufficient size and influence, to national meetings of Polish Jewry—the Council of Four Lands.

Royal charters and privileges guaranteed Jews not only residential and occupational rights but also a kind of autonomy that in some ways approached self-government. As the historian Simon Dubnow wrote: "From the days of the Medieval centres in Babylon and Spain, no other land had such a large concentration of Jews and such wide latitude for autonomous development."[22] Indeed, Polish Jewry developed the most elaborate and ramified institutional structures in European Jewish history: from artisan guilds and voluntary societies, communal governments, and

20. These rabbis taught, for example, a virtually predestinarian doctrine to the effect that the wealth and authority of the learned were an indication of providential divine blessing. Ben-Sasson, *Hagut vehanhagah,* esp. n. 42, p. 89.

21. Jacob Katz, *Tradition and Crisis: Jewish Society at the End of the Middle Ages,* 2d ed., trans. Bernard D. Cooperman (New York, 1993). For additional references, see Gershon Hundert and Gershon Bacon, *The Jews in Poland and Russia: Bibliographical Essays* (Bloomington, Ind., 1984), 17–20. And see also chapter 5 below.

22. Simon Dubnow, *History of the Jews in Russia and Poland from the Earliest Times until the Present Day,* trans. Israel Friedlaender (Philadelphia, 1916–1920), 1: 123. See also Gershon Hundert, "On the Jewish Community in Poland during the Seventeenth Century: Some Comparative Perspectives," *Revue des études juives* 142 (1983): 349–72.

regional assemblies to a national council or parliament called the Council of Four Lands (Va'ad arba aratsot). In these institutions the Jews saw, as Dov Ber Birkenthal, an eighteenth-century memoirist, put it, "a fragmentary redemption and a bit of honor" (*ge'ulah ketanah ume'at kavod*).[23] He also suggested that the subsequent partitions of Poland were divine retribution for the disestablishment of the Council of Four Lands in 1764.[24] The importance of the council is further reflected in the lament of the preacher, Hillel ben Ze'ev Wolf: "Without the council, there is no one to go to the lords of the land and the king to bow down and to make requests because of the weight of taxes and evil decrees."[25]

The Council of Four Lands appeared some time during the second half of the sixteenth century.[26] The exact date of its founding is uncertain because the minute books of the council have not survived. It normally met twice annually, usually at the great fairs in Lublin and Jarosław. The council was a sort of bicameral parliament, composed of a lay assembly and a council of rabbis, but the latter ceased to function in about 1720. The two "houses" collaborated on the formulation and execution of legislation. The assembly would identify an issue needing attention, and the rabbinic council would formulate the legislation or edict in accordance with the usages of halakah. The rabbinic council also functioned as an appellate court. Execution of the law was the responsibility of the assembly. The chief preoccupation of the lay assembly, however, was the apportionment of the burden of taxes owed the crown among the regions and communities. That is, from at least 1581, the Council of Four Lands collectively paid the particular tax owed the Treasury by Jews. The nobility complained continually that lump-sum payments of what was intended to be a capitation tax resulted in great losses. Finally, in 1764, in the course of a fiscal

23. See Dov Ber (of Bolechów) Birkenthal, *The Memoirs of Ber of Bolechow (1723–1805)*, ed. and trans. M. Vishnitzer [Mark Wischnitzer] (London, 1922), 40; Dov Ber (of Bolechów) Birkenthal, *Zikhronot R. Dov me-Bolihov (483–565)*, ed. M. Vishnitzer [Mark Wischnitzer] (Berlin, 1922), 149–51.

24. *VL*, 7: 44.

25. Hillel ben Ze'ev Wolf, *Heilel ben shahar* (Warsaw, 1804), 22b.

26. Among the more recent literature on the Council of Four Lands, see M. J. Rosman, "A Minority Views the Majority," 39–49. Cf. *PVAA;* Jacob Goldberg, "The Jewish Sejm: Its Origins and Functions," in *The Jews in Old Poland 1000–1795*, ed. Antony Polonsky, Jakub Basista, and Andrzej Link-Lenczowski (London, 1993), 147–65, published in Polish as "Żydowski Sejm Czterech Ziem w społecznym i politycznym ustroju dawnej Rzeczypospolitej," *Żydzi w dawnej Rzeczypospolitej*, ed. Andrzej Link-Lenczowski (Wrocław, 1991), 44–58, and in Hebrew as "Va'ad arba aratsot bamishtar hamedini vehahevrati shel mamlekhet Polin-Lita," in Jacob Goldberg, *Hahevrah hayehudit bemamlekhet Polin-Lita* (Jerusalem, 1999), 125–42.

reform, the Polish government disestablished the Council of Four Lands.[27] A phantom council continued to function for some years thereafter, chiefly occupied with the disposition of significant debts that it had accumulated.[28] A census intended to establish the actual Jewish population and provide a basis for a true capitation tax was carried out in 1764–65. It is from these data that we derive our best information about the number of Jews in the Commonwealth at that time.

By the seventeenth century, the Jewish community of Poland-Lithuania had become the largest in the Diaspora and seemed to some observers to be expanding at an astonishing rate. In about 1618, the Kraków city council apparently commissioned Sebastian Miczyński, a professor at the Jagiellonian University, to write a book in the service of the struggle of Christian merchants of the city against their Jewish competitors.[29] He drew attention to the rapid increase in Jewish numbers and noted that "[n]one of them dies in war or of the plague. . . . Moreover, they marry when they are twelve . . . and so multiply rampantly."[30] Miczyński's explanation is incorrect: the Jewish rate of growth was due, not to a higher birthrate, but to the fact that rates of infant mortality were lower among Jews than Christians. Thus the proportion of young people among Jews expanded throughout the period.

Expanding Jewish numbers contributed to stimulating the movement of Jews to Ukrainian lands, which began to be settled more intensively by them after the Union of Lublin in 1569 led to these territories being transferred to the Polish crown. The monarch bestowed vast tracts on powerful noblemen who wished to develop their newly acquired estates and towns. Although there were Jewish craftsmen and merchants in Ukraine, all the sources agree that the most visible economic activity was leasing parts of holdings or various monopolies from Polish noblemen. The most common type of lease was of "propination" rights, that is, the exclusive right to manufacture, distribute, and sell alcoholic beverages,

27. *VL*, 7: 44–50. Technically, the word "disestablished" is inappropriate, since no official government act establishing the Council is known. Nevertheless, government documents over almost two centuries certainly granted implicit official standing to the Jewish institution.

28. Emanuel Ringelblum, "Shmuel Zbytkower: Askan tsiburi-kalkali bePolin bimei halukatah," *Zion* 3 (1938): 246–66; 337–55.

29. *Zwierciadło korony polskiey urazy ciężkie, y utrapienia wielkie, ktore ponosi od Żydów* (Kraków, 1618). Cf. Adam Teller, "'Ha'aspaklariyah shel malkhut Polin' me'et Sebastian Miczynski—He'arot makdimot," in *Kroke—Kazimierz—Krakow: Mehkarim betoledot yehudei Krakow*, ed. Elchanan Reiner (Tel Aviv, 2001), 329–37.

30. Sebastian Miczyński, as quoted in Janusz Tazbir, "Żydzi w opinii staropolskiej," in his *Świat panów Pasków* (Łódz, 1986), 220.

which was the monopoly of the noble owner. The Jewish innkeeper, distiller, or brewer became a characteristic figure in the region, so much so that the terms *arendarz* (leaseholder) and "Jew" became synonymous. To many residents of Ukraine, the Poles had "subjected them to the enemies of Christ, the Jews."[31] Ukrainian peasants resented their Polish lords not only on economic grounds but also on religious and national grounds. The Cossacks too felt their rights were abridged by the Polish state, and their resentment was sometimes couched in religious terms. In the late sixteenth century, an Orthodox religious and cultural revival erupted in Ukraine and Belarus, motivated substantially by a desire to resist both Jesuit and Protestant advances. The Union of Brest (1596) creating the so-called Greek Catholic, or Uniate, Church, which followed Orthodox practice but paid allegiance to the pope in Rome rather than the patriarch in Constantinople, further complicated the matter. The Cossacks saw the bishops who accepted the Union of Brest as traitors. Finally, there was a national dimension to this struggle. When Bohdan Khmelnytskyi (1595–1657), the leader of the uprising that exploded in 1648, entered Kiev in January 1649, after initial victories against the Poles, he was hailed as the Moses of Ukraine, ruler of the Ruś (i.e., Ukrainian) people, liberator of Ukraine from Polish slavery, and Batko (Father) Bohdan. To the people of Ukraine, Catholic priests, Polish noblemen, and Jews were all oppressors.

For Jews, the period of almost twenty years of chaos that began with the Cossack uprising in the middle years of the seventeenth century was the worst, in terms of the number of lives lost, in European Jewish history to that date. In the years following 1648, Jews were attacked and murdered in succession by Cossacks and peasants, by the Russian army that invaded Poland, ostensibly in support of the Cossacks, and by Polish forces during their struggle against yet another invader—the Swedes. Thousands of Jews lost their lives; others fled westward.[32] The Jewish population, however, recovered rather quickly from these blows. Major centers of Jewish settlement were reestablished precisely in the regions of the Cossack attacks, except for the eastern portion of Ukraine that was annexed by

31. Maria Kowalska, ed., *Ukraina w połowie XVII wieku w relacji arabskiego podróżnika Pawła, syna Makarego z Aleppo* (Warsaw, 1986), 19.

32. Shaul Stampfer is preparing a book that includes an attempt to calculate Jewish losses in the mid seventeenth century. His calculations, based on a careful evaluation of demographic information from before and after the catastrophic years, reduce the absolute number of victims to about 13,000 but maintain the tragic proportions of the loss of Jewish lives in Ukrainian lands in those years.

Russia, where Jews were forbidden to reside.[33] The poisonous mix of national, economic, and religious hatred, however, continued to infect Ukraine. Still, the reign of Jan Sobieski (1674–1696) saw considerable recovery and rebuilding.

The first decades of the eighteenth century were a period of almost complete chaos in Poland-Lithuania. The Northern War (1700–1721) against Sweden and the internecine strife within Poland that accompanied it were attended by enormous destruction, epidemics, and famine.[34] Jewish communities suffered along with the rest of the country.[35] In a striking reflection of the links that tied together Jews in various parts of Europe, Sephardi Jews in London allocated £276 9s. (1,595 Reichstalers) in 1710 "for our poor brethren in Poland in view of their calamities," to be distributed among more than two dozen communities, including Poznan, Kalisz, Krotoszyn, Kraków, Opatów, Pińczów, and Szydłów.[36] Even before the outbreak of the Northern War, renewed Cossack insurgency had begun in the 1680s and continued until about 1715. Struggles between Haidamaks, or Cossacks, and Polish authorities began again in the 1730s, culminating at Humań (Uman) in 1768.

When Stanisław August Poniatowski was elected king of Poland on September 6, 1764, he immediately set about attempting to reform the Polish political system. He was stymied by Russian opposition and was only able to implement the fiscal reform referred to earlier that included the disestablishment of the Council of Four Lands. In fact, the Russians virtually controlled Lithuania and had troops stationed in Ukrainian lands from at least the 1740s on. Frustration among magnates and noblemen led to the Confederation of Bar in 1768, a legal rebellion or civil war between the reformers and their Russian-backed opponents. The confederates evaded defeat by the Russians for four years, until growing interference

---

33. Weinryb, *Jews of Poland,* 195–99; Mordechai Nadav, "Toledot kehillat Pinsk: 1506–1880," in *Pinsk: Sefer edut vezikaron,* ed. W. Z. Rabinowitsch (Tel Aviv, 1973), 99–103.

34. Acting without the agreement of the Polish Sejm, Augustus II's attempt to conquer Livonia brought Poland into the war with Sweden. Polish troops were no match for the Swedes, and Charles XII's armies marched across the country. The Polish nobility split into pro-Swedish and pro-Saxon confederations. Eventually, the pro-Saxon Sandomierz Confederation defeated the pro-Swedish forces.

35. Mordechai Nadav, "Iyun behitrahashuyot beshalosh kehilot bePolin-Lita biyemei milhemet hatsafon ule'ahareha," *Proceedings of the Eighth World Congress of Jewish Studies,* Division B, 2 (Jerusalem, 1982): 89–96.

36. R. D. Barnett, "The Correspondence of the Mahamad of the Spanish and Portuguese Congregation of London during the Seventeenth and Eighteenth Centuries," *Jewish Historical Society of England: Transactions* 20, sessions 1959–61 (1964): 1–50, and see there esp. 41, 42.

in Polish affairs by Austria, France, Prussia, and Russia culminated in the first partition of Poland in 1772. This foreign interference led to the annexation and progressive disappearance of Poland from the map of Europe in successive partitions of Poland in 1772, 1793, and 1795.

Military disorder in the state and national, religious, and economic complaints in Ukraine, as well as rumors that the Bar Confederates intended to extirpate Orthodox Christianity, led to the great Cossack (Haidamak) and peasant uprising of 1768, the Kolishchyzna, led by Maksim Zalizniak (Żeleźniak), which was ultimately put down by combined Polish and Russian forces. At the height of the rebellion, the rebels controlled almost all of Kiev and Bracław (Bratslav) provinces and parts of Volhynia. There were ferocious murders of Polish noblemen, Catholic priests, and Jews. In the worst episode, at least two thousand Catholic noblemen and Jews who had taken refuge in the town of Humań (Uman) were ruthlessly murdered. The commander of the Polish forces, Ivan Gonta, betrayed the Jews and his own comrades and joined the Haidamak forces. Then, as one chronicler described, "They marched together on Humań. On their way, wherever they found Jews or gentry, these were cut to pieces . . . and they filled the whole town of Humań with corpses. The deep well in the marketplace was filled with the bodies of dead children. The peasants in the [surrounding] villages robbed and killed the Jews and their children." The slaughter in Humań came only after Jews had participated in significant numbers in the military defense of the town, led by Leib Sharogorodski and Moses Menaker.[37]

As mentioned, the military chaos and vast destruction of the period of the Bar Confederation came to a halt with the partitioning of Poland-Lithuania in 1772 by Russia, Prussia, and Austria. The Commonwealth lost about 30 percent of its territory and a slightly larger percentage of its

---

37. Adam Moszczeński, *Pamiętniki do historii polskiej w ostatnich latach panowania Augusta III i pierwszych Stanisława Poniatowskiego* (Poznan, 1858), 142, 144. According to W. Serczyk, *Koliszczyzna* (Kraków, 1968), 90–101, at Uman (Humań) more than 600 nobles and 1,400 Jews were massacred (the conventional count had been 5,000 nobles and 7,000 Jews killed). S. Bernfeld, *Sefer hadema'ot*, vol. 3 (Berlin, 1926), 290–302; S. Dubnow, "Der tsvayter khurbn fun Ukrayne (1768)," *Historishe shriftn* 1 (1929): 27–54; Anna Zuk, "A Mobile Class: The Subjective Element in the Social Perception of Jews: The Example of the Eighteenth Century," *POLIN* 2 (1987): 163–78; Jaroslav Pelenski, "The Cossack Insurrections in Jewish Ukrainian Relations," *Ukrainian-Jewish Relations in Historical Perspective*, ed. Howard Aster and Peter J. Potichnyi (Edmonton: Canadian Institute of Ukrainian Studies, 1988), 36; id., "The *Haidamak* Insurrections and the Old Regimes in Eastern Europe," in *The American and French Revolutions 1776–1848: Sociopolitical and Ideological Aspects*, Proceedings of the Second Conference of Polish and American Historians, Iowa City, 29 September–1 October 1976, ed. Jaroslav Pelenski (Iowa City, 1980), 237.

population. Within the remaining territory, Russia retained its dominance by diplomacy, the threat of arms, and bribing key officials.

In the course of the eighteenth century, millions of Jewish lives were lived on the lands of Poland-Lithuania. Virtually all of the heterogeneity and diversity that so large a human community is capable of was played out there during that century. Fasting and feasting; perfunctory prayer and mystical intensity; chastity and licentiousness; proprietary sadness and God-intoxicated joy; vast wealth and dire poverty; orderly patriarchal solemnity and impudent, rebellious youth were all part of Jewish life. Such extremes of experience were nevertheless bounded by commonalities and shared patterns that gave structure to communities and defined their Jewish aspect. The Jewish calendar defined the rhythm of the day, the week, and the year; the language in which life was apprehended was Yiddish; the commandments that were observed or transgressed were the defining categories of value. And what distinguished Polish Jewry from other Jewish communities, aside from sheer numbers, was its extraordinary vitality. This vitality expressed itself in the ramified autonomous institutions, the cultural creativity, and the singular sense of both independence and rootedness that characterized the Jewish community of Poland-Lithuania. Eighteenth-century Polish-Lithuanian Jewry inhabited a cultural universe constructed of elements that arose out of its own traditions. It was, in the Weberian sense, a "traditional society." The basic values and patterns of behavior by which most Jews lived their lives were unexamined and unselfconscious.

The most recurrent observation about Jews in Poland-Lithuania in the travel literature of the period was how numerous Jews were. Nathaniel William Wraxall (1751–1831), an English diplomat and member of parliament, visited Warsaw in the late 1770s, at a time when Jews constituted no more than 5 percent of the city's population. Yet he was impressed with the size of the Jewish population and noted that "Warsaw is . . . crowded with Jews, who form a considerable portion of the inhabitants."[38] In the villages and smaller towns, other travelers also seemed to find only Jews: "a village called Marienpoint . . . is inhabited by a few families, chiefly Jews."[39] Synatine (Szniatyn?) "is . . . a poor village inhabited by

38. Nathaniel William Wraxall, *Memoirs of the Courts of Berlin, Dresden, Warsaw and Vienna in the Years 1777, 1778, 1779* (London, 1800), 2: 8.

39. Adam Neale, *Travels through Some Parts of Germany, Poland, Moldavia and Turkey* (London, 1818), 143. Neale (d. 1832) was a physician attached for some time to the British embassy in Istanbul.

Jews."[40] "Kroupki is a small bourg. . . . The houses are entirely of wood, with a population of about three hundred Jews."[41] Impressions were the same in Lithuania. The town of Orcha, Robert Johnston, an English observer, reported, had a population of about two thousand, "and consists mostly of Jews."[42] The village of Liadi was "inhabited by a colony of Jews."[43] Archdeacon William Coxe, perhaps the best known of the English travelers of this period, as well as the most scholarly, asserted that Jews in Lithuania were even more numerous than those of Poland. Indeed, they "seem to have fixed their headquarters in this duchy. If you ask for an interpreter, they bring you a Jew: if you come to an inn, the landlord is a Jew; if you want post-horses, a Jew procures them, and a Jew drives them; if you wish to purchase, a Jew is your agent: and this is perhaps the only country in Europe where Jews cultivate the ground: in passing through Lithuania, we frequently saw them engaged in sowing, reaping, mowing and other works of Husbandry."[44] John Thomas James (1786–1828), an English academician who took holy orders when he returned from the Continent and eventually became bishop of Calcutta, offered similar observations but added a plausible explanation:

We now crossed the frontier of Poland, and passed from the land of the credulous to the habitations of the unbelievers, for every house we saw was in the hands of Jews. They seemed, indeed, the only people who were in a state of activity, exercising almost all professions, and engaged in every branch of trade; millers, whitesmiths, saddlers, drivers, ostlers, innkeepers, and sometimes even as farmers. Their constant bustle makes them appear more abundant in number than they really are; and although the streets of Zytomir [Żytomierz; Zhytomyr] seemed full of them, we were informed that out of a population of 6,000, not more than one third were of this sect, . . . we could easily have imagined the contrary to have been the fact.[45]

Jews were usually identifiable by their costumes and appearance, which also made them stand out in the eyes of foreign visitors.

40. Ibid., 150.

41. Robert Johnston, *Travels through Part of the Russian Empire and the Country of Poland along the Southern Shores of the Baltic* (New York, 1816), 333. Johnston (ca. 1789–ca. 1853) was a British scholar.

42. Ibid., 331.

43. Ibid., 327.

44. William Coxe, *Travels into Poland, Russia, Sweden and Denmark Interspersed with Historical Relations and Political Inquiries* (London, 1784), 1: 163. Coxe (1747–1828) was an accomplished biographer and historian. He tutored wealthy young men on their grand tours of Europe.

45. John Thomas James, *Journal of a Tour in Germany, Sweden, Russia, Poland, in 1813–1814* (London, 1819), 2: 367.

Both the identifiability and the activity of Jews contributed to the virtually unanimous observation among travelers that "nearly the whole retail trade of Poland is in the hands of the Jews."[46] Archdeacon Coxe observed that "[t]he number of Jews is now prodigious, and they have in a manner engrossed all the commerce of the country; yet this flourishing state of affairs must not be attributed solely to the edicts of Casimir in their favour, but to the industry of those extraordinary people, to the indolence of the country, and oppressed condition of the peasants."[47] Robert Johnston asserted flatly that "the whole trade of Lithuania and Poland is carried on by the Jews."[48] Dr. Adam Neale's remarks were only slightly qualified: "Masters of all the specie, and most of the commerce of Poland, mortgagees of the land, and sometimes masters of the glebe, the Jewish interlopers appear to be more the lords of the country than even the Poles themselves."[49]

It was not only trade that Jews seemed to dominate, but transportation and innkeeping. Coxe noted that "the only places of reception for travellers were hovels, belonging to Jews, totally destitute of furniture and every species of accommodation."[50] John Ledyard, an American traveler, found that Jews "keep the Stage houses on the Road."[51]

At least for the eastern half of the Polish Commonwealth, the travelers' impressions were not far from wrong. Overall, in 1765, 750,000 Jews formed about 5.35 percent of the population of the Polish Commonwealth, which is estimated to have been between 12.3 and 14 million.[52] The density of Jewish settlement, however, increased dramatically from west to east. Only 12 percent of Polish-Lithuanian Jews lived in Great Poland and 17 percent in Little Poland, whereas 27 percent lived in Lithuania-Belarus, and 44 percent in Ukraine-Ruthenia. In fact, the Jewish experience in the Polish Commonwealth cannot be understood without careful consideration of the demography of the community.

---

46. George Burnett, *View of the Present State of Poland* (London, 1807), 137.
47. Coxe, *Travels,* 1: 193.
48. Johnston, *Travels,* 381–82.
49. Neale, *Travels,* 146.
50. Coxe, *Travels,* 1: 194.
51. Stephen D. Watrous, ed., *John Ledyard's Journey through Russia and Siberia: The Journal and Selected Letters* (Madison, Wis., 1966), 204.
52. W. Czapliński and T. Ładogórski, eds., *Atlas historyczny Polski* (Warsaw, 1993); Irena Gieysztorowa, "Ludność," *Encyklopedia historii gospodarczej Polski do 1945 r.* (Warsaw, 1981), 430; R. Mahler, *Yidn in amolikn Poyln in likht fun tsifern* (Warsaw, 1958); Shaul Stampfer, "The 1764 Census of Polish Jewry," *Bar Ilan: Annual of Bar-Ilan University,* Studies in Judaica and the Humanities 24–25 (1989): 41–147.

CHAPTER I

The Largest Jewish Community in the World

When Is a Minority Not a Minority?

A consideration of demographic history is indispensable to an understanding of the Polish Jewish experience. The large numbers of Jews, their residence mainly in urban settlements, their concentration in the eastern half of the Polish Commonwealth, and their continuing expansion all profoundly affected, not only the relations of Jews with the Polish state and their relations with their non-Jewish neighbors, but also the quality of Jewish culture in East Central Europe.

The term "minority" is used to describe groups outside of the imagined homogeneous citizenry in modern nation-states. It has a set of connotations that are misleading when applied to Jews in the Polish Commonwealth. First of all, identity in premodern European society was characterized by a multiplicity of loyalties and memberships. Indeed, there was no majority as we now understand the term. Local patriotism was the order of the day, and there was little sense of belonging to a nation, let alone a nation-state. Even in the eighteenth century, ethnic Poles were not a majority in Poland-Lithuania. In addition to autochthonous Lithuanians, Ukrainians, and Belorussians, as well as Tatars and Romany, many of the cities and towns were distinguished by ethnic and religious diversity: their inhabitants included Germans, Italians, Scots, Armenians, and Greeks. Therefore, Jews cannot be seen as a minority group when less than 20 percent of the population of the country was urban, and only 40 to 60 percent was ethnically Polish.

More important, however, is the fact that about half of the urban population of the Polish Commonwealth was Jewish. A significant proportion of Jews lived in towns where there was a Jewish majority, and an even larger proportion can be said to have *experienced* living in towns where there appeared to be a Jewish majority because so many of the Christian townspeople had turned to agriculture. A substantial majority of Jews lived in communities of five hundred or more.[1] Thus, most of the shops and marketplace stalls, as well as the inns and the taverns, would have belonged to Jews. Indeed, most of the people moving through the streets would have been Jews. In other words, most Jews lived in communities that were quite large enough to support the living of the dailiness of life in a Jewish universe. For these reasons, the term "minority group" is utterly misleading.[2]

The best estimate of the number of Jews in Poland-Lithuania is the one arrived at by Raphael Mahler based on his analysis of the fiscal census carried out in 1764–65 (see table 1). The occasion was the abolition of the Council of Four Lands by the Sejm and the decision to collect the capitation tax on the basis of the actual number of Jews. The actual count was 429,587 for Poland and 157,649 for Lithuania. After correcting for children under one year of age (6.35 percent) and underreporting (20 percent), Mahler concluded that there were 750,000 Jews (549,000 in Poland, 201,000 in Lithuania) in the Polish Commonwealth in 1764–66.[3] While tax records are not the best place to seek the truth about any population, Mahler's corrected figures for 1764–66 are a sound beginning point, and I shall use them in the analysis below.

Mahler's figures can be used to estimate the number of Jews in earlier periods. Assuming a moderate rate of growth of 1.6 percent per year, there would have been about 150,000 Jews in Poland-Lithuania in 1660, and 375,000 in 1720.[4] The Jewish proportion of the total population of the

1. Raphael Mahler, "Di Yidn in amolikn Poyln," in *Yidn in Poyln* (New York, 1946), vol. I, col. 179.

2. The idea that the term "minority" is inappropriate was suggested to me long ago by Professor Shmuel Ettinger when he asked me a question after a talk I presented at Harvard, where he was visiting in 1982.

3. Unless otherwise indicated, all of the figures for 1764–65 mentioned in this chapter follow the analysis of Raphael Mahler, *Yidn in amolikn Poyln in likht fun tsifern*, 2 vols. (Warsaw, 1958). In general, this chapter depends heavily on Mahler's work. His data and procedures have been reviewed by Shaul Stampfer, who concluded that "Mahler's estimates appear more reasonable than . . . any others." Stampfer, "The 1764 Census of Polish Jewry," *Bar Ilan: Annual of Bar-Ilan University*, Studies in Judaica and the Humanities 24–25 (1989): 72. See also, Zenon Guldon and Jacek Wijaczka, "Die zahlenmäßige Stärke der Juden in Polen-Litauen im 16.–18. Jahrhundert," *Trumah: Zeitschrift der Hochschule für Jüdische Studien, Heidelberg* 4 (1994): 91–101.

4. B. D. Weinryb proposed a rate of growth of 2 percent per annum of the Jewish population between 1667 and 1765. This, if correct, would reduce the estimate for 1660 to about 100,000. Weinryb, *The Jews of Poland: A Social and Economic History of the Jewish Community in Poland from 1100 to 1800* (Philadelphia, 1973), 320. Raphael Mahler has suggested that the Jewish population did not exceed 190,000 in 1675.

TABLE 1. The Largest Jewish Communities
in Poland-Lithuania in 1764–65

Brody[a] (P)	8,600
Lwów	7,400
Leszno (P)	6,000
Kraków[b]	4,150
Wilno (Vilnius; Rus., Vilna)	ca. 3,900
Brześć Lit. (Brest Litovsk)	ca. 3,800
Grodno (Hrodna)	ca. 2,800
Pinczów (P)	2,600
Zasław (Zaslav) (P)	2,600
Dubno (P)	2,550
Poznań[c]	2,500
Międzyboż (P)	2,500
Żółkiew (P)	2,400
Ostróg (P)	2,250
Opatów (P)	2,150
Krotoszyn (P)	2,100

SOURCE: Raphael Mahler, *Yidn in amolikn Poyln in likht fun tsifern* (Warsaw, 1958), 1: 62.

NOTES: Figures corrected to take into account children under one year of age (6.35 percent) and underreporting (20 percent). The symbol (P) indicates a private town. In 1787, Lublin had a total population of 8,550: 4,320 Christians, and 4,230 Jews (Władysław Cwik, *Miasta królewskie lubelszczyzny* [Lublin, 1968], 18).

[a]Brody had a total population in the 1760s of ca. 10,000.

[b]Kraków had a total population in 1750 of ca. 5,000; in 1791, of ca. 10,000.

[c]Poznań had a total population in 1733 of ca. 5,000; in 1793, of ca. 12,000.

Commonwealth—Jews formed less than 0.5 percent of the Polish population in 1500, increasing to about 3 percent in 1672, and about 5.35 percent in 1765—shows that the Jewish population was growing at a rate substantially faster than the general rate of growth.[5] The usual estimate of the Polish population for the last decade before the first partition in 1772

5. Some have suggested a larger proportion. For example, Jerzy Topolski has written that before the First Partition of Poland, Jews made up 9 percent of the total population and between 40 and 50 percent of the urban population of the country. Topolski, "On the Role of the Jews in the Urbanization of Poland in the Early Modern Period," in *The Jews in Poland,* ed. Andrzej K. Paluch (Kraków, 1992), 1: 47; id., "The Role of the Jews on the Polish Home Market in the Early Modern Period" (typescript), 6–7.

is between 12.3 and 14 million.[6] As indicated earlier, this faster rate of growth was due less to higher birthrates than to lower death rates, since the incidence of infant mortality was lower among Jews. Zdzisław Budzyński studied twenty-six sets of data from various years between 1777 and 1799 for the following nine localities: Jasło, Nowy Sącz, Przemyśl, Żółkiew (Zhovkva), Bełz, Rzeszów, Sambór (Sambir), Sanok, and Lwów. In twenty-five of the twenty-six cases, the Jewish death rate was lower, and generally significantly lower, than the rate for Christians. The Jewish birthrate was higher in fifteen cases. In Bukovina, for example, between 1790 and 1799, the Christian birthrate was 40.2, and the Jewish birthrate was 38.8; the Christian death rate was 21.9, and the Jewish death rate was 17.2; in that decade, the Christian population increased 2.2 times, the Jewish population increased 3.7 times.[7]

The Jewish population was clearly expanding more rapidly when compared with the entire Christian population of the country. There can be no single explanation of this phenomenon. To a certain extent, the existence of systems of support within the Jewish community undoubtedly helped poorer people in the community to find the shelter and nourishment necessary for nurturing children. The relative stability of the Jewish family, which may well have meant lower incidence of sexually transmitted diseases and relatively lower rates of alcoholism, probably also contributed to lower rates of infant mortality among Jews. Finally, the system of *kest*, in which a newly married couple lived most often with the parents of the bride, also helps to account for the lower rates of infant mortality. The age at marriage of those who expected to be supported by their parents in this way was generally low. Statistics published by Jacob Goldberg show that early marriage and the practice of *kest* was characteristic of about 25 percent of Jews.[8] These were from the wealthier stratum of Jewish society. The housing and provisioning of additional "mouths to feed," that is, the young couple and newborn children, was possible only for the wealthier members of the community. Thus, in the families best able to provide heat, clothing, and food, the age of the mother at first birth was likely to have been the lowest.

6. Although some have put it higher, Emanuel Rostworowski has estimated the proportion of the *szlachta* as a whole at this time at between 6 and 6.5 percent. Rostworowski, "Ilu było Rzeczypospolitej obywateli szlachty?" *KH* 94 (1987): 31.
7. Zdzisław Budzyński, *Ludność pogranicza polsko-ruskiego w drugiej połowie XVIII wieku: Stan rozmieszczenie, struktura wyznaniowa i etniczna* (Pzemyśl-Rzeszów, 1993), 1: 102–8.
8. Jacob Goldberg, "Jewish Marriage in Eighteenth-Century Poland," *POLIN* 10 (1997): 3–39.

The data analyzed by Mahler for 1764–65 suggest that the average size of a Jewish family in Poland was 3.4 persons. On the basis of comparative data from other years and other regions, however, Mahler proposed that the most reasonable overall estimate of the average size of a Jewish Polish family was five. In this case, Mahler's procedure has been questioned. The more likely figure is probably closer to the one that emerges from the data themselves. Rural Jewish family units were larger than urban ones by about 25 percent.[9] The number of Jews per dwelling varied in different regions, and a global average is thus neither useful nor reliable.[10] The data on the growth in Jewish numbers, on the other hand, are incontrovertible. And if this growth was, as I have maintained, largely because of a lower rate of infant mortality, it means that the proportion of young people among Jews was expanding continuously. The implications of this aspect of the demographic situation will be explored in later chapters.

The Jewish population was unevenly distributed: 44 percent lived in the south-east (Ruthenia-Ukraine) and 27 percent in the north-east (Lithuania-Belarus); 17 percent lived in the central areas (Małopolska, Little Poland), and only about 12 percent lived in the west (Wielkopolska, Great Poland). That is to say, more than 70 percent of the Jewish population of the Polish Commonwealth was concentrated in the eastern half of the country. Five of the six provinces (województwa) with the largest Jewish populations were in the east: Ruś (100,111); Volhynia (50,792); Podolia (38, 384); Troki (Trakai) (33,738); and Wilno (Vilnius; Vilna) (26,977). The sixth was Sandomierz, in Little Poland (42,972). The distribution of larger communities followed the same pattern. Of forty-four towns in which more than one thousand Jews lived, four were in the west, seven in the center, five in Lithuania-Belarus, and twenty-seven in Ruthenia-Ukraine. One, Warsaw, was in Mazovia. That is to say, the Jewish population became more concentrated as one moved eastward. (See maps 1 and 2.)

Slightly more than two-thirds of Jews lived in urban settlements, although many of these were rather small towns, the characteristic form of

9. Stampfer, "1764 Census," 47–49.

10. Adam Teller, "Warunki życia i obyczajowość w żydowskiej dzielnicy Poznania w pierwszej połowie XVII wieku," in Żydzi w Wielkopolsce na przestrzeni dziejów, ed. J. Topolski and K. Modelski (Poznan, 1999), 57–70. Using tax rolls as a base, Pawel Fijalkowski, Żydzi w województwach łęczyckim i rawskim w XV–XVIII wieku (Warsaw, 1999), 35, found that in the small town of Parczew (Łęczyca province), the average number of Jews per dwelling was 7.1 in 1775 and 14.8 in 1793–94. This seems unlikely.

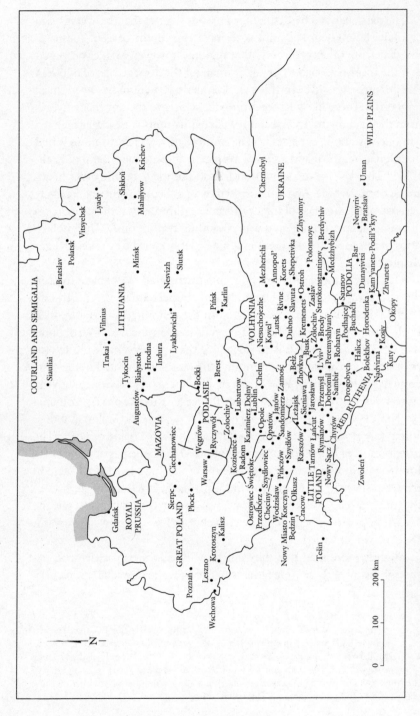

MAP 1. Poland-Lithuania in the eighteenth century

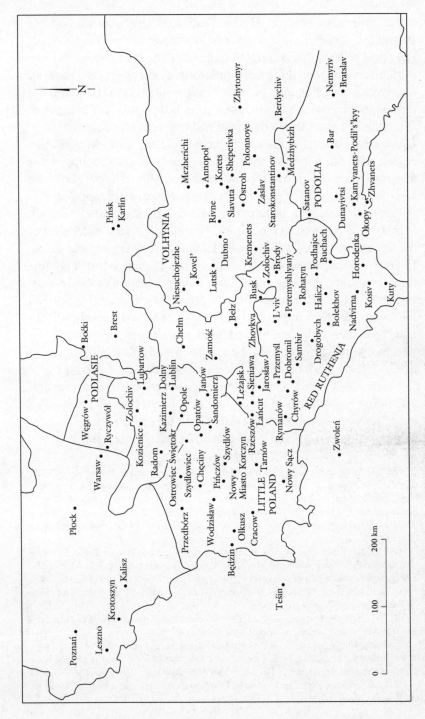

MAP 2. Little Poland, Red Ruthenia, Volhynia, and Podolia

urban settlement in Poland. Hubert Vautrin, a Frenchman who lived in Poland for several years, wrote that he would not use the French words *ville* (city) or *bourg* (market town) to translate the Polish *miasto,* because the term denotes something that is little more than a village, and the word simply had no analogue in French.[11] Even at the end of the eighteenth century, not more than twelve Polish cities had populations in excess of 10,000, while more than a thousand had fewer than 2,000 inhabitants. Despite their small size, those settlements were not agricultural villages, at least not with respect to their Jewish populations. In contrast, most Christian townspeople (60 percent) tended actually to be burghers who had turned to cultivating plots on the edges of the town to support themselves; some were both artisans and farmers at the same time.[12] In light of this, it will easily be seen how much, particularly in the eastern half of the Commonwealth, Jews dominated urban commerce and production. In Great Poland, where there was a substantial ethnic German population, Jews made up about 16.5 percent of the population of the towns.[13] Archdeacon Coxe's impression that Jews had "in a manner engrossed all the commerce of the country" thus becomes easier to comprehend.[14] In 1765, the cities with the largest Jewish populations were Brody (ca. 7,000), Lwów (ca. 6,000), and Leszno (ca. 5,000). Kraków, Wilno, and Brześć-Litewski each had about 3,500 Jewish residents. (See table 1.)

There were significant regional variations in the urban-rural distribution of the Jewish population. In parts of Western Poland, 2 percent or less of Jewish residents lived in villages.[15] In the eastern regions, the rural proportion of the population sometimes exceeded one-third.

11. "Tout ce qui porte le nom de ville ne mérite pas même celui de bourg; la plupart ne sont habitées que par des Juifs et des serfs: on les appelle miasto dans la langue du pays; je leur conserverai cette dénomination de miastes, parce qu'elle n'a point d'analogue dans la langue française." Hubert Vautrin, *La Pologne du XVIIIe siècle vue par un précepteur français,* ed. Maria Cholewo-Flandrin (Paris, 1966), 61. First published as *L'Observateur en Pologne* (Paris, 1807).

12. Emanuel Rostworowski, "Miasta i mieszczanie w ustroju Trzeciego Maja," in *Sejm Czteroletni i jego tradycje,* ed. Jerzy Kowecki (Warsaw, 1991), 138–51; Jacob Goldberg, *Stosunki agrarne w miastach ziemi wielunskiej w drugiej połowie XVII i w XVIII wieku* (Łódz, 1960).

13. Jacob Goldberg, "Polacy-Żydzi-Niemcy w Polsce w XVII–XVIII wieku," in *Między Polityką a Kulturą* (Warsaw, 1999), 176.

14. William Coxe, *Travels into Poland, Russia, Sweden and Denmark Interspersed with Historical Relations and Political Inquiries* (London, 1784), 1: 193.

15. On the village population in Western Poland, see Stefan Cackowski, "Wiejscy Żydzi w województwie chelmińskim w 1772r.," *Acta Universitatis Nicolai Copernici: Historia* 28 (1993): 61–72, and the references there. See also Antoni Podraza, "Jews and the Village in the Polish Commonwealth," in *The Jews in Old Poland, 1000–1795,* ed. Antony Polonsky et al. (London, 1993), 299–321.

TABLE 2. Rural Jewish Population as a Percentage of
the Total Jewish Population of Selected Provinces
and Regions of Poland-Lithuania in 1764–65

Kalisz	1.2
Gniezno	1.6
Inowrocław	9.0
Kraków	31.0
Lublin	30.5
Sandomierz	32.0
Ruś[a]	19.0
Volhynia	28.5
Kiev	36.0
Podlasie	55.0
Wilno (Vilnius; Rus., Vilna)	25.0

SOURCE: Raphael Mahler, *Yidn in amolikn Poyln in likht fun tsifern*
(Warsaw, 1958).

[a] Data unavailable for Przemyśl and Sanok districts.

Overall, almost 27 percent of Polish Jews inhabited villages in 1764–65.
A significant proportion of village Jews, however, were only temporarily
rural and either maintained residences in towns or returned to an urban
center after the expiration of their *arenda* (lease) contracts. On average,
fewer than two Jewish families (7.1–9.6 people) lived in a village. Moreover, from the last decades of the eighteenth century on, the number and
proportion of Jews living in villages constantly diminished. Most Polish
villages had no Jewish population. In the Kraków province, for example,
Jews lived in fewer than one-third of 2,628 villages. In Galicia in 1785, village Jews accounted for less than 3 percent of the total rural population.[16]
The Jewish population, in general, was quite mobile, especially the most
prosperous and those at the opposite end of the economic scale, the vocationless, itinerant poor. It should be stressed that not only was the Jewish population essentially urban, but that it lived in the midst of a society that was overwhelmingly rural and agricultural. The consequence of
this was that half of the urban population, and in large parts of the country more than half, was Jewish. (See table 2.)

Questions related to the quality of the exchanges between Jews and
Christians in the eighteenth century will often appear in the following

16. Budzyński, *Ludność pogranicza*, 1: 324–25.

chapters. Perhaps it is best to state from the outset that a simple dichotomous view is not nearly complex enough to reflect the actual situation. Nevertheless, it would appear, at least at first, that the demographic situation argues for Jewish insularity and apartness within the context of Polish-Lithuanian society. The dramatic contrast between the rate of expansion of the Jewish population and that of the Commonwealth's population as a whole suggests cultural and physical isolation. Culturally, the phenomenon suggests Jewish distinctiveness in matters related to marriage, hygiene, diet, and child rearing. It suggests physical isolation protecting Jews from infection and the spread of communicable diseases. This apparently powerful argument, however, is flawed. It takes the population as a whole, which was overwhelmingly agrarian, as its comparison group. Jews, as noted earlier, were mainly urban. Still, it might be answered, urban European populations in this period, including those in Poland, were unable to reproduce themselves. Yet, the upper socioeconomic strata of those cities did succeed in increasing their numbers, and it may well be that this is the group with which Jews should be compared. For the moment, unfortunately, there are no such finely tuned studies of Polish urban demography in the eighteenth century.

Moreover, the argument for insularity is vitiated considerably by a review of the patterns of residence of Jews. Except for large crown cities like Poznan and Lwów, there was no residential segregation. The degree of concentration of Jewish homes varied somewhat, but in many if not most cases, Jews and Christians lived interspersed.[17] The tendency of Jews to live on the marketplace *(rynek)* intensified this phenomenon. For example, Jews occupied more than half the dwellings on the marketplace in Dobromil (68 percent), Łańcut (84 percent), Chyrów (59 percent), and Sieniawa (87 percent). Overall, of six towns in the Przemyśl-Sanok region studied by Jerzy Motylewicz, Jews occupied 119 of 208 houses on the mar-

17. Gershon Hundert, "Jewish Urban Residence in the Polish Commonwealth in the Early Modern Period," *Jewish Journal of Sociology* 26 (1984): 25–34; M. J. Rosman, *The Lords' Jews: Magnate-Jewish Relations in the Polish-Lithuanian Commonwealth during the Eighteenth Century* (Cambridge, Mass., 1990), 42–48. In 1764, in the private town of Uła (Połock province), there were nine streets, and Jews lived or owned real estate on seven of them. *Istoriko-iuridicheskie materialy, izvlechennye iz aktovykh knig gubernii Vitebskoi i Mogilevskoi, khraniaschchikhsia v tsentralnom arkhivie v Vitebskie* 22 (Vitebsk, 1891), 420–50. Cf. Jacek Wijaczka, "Raport Ignacego Husarzewskiego o domach i placach żydowskich w Kozienicach z 1767 roku," *Studia Historyczne* 43 (2000): 503–12; Jerzy Motylewicz, "Ulice etniczne w miastach ziemi przemyskiej i sanockiej w XVII i XVIII wieku," *KHKM* 47 (1999): 149–55.

ketplaces. In Biłgoraj, Jews owned fifty-six of sixty-eight houses on the marketplace in the latter decades of the eighteenth century.[18]

The numbers presented here constitute a powerful argument supporting my general contention about the formation of an eastern European Jewish mentality. The dense and growing concentration of Jews in the eastern half of the Polish Commonwealth contributed in a vital way to the creation of conditions—the experience of living in a substantially Jewish universe, of being a minority that is not a minority—in which that mentality could develop.

There is no doubt that some degree of material prosperity was a necessary condition for the expansion of the Jewish population. As important, the crucial role Jews played in the economy of the state not only contributed to their physical security but to the self-confidence that characterized their community.

18. Jerzy Motylewicz, "Żydzi w miastach ziemi przemyskich i sanockiej w drugiej połowie XVII i w XVIII wieku," in *Żydzi w Małopolsce: Studia z dziejów osadnictwa i życia społecznego,* ed. Feliks Kiryk (Przemyśl, 1991), 121. Jerzy Markiewicz et al., *Dzieje Biłgoraja* (Lublin, 1985), 47. Sometimes churchmen objected to Jews living on the marketplace, where Church processions took place. They viewed the presence of Jews and particularly of a synagogue as blasphemous. Adam Kaźmierczyk, *Żydzi Polscy 1648–1772: Źródła* (Kraków, 2001), no. 21, p. 32 (1725).

CHAPTER 2

Economic Integration

The role of Jews in the economy of Poland-Lithuania became progressively more significant in the course of the eighteenth century.[1] This was largely a consequence of three trends. It was mainly Jews who managed the transformation in the use of grain (rye) from primarily an export

1. On this subject, the basic work remains Ignacy Schiper, *Dzieje handlu żydowskiego na ziemiach polskich* (Warsaw, 1937). More recent works on the economic activities of Jews in the eighteenth century include Jacob Goldberg, "Hamishar hakim'oni hayehudi bePolin bame'ah ha18: Takanot lahenvanim beZaslav uveBrody veshe'elat hamekorot ha'ivriyim-hapolaniyim letoledot hamishar vehahevrah hayehudiyim," in *Studies on Polish Jewry: Paul Glikson Memorial Volume,* ed. Ezra Mendelsohn and Chone Shmeruk (Jerusalem, 1987), 11–64, also published in a shorter Polish version: "Żydowski handel detaliczny w Polsce w XVIII wieku w świetle polsko-hebrajskiego 'Porządku kramarzów miasta Zasławia 1771 anno,'" *Przegląd humanistyczny* 4 (1993): 45–57; id., "Żyd i karczma miejska na Podlasiu w XVIII wieku," *Studia Podlaskie* 2 (1989): 27–38, also in id., *Hahevrah hayehudit bemamlekhet Polin-Lita* (Jerusalem, 1999), 241–50; id., "Żyd a karczma wiejska w XVIII wieku," *Wiek Oświecenia* 9 (1993): 205–13, also in id., *Hahevrah hayehudit,* 232–40; id., "Manufaktura żelazna księdza infulata Kazimierza Lipskiego i Szlamy Efraimowicza w Choczu: Inicjatywy gospodarcze Żydów w XVIII wieku," in *Żydzi w Wielkopolsce na przestrzeni dziejów,* ed. J. Topolski and K. Modelski (Poznan, 1999), 83–99, also in id., *Hahevrah hayehudit,* 251–63; Gershon Hundert, "The Role of the Jews in Commerce in Early Modern Poland-Lithuania," *Journal of European Economic History* 16 (1987): 245–75; Yehudit Kalik, "Hayahas shel hashlakhta lamishar hayehudi," *Gal-Ed* 13 (1993): 43–57; M. J. Rosman, *The Lords' Jews: Magnate-Jewish Relations in the Polish-Lithuanian Commonwealth during the Eighteenth Century* (Cambridge, Mass., 1990); Adam Teller, "Tafkidam hakalkali uma'amadam hevrati shel hayehudim be'ahuzot beit Radziwill beLita bame'ah ha18" (Ph.D. diss., Hebrew University, Jerusalem, 1997); Adam Teller, "Hape'ilut hakalkalit shel hayehudim bePolin bemahatsit hasheniyah shel hame'ah ha17 uveme'ah ha18," in *Kiyum veshever,* ed. I. Bartal and I. Gutman (Jerusalem, 1997), 209–24; Teresa Zielinska, "Kariera i upadek żydowskiego potentata w dobrach radziwiłłowskich w XVIII wieku," *KH* 98 (1991): 33–49.

commodity to its use in the production of alcoholic beverages. This activity accounted for a very large proportion of the income from rural estates. Secondly, the role of Jews as lessees of estate monopolies temporarily counteracted the continuing decline in the efficiency of serf labor. And, finally, growing Jewish numbers and other developments discussed below led to Jews being highly prominent in commerce. The indispensability of Jews to the economy of the Commonwealth contributed substantially to their relative security and self-confidence. It was also a significant influence on the character of their relations with their neighbors.

As we saw in the previous chapter, the growing number of Jews was overwhelmingly concentrated in the eastern and southern provinces, and Jews constituted even more than 50 percent of the urban population in numerous regions. The role of Jews in commerce, and particularly in the domestic market, was crucial. In some towns, as many as 80 or 90 percent of all merchants were Jewish: in the late seventeenth and early eighteenth centuries, of 473 merchants in the town of Rzeszów mentioned in the sources, 412 were Jews. In Przemyśl, in the same period, of 137 merchants, 111 were Jews. In the eighteen largest towns of the Przemyśl-Sanok region, 745 (76.3 percent) of the 976 merchants were Jews. "Among us you do not have a single Christian merchant, Jews conduct all of the trade," the Christian burghers of Jarosław declared in 1723.[2] In Nowy Sącz, in 1733, a municipal official remarked offhandedly to the governor of the province that only Jews were occupied with commerce in that town.[3] In Tarnów, Jewish shopkeepers were accused of conducting business, contrary to law, on a Christian holy day. The complaint named forty-three Jewish shopkeepers.[4] A sample consisting of the data from twenty-three (out of sixty) tariff payment toll stations in 1764–67, found references to

2. "Już między nami z Chrześcian żadnego . . . kupca nie masz . . . ale Żydzi wszystkie handle . . . prowadzą." Jan Pęckowski, *Dzieje miasta Rzeszowa do końca XVIII wieku* (Rzeszów, 1913), 301.

3. Jerzy Motylewicz, "Żydzi w miastach ziemi przemyskich i sanockiej w drugiej połowie XVII i w XVIII wieku," in *Żydzi w Małopolsce: Studia z dziejów osadnictwa i życia społecznego,* ed. Feliks Kiryk (Przemyśl, 1991), 124; A. Tomczak, ed., *Lustracja województw wielkopolskich i kujawskich 1789 r.,* pt. 3 (Warsaw, 1977), 17; Rosman, *Lords' Jews,* 76; R. Mahler, *Sefer Sants* (Tel Aviv, 1970), 54. In Ożarów in 1728, a church inventory reported that "trade is in Jewish hands." Cf. Mariusz Kulczykowski, *Kraków jako ośrodek towarowy Małopolski zachodniej w drugiej połowie XVIII wieku,* Studia z Historii Społeczno-Gospodarczej Małopolskiej, no. 6 (Warsaw, 1963), 139–40.

4. Among them six women, all but one identified as widows. Adam Kazmierczyk, *Żydzi Polscy 1648–1772: Źródła* (Kraków, 2001), no. 103, pp. 180–82.

5,888 Jews among a total of 11,485 merchants.[5] Generally speaking, and bearing in mind the concentration of Jews in the eastern half of the Polish Commonwealth, 50 to 60 percent of domestic trade was in the hands of Jewish traders. Even in foreign trade, Jewish numbers were quite significant, especially during the last quarter of the century.[6] At that time, for every Christian merchant from Poland at the fairs in Leipzig, there were seven Jewish merchants.[7]

Forty-one merchants came to Leipzig from the Polish Commonwealth for the Easter fair in 1748. Of these, thirty-two were Christians and nine were Jews. A few years later, the situation had changed dramatically. Between 1766 and 1800, 18,609 merchants from Poland-Lithuania visited Leipzig trade fairs. Of these, 16,100 (86.5 percent) were Jews. For the most part, they exported furs, skins, tallow, saltpeter, and wax and imported finished goods, especially textiles and metal products. The value of imports exceeded the value of exports, with the balance obtained on credit. As early as 1753, Jewish merchants from the great trading emporium in Brody had their own place of prayer in Leipzig.[8] Even in the first decades of the eighteenth century, J. P. Marperger noted that Polish Jews particularly brought a range of Levantine, Turkish, and Ukrainian goods to the Leipzig fairs.[9] It was not until after 1772, however, that Jewish merchants from Poland-Lithuania were diverted in massive numbers from Frankfurt and Breslau to Leipzig. Indeed, they exerted a decisive influence on Leipzig, which was experiencing its heyday in those decades between the First Partition of Poland and the Napoleonic wars. The two ingredients most responsible for the massively increased intensity of commercial travel between Polish lands and the Saxon trade fair after 1772 were the improvement in the Polish economy and the removal of discriminatory taxation on Jews attending the Leipzig fairs.[10]

5. This enumerates references; many individuals would have been represented two or more times in the records. AGAD, Archiwum Kameralne III.

6. Sometimes Jewish merchants misjudged their market. The inventory of a Jewish merchant in Tarnów in the 1720s included goods from Gdańsk, Wrocław, Moscow, France, and Venice. The document was prepared in connection with his bankruptcy. Tomasz Opas, "Rynek lokalny Tarnowa w XVIII wieku," *Roczniki dziejów społecznych i gospodarczych* 36 (1975): 42.

7. Max Freudenthal, *Leipziger messgaste; die jüdischen besucher der Leipziger messen in den jahren 1675 bis 1764* (Frankfurt a/M, 1928); Richard Markgraf, *Zur Geschichte der Juden auf den Messen in Leipzig von 1664–1839* (Bischofswerda, 1894); Josef Reinhold, *Polen/Litauen auf den Leipziger Messen des 18. Jahrhunderts* (Weimar, 1971).

8. Adolf Diamant, *Chronik der Juden in Leipzig* (Leipzig, 1993), 59–60, 263.

9. *Abriss der kommerzien und Manufakturen des Kurfürstentums Sachsen und seiner inkorporierten Länder* (Dresden, 1718) as quoted by Reinhold, *Polen/Litauen*, 16.

10. On the latter see Reinhold, *Polen/Litauen*, 67–75.

Among the most prominent towns of origin of these Jewish merchants were Brody, Leszno (Lissa), Szklów (Shklov), Dubno, and Berdyczów (Berdychiv). Leipzig, of course, was not the only emporium utilized by Polish Jewish merchants. Szklów merchants, for example, in addition to active ties to Königsberg (Kaliningrad), corresponded with firms in Moscow, Berlin, Hanover, Breslau (Wrocław), Altona, and Amsterdam.[11] One of the greatest traders at Leipzig was identified in the records as Nathan Chaim of Szklów. In 1786, he brought forty wagons of furs worth a half-million Reichstalers to the Michaelmas fair.[12] This was Natan Nota b. Hayim, known as Nota Khaimovich Notkin (d. 1804), a friend of the enlightened Jews of Berlin and an associate of Count Grigorii Potemkin.[13] Notkin was not the only one in whom involvement in international trade and attraction to new cultural trends were linked. As early as 1783, a certain Jacob Hirsch, a German Jewish expatriate involved in the Belorussian wool industry, sought permission from Catherine to establish a network of modern Jewish schools. He claimed to have support among the local Jews for his plans:

I was born to Jewish parents and continue to this day to be attached to the religion of my ancestors, but I also respect the religion of the Christians and its scholars. I have always wanted to address the problem of ignorance, which is the source of the lowly condition of my poor brethren. This desire has been intensified as I see many Christians of noble spirit addressing the same issue . . . I have consulted with the most honorable of my brethren in the province of Mohylew and can rely on their support. . . . At least at the beginning the teachers must be Jews. I can obtain them in exchange for low wages. Some will be local and some will be invited from German lands through the good offices of the learned Moses Mendelssohn.[14]

The second element underlying the importance of Jews to the Polish-Lithuanian economy was the continuing decline in the efficiency of serf labor. The phenomenon of peasants paying labor dues instead of money

---

11. "Jüdische Kaufmannsbriefe aus den Jahren 1780 bis 1804," *Jüdische Familien-Forschung* 5, no. 4 (1929): 203.

12. Reinhold, *Polen/Litauen,* 149–52.

13. David E. Fishman, *Russia's First Modern Jews: The Jews of Shklov* (New York, 1995), s.v. "Notkin." And see above around n. 8.

14. *Regesty i nadpisi; svod materialov dlia istorii evreev v Rossii (80 g.–1800 g.)* (St. Petersburg, 1913), 3: 240–43; Y. Slutsky, "Hatsa'ato shel hayehudi Ya'akov Hirsh lehakim beit sefer yehudi rashi beMohilev vesidur batei sefer aherim kedugmato beBelorusiyah (1783)," *Heavar* 19 (1972): 78–80; David Fishman, *Russia's First Modern Jews,* 61–62. To my knowledge, the subject of the migration of central European Jewish entrepeneurs to eastern Europe in the late eighteenth century has not been studied.

rents created, at least in some regions, what is sometimes called a "second serfdom." According to Jerzy Topolski, Jewish activity counteracted the negative effects of this decline by maintaining sources of income for the estate owners.[15] In this way, Jews contributed to the preservation of the manorial serf economy. It should be recalled in this context that two-thirds of the towns of the Commonwealth were private towns, and that Jews tended to live in such towns to the benefit of the estate owners.[16] At least in the eastern half of the country, urban economic vitality depended on Jews. In a very substantial number of towns, Jews were the only commercially active segment of the population. In 1719, an official of the Czartoryski holdings in Podolia was instructed to settle the maximum possible number of Jews. The eighteenth-century noble memoirist Marcin Matuszewicz recorded that after they acquired an abandoned townlet (miasteczko) called Rosna, which had been ruined, enfeebling the fairs held there, "My parents wanted to restore the fortunes of the town— to settle some Jews" (emphasis added).[17]

Thirdly, while the heart of the Polish national economy in the sixteenth and seventeenth centuries had been the cultivation of grain in the central and eastern portions of the Commonwealth for export, Jews managed the transformation in how that grain was used in the eighteenth century. The production of alcoholic beverages for local consumption substantially replaced grain exports. Jacob Goldberg has suggested three strands of explanation of this phenomenon.[18] First, the price of beer and alcohol was

15. Jerzy Topolski, "The Role of the Jews on the Polish Home Market in the Early Modern Period" (typescript).

16. A comparison with private towns in Hungary, Moldavia, and Transylvania in this period might yield interesting results. In Hungary in the eighteenth century, there were 600 private towns, all but 44 owned by noblemen. Józef Mazurkiewicz, "O niektórych problemach prawno-ustrojowych miast prywatnych w dawnej Polsce," Annales Universitatis Mariae Curie-Skłodowska, sec. G, vol. 11 (1964): 100. The subject of the legal status of Jews on private holdings in general is addressed by Adam Kaźmierczyk, Żydzi w dobrach prywatnych w świetle sądowniczej i administracyjnej prakyki dóbr magnackich w wiekach XVI–XVIII (Kraków, 2002).

17. Kaźmierczyk, Żydzi w dobrach prywatnych, 24; "Rodzice tedy moje chcieli miasteczko znowu restaurować Żydów osadzali." Marcin Matuszewicz, Diariusz życia mego, vol. 1: 1714–1757, ed. Bohdan Krolikowski, commentary by Zofia Zielinska (Warsaw, 1986), 116–17. For similar attitudes, at least regarding the presence of Jews as a stimulus to trade, see the privilege granted to the Jews of Lubraniec published by Jacob Goldberg, Jewish Privileges in the Polish Commonwealth: Charters of Rights Granted to Jewish Communities in Poland-Lithuania in the Sixteenth to Eighteenth Centuries (Jerusalem, 1985), 165.

18. Jacob Goldberg, "Hayehudi vehapundak hakafri," in id., Hahevrah hayehudit bemamlekhet Polin-Lita (Jerusalem, 1999), 232–33. Cf. Jerzy Topolski, Gospodarka polska a europejska w XVI–XVIII wieku (Poznan, 1977), 39.

rising faster than the price of grain; second, marketing of beverages was easier and brought faster returns than exporting grain; and third, the consumption of alcohol increased in this period, because vodka joined beer as a common drink and the drink of commoners. Income from the sale of vodka as a percentage of the total income on royal estates rose from 6.4 percent in 1661 to 40 percent in the second half of the eighteenth century. This was a highly profitable enterprise, involving less risk than the export of grain, since prices could be controlled much more easily. For example, on the vast Zamoyski estates, alcohol sales returned a net profit of 124 percent on production and retail costs. In 1800, Józef Czartoryski described his distilleries as "mints, as it is only through them that in years of plenty we may convert our grain into cash." On certain crown lands in Małopolska the percentage of total revenues derived from sales of alcohol rose from 6 percent in 1664 to 33.3 percent in 1764 and exceeded 40 in 1789. On the Zamoyski estates, the proportion averaged about 30 percent, reaching 46.2 percent in 1791.[19] The percentages were highest in the remote regions of Ukraine. In general, the more variegated and dynamic a region's economy, the less important *propinacja* (the licensing of the monopoly on the production and sale of alcoholic beverages) was likely to be. In the districts of Poznan and Kalisz, the proportion of income derived from the sale of alcohol was usually under 10 percent. In the eastern half of the country, as already noted, Jews managed this entire sector of the economy.[20] As much as one-third of the Jewish population of the Commonwealth was involved in occupations related to the manufacture, distribution, and sale of alcoholic beverages, although the lion's share of the profits went to the lords.

In sum, then, in the Polish Commonwealth during the eighteenth century, Jews can usefully and with some accuracy be described as a colonized economic group. They performed indispensable services and played a crucial role in the economy, but the primary beneficiaries were

19. Jerzy Tadeusz Lukowski, *Liberty's Folly: The Polish-Lithuanian Commonwealth in the Eighteenth Century, 1697–1795* (New York, 1991), 27. Cf. Andrzej Burzynski, "Struktura dochodów wielkiej własności ziemskiej XVI–XVIII wieku (Próba analizy na przykładzie dóbr królewskich województwa sandomierskiego)," *Roczniki dziejów społecznych i gospodarczych* 34 (1973): 31–66; Józef Kasperek, *Gospodarcza folwarczna ordinacji Zamojskiej w drugiej połowie XVIII wieku* (Warsaw, 1972), table 59, 162–63; Tomasz Opas, "Rynek lokalny Tarnowa w XVIII wieku," 47–48.

20. According to Jerzy Topolski, no more than 5 percent of the innkeepers in Great Poland were Jews. Topolski, "Uwagi o strukturze gospodarczo-społecznej Wielkopolski w XVIII wieku czyli dlaczego na jej terenie nie było żydowskich karczmarzy?" in *Żydzi w Wielkopolsce na przestrzeni dziejów,* ed. id. and K. Modelski (Poznan, 1999), 71.

their patrons, the magnate-aristocrats.[21] Indeed, from the second half of the eighteenth century on, the involvement of Jews in this sector, particularly in the countryside, became an increasingly prominent concern among politicians and pamphleteers vis-à-vis both the situation of the peasants and the occupational distribution of Jews. Simultaneously, in some regions, there were attempts to limit Jews from pursuing such occupations, not for ideological reasons, but as a result of landlords' efforts to rationalize the administration of their estates. The role of Jews in the liquor industry subsequently diminished somewhat, but it remained important.

The Economic Alliance of Jews and Nobles

The relationship between Jews and magnate-aristocrats was both instrumental and reciprocal.[22] Jews found relative security in the protection and support they received from the magnate-aristocrats. The magnate-aristocrats, in turn, benefited from the financial, managerial, and commercial expertise of Jews and the income they generated. What helped to balance the gulf in power between Jews and the magnates who owned the estates on which they lived was precisely the financial utility of the economic activities of the Jews. If Jews felt that the protection of their rights or the guarantees of their security were not being upheld, they threatened to leave. And this would have been very costly to their patrons.[23]

On the other hand, magnates were likely to find Jews at least as dis-

---

21. In using the term "magnate-aristocrat," I have been trying, as the Yiddish expression has it, "to dance at two weddings." The imprecise but widespread use of the term "magnate" in Polish historiography has been criticized by Andrzej Kaminski, who suggests that the term "aristocrat" is best used to denote the small (not more than 15–20 families), elite group of powerful families in Poland-Lithuania. "The Szlachta of the Polish-Lithuanian Commonwealth and Their Government," in *The Nobility in Russia and East Central Europe,* ed. Iwo Banac and Paul Bushkovitch (New Haven, 1983), 17–45. Cf. Teresa Zielińska, *Magnateria polska epoki saskiej* (Wrocław, 1977). Cf. Gershon Hundert, "On the Problem of Agency in Eighteenth-Century Jewish Society," *Scripta Hierosolymitana* 38 (1998): 83–84.

22. There are three recent monographs devoted to relations between Jews and magnate-aristocrats in Poland-Lithuania in the eighteenth century: Rosman, *Lords' Jews,* Adam Kaźmierczyk, *Żydzi w dobrach prywatnych,* and Teller, "Tafkidam hakalkali." Important dimensions of the problem have also been studied by Jacob Goldberg, see the references below and above, n. 1.

23. Eliyahu ben Yehezkel, *She'elot uteshuvot har hakarmel* (Frankfort a/O, 1782), "Hoshen mishpat," p. 24a, qu. 30: "and therefore, every nobleman in his town, because it belongs to him, decrees that no one will live in his territory unless they bring him some profit." Cf. p. 24b.

tasteful as anyone else in Polish Christian society. An analysis of twenty-nine diaries of noblemen found that the authors shared a distinct tendency to xenophobia and disliked Jews most of all.[24] Personal attitudes, however, were mitigated by the desire to protect the significant income generated by the presence of Jews in their towns and in the villages. Self-interest thus led nobles to grant dozens of privileges to Jewish communities that guaranteed this.[25] In almost every case, the town owner promised to ensure the Jews' freedom to trade in any commodity, anywhere, and at any time.

While a magnate was vastly more powerful than Jews who negotiated contracts to lease monopolies, the typical leaseholder "was by no means a cowering sycophant, but a man as much aware of his rights as his obligations."[26] Nonetheless, it was not uncommon for noblemen either to use force or to hold their leaseholders' wives and children hostage to extract payment from them. Clauses to this effect appear in contracts between Jews and their patrons.[27] A rabbinic responsum from this period took up the question of whether a wife, held hostage in this way, was "permitted" to her husband if he was a *kohen* (of priestly descent). Zalman Kohen held the *arenda* on a village, but his house and the implements in it were destroyed in a fire. The lord of the village and Zalman agreed on a settlement of the latter's debts. "And the lord held [the Jew's] wife until he brought the sum agreed upon." She must have been held for at least a week, since the responsum records that "every two or three days, Jews would come and visit with her through the window of her cell." After considering various precedents in the legal literature, and after announcing his determination to try to find a way to "permit" the wife to him, the last paragraph adds a further consideration:

24. Joanna Partyka, "Szlachecka silva rerum jako źródło do badań etnograficznych," *Etnografia Polska* 32 (1988): 67–94.

25. Będzin, Dębno, Dobromil, Kałusz, Kamionka, Kazimierz Dolny, Kobylin, Kowal, Łask, Leżajsk, Łosice, Mordy, Nowy Korczyn, Płock, Przedbórz, Swarzędz, Warta, Zwoleń: Jacob Goldberg, *Jewish Privileges*, s.v.; Niemirów, Toporów, Dobromil, Tomaszów Lubelski: Maurycy Horn, *Żydzi na Rusi Czerwonej w XVI i pierwszej połowie XVII w.: Działalność gospodarcza na tle rozwoju demograficznego* (Warsaw, 1975), 163–64; Tarnopol: P. Korngruen, ed., *Tarnopol* (Jerusalem, 1952), col. 28; Brody: Nathan Michael Gelber, *Toledot yehudei Brody 1584–1943*, "Arim ve'imahot beYisra'el," vol. 6 (Jerusalem, 1955), 25. Many more examples could be added.

26. Rosman, *Lords' Jews*, 131.

27. Ibid.; Goldberg, "Poles and Jews," 261; Goldberg, *Hahevrah hayehudit*, 42, 236–37; Gershon D. Hundert, "Approaches to the History of the Jewish Family in Early Modern Poland-Lithuania," in *The Jewish Family: Myths and Reality*, ed. S. M. Cohen and P. E. Hyman (New York, 1986), 20.

Another deduction supports permitting [the wife]. There is a distinction that applies to this case that depends on whether Jews or Gentiles have the upper hand. If Jews have the upper hand, the Gentile would be afraid to pollute the woman, because then he would lose his money. If the Gentiles have the upper hand, he would not be afraid [to do so]. In this case, the husband has handed her over to the lord and told the lord that he was going to find the money for him in order to redeem his wife. Surely the Gentile would know, by his own reason, that if he pollutes the wife, the husband would not wish to redeem her in that state. Therefore, he would definitely fear losing his money, since the husband would not want to redeem her.[28]

What gave the Jew the "upper hand" was the financial dependence of the lord on him. On the other hand, even before the eighteenth century, noblemen would sometimes order a Jew to "dance a *mayufes*." The Yiddish word corresponds to the first two Hebrew words of a Sabbath hymn, but the word came to be both a noun designating a song, or song and dance, that a cowering Jew performed for a nobleman and an adjective describing the noun "Jew" and connoting a cringing and/or toadying Jew. The first recorded reference dates to 1763.[29]

While the growing dominance of great magnate-aristocrats in the distribution of power in the Polish Commonwealth is undeniable, they were not unified in their interests, programs, ideologies, or allegiances to neighboring states. Very frequently, the motivation behind the actions of a magnate should be understood as related to his material interests, especially to the expansion of his share of lucrative patronage positions. In the western part of the country, the estates of the gentry were characteristically small; great latifundia became larger and more common as one moved eastward toward Ukraine, Belorussia, and Lithuania, precisely the areas where the Jewish population was concentrated. In those regions, economic decline characteristically had forced middle gentry to surrender their estates to their magnate neighbors, whose holdings became enormous. Roughly 90 percent of the land in Poland-Lithuania was owned by noblemen, although perhaps no more than 25 percent of noblemen actually owned land.

Vast wealth and enormous power were characteristic of the magnates. They had private armies. Radziwiłł, for example, employed 2,000 troops

28. Menahem Mendel ben Moses Auerbach of Krotoszyn (d. 1760). Published by Tsevi Halevi Ish Horowitz, *Letoledot hakehillot bePolin* (Jerusalem, 1978), 91–92. And see there p. 55, where the date of the rabbi's death is recorded on the basis of an entry from the records of the Burial Society of Krotoszyn. An incorrect date is given in the *Encyclopaedia Judaica*.

29. Chone Shmeruk, "*Majufes:* A Window on Polish-Jewish Relations," *POLIN* 10 (1997): 273–86.

with foreign officers and operated his own cadet school. Radziwiłł's soldiers were more modern in their weaponry and tactics than the Polish army was. The Zamoyski estates in the 1770s included ten towns, 220 villages, and a population of over 100,000.[30] In 1748, the total public revenue of Poland-Lithuania was eight million florins. Michael Radziwiłł's income that year was five million and that of F. S. Potocki three million; the Zamoyski estates returned about one million florins per year. There were considerable variations in the rates of return on magnate estates, which were vulnerable because of their concentration in the cultivation of grain.[31]

The *szlachta,* or gentry, constituted at least 6 percent of the population of the Commonwealth. The *szlachta* was not a class, however, and was quite highly differentiated, although there were no formal hierarchical distinctions of title and rank within it. Even though there were members of the *szlachta* who were landless and virtually indistinguishable from peasants, in principle they were all brothers, from the greatest magnate-aristocrat to the poorest gentleman. All were equals and all were entitled to participate in the deliberations of the local assemblies of the nobility *(sejmiki)* and to elect their delegates to the Sejm, or parliament. The petty gentry were more hostile to Jews in practice and in the legislation they advocated than were the great magnate-aristocrats.[32] This was a reflection of economic competition between gentry and Jews in the areas of the leasing of property from the magnates and in certain forms of commerce. It was from the *szlachta* that the demands to limit Jewish commercial activity arose. Nevertheless, they, too, perhaps under pressure from their magnate patrons, had to recognize the significance of Jewish commerce.

Thus, for example, throughout the seventeenth century, there were demands that Jews and others be forbidden to travel to Hungary to import wine.[33] These demands were repeated again early in the eighteenth

30. Lukowski, *Liberty's Folly,* 26. J. Kasperek, *Gospodarka folwarczna ordynacji zamojskiej w drugiej połowie XVIII wieku* (Warsaw, 1972); R. Orłowski, *Działalność społeczno-gospodarcza Andrzeja Zamoyskiego 1757–1792* (Lublin, 1965).

31. The income of Zamoyski estate in 1786–87 was about 64 percent less than it had been in 1777–78. Lukowski, *Liberty's Folly,* 15, 27. Cf. Kasperek, *Gospodarka folwarczna ordynacji zamojskiej;* Orłowski, *Działalność społeczno-gospodarcza Andrzeja Zamoyskiego.*

32. See Jacob Goldberg, "Poles and Jews in the Seventeenth and Eighteenth Centuries: Rejection or Acceptance," *Jahrbücher für Geschichte Osteuropas,* n.s., 22 (1974): 261–62, also in an expanded Hebrew version, "Al yahas hahevrah hapolanit kelapei hayehudim," *Hahevrah hayehudit bemamlekhet Polin-Lita,* 37–44, for a slightly different view.

33. Gershon Hundert, "The Implications of Jewish Economic Activities for Christian-Jewish Relations in the Polish Commonwealth," in *The Jews in Poland,* ed. Antony Polonsky et al. (Oxford, 1986), 231, n. 43.

century.[34] Such legislation had little impact on Jewish importers. On one occasion, representatives of the gentry of Podolia intervened on behalf of Jewish wine importers "because they have so very few sources of income."[35] We learn from his memoirs that a Jewish merchant in Bolechów, Dov Ber Birkenthal, and his father before him had prospered in the Hungarian wine trade. Indeed, by 1740 and 1744, the resolutions of the *sejmik* (regional assembly) of Wisznia included clauses advocating *permitting* Jews to import wine, "because the revenue generated by this trade is significant."[36] The legislation and policies adopted depended on the resolution of the contradictions among a number of competing interests and forces. In addition to the desire of the magnates to protect their revenue-producing Jews and to a generally expressed desire to increase state revenues, it was understood that Jewish competition in the import and sale of various commodities would help keep prices down. Members of the petty *szlachta* often competed directly with Jews in certain sectors of the import market and generally displayed more sympathy for the interests of Christian merchants, but for the most part, the magnates' interests triumphed.

The decade of the most extensive Jewish involvement in leasing monopoly rights for the production and sale of alcoholic beverages was probably the 1760s. In some regions, as many as 55 percent of rural Jews and 25 percent of urban Jews were primarily involved in this occupation. Pressure to oust Jews from this industry coming from the Catholic clergy,[37] as well as from the *szlachta,* led the Sejm in 1768 to forbid Jews to keep inns and taverns without a pact or agreement with municipal authorities.[38] Although many magnates ignored the legislation, according to some scholars, there was a substantial reduction in the number of Jews in this sector, particularly in the eastern regions of the Commonwealth, beginning in the 1770s.[39]

---

34. *AGZ*, vol. 22: *244–42,* p. 615; *267–42,* p. 675 (italicized figures refer to section and subsection numbers). Cf. Yehudit Kalik, "Hayahas shel hashlakhta lemishar hayehudi," 43–57.

35. Including Wojewoda kijowski Józef Potocki, wojewoda podolski Stefan Humiecki, wojewoda belski Stefan Potocki and others. Henryk Gmiterek, *Materiały źródłowe do dziejów Żydów w księgach grodzkich lubelskich z doby panowania Augusta II Sasa 1697–1733,* "Judaica Lublinensia," vol. 1 (Lublin, 2001), no. 1346, p. 252 (1719); no. 1435, p. 267 (1720).

36. *AGZ*, vol. 23: *76–7,* p. 193; *93–9,* p. 228.

37. Goldberg, "Hayehudi vehapundak hakafri," 233, 240.

38. *VL,* 7: 755 (352).

39. Maurycy Horn, "Rola gospodarcza Żydów w Polsce do końca XVIII wieku," in *Żydzi wśród Chrześcijan w dobie szlacheckiej Rzeczypospolitej,* ed. Waldemar Kowalski and Jadwiga Muszynska (Kielce, 1996), 27; Schiper, *Dzieje handlu żydowskiego,* 225–31, 316–19, 350; Daniel Stone, *The Polish-Lithuanian State, 1386–1795* (Seattle, 2001), 304–5.

One success that the petty *szlachta* achieved was to gain the right to control the leasing of the lands and estates of magnates. The monopolies on distilling and brewing were virtually entirely in Jewish hands, but, by the eighteenth century, leaseholdings involving the territory together with the inhabitants came mainly into the hands of the petty *szlachta*. There were exceptions to this pattern, and at least one of them is notorious.

Usually, poorer noblemen leased estates or parts of estates on which there were peasants and other residents, and the standard contract gave the lessee jurisdiction over at least the peasant population. Jews rarely held such leases in the eighteenth century, but when they did, estate owners modified the conventional wording. Thus, in a contract for the lease of four villages in Małopolska in 1754, we read that "this Jew will have not even the slightest authority over the Christians, he must not dare to strike or oppress them. If they fail to heed him, he should appeal to the administrator."[40]

The powerful and wealthy brothers, Shmu'el and Gedaliah Ickowicz, lessees of the Radziwiłł estates during the 1720s, 1730s, and 1740s were an exception to the tendency of Jews in the eighteenth century not to lease whole estates.[41] The memoirist Solomon Maimon (ca. 1753–1800) calls them tyrants *(tyrannen)*, and in letters to them, Marcin Radziwiłł addressed them as he would have done a *szlachcić*, as *waszmość* ("Your Excellency") and *jego mości pan*.[42] Shmu'el's activities were "indispensable to [Anna z Sanguszków] Radziwiłł; he was one of her main providers of liquid capital and her closest advisor in financial matters."[43] Nevertheless, in 1736, when Marcin Radziwiłł leased Biała to Shmu'el Ickowicz, the contract specified, "I order Shmu'el, my agent, that he neither punish nor judge himself; no Jewish hand shall be raised against a Christian on pain of a heavy punishment." Officials with detailed instructions would enforce

---

40. AP Krakow, Castr. Biec. 380, p. 3 as quoted by Jacob Goldberg, "Hokhrei ha'ahuzot hayehudim," *Hahevrah hayehudit bemamlekhet Polin-Lita,* 167.

41. See also the remarkable case of Yisrael Rubinowicz, general manager *(ekonom)* of the Rytwiany-Lubnice complex in the administration of the Sieniawski-Czartoryski holdings described in detail by Rosman, *Lords' Jews,* 154–84.

42. AGAD, Arch. Radziwiłłów, dz. IV, no. 122, p. 26; 995: letters of November 2, 1740, to Gedaliah and April 22, 1742, and May 5, 1745, to Shmu'el, quoted by Goldberg, *Hahevrah hayehudit,* 164. The most extensive discussion of the Ickowicz brothers is in Teller, "Tafkidam hakalkali," 98–148. Cf. Teresa Zielińska, "Kariera i upadek żydowskiego potentata."

43. Wanda Karkucińska, *Anna z Sanguszków Radziwiłłowa* (Warsaw, 2000), 26. The author comments that she finds this central role played by the Jewish advisor *(kasjer)* "in a certain sense, strange, and for me until now an unsolved question."

the law, "not the Jews."[44] Those officials, on the other hand, were not to interfere in the affairs of the Jewish lessee. In any case, there is room to doubt that Ickowicz adhered to the terms of the contract.

During the twenty years (1727–47) that the Ickowicz brothers leased the Krzyczew (Krichev) estates, the number of villages doubled and the income generated by those lands also almost doubled. But there were strident complaints against the brothers, not only from the peasantry, but also from the petty gentry and from Jewish sub-lessees.[45] In 1740, when the petty gentry and the peasantry rebelled against their Jewish oppressors, the Radziwiłłs supported the Ickowicz brothers against the rebels.

Woszczyłło, the leader of the revolt, presented himself as the grandson of (Bohdan) Khmelnytskyi[46] and styled himself as head of the armies for the defense of Christianity and the destruction of the Jewish people. He insisted that, contrary to the Jewish rumor, his movement was not directed against the government or against the nobility. He was opposed only to Jews who denied Christians an opportunity to make a living, attacking, murdering, and robbing Christians. He claimed that Jews leased churches and that no child could be baptized without their permission. The community of Mstislavl (known by Jews as Amtshislav) observed an annual fast day followed by a communal Purim in memory of the events of 1739–40 because the revolt led by Woszczyłło was put down before the rebels could reach them. The communal minute book explained the attacks as arising from the rebels' jealousy of the prominence, wealth, and power of the Ickowicz brothers, which led them to attack the people to whom these great men belonged.[47]

Christian Burghers and Jewish Merchants

During the sixteenth, seventeenth, and eighteenth centuries, the relative power of the magnate-aristocrats increased at the expense of the crown and the gentry. Jewish "foreign policy" in other times and places had been

44. Goldberg, *Hahevrah hayehudit,* 167.

45. Marian Lech, "Powstanie chłopów białoruskich w starostwie krzyczewskim 1740r.," *Przegląd Historyczny* 51 (1960): 323n.

46. This may be an indication that the romantic view of Khmelnytskyi as defender of the interests of the peasants transcended the boundaries between Belarus and Ukraine; or was it that religious solidarity was the source of the power of the association?

47. Israel Halpern, *Yehudim veyahadut bemizrah Eiropah: Mehkarim betoledoteihem* (Jerusalem, 1968), 286.

predicated on the forging of alliances exclusively with the crown or with the highest authority in the state. In the Polish Commonwealth, it became necessary to adjust that strategy to conditions of increasing decentralization of power. The close links and the partial identity of interests of Jews and magnates may be inferred from the fact that by the eighteenth century, between one-half and three-quarters of all Polish-Lithuanian Jews lived in cities, towns, and villages belonging to magnates.[48]

In these private towns, Jews were likely to dominate commercial life and to enjoy the protection of the town owner. This contrasted sharply with the situation in older crown cities like Kraków, Lwów, Lublin, and Poznan, where competition between Jewish and Christian merchants and artisans was fierce. The privilege for the Jewish community in Kutów (Kuty) issued by Józef Potocki in 1715 promised exemption from taxes for five years to any merchant who would settle in the town, including Jews ("Żydom talmudowym hebrajskim").[49] Perhaps the ultimate test of status was the value accorded a Jewish life. Was a Jewish life equal in value to a Christian life? In the private town of Żółkiew in 1746, a miller was convicted of murdering a Jewish merchant, Gershon Lewkowicz, his wife, and his two daughters, Esther and Chajka. The murderer was hanged, then beheaded, and his skull was placed on the gates of the town by the court.[50] Assuming that Jews were similarly valued elsewhere by the magnates, the Jewish preference for private towns is not difficult to understand. Additionally, as a general rule, private towns were more attractive economically than the crown cities, which were frequently stagnant.

In crown cities, residential segregation tended to be stricter, competition more intense, and animosities more dangerous than in the private towns. This was true of Kraków, Poznan, Lwów, and, although it was a somewhat special case, Warsaw as well. Dozens of crown cities, including Kraków, Wilno, Lublin, and Warsaw, as well as almost all towns owned by the Church, attempted to exclude Jews from residing in their jurisdictions. In November 1789, Jewish representatives of the communities in Poland assembled in Warsaw and submitted what they called "A Humble Request to the Sejm." They claimed that there were 301 royal and ecclesi-

48. Weinryb, *Jews of Poland,* 120. Rosman, *Lords' Jews;* Gershon Hundert, *The Jews in a Polish Private Town: The Case of Opatów in the Eighteenth Century* (Baltimore, 1992).

49. Goldberg, *Jewish Privileges,* 142.

50. N. M. Gelber and Y. Ben-Shem, eds., *Sefer Zolkvah* (Jerusalem, 1969), col. 50; S. Buber, *Kiryah nisgavah, hi ir Zolkvah* (Kraków, 1903), 3; Patrycja Gąsiorowska and Stefan Gąsiorowski, "Inducta rzeczy spisanych po zabitym Gerszonie w roku 1746," *Studia Judaica* 1 (1998): 88–94.

astical towns, of which 200 forbade Jewish residence.[51] This proposition was a piece of rhetorical exaggeration and did not accurately reflect the situation, although it did reflect the perception of Jews, who felt themselves to be victims of discriminatory legislation. The Jewish response to intense competition was typically to seek a more hospitable place. In the smaller crown town of Krzemieniec (Kremianets') in Volhynia, the Christian burghers' struggle to limit Jewish economic activity intensified in the 1770s and 1780s. By 1789, a royal surveyor reported that the complaints of the burgers had led to Jews abandoning the town, which was now in ruins.[52]

Limitations on Jewish commerce and artisanry were often enacted in municipalities. The aim was to reduce, if not eliminate, Jewish competition. Typically, Jews would be classed as foreign merchants and forbidden to engage in retail trade, Jewish wholesale merchants were limited to certain specific commodities, or Jews were forbidden to lease shops or stores on the town marketplace. Frequently, the charters of artisan guilds not only excluded Jews but insisted that they be prohibited from acquiring the raw materials used by members of the guild, as for example the hides needed by shoe- and bootmakers. At times, too, Jews were prohibited from selling imported products of the same type as those produced by the artisans. All this legislation, it bears repeating, was much more characteristic of crown towns than of private towns. In Kraków, for example, the struggle of Jews for rights of residence anywhere in the city and for the abolition of restrictions on their commercial activities continued well into the nineteenth century.[53] By contrast, in one private town, at the beginning of the eighteenth century, the Christian municipality complained to the town owner about the local Jews, noting that, according to municipal law, it was forbidden for Jews to conduct business anywhere except on their own street: "And now they brew beer and mead, sell wine, grain, fish, salt, candles, meat, etc., in our marketplace. They even sell pork, which they do not eat."[54]

The town owner's reply rejected the complaint out of hand, stressing the rights and privileges of Jewish residents. Their *privilege*, in which they were accorded the right to buy and sell any commodity in any location, was quoted. The magnate added here, "The burgers must obey the law." And, what is more, "Żydzi cieszać się prawami i przywileiami miasta, iako

---

51. *MDSC*, 6: 129–32.

52. C. Shmeruk and S. Ettinger, "Letoledot hayishuv hayehudi beKremenits," in *Bein Polin leRusiyah* (Jerusalem, 1994), 345, originally published in *Pinkas Kremenits,* ed. A. S. Stein (Tel Aviv, 1954), 9–45.

53. Majer Bałaban, *Historia Żydów w Krakowie i na Kazimierzu,* 2 vols. (Kraków, 1931, 1936).

54. Hundert, *Jews in a Polish Private Town,* 135.

wspól mieszczanie, equali juri gaudere maią": that is, by law, Jews are equal to other burghers in every respect.[55]

Even in the cities that pursued such policies, however, a certain inconsistency arose because of the significance of the Jewish role in the home market. Thus, most of the localities that had the policy *de non tolerandis Judaeis* nevertheless permitted Jews to enter the town and remain for periods of time during fairs and on market days. This was true, for example, of Toruń and Gdańsk and numerous smaller towns.[56] The growing importance of Jews in commerce also meant that the force of the various exclusionary and limiting measures weakened during the late seventeenth and early eighteenth centuries. However, during the course of the last decades of the eighteenth century, in certain crown cities, there was a distinct intensification of the pressures on Jewish merchants and artisans. This was due, on the one hand, to the increasing economic significance of commerce and of the urban merchants, and on the other hand, to the beginnings of the dawning of national political consciousness among some elements of the urban Christian population.

It would be misleading to speak in general of a Polish Christian bourgeoisie during much of the eighteenth century. One of the keys to the flourishing of Polish Jewry was the political impotence of the Christian city-dwellers.[57] The birth of the Polish bourgeoisie came only at the end of the eighteenth century and with it an increasing enmity toward Jewish competitors, especially as the Polish bourgeoisie acquired political consciousness, together with some limited political influence. Still, in eighteenth-century Poland, a true bourgeoisie was largely restricted to Warsaw.

Jewish Economic Attitudes

Three predominant Jewish worldviews as to the nature and value of economic activity seem to have coexisted during this period.[58] The first is

55. Ibid.

56. See Jacob Goldberg, "*De Non Tolerandis Iudaeis:* On the Introduction of the Anti-Jewish Laws into Polish Towns and the Struggle against Them," in *Studies in Jewish History Presented to Professor Raphael Mahler on His Seventy-Fifth Birthday* (Merhavia, Israel, 1974), 39–52.

57. Benzion Dinur, "Darkah hahistorit shel yahadut Polin," in id., *Dorot vereshumot* (Jerusalem, 1978), 193–201.

58. The three paradigms are meant to be emblematic and certainly not comprehensively to reflect all of the existing economic attitudes of Polish-Lithuanian Jews in the eighteenth century. My goal is to buttress my general insistence on seeing the vast heterogeneity of this community.

seen in the immense popular medieval ethical work *Hovot halevavot* ("Duties of the Heart") by Baḥya ben Joseph Ibn Paquda.[59] The author advocated a life of pious self-deprivation, and the idea of *perishut*, or voluntary separation from the material world, became widely accepted. This paradigm justified communal support for those devoting themselves to spiritual pursuits.

The second view, emerging from the 1770s on, is seen in the rapid spread of the movement of religious revival known as Hasidism. While the economic doctrines of the early Hasidic masters have yet to be systematically studied, it is evident that those teachings, with some exceptions, involved a rejection of the notion of poverty and self-deprivation as positive religious values. The Hasidic masters neither railed against the differences between rich and poor nor generally deprived themselves of material comfort. *Bitahon,* the confidence that the Lord would provide for His servants, characterized Hasidic teaching. At this point, and only impressionistically, one can say only that Hasidism did not discourage an entrepreneurial outlook.

For example, in 1783 the Russian government, having annexed Polish territory roughly coterminous with Belorussia in 1772, enacted various restrictions on the production and sale of alcohol that had the effect of virtually removing Jews from access to that industry.[60] Some of the Hasidim of the region wrote complaining of the edict to their rebbe, Menahem Mendel of Witebsk (Vitsyebsk; Vitebsk) (1730–1788), who was in the Land of Israel. His response, from which the following is abstracted, reflects the Hasidic view of the matter:

There is a note of despair in your letter because of the campaign of the king and his ministers to destroy your livelihood [*sibbat parnasatam*] of innkeeping [*hakabak*]. I was not disturbed to hear this, because to me it was nothing new. I have seen [this] in earlier times when I dwelt there under their rule, the weight of which increases greatly. . . . "Neither poverty nor wealth come from one's occupation

59. *Hovot halevavot* appeared in at least thirty-one editions during the seventeenth and eighteenth centuries. Cf. Allan Lawrence Nadler, *The Faith of the Mithnagdim: Rabbinic Responses to Hasidic Rapture* (Baltimore, 1997), 78, 216 n. 5.

60. Richard Pipes, "Catherine II and the Jews: The Origins of the Pale of Settlement," *Soviet Jewish Affairs* 5 (1975): 10–13; John Klier, *Russia Gathers Her Jews: The Origins of the "Jewish Question" in Russia, 1772–1825* (De Kalb, Ill., 1986), 69; Simon Dubnow, *History of the Jews in Russia and Poland from the Earliest Times until the Present Day,* trans. Israel Friedlaender (Philadelphia, 1916–20), 1: 310–14; Eugeniusz Aniszczenko, "Rządowa organizacja kahałów Bialorusi Wschodniej na terytorium anektowanym przez Rosje w 1772 r.," *Prawo* (Wrocław) 251: *Studia historyczno-demograficzne,* ed. Tadeusz Jurek and Krystyna Matwijowski (1996), 65–76.

[God is the one true source of wealth]" [BT Kiddushin 82b]. The *sibbah* [reason; thought] is not the main thing but the deed. As the verse says: "And the Lord your God will bless you in all that you do" [Deut. 15:18]: One must believe in God, the Reason of all reasons. . . . If you cannot pursue one occupation, pursue another. In my view, even if the decree of the government is rescinded and you are permitted to engage in the business of beverages, you should keep it as far from yourselves as possible. For it is condemned and no blessing attends it. There were numerous communities and the entire province of Podolia where in my day this occupation was forbidden them. [At the time] all of their lives were dependent on it. [This was] in the days of the BeShT and the days of my teacher the rabbi [Dov Ber the Maggid of Międzyrzecz (Mežyrič), d. 1772] (their souls are in heaven). And we saw this [decree] as humorous. Who cares if one's occupation changes? And thus it was. They prospered ever more greatly after they changed to other occupations and commerce. God blessed all that they did. The land was filled with money, but earlier, when they pursued that occupation, the land had been poor and destitute. Later when it was taken from them, the Source of Blessing blessed them.[61]

A third viewpoint was held by the nascent Jewish bourgeoisie found primarily in Warsaw, but also in trading emporia like Szkłów and Brody in the second half of the century. These were Jews, some of them immigrants from the west, who were adapting successfully to the general changes in the European economy and consciously or unconsciously incorporating the most modern currents of thought, behavior, and attitude into their outlook.[62]

On May 30, 1790, an anonymous member of the emerging Jewish bourgeoisie of Warsaw addressed an open letter to the delegates representing the towns. The missive was brimming with references to the slogans of the French Revolution and the Rights of Man. The author, David Königsberger, a Silesian Jewish merchant, demanded that the natural rights of Jews be respected. At about the same time, a number of prosperous Warsaw Jews submitted a petition to the Sejm asking that the rights of citi-

61. Menahem Mendel ben Moshe, *Peri ha'arets* (Kapust, 1814), 29b; *Likkutei amarim* (Lwów, 1811), pt. 2, letter 6, pp. 9b–12b; Yaakov Barnai, *Igerot hasidim me'erets-yisra'el* (Jerusalem, 1980), 117–24. Cf. Nahum Karlinsky, *Historiyah shekeneged: Igerot hahassidim me'erets-Yisra'el: Hatekst vehakontekst* (Jerusalem, 1998), 23–34, 49–72, and see the references there on the changing Hasidic idea of *"bitahon."*

62. Moshe (Wolfgang) Heymann (originally from Breslau) was a merchant-banker in Warsaw and a leader of the incipient Jewish bourgeoisie. He was among the delegation that presented the celebratory poem composed for the Warsaw Jewish community in honor of the first anniversary of the Constitution of the 3rd of May to the Polish monarch in 1792. Subsequently, he became involved in espionage and was hanged as a Prussian spy on July 24, 1794. Jacob Shatzky, *Di geshikhte fun Yidn in Varshe* (New York, 1947), 1: 141.

zenship be extended immediately to 250 Jewish families in Warsaw. These families probably encompassed the entirety of the embryonic polonizing Jewish middle class in Warsaw.[63]

On the level of individual contacts between Jews and Christian burghers, it is safe to say that the legislation attempting to limit and circumscribe Jewish economic activity faithfully reflects norms but not necessarily behavior. The prescribed relationship was one of general distrust, if not hostility. Jewish attitudes and norms, no less than those of Christians, advocated segregation and keeping far from the "other." Thus a rabbi in the mid eighteenth century remarked without special emphasis that a Gentile making a purchase from a Jew certainly "would not do so except before witnesses and a court."[64] A preacher warned in a book published earlier in the century: "In our day people are lenient in the matter of partnerships [with Gentiles], and even more so [regarding] doing business with them without a partnership. He who would preserve his soul should always keep far away from them."[65] Jewish communal legislation repeatedly prohibited partnerships, and even temporary agreements, with Gentiles. These insistent prohibitions suggest that the proscribed behavior was common enough to warrant continual attention.

The *kahal*'s concern was not only to uphold Jewish law, but also to defend the community that would be likely to be held responsible for losses incurred by the Christian partner. Furthermore, the solidarity of the community was a fundamental part of its security, and there were constant condemnations and bans of excommunication against those who revealed "the secrets of Israel" to merchants or noblemen. A Jew who pooled his interests with a Christian defied heaven and the sanctions of his community.[66] Sometimes, however, the profits were worth the risk of social condemnation. In any case, if the Christian patron or partner were sufficiently powerful, the individual could often avoid the prescribed ostracism.

Commercial and business relations had an instrumental character. Jews were convinced of the superiority of their own culture to that of their neighbors, whom they viewed as overwhelmingly immoral, violent, prone to drunkenness, and often dangerously hostile. The culture of Polish Christian townspeople, not to speak of peasants, held no attraction

63. *MDSC*, 6: 188–90; Artur Eisenbach, *The Emancipation of the Jews in Poland 1780–1870*, trans. Janina Dorosz, ed. Antony Polonsky (Cambridge, Mass., 1991), 90–91.

64. Eliyahu ben Yehezkel, *She'elot uteshuvot har hakarmel*, "Orah hayyim," p. 10b, qu. 13.

65. *Sefer toharot hakodesh* (Amsterdam, 1733) written in the second half of the seventeenth century, pt. 1, 30b. See also pt. 2, 38b.

66. Hundert, "Implications of Jewish Economic Activities," 61.

for Jews. It was urgently desirable, moreover, to keep as much distance as possible from this hostile "other." The demand in the minute book of the Jewish community of Ivanits (Iwaniec, near Mińsk) in 1759 that no Jew live in a Gentile's courtyard on pain of a fine and public shaming, for example, was not only a matter of social control.[67] Living too close to Gentiles carried with it the danger of corruption and of attack.

Nevertheless, the environment of the Polish Commonwealth profoundly affected Jews. Such influence could not have occurred without the intimate encounter of Jews and Christians. Similarly, the "thousands and thousands of words" that entered the Yiddish language from Polish are clear evidence that Jews were not socially isolated in Poland-Lithuania.[68] Jews' clothing likewise resembled the dress of their Polish neighbors, in form if not in color.[69]

There is also anecdotal evidence of various kinds that indicates the traversing of boundaries between Jews and Christians not only in the marketplace but in the towns as well. Reports of romances, of drinking together in taverns, and of intellectual conversations are quite abundant. In Żółkiew in the eighteenth century, we know of two affairs between Jewish householders and non-Jewish domestics. In one case, both the girl and her lover were lashed in public and expelled from the town. In the 1780s, it was reported that a Jew had had sexual relations with a Christian woman in Łęczyca. She was executed, but he was freed—according to municipal authorities, the Jewish community bribed the judges. Tavern discussions could be dangerous. In Rzeszów, in 1726, what began as a conversation in a tavern between a Jew and some Christian municipal officials about the coming elections in the town ended with the Jew being tried for blasphemy.[70] The frequency of such occurrences should not be exaggerated, however. There were no trends in Poland reflecting a model of integration of Jews and Christians in a civil society, though Jewish individuals did transgress the ethnic-religious divide in defiance of communal discipline.

67. I. Vernadsky Library of the Ukrainian Academy of Sciences, Kiev, Op. 1, 33: *Pinkas dekahal Ivanets.*
68. Max Weinreich, *Geshikhte fun der yidisher shprakh* (New York, 1973), 2: 185; 4: 250–52.
69. See chapter 4 below.
70. For romances, see Bogdan Baranowski, *Życie codzienne małego miasteczka w XVII i XVIII wieku* (Warsaw, 1975), 155: Jewish wife and Christian lover: 1765 in Tuszyn; Gelber and Ben-Shem, eds., *Sefer Zolkvah*, col. 40; Goldberg, "Poles and Jews," 277, and see there 259, 263, and 277 for numerous other examples. On the Rzeszów incident, see Kaźmierczyk, *Żydzi Polscy*, nos. 85, 86, 97, pp. 147–51, 169–71. On camaraderie in taverns, see also Hundert, *Jews in a Polish Private Town,* 70–71.

For instance, the nobleman memoirist, mentioned earlier, Marcin Matuszewicz, visited Brody in 1760 and stayed at the great stone house (kamienice) of a wealthy Jew. This Jew, who significantly is not named in the memoir, apparently ate off of silver plates and, what was more striking to Matuszewicz, "often had even noblemen at his table."[71] In the eighteenth century, a Jewish artist, Herszek Lejbowicz, prepared copies of portraits of the entire Radziwiłł family as woodcuts.[72] The sociocultural significance of Lejbowicz's commission is greater than the aesthetic standard of the work, which is not very distinguished.

It may be that another form of resistance or defiance of communal norms was located among Jewish women engaged in certain forms of trade and commerce.

WOMEN, COMMERCE, AND COMMUNITY

One of the very first items taken up by the Lithuanian council when it met in 1712 after an apparent hiatus of thirty years was the unseemly participation of women in commerce and especially in peddling. Some husbands, the council complained, had exposed and abandoned their wives in this way, permitting them to travel alone from house to house, and left the support of their households to their wives. Consequently, their children were as if illegitimate. The communities could not punish these women because they constituted nearly a majority and were supported by the Gentile powers. Therefore, they ordered, "From today, no woman with goods of any kind may enter a gentile house or that of a priest or ruler, even two or three together." The council went on to demand the eradication of the phenomenon of female peddlers, or tendlerkes. A ban was to be placed on storekeepers and merchants who provided them with goods for sale. They were to be pursued, expelled, and ostracized from the community of Israel. Anyone seeing a female peddler was empowered, without resort to authority, to destroy her goods in any way possible. The enactment was repeated in 1761.[73] What we may be seeing here is that women were evading the authority of the kahal and seeking (economic) independence. If so, it sug-

71. Marcin Matuszewicz, Diariusz życia mego, vol. 2: 1758–1764, 105. See also ibid., vol. 1: 1714–1757, 96 and 385–86.

72. Hanna Widacka, "Działalność Hirsza Leybowicza i innych rytowników na dworze nieświeskim Michała Kazimierza Radziwiłła 'Rybeńki' w świetle badań archiwalnych," Biuletyn Historii Sztuki 39 (1977): 62–72; Laima Šinkunaite, XVII a. Radvilu portretai (Kaunas, 1993).

73. PML, no. 947, 257; repeated: no. 1005, 270 (1761).

gests corporate female activity for economic independence in defiance of the male establishment. Some support for this possibility is found in a petition submitted to the Kraków municipal authorities by a group (guild?) of Jewish women peddlers, who sought permission to continue their commercial activities from the municipality, "because we do not belong to the elders of the community of Kazimierz [the Jewish "town" next to Kraków] but only to the treasury of the city of Kraków."[74]

Of course, most participation by women in the economy was not a form of resistance but collaboration with their husbands. It is thus difficult to compute the degree of female commercial and artisanal activity, which was accounted as part of their husbands' business.

OCCUPATIONAL STRUCTURE

It is impossible to determine the occupational structure of Polish-Lithuanian Jewry with great precision, chiefly because people tended not to engage consistently and permanently in one precise category of livelihood. Moreover, one cannot assume that the lists of taxpayers that sometimes indicate occupations utilized those designations consistently. A person classified as a *szmuklerz* (haberdasher) on one list might appear on another as a *kupiec* (merchant). Jewish economic activity was characteristically fluid and entrepreneurial; artisans marketed the goods they produced; merchants were also artisans and lent money at interest; rabbis and other religious functionaries engaged in commerce; the holder of an *arenda* contract might well also trade in imported cloth.[75] Generally, one can say that by the second half of the eighteenth century, roughly equivalent proportions of Jews were engaged in artisanry and in trade in urban settlements. In the villages, about 80 percent of Jews were engaged in occupations related to the liquor trade. During the eighteenth century, while the Jewish share of domestic and international commerce in Poland-Lithuania grew, the proportion of the Jewish population engaged in artisanry also expanded.

Jewish involvement in artisanry increased together with the growing Jewish population in the eighteenth century. Most Jewish artisan guilds founded then were in fields related to textiles and furs.[76] They functioned

74. AP Kraków, Akta Żydowskie III/11/8, unpaginated; Hundert, "Approaches to the History of the Jewish Family," 22–23; Teller, "Tafkidam hakalkali," 259–67.

75. Rosman, *Lords' Jews*, 48–51.

76. Maurycy Horn, *Żydowskie bractwa rzemieślnicze na ziemiach polskich, białoruskich i ukrainskich w latach 1613–1850* (Warsaw, 1998). On this subject, in addition to the many works cited by Horn, see Mark Wischnitzer, *A History of Jewish Crafts and Guilds* (New York, 1965).

as Christians guilds did; they controlled prices and sought monopolistic control of their craft. Some guilds had their own places of worship, clerical leadership, courts, annual banquets, and guild banners.[77] Guilds attempted to defend Jewish artisans from their Christian competitors.[78] This competition could become quite intense, particularly in royal towns.

Even among artisans, however, there was frequently a complementary relationship, an ethnic division of products, as was the case, occasionally, among merchants.[79] In Opatów, in the late eighteenth century, for example, all saddlers and shoemakers were Christians, while all hat makers and all but one furrier were Jews. All smiths and coopers were Christians, but all save two of the haberdashers and tailors were Jews. In Łęczyce, by 1765, there were only two Christian tailors and twenty-five Jewish tailors.[80] In general, Jews were most likely to be involved in trades related to textiles and furs (drapers, haberdashers, tailors, cap makers, furriers). They were also goldsmiths, jewellers, glaziers, and bookbinders.[81] Jewish butchers, bakers, brewers, distillers, and workers in related trades associated with food were also common. Indeed, Jews were frequently as dominant in the meat trade as they were in tailoring. They were least likely to be smiths, carpenters, and shoemakers.

While the number of Jews involved in publishing was very small, this industry was crucial to the cultural life of Polish-Lithuanian Jewry. The commercial history of this industry has not yet been studied.[82] The issue that is most puzzling is the fact that the massive market for Jewish books

77. The owner of Zasław recognized a guild of tailors and furriers with the right to its own preacher and place of prayer "on the model of my other towns" (przykladem innych miast moich) in 1735. The original founding text (in Hebrew) had been approved by the estate administrator three years earlier. Kaźmierczyk, Żydzi Polscy, no. 29, pp. 48–50.

78. Stefan Gąsiorowski, "Walka chrześcijanskich cechów z konkurencja żydowska w Żółkwi w świetle przywilejów z XVII i pierwszej połowy XVIII wieku," Prawo 251: Studia historyczno-demograficzne, ed. Tadeusz Jurek and Krystyna Matwijowski (Wrocław, 1996), 39.

79. Hundert, "Implications of Jewish Economic Activities," 57, and see also Hundert, Jews in a Polish Private Town, 48–51; T. Opas, "Sytuacja ludności żydowskiej w miastach szlacheckich województwa lubelskiego w XVIII wieku," BZIH 67 (1968): 17; Teller, "Tafkidam hakalkali," 57–67.

80. Tomczak, ed., Lustracja województw wielkopolskich i kujawskich 1789 r., pt. 3, 11.

81. A number of Jewish goldsmiths enjoyed Radziwiłł patronage. Karkucinska, Anna z Sanguszków Radziwiłłowa, 150–51, 170. For further references to Jewish metal workers, see Majer Bałaban, Zabytki historyczne Żydów w Polsce (Warsaw, 1920), 12–14.

82. Most of the older sources are cited by Israel Halpern, "Va'ad arba aratsot bePolin vehasefer ha'ivri," in id., Yehudim veyahadut, 78–107 (with appendices). See also Emanuel Ringelblum, Kapitlen geshikhte fun amolikn yidishn lebn in Poyln (Buenos Aires, 1953), 389–456; id., "Johann Anton Krieger, Printer of Jewish Books in Nowy Dwór," POLIN 12 (1999): 198–211. And see below.

in the Commonwealth was served by only one domestic center of production during the entire period between 1692 and about 1760. This was the press founded in the private town of Żółkiew by Uri (Phoebus) ben Aaron Halevi (also called Uri Witzenhausen or Witmund; 1625–1715), formerly of Amsterdam.[83] A total of 259 books were published in Żółkiew between 1692 and 1762. The size of the press runs for these books is unknown. Fifteen other presses were created in Poland in the years following about 1760, and the volume of publication increased substantially, partly as a result of the intervention of Polish government officials. From 1763 to 1795, 781 titles were published in Poland. By contrast, in Amsterdam, the center of Hebrew publishing, a total of 1,597 titles appeared in the course of the eighteenth century.[84]

As far as we know, no books were published in Kraków or Lublin during the whole of the eighteenth century. Part of the reason for this may be traceable to legislation adopted by the Council of Four Lands intended to protect the newly founded press in Żółkiew at the end of the seventeenth century. In 1697 and again in 1699, the council condemned publishers in Kraków and Lublin for competing unfairly with the presses of Żółkiew and sought to eliminate the problem.[85] The language of the resolutions provides the solution to this puzzle. Both resolutions forbade publishers in Kraków and Lublin to publish in other countries and import the books back into Poland. It is possible that the products of these presses have been lost to posterity. This possibility is strengthened by a specific reference in the resolutions to pamphlets in Yiddish of ten or fewer pages. Such material is ephemeral and not likely to survive over long periods of time. Nevertheless, it is much more likely that the practice of importing books published elsewhere was dominant. A Warsaw newspaper devoted to commerce estimated as late as 1786 that Polish Jews annually imported books with a value of at least one million florins.[86]

In Żółkiew, in the mid eighteenth century, nine presses were in operation. This highly profitable enterprise did not escape the attention of the magnates who owned the town. In 1750, Michał Kazimierz Radziwiłł issued an "ordinance" setting the tax due him from each Żółkiew publisher

---

83. H. D. Friedberg, *Toledot hadefus ha'ivri bePolanyah* (Tel Aviv, 1950), 62–64.

84. Yishayahu Vinograd, *Thesaurus of the Hebrew Book*, 2 vols. (Jerusalem, 1995). Ze'ev Gries, *Hit'orerut ha'inteligentsiyah haredumah: Hadpasat sefarim bame'ah ha18 bikhlal velakahal hakor'im bemizrah Eiropah bifrat kevitui letahalikhei temurah veshinui bahinukh yehudi* (typescript, Jerusalem, 1996), 58, n. 32.

85. *PVAA*, no. 510, pp. 237–38; no. 520, pp. 242–44.

86. *Dziennik handlowy*, 1787, p. 364, as quoted by Schiper, *Dzieje handlu żydowskiego*, 313.

at 20 ducats, or "red" florins, that is, the equivalent of 360 florins.[87] The ordinance also sought to eliminate competition among the three owners of the nine presses (Gierszon—three presses; Chaimek—four presses; Dawidek—two presses). There were clauses demanding that only good-quality paper be used; that two copies of each book be deposited in the lord's archive; and that the wages of the various skilled workers be regulated. The highest-paid workers apparently were paid 1 ducat (18 florins) weekly, an extraordinarily high rate. There were also agreements negotiated among the publishers themselves seeking to divide the market and to avoid competition.[88]

In a way, the saga of the Jewish publishing industry in eighteenth-century Poland-Lithuania might be said to constitute evidence of the degree to which the economic destiny of the Jewish population was dependent on macroeconomic and political developments outside of their control. The failure to develop economic interventionist policies by successive Polish governments led to reliance on imported industrial products. The role of the powerful Radziwiłłs in protecting their own interests was likely the critical ingredient in this story. Only in the very last decades of the eighteenth century did their monopoly erode. The dependence of the domestic Jewish publishing industry on one powerful magnate and the consequent demand for books imported from Amsterdam and German lands until the 1770s and 1780s mirrored the general economic evolution of the Commonwealth.

In the last years of the eighteenth century, the beginnings of a secular trend of disintegration of the "feudal" system were intensified by the partitions of Poland. Jews, whose integration in the economic system of the old regime has been demonstrated in the foregoing pages, experienced displacement and dislocation because of the economic changes that developed at a growing pace in the nineteenth century. Before the end of the eighteenth century, however, the signs of the coming disintegration were discernible, particularly in the movement to remove Jews from the rural production and sale of alcohol. Jews continued during that period to be crucial to the functioning, as inefficient and backward as it was, of the magnate-dominated economy of the Polish Commonwealth, but their economic integration did not mean cultural integration. The crucial ingredient in Polish culture that kept the Jews alien and foreign was the Church.

87. AGAD, AR, dz. XXIX, rkps no. 6, published by Kaźmierczyk, *Żydzi Polscy*, 100–102.
88. Yehoshua Mondshine, "Ma'amad shene'erakh bein hamadpisim beLevov veZolkiew," *Sefer hazikkaron lerabbi Moshe Lifshits*, ed. R. Rozenbaum (New York, 1996), 898–916.

CHAPTER 3

The Polish Church and Jews, Polish Jews and the Church

By the beginning of the eighteenth century, being Polish had come to imply being Catholic.[1] The Reformation churches had found numerous adherents in Poland-Lithuania in the sixteenth century, when Lutheranism was popular among burghers, and Calvinism proved particularly appealing to members of the *szlachta*. Indeed, around the late sixteenth century, a majority of the Polish nobility was not Catholic. By the end of the seventeenth century, however, the triumph of the Counter-Reformation Church in Poland was virtually complete. Although the eighteen Latin Catholic bishops continued to sit in the Senate during this period, churchmen of other denominations, even at the height of the acceptance of the Reformed churches, never joined them. The Jesuits' near dominance in the field of education meant that they were responsible for the training of a majority of each generation of gentry.[2]

Political events also fostered the identification of Polish nationality with Catholicism. All of the invading powers that attacked Poland from every side in the mid seventeenth century were non-Catholic. Poles attributed their successful resistance to the Protestant Swedish siege of the town of Częstochowa in 1655 to the icon of the Madonna in the Jasna Góra monastery there. The victory was seen as a miracle and bolstered a Pol-

---

1. Janusz Tazbir, *Świat panów Pasków* (Łódz, 1986), 31.
2. The conventional estimate for the mid eighteenth century is about sixty-seven Jesuit and about thirty Piarist colleges. The abolition of the Jesuit Order by Pope Clement XIV led to a crisis addressed by the establishment of the Commission for National Education in 1773. See K. Mrozowska, *Funkcjonowanie systemu szkolnego Komisji Edukacji Narodowej na terenie Korony w latach 1783–1793* (Wrocław, 1985).

ish Catholic "crusade" against the Swedes. It was much repeated at the time that King Charles X of Sweden had boasted to Cromwell that soon not a single Papist would be left in Poland. What happened was the reverse of the king's prophecy. The number of Catholic clergy tripled in the course of the seventeenth century. The expression of patriotism in the Church and of Catholic piety in the Polish parliament became normal. Mary, the Mother of God, was queen of Poland.[3]

The triumph of the Counter-Reformation Church and the symbiotic relationship between the Church and the beginnings of Polish national consciousness were important ingredients in the development of Polish Catholicism in the eighteenth century. Guided by industrious bishops, preachers, and polemicists, the Church grew in numbers and influence, and its leadership displayed energy and renewed vigor. The construction of churches, monasteries, and convents in the eighteenth century was dramatically greater than in earlier periods.[4] While in the latter half of the century, there were divisions between those attracted to new trends in European thinking and those who reacted against the novel ideas of the Enlightenment, the general trends through the first six decades of the century were toward ever-greater xenophobia and intolerance.[5] Nor were

3. See, e.g., Andrzej J. Baranowski, "Oprawy uroczystości koronacyjnych wizerunków Marii na Rusi Koronnej w XVIII w.," *Biuletyn Historii Sztuki* 57 (1995): 299–322 and the references there.

4. Stanisław Litak, "Jezuici na tle innych zakonów męskich w Polsce XVI–XVIII wieku," in *Jezuici a kultura polska*, ed. L. Gzebień and S. Obirek (Kraków, 1993), 185–98. J. A. Chrościcki, "La Reconquête catholique dans l'architecture et la peinture religieuses," *XVIIe siècle* 199 (1998): 350–51.

5. On the Church and the Jews in Poland, see Jacob Goldberg, *Hamumarim bemamlekhet Polin-Lita* (Jerusalem, 1985); N. M. Gelber, "Die Taufbewegung unter den polnischen Juden im XVIII. Jahrhundert," *MGWJ* 68 (1924): 225–41; Yehudit Kalik, "Hayahasim bein hakenesiyah hakatolit layehudim bemamlekhet Polin-Lita," in *Kiyum veshever*, ed. Israel Bartal and Israel Gutman (Jerusalem, 1997), 1: 193–208; Waldemar Kowalski, "W obronie wiary: Ks. Stefan Żuchowski–między wzniosłością a okrucieństwem," in *Żydzi wśród Chrześcian w dobie szlacheckiej Rzeczypospolitej*, ed. Waldemar Kowalski and Jadwiga Muszyńska (Kielce, 1996), 221–33; Jacek Krochmal, "Hayahasim bein ha'ironim vehakenesiyah bePrzemysl levein hayehudim bashanim 1559–1772," *Gal-Ed* 15–16 (1997): 15–33; Daniel Tollet, "Le Goupillon, le prétoire et la plume: Stéfan Żuchowski et l'accusation de crimes rituels en Pologne à la fin du XVII siècle et au début du XVIII siècle," in *Żydzi wśród Chrześcian*, ed. Kowalski and Muszyńska, 207–20; K. S. Wirszyłło, "Stosunek duchowieństwo katolickiego na Wolyniu do Żydów XVIII wieku," *Miesięcznik Diecezjalny Lucki* 9 (1934): 18–25; Bogdan Rok, "Stosunek polskiego Kościola katolickiego do sprawy żydowskiej w 1. połowie XVIII wieku," in *Z historii ludności żydowskiej w Polsce i na Śląsku*, ed. Krystyn Matwijowski (Wrocław, 1994), 85–97. There are two as yet unpublished doctoral dissertations related to this subject: Yehudit Kalik, "Hakenesiyyah hakatolit vehayehudim bemamlekhet Polin-Lita bame'ot ha17–18" (Ph.D. diss., Hebrew University, Jerusalem, 1998), and Magdalena O. Teter,

such attitudes necessarily displaced by the adoption of ideas influenced by the Enlightenment.

The increased intensity of pressures on marginal groups in a society that was seeking to achieve religious and national conformity and where political and economic conditions were difficult is not surprising. These pressures manifested themselves in the large number of witch trials during the Saxon period (1697–1763),[6] as well as of trials of Jews accused of ritual murder and the ritual use of Christian blood. In the eighteenth century, there was, too, a new effort on the part of certain churchmen to convert Jews.

Relations between the Polish Church and Polish churchmen, on the one hand, and Polish Jews, on the other, were complex. Pope Benedict XIV issued his encyclical *A Quo Primum* on Jews in Poland to the leaders of the Polish Church on June 14, 1751, and it was published the following year in Poland in Latin and Polish, and repeatedly thereafter.[7] After recalling the beginnings of Christianity in Poland, the pope reminded his readers of "the many successful councils and synods that gloriously defeated the Lutherans." He invoked particularly the 1542 council of Piotrków, which had "prohibited the principle of freedom of conscience." That is, the pope implied that the victory over Protestantism in Poland was complete.[8] (In fact, the victory of Catholicism had been consolidated

---

"Jews in the Legislation and Teachings of the Catholic Church in Poland (1648–1772)" (Ph. D. diss., Columbia University, 2000).

6. "In the seventeenth century and at least the first part of the eighteenth century, belief in witches and witchcraft was well-nigh universal, including [among] the upper classes." Joanna Partyka, "Szlachecka silva rerum jako źródło do badań etnograficznych," *Etnografia Polska* 32 (1988): 74.

7. Benedict XIV, *Epistola encyclica ad Primatem, Archipiscopos, et Episcopos Regni Poloniae. De his, quae vetita sunt Hebraeis habitantibus in iisdem civitatibus et locis in quibus habitant Christiani,* in *Sanctissimi Domini Nostri Benedicti Papae XIV Bullarium* (Venice, 1778), 3: 175–77. The Polish "translation" embellished the Latin version at times. Both Bishop Franciszek Kobielski and Bishop Eustachy Szembek published it in 1752. Biblioteka Czartoryskich, Kraków, MS IV 589, k. 291–306. It was also reprinted in Gaudenty Pikulski, *Złość żydowska Przeciwko Bogu y bliźnemu Prawdzie y Sumnieniu na obiasnienie Talmudystów. Na dowód ich zaślepienia, y Religii dalekiey od prawa Boskiego przez Moyzesza danego. Rozdzielona na trzy części opisana* (Lwów, 1758), 460–71. The text is available in English in Claudia Carlen, *The Papal Encyclicals, 1740–1878* (Wilmington, N.C., 1981), 1: 41–44. Cf. Majer Bałaban, *Letoledot hatenu'ah haFrankit* (Tel Aviv, 1934), 1: 99; N. M. Gelber, ed., *Toledot yehudei Brody [Arim ve'imahot beYisra'el,* vol. 3] (Jerusalem, 1955), 104–5; Kalik, "Hakenesiyyah hakatolit," 63, 75, 91; Teter, "Jews in the Legislation and Teachings of the Catholic Church in Poland." Benedict XIV's papal reign extended from 1740 to 1758.

8. We might recall here that the proceedings of a Church synod in Płock in 1733 included the telling observation that there remained no heresy in the diocese except "the perversity of the Jews." "Z całej duszy ubolewać musimy nad tem, *że w dyecezyi naszej Płockiej, gdzie inne zresztą nie gnieżdżą się kacerstwa, sama tylko żydów przewrotność, która Bogu jest nieprzy*

in the Sejm in 1733, when the political rights of non-Catholics were restricted and their ability to build new places of worship or to repair old
ones was limited.)[9] The papal document went on to mention the 1267
synod of Gniezno Province in Breslau, which had decreed various policies to ensure the separation of Jews from Christians. Now, however, "the
number of Jews in that country has greatly increased" and violations of
canon law regarding both the segregation of Jews and the prohibition of
allowing Jews authority over Christians were widespread. It further
noted that in some cities and towns, there were only a few Christians.
Jews dominated commerce and trade and controlled the income from alcoholic beverages. The pope reproved the magnates for permitting Jews
to hold leases on inns and villages. It was unacceptable for Jews to be able
to give orders to fine Christians, or even to have them whipped, to a Christian official, who if he did not comply would lose his post.[10] Moreover,
Jews were serving as officials of the noblemen, living in the same houses
as Christians, where "they also ceaselessly exhibit and flaunt authority over
the Christians they are living with." Worse, still, Jews had Christian domestics living in their houses. The pope complained particularly about
Christians loaning money to the Jews' *kahals:* "Even if they borrow money
from Christians at heavy and undue interest, with their synagogues as
surety, it is obvious to anyone who thinks about it that they do so to em-

---

jazną miasta zajmuje i na równi z katolikami się stawią [emphasis added] Wiemy wprawdzie,
że w innych Królestwa prowincyach jakoteż w obcych krajach, niewiemy ten lud cierpianym
jest, a to z tej przyczyny, aby resztki Izraela nawrócili się, i ponieważ pień utrzymanym być
musi dla piękność kwiatu, który z niego wykwitl, dalej dla tego, aby żyjąć z nami, przy-
pominali nam męki Chrystusa Pana, aby z pogardy ich i kary, która jako niewolnicy nasi
znoszą, jasno się okazała Boska sprawiedliwość, nareszcie aby rozproszeni przez cały świata
okrąg wszędzie musieli być świadkami i patrzyć się na tę wiarę którą nienawidzą." Ludwik
Gumplowicz, *Prawodawstwo Polskie względem Żydów* (Kraków, 1867), 105–6. Also cited by
Simon Dubnow, *Toledot hahassiduth* (Tel Aviv, 1967), 14. Cf. Jakub Sawicki, *Conciliae Poloniae: Źródła i studia krytyczne, Synody diecezji płockiej i ich statuty,* vol. 6 (Warsaw, 1952), 171.
Compare also the report of the bishop of Kraków, Kazimierz Lubienski, in 1716: "Haeretici
partim calvinistae partim lutheranae sectae tam genere nobiles quam plebei in civitatibus et
villis non tamen in magno numero reperiuntur." Wiesław Müller, *Relacje o stanie diecezji
krakowskiej 1615–1765,* Materiały do Dziejów Kościoła w Polsce, vol. 7 (Lublin, 1978), 110. For
the situation of Protestants in Poland in the eighteenth century, see Wojciech Kriegseisen,
*Ewangelicy polscy i litewscy w epoce saskiej 1696–1763: Sytuacja prawna, organizacja i stosunki mi-
ędzywyznaniowe* (Warsaw, 1996).

9. *VL,* 6: 581. Kriegseisen, *Ewangelicy polscy i litewscy,* 19–22. Cf. *VL,* 6: 253–54.

10. Jews could not directly impose punishments on Christians. See Jacob Goldberg, *Hahevrah hayehudit bemamlekhet Polin-Lita* (Jerusalem, 1999), 159–70, and id., "Władza dominialna Żydów-arendarzy dóbr ziemskich nad chłopami w XVII–XVIII wieku," *Przegląd
Historyczny* 81 (1990): 189–98.

ploy the money borrowed from Christians in their commercial dealings. This enables them to pay the agreed interest and simultaneously increase their own store." At the same time, he astutely added, because of their borrowing, Jews "gain as many defenders of their synagogues and themselves as they have creditors."

Two of the nine items in the encyclical are devoted to the debate among churchmen dating back to the reigns of Pope Innocent IV (1243–1254) and King Louis IX of France (1226–1270) over whether Jews ought to be destroyed or expelled. These sections constituted a response to demands for the expulsion of Jews from Poland that had been raised since the middle of the seventeenth century, when the radical Protestant Arians, suspected of collaborating with the Protestant enemies of Poland, had been driven out of the country.[11] The document invokes with approval the insistent opposition of Bernard of Clairvaux (1090–1153) to the "immoderate and maddened zeal" against Jews of the Cistercian monk Radulph at the time of the Second Crusade: "The Jews are not to be persecuted; they are not to be slaughtered; they are not even to be driven out." It also commended the example of Peter the Venerable, abbot of Cluny (1090–1156), who urged King Louis VII not to permit the destruction of the Jews. At the same time, Peter insisted that Jews be punished for their excesses and stripped of property and gains from usury from Christians. "In this matter [destruction/expulsion of the Jews?], as in all others," Benedict wrote, "We adopt the same norm of action as did . . . our venerable predecessors." Next, the prohibitions by Alexander III and Innocent III against Christians accepting domestic employment with Jews were cited, along with the ban on promoting Jews to public office. Thus, the position of the pope seems to have been to oppose expulsion and violence against Jews so long as their role in society reflected their proper status "as servants rejected by their Lord for whose death they evilly conspired. Let them realize that the result of this deed is to make them servants of those whom Christ's death made free."

The last paragraph in this section, however, is puzzling:

Innocent IV, also, in writing to St. Louis, King of France, who intended to drive the Jews beyond the boundaries of his kingdom, *approves* [emphasis added] of this plan since the Jews gave very little heed to the regulations made by the Apostolic See in their regard: "Since We strive with all Our heart for the salvation of souls, We grant you full power by the authority of this letter *to expel the Jews* [emphasis added], particularly since We have learned that they do not obey the said statutes issued by this See against them."

---

11. By a decision of the Sejm in 1658. *VL,* 4: 515.

Two features of the passage are striking. First, although the weight of the encyclical supposed a continuing Jewish presence in Poland, the lines cited above express Benedict's ambivalence about expelling the Jews. What is truly remarkable, however, is the fact that the lines attributed to a letter from Innocent IV to King Louis were in fact not addressed to the king of France but rather to the archbishop of Vienne.[12] Although Innocent IV insisted on the segregation of French Jews, he never authorized or supported their expulsion.[13] Whatever the reason for the mistaken citation, its effect was to suggest that the papacy was not unalterably opposed to expulsion.[14]

Following the quotation from Innocent IV, Benedict summarized his position on Jews living among Christians in Poland: "All those activities that are now allowed in Poland are forbidden." The pope demanded that the Polish clergy observe the neglected synodal statutes and precepts, so that they would "be able to give these orders and commands easily and confidently." They were neither to lease their lands or their monopoly rights to Jews nor to provide them with money or credits. "Thus, you will be free from and unaffected by all dealings with them."[15]

The papal document touched on some of the most important aspects of the Church's effect on Jews in Poland-Lithuania in the eighteenth century. These were canon (and synodal) legislation; the protective role of

12. Solomon Grayzel, *The Church and the Jews in the XIIIth Century,* rev. ed. (New York, 1966), no. 131. It is possible that this was an oversight. The papal document cited item 34 for the year 1253 in Odoricus Raynaldus, *Annales Ecclesiastici ab anno MCXCVIII ubi Card. Baronius desinit,* vol. 12 (Rome, 1646), 398. That item does refer to St. Louis but then goes on to attribute the passage we are concerned with as follows: "ex literis Vienensi archiepiscopo ab Innocentio hoc anno missis." A sloppy clerk could have conflated the reference to Louis with the quotation from the papal letter. On the other hand, the quotation in the papal document omits the words "de ipsa provincia" that follow the word "expellendi" in Raynaldus, *Sanctissimi Domini,* vol. 176, no. 5.

13. See, e.g., Robert Chazan, *Medieval Jewry in Northern France: A Political and Social History* (Baltimore, 1973), 120f., 128–31; Grayzel, *Church and the Jews,* nos. 104, 119.

14. For a different interpretation of the encyclical, without notice of the problematic passage, see Kalik, "Hakenesiyyah hakatolit," 90–91.

15. "Co łatwiey y bespieczniey roskazać inszym będziecie mogli ieżeli ani waszych Dobr, ani praw Żydom niepowierzycie, żadney sprawy w pozyczaniu albo daniu pieniędzy zniemi niemaiąc, iednym słowem (iako mamy od godnych sobie świadków doniesiono) od wszystkich handlów z Żydami wolni będziecie." Pikulski, *Złość żydowska,* 470. Wiesław Müller has shown that Bishop Andrzej Stanisław Załuski (bishop of Kraków, 1746–1758) had requested a papal breve that would strengthen the demands of the episcopate that the nobility and the monastic orders comply with canon law. Müller, "Jews in the *ad limina* Reports of Polish Bishops in the Seventeenth and Eighteenth Centuries" (typescript), 9; N. M. Gelber, "Taufbewegung."

the magnates; the numerical and economic strength of the Jewish community; and the substantial economic ties between Church institutions and Jews and Jewish communities.

The segregation of Jews from Christians and the restriction of their contacts were ancient and continuing conventions of canon law, and were stressed in the first Polish synods in the thirteenth century.[16] Segregation continued to be the dominant motif in the enactments of Church synods and the letters of instruction issued by bishops in Poland in the eighteenth century. Interestingly, the detailed wording of some of these demands for eliminating contact between Christians and Jews reveals that such contacts in fact were lively and multifaceted. The enactments of the synod in Luck (Lutsk) in 1726 included the traditional prohibitions forbidding Christians to dwell or bathe with Jews; to eat with them; or to serve them. Other clauses, however, forbade Christians to guard Jewish cemeteries; light and extinguish candles on Jewish holidays; and to eat *matsot* or play the role of Haman (in Purim comedies).[17] A book published under Jesuit auspices in Warsaw in 1724 and in Wilno in 1728 forbade Christians to eat "Jewish *kugel* and other Jewish dishes."[18] Similarly, a decree of Wacław Sierakowski, bishop of Przemyśl, on July 10, 1743, listed the following prohibitions: celebrations during Lent were forbidden to Jews, and at Lent, or during any other solemn season, Jews were not to celebrate weddings with processions of candles and torches. Jews were specifically forbidden to have music, to sing, to fire gunshots, to shout, or otherwise to make noise when leading a bride and groom to the synagogue or the wedding house. All these actions were prohibited in the marketplace, in the

16. See the references in Salo Wittmayer Baron, *A Social and Religious History of the Jews,* vol. 10 (New York, 1965), 33–34.

17. Jacob Goldberg, "Poles and Jews," 252–57; Adam Kaźmierczyk, "The Problem of Christian Servants as Reflected in the Legal Codes of the Polish-Lithuanian Commonwealth during the Second Half of the Seventeenth Century and in the Saxon Period," *Gal-Ed* 15–16 (1997): 23–40. Waldemar Kowalski, "Ludność żydowska a duchowieństwa archidiakonatu sandomierskiego w XVI–XVIII wieku," *Studia Judaica: Biuletyn Polskiego Towarzystwa Studiów Żydowskich* 1 (1998): 177–99. For other prohibitions of the playing of the role of Haman, see Joannes Alexander Lipski, *Epistola Pastorales ad Clerum et Populum Diecesis Cracoviensis* (Kraków, 1737), as cited by Kalik, "Hakenesiyyah hakatolit," 67–73. In a later document, the holiday is referred to as "Aman," on which Jews were forbidden to dress as Germans or Poles and to shoot: "Na Amana abyście się nie ubierali w suknie Polskie lub Niemieckie, y w te dni nie strzelali." Franciszek Antoni Kobielski, *Światło na oświecenie narodu niewiernego to iest kazania w synagogach żydowskich miane, oraz reflexye y list odpowiadaiący na pytania synagogi brodzkiey* (Lwów, 1746), 191; Mojżesz Schorr, *Żydzi w Przemyślu do końca XVIII wieku* (Lwów, 1903, reprint, Jerusalem, 1991), 41–42; "Materials," no. 136, 213–26.

18. Goldberg, "Poles and Jews," 254.

streets of the town, and even on the Jewish street. Any Christian who had contact with Jews, whether it be talking, drinking, or eating with them or attending their weddings or dances, would be excommunicated from the Church. If Jews despised Christian food and utensils, so even more should Christians despise those of Jews. Jews were not to use Christians to light the candles in the synagogue on their holidays on pain of a large fine of 500 *grzywień* (= 800 florins) for the *kahal* and a month in prison for the rabbi. "Should a Christian play Haman and be led about and insulted and abused" on the holiday of Purim, the *kahal* would incur a huge fine of 1,000 *grzywień* and the rabbi would serve a year in prison. The decree further forbade Jews and *"bachurs"* (young men), dressed like Turks and others, to carry torches, burn straw in triumphal fires in front of the synagogue, shoot rifles in the streets, beat drums, and make clamorous noises. No Jewish ceremony of any kind was to be held that might interfere with Church ceremonies and processions. An enormous fine of 5,000 *grzywień* would be imposed on Jews for imitating Christian ceremonies, should they be found, for example, parading in the synagogue wearing a silver crown similar to that of the bishop.[19]

These discriminatory enactments that delimited boundaries were often repeated in synodal and other Church legislation. They were also reproduced in catechisms, in sermons, and in lessons in the schools, as well as in contemporary literature. Their constant repetition undoubtedly had an effect on the shaping of Catholic attitudes to Jews. Yet while the psychological distance between Christian and Jew widened, the actual enforcement of such segregationist provisions was rare. Obviously, the highly specific and repeated references aimed at separation reflect regular and continuing contacts of all sorts between Jews and Christians.

This is very far indeed, however, from saying that the Church had little effect on the lives of Jews. From the mid sixteenth century on, for example, Jews were obliged to obtain permission from the local bishop to build a new synagogue, repair an old one, or establish a cemetery. In the

19. Mojżesz Schorr, *Żydzi w Przemyślu do końca XVIII wieku,* 41–42; "Materials," no. 136, 213–26; Jacek Krochmal, "Dekret biskupa W. H. Sierakowskiego z 19 lipca 1743 roku w sprawie Żydów przemyskich," *Rocznik Przemyski* 29–30 (1993–94): 285–99. See the similar regulations issued by the same bishop to the Jewish community of Rzeszów in connection with his confirmation of their right to the existing synagogue and cemetery. Adam Kaźmierczyk, *Żydzi Polscy 1648–1772: Źródła* (Kraków, 2001), no. 36, 62–65 (1745). And see the similar demands made earlier by the bishop of Kraków, Konstanty Felicjan Szaniawski, of the Jews of Ożarów, who had repaired their synagogue and cemetery without his permission. Ibid., no. 98, 171–73.

seventeenth and eighteenth centuries, there were occasional complaints that these rules were not being observed. Powerful magnates did sometimes protect "their" Jews from the expenses involved in following this rule. After their synagogue was destroyed by fire in 1714, the Jews of Ostrowiec Świętokrzyski built another without permission from the bishop of Kraków. Bishop Mikołaj Dembowski asserted in 1745 that the Jews of Międzyboż had built a second synagogue without his permission.[20] Still, these requirements on the whole were honored. In 1750, Bishop Młodziejowski granted the Jews in Iłów permission to build a synagogue. In 1780, the archbishop of Gniezno, Antoni Ostrowski, at the request of Mikołaj Małachowski, owner of the town of Końskie, granted Jews permission to erect a new place of worship. The same archbishop permitted the construction of new synagogues in Żychlin in 1780 and in Łęczyce in 1782.[21] In granting permission for new synagogues, which was contrary to the strict letter of canon law, bishops often attached conditions obliging Jews to agree to observe synodal legislation.[22] They also collected substantial payments in return for their authorization.[23]

In a well-known case, the local bishop sealed the synagogue in Husiatyn, which had been built without his permission to replace one destroyed by fire, and ordered the community to pay a large fine. The town

20. Jacek Kaczor, "Kahał ostrowiecki w XVII–XVIII wieku," in *Żydzi wśród Chrzescijan w dobie szlacheckiej Rzeczypospolitej*, ed. Waldemar Kowalski, Jadwiga Muszynska (Kielce, 1996), 64. Kaźmierczyk, *Żydzi Polscy*, no. 139, 238–39.

21. Hundert, *Jews in a Polish Private Town*, 41. Kraków, AP, Archiwum Dzikowskie Tarnowskich, sygn. 105. Paweł Fijalkowski, "Kultura Żydów pogranicza wielkopolsko-mazowieckiego w XVI–XVIII wieku," in *Żydowskie gminy wyznaniowe*, ed. Jerzy Woronczak (Wrocław, 1995), 30–31; id., *Żydzi w województwach łęczyckim i rawskim w XV–XVIII wieku* (Warsaw, 1999), 77; Kalik, "Hakenesiyyah hakatolit," 76, 140–47. The archbishop of Polock permitted Jews in Witebsk to establish a cemetery. *Istoriko-iuridicheskie materialy, izvlechennye iz aktovykh knig gubernii Vitebskoi i Mogilevskoi, khraniaschchikhsia v tsentralnom arkhivie v Vitebskie* 18 (Vitebsk, 1888), nos. 24–25, pp. 196–202. Cf. Jacob Goldberg, *Jewish Privileges in the Polish Commonwealth: Charters of Rights Granted to Jewish Communities in Poland-Lithuania in the Sixteenth to Eighteenth Centuries* (Jerusalem, 1985), 17–18. In a recent article, Jacob Goldberg draws attention to six previously unknown bishops' privileges for the building of synagogues and the establishment of cemeteries and discusses the relevant issues: Goldberg, "O przywilejach biskupich dla gmin żydowskich w dawnej Rzeczypospolitej," in *Christianitas et cultura Europae: Księga jubileuszowa Profesora Jerzego Kłoczowskiego*, ed. H. Gapski, pt. 1 (Lublin, 1998), 625–29.

22. In addition to material already cited, see Maurycy Horn, *Regesty dokumentów i ekscerpty z Metryki Koronnej do historii Żydów w Polsce, 1697–1795* (Wrocław and Warsaw, 1984–88), 3: 6.

23. Kalik, "Hakenesiyyah hakatolit," 87–88; Gelber, *Toledot yehudei Brody*, 47; B. D. Weinryb, *The Jews of Poland: A Social and Economic History of the Jewish Community in Poland from 1100 to 1800* (Philadelphia, 1973), 355, n. 4; Raphael Mahler, *Toledot hayehudim bePolin: Kalkalah, hevrah, hamatsav hamishpati* (Merhavia, Israel, 1946), 333–34.

owner, Michał Potocki, intervened on the side of "his" Jews, reopened the synagogue, and informed the bishop that no fine would be paid, saying that he would "not allow his Jews to be harmed."[24] The closing and sealing of synagogues by bishops and other churchmen was usually due to the failure of the local community to meet the required loan payments owed to the bishop or another Church institution. This was apparently the case in Bolechów, as described by the local wine merchant Dov Ber Birkenthal, in about 1760.[25]

Although magnates frequently intervened in defense of the Jews on their hereditary estates, it was no simple matter to defy a bishop. The case of Michał Potocki, mentioned above, was unusual. More representative was the success of Franciszek Antoni Kobielski (1679–1755), bishop of Łuck and Brześć, who persuaded various magnates, although not, as he said, without difficulties, to allow missionizing sermons in the synagogues of the area under his rule.

In the sixteenth century (1584), in the midst of the Counter-Reformation, Pope Gregory XIII had revived the practice of his thirteenth-century predecessors of using sermons as a conversionary device. He ordered weekly sermons in the synagogues of Jews to teach them "the truth of the Catholic faith, the nature of their desolation, and the error of their messianic hopes and beliefs." These measures were to be applied wherever Jews lived, especially in Germany and Poland,[26] but during the sixteenth and early seventeenth centuries, the papal injunction had no effect in Polish lands. Pope Clement XI, in his own edict of 1704, included an exhortation to revive the practice ordered in the 1584 papal bull. Kobielski, in his writings, explicitly cited the sixteenth-century edict, but he was

24. Mahler, *Toledot hayehudim bePolin*, 333; Weinryb, *Jews of Poland*.

25. Dov Ber Birkenthal, *Zikhronot R. Dov meBolihov (483–565)*, ed. M. Vishnitzer [Mark Wischnitzer] (Berlin, 1922), 68. For a similar case, see Mordecai ben Samuel, *Sha'ar hamelekh* (Żółkiew, 1762), pt. 1, gate 1, ch. 8. Cf. also Jacob Goldberg, *Jewish Privileges in the Polish Commonwealth* (Jerusalem, 1985), 18; id., "O przywilejach biskupich dla gmin żydowskich w dawnej Rzeczypospolitej"; Yehudit Kalik, "Patterns of Contact between the Catholic Church and the Jews in the Polish-Lithuanian Commonwealth: The Jewish Debts," in *Studies in the History of the Jews in Old Poland in Honor of Jacob Goldberg*, Scripta Hierosolymitana, vol. 38, ed. Adam Teller (Jerusalem, 1998), 118 (Franciscans), 120 (Dominicans); M. J. Rosman, "The Indebtedness of the Lublin Kahal in the Eighteenth Century," in ibid., 180 (Jesuits); M. Schorr, *Żydzi w Przemyślu do końca XVIII wieku* (Lwów, 1903), 14. See also the case in Lublin in 1708: Henryk Gmiterek, ed., *Materiały źródłowe do dziejów Żydów w księgach grodzkich lubelskich z doby panowania Augusta II Sasa 1697–1733*, Judaica Lublinensia, 1 (Lublin, 2001), no. 745, 154 (Dominicans).

26. Kenneth R. Stow, *Catholic Thought and Papal Jewry Policy, 1555–1593* (New York, 1977), 20–21, 210–11.

the only Polish bishop who responded energetically. A few other contemporary churchmen are said to have preached in synagogues, among them Wawrzyniec Owłocymski (1724–1763), a Dominican who preached in Brześć, and a certain Bernardine, Wyktoryn Adrian Krzywiński, author of the text of a sermon delivered in a synagogue in 1742.[27]

The priest Józef Szczepan Turczynowicz (d. 1773) founded an order of nuns (Congregatio Mariae Vitae) in Lithuania in 1737 whose primary mission was to convert Jewish women. In addition to its headquarters in a church in Wilno, he established seventeen small convents, members of which, encouraged by their founder, kidnapped and baptized Jewish children. Turczynowicz claimed to have converted five hundred Jewish women, and by 1820, the group claimed two thousand converts.[28] In 1783, Ignacy Massalski, the bishop of Wilno, published a pastoral letter rebuking the members of his diocese for being overzealous. He argued that the forcible kidnapping of children of unbelievers in order to baptize them caused trouble and harm to the Church.[29] The primate of Poland, Michał Poniatowski, issued a similar statement in 1785. Both men were among the senior Polish churchmen associated with Enlightenment ideas.[30]

The conversionary efforts of Franciszek Kobielski, which began when he became bishop of Łuck and Brześć in 1739 and continued until his death in 1755, are well documented.[31] In a step that was unusual for its time and,

27. Kalik, "Hakenesiyyah hakatolit," 98; Rok, "Stosunek polskiego Kościoła," 87, 92. Kalik also cites a collection of sermons "On the Errors of the Jews" delivered to the community of Komarno in 1797 and published in 1803. Kalik, "Hakenesiyyah hakatolit," 100f. Citing *Wiadomości Warszawskie* for February 9, 1763, N. M. Gelber writes: "Auch Mönche veranstalten um diese Zeit unaufhörlich Predigten in den jüdischen Synagogen." He adds: "So muste die Judenschaft von Brześć jede Woche, mit dem Kahal an der Spitze, einmal wöchentlich in der Synagoge, das andere Mal wieder vor dem Missionsgebäude, welches der Starost für die Mönche bauen lies, die Predigten der Dominikaner anhören." Gelber, "Taufbewegung," 233. This probably refers to Owłocymski and is likely based on the memoirs of Julian Ursyn Niemcewicz. See the excerpt in *Nietolerancja i zabobon w Polsce w XVII– XVIII wieku,* ed. Bohdan Baranowski and Władysław Lewandowski (Warsaw, 1987), 19–20.

28. Krzysztof Lewalski, "Szkic do dziejów misji Chrześcijańskich wśród Żydów na ziemiach polskich w XVIII–XX wieku," *Studia Historyczne* 36 (1993): 185–202.

29. Bałaban, *Letoledot,* 1: 92–93; Goldberg, *Hamumarim,* 38; Kalik, "Hakenesiyyah hakatolit," 102–3; Lewalski, "Szkic," 185. On Massalski, see the massive biography by Tadeusz Kasabula, *Ignacy Massalski biskup wileński* (Lublin, 1998).

30. Kalik, "Hakenesiyyah hakatolit," 104–5.

31. Kraków, AP, 2347/1: Odpowiedź Chrześcijańska na odpowiedź żydowska przeciwko kazaniu JMCi X. Kobielskiego Biskupa Łuckiego [CAHJP: HM 6738]; L'viv, Stefanyk Lviv Scientific Library of the Academy of Sciences of Ukraine, Fond 5, Opis 1, Dzial 310: Odpowiedź Biskupa Łuckiego do synagogi m. Brody w sprawach religijnych [CAHJP: HM 2/8111.9], henceforth cited as L'viv 310; Kobielski, *Światło na oświecienie narodu niewiernego.* A printed broadsheet containing the text of the letter from Kobielski to the Jews of his

in fact, very rare at any period in Polish history, Bishop Kobielski ordered that sermons be delivered in the synagogues under his jurisdiction no fewer than four times annually and even published the texts for priests to read. He apparently preached in the synagogue in Luck and, on at least one occasion, in January 1743, in the synagogue in Brody. Moreover, he organized disputations in Brody and Ostróg on the model of those held in medieval western Europe.

In 1741, Bishop Kobielski published an epistle addressed to the Jews of his dioceses (Luck and Brześć) ordering them to adopt the True Faith.[32] No other bishop, as far as I know, ever addressed a pastoral letter to Jews. They were to attend sermons given by his priests in their synagogues at least once in every four months so as to hear the truth in the words of their own prophets. The letter, which was to be read aloud in the synagogues and posted on their doors, elaborated a set of ordinances that in addition to generally reflecting the tenor of synodal enactments of the period included some novel details. Kobielski commented that Jews hired Christians because every Jew wished to be a lord and even the poorest of them refused to act as servants. As a result, theft was widespread among poor Jews (who refused employment as domestics), especially the robbery of churches. The bishop went on to forbid Jewish merchants traveling abroad to hire Christian teamsters.[33] Rabbis were enjoined not to demand unfairly high taxes from the poor and to prevent itinerant poor Jews from entering their towns. Asserting that Jews required their sons to study only the Talmud and to despise artisanry and because such great poverty came from studying the Talmud, the bishop ordered an inventory of all the books in all the synagogues of the diocese to be made and submitted to him. He further forbade Jews to publish any new book without the permission of his archdeacon.[34] Furthermore, repairing synagogues without permission was forbidden, as were processions to syna-

---

dioceses, and especially to their rabbis and elders, dated 1741, was published in Goldberg, *Hamumarim*, 75–81. Cf. Bałaban, *Letoledot*, 1: 95–100; Gelber, "Taufbewegung," 225–41; id., *Toledot yehudei Brody*, "Ma'assei hahegemon Kobielski," 95–105; Wirszyłło, "Stosunek duchowieństwo katolickiego na Wołyniu do Żydów," 18–25. See also Teter, "Jews in the Legislation and Teachings of the Catholic Church in Poland."

32. Czartoryski Library, Kraków, MS IV 589, k. 290. The document has been published by Goldberg, *Hamumarim*, 75–81, and by Kaźmierczyk, *Żydzi Polscy*, no. 32, pp. 53–57.

33. Gelber, *Toledot yehudei Brody*, 97, reports that many memoir books of the eighteenth century accused Jews of selling Christian peasants to the Prussians.

34. What is striking here is the emphasis on Jews adopting "useful" occupations. It is tempting to suggest a connection to what would become the support of the Church for the Frankists who were designated "antitalmudists."

gogues. Even establishing a place of prayer in a private dwelling would be subject to a huge fine. The bishop's special anxiety was reserved for the dangers presented by Christian women working in Jewish households. He was not alone in this preoccupation. A contemporary remarked:

On this occasion, it is worth bringing into the open what these unvirtuous women do in the company of Jews, what illicit acts and sins against the flesh they commit with Jews and with Christians. . . . On the Sabbath [*W Szabasz*] they eat meat with Jews, they do not keep Church days of fast and abstinence, they attend Jewish worship services, on holy days and Sundays they do not go to church ([saying] what does it profit us to go to that God of wood?); they also keep kosher [*koszerują się*] like the Jews.[35]

According to Kobielski, Christian women who were servants in Jewish homes often prayed with Jewish children in Hebrew. He reminded the Jews: "You are forgetting that you are exiles in our country and have no right to such freedoms." He ordered that a register listing of every Jew in each town was to be submitted annually to the Church. Thus, when a Christian child disappeared "because of you" ("bo kiedy chrześciańskie dziecię przez ręce wasze zaginie"), evidence would be readily available, whether against a Christian or a Jew. Finally, Jews were to make two annual payments to the Church, both confirming the superiority of the holy Catholic faith in Poland and also as recompense to the Church for the harm done to it by Jews.[36]

35. Cf. Pikulski, *Złość żydowska*, 395.
36. Another set of edicts, promulgated by Kobielski in the same year, apparently was more conventional. Its provisions included the following:
   1. Christian servants working for Jews in any capacity, on contract for a half-year or at most a year, are forbidden to sleep in Jews' houses.
   2. Jews are forbidden to hold public processions to their synagogues.
   3. Jews are forbidden to dress on "Aman" [Purim] in Polish or German costume, and gunshots are forbidden on this holiday.
   4. It is forbidden to employ Christian servants to extinguish candles on the Day of Atonement.
   5. It is forbidden to employ Christian wet nurses.
   6. Corpses may not be carried through the city during the day, only in the evening. And even then without any illumination, song or voiced cries.
   7. No cemetery may be near the road or the city.
   8. The beadles may not call out to people to come to the synagogue or knock loudly for that purpose. The beadle must go silently to each house to announce the hour of prayer.
   9. No more candles may be kindled in the synagogue than are lit in the poor Christian churches. Jews must give candles to the churches.
   10. Jews are forbidden to have contact of any kind with converts.
   11. No Christian may be hired as a teamster for a journey abroad. For we have reached a situation in which you have sold many a Christian from most of

It is unlikely that Kobielski's industrious and expansive campaign to convert Jews met with much success. On one occasion, he admitted that the Jews were not yet persuaded. On another, he claimed that only a few had been persuaded. In a letter accompanying the text of the bishop's responses to the answers of the Jews in Brody, an assistant to the bishop said that his superior still hoped to save at least a single soul from among the Jews of Brody.[37]

The bishop was singularly unsuccessful in converting them, however, and he turned to attempting to enforce his ordinances. Jews complained to the Vatican, and the pope asked his nuncio in Warsaw to investigate. The latter wrote to Kobielski on December 12, 1752, to inquire whether the Jews' complaints had any basis in fact. If it were true that Jews were being persecuted and oppressed in his bishopric, "those responsible must be punished and tried immediately so that the priests will not become accustomed to permitting themselves such hateful deeds toward this wretched people."[38]

Historical opinions about Kobielski differ markedly. He has been seen both as "a member of the group of extreme Jew-haters" and as "pro-Jewish."[39] A nuanced assessment of the importance of the career of this eminent and energetic bishop, and his actions relative to Jews, must consider his time and place. First of all, he was a believing Christian who wanted to save Jews from eternal damnation by bringing them to what he genuinely saw as the True Faith. Faith alone, however, does not explain the urgency of his actions and his devotion to his mission to the Jews. Other factors played a real, if unarticulated, role. To understand them, it is important to remember that these years saw the consolidation of the Polish Church and its struggle with the nobility, which wanted to reduce the Church's power, coupled with the beginnings of the crystal-

the towns in our jurisdiction to Turks and to Prussians. These sales give us factual evidence of the dishonest Talmud to which you will not admit publicly. However, if some merchant is unable to travel without a Christian teamster, and the latter offers his services for the sake of his own livelihood, you may hire him but only with the explicit permission of the priest of the town or village where he lives and after you have given the priest an explicit promise to return the teamster home after his journey.

Kobielski, *Światło*, 190–92; cf. Gelber, *Toledot yehudei Brody*, 96

37. Kobielski, *Światło*, 56–68, 177. "Jednakże nie traci ten żarliwi Pasterz W woyej nadziei że przynaymniey jedną duszę z całey Synagogi na zbawienną zaprowadzi drogę." L'viv, 310: 54r.

38. Bałaban, *Letoledot*, 1: 99–100.

39. Ibid., 95; Kalik, "Hakenesiyyah hakatolit," 99.

lization of a Polish national identity. It was not unusual in Church documents of the eighteenth century for the term "Polak" to be used as a synonym for (Latin) Catholic.[40] An attempt to explain the general phenomenon of which Kobielski's missionizing campaign formed one part is taken up below.

Whatever one may think about Kobielski's motives, what is particularly striking, especially in light of the tendency in recent historiography to emphasize the positive consequences of the alliance between Jews and magnates in eighteenth-century Poland, is the fact that he focused on the Jews of Brody, which was not only home to one of the Commonwealth's largest and most prosperous Jewish communities but a private town. The Church's challenge to magnate-aristocrats who protected Jews should not be minimized. Although he apparently resisted at first, Brody's owner, the powerful magnate Józef Potocki, evidently was unable to protect "his" Jews from Kobielski's missionary efforts. The nobility sought to halt the growth of Church power by demanding restrictions on its fiscal and juridical privileges, but in the first half of the eighteenth century, in contrast to the administrative apparatus of the Polish state, which was in disarray, the wealth and the property of the Church and the efficiency of its administration increased.[41] Moreover, a bishop was a powerful man who could not be resisted easily or without risking one's soul.

Kobielski's missionary campaign led him to rise in the Sejm in 1748 to oppose a proposal to impose higher taxes on Jews that would be collected directly and without the mediation of their autonomous institutions. "Though this people is despised and scattered in all lands, nevertheless, no one can deny that they are close to us. If, eventually, a higher tax is imposed, it would be wise to supervise their rabbis closely lest they oppress the poor."[42]

Just as Jews served the economic interests of magnate-aristocrats, they were useful to certain Church institutions and high officials in the ecclesiastical hierarchy. And since members of magnate families usually held the highest offices in the Polish Church, the interests of the members of

40. Zdzisław Budzyński, *Ludność pogranicza polsko-ruskiego w drugiej połowie XVIII wieku: Stan rozmieszczenie, struktura wyznaniowa i etniczna*, vol. 1 (Pzemyśl-Rzeszów, 1993), 340–41. Another part of the explanation would be that Kobielski and his fellow bishops were giving voice and form to the economic resentments of the Jews' urban competitors, but this must be considered, at most, a minor motif in the explanatory schema.

41. Bolesław Kumor and Zdzisław Obertynski, eds., *Historia Kościoła w Polsce* (Poznan, 1974), 1: 173–75; Jerzy Kłoczowski, ed., *Kościół w Polsce* (Kraków, 1968), 2: 39–42, 123–31.

42. Władysław Konopczyński, *Diarjusz Seymu r. 1748* (Warsaw, 1911), 1: 29–30.

the two groups often coincided. Jews sometimes managed monopolies on Church estates. Indeed, when Bishop Kobielski complained that magnates placed Christians under Jewish authority, his own priests in Łuck responded saying that not only the magnates but also the bishops were guilty of this defiance of canon law.[43] A more important moderating influence on the Church's policies toward Jews was the fact that monasteries and other Church institutions lent or invested significant sums in the communal and intercommunal organizations of Jews. This practice was very widespread; there was hardly a Jewish community in the country that did not benefit from such credits.[44] While these debts often served to temper radical measures against Jews, the Church did not shy away from extreme actions such as trials, accompanied by torture, of Jews accused of the ritual murder of Christians, or of using Christian blood in their ceremonies, or of desecrating the Host.

The number of actual trials based on charges of ritual murder and the blood libel in Polish lands was about the same in the eighteenth century as in the previous one.[45] Two changes, however, characterize the eighteenth century. The Church was much more involved in fomenting and carrying out trials. We know of six cases in which bishops were involved. Secondly, the number of victims of judicial murder at the hands of Polish courts was greater. In the eighteenth century, more than one hundred Jews and several non-Jews are known to have been victims of the libel that the murder of Christians and/or the use of their blood was a requirement of Judaism. The actual number of victims may well have been higher. When the Polish parliament abolished torture in 1776, incidents of judicial murder fell off sharply. There was also an attitude of repugnance toward such trials on the part of some. Stanisław Poniatowski, the future King Stanisław II, in conversation with a Jew in Amsterdam in about 1753, expressed his disgust at the actions of the then auxiliary bishop of Kiev, Kajetan Sołtyk, who had caused the execution

43. Kalik, "Hakenesiyyah hakatolit," 76–77.
44. Hundert, *Jews in a Polish Private Town*, 104–6; Rosman, "Indebtedness of the Lublin Kahal," 166–83; Kalik, "Patterns of Contact," 102–22.
45. The number of actual trials was in the low twenties in each century. See, most conveniently, Zenon Guldon and Jacek Wijaczka, "The Accusation of Ritual Murder in Poland, 1500–1800," *POLIN* 10 (1997): 99–140. To the list there I can add one further, late, incident: near Kowel in 1791. YIVO Institute for Jewish Research, New York, RG 87: 939: II 18b. The date of the execution of the young woman, Adel of Drohobycz, should be August–September 1718. S. Buber, *Anshei shem asher shimshu bekodesh be'ir Levuv* (Kraków, 1895), 19. Daniel Tollet, *Accuser pour convertir: Du bon usage de l'accusation de crime rituel dans la Pologne catholique à l'époque moderne* (Paris, 2000).

of eleven Jews.[46] And eleven Jews were indeed executed at Żytomierz in May of 1753, after being tortured.[47] Nevertheless, at the end of the eighteenth century, the preacher Hillel ben Ze'ev Wolf felt that the period of blood libels had passed.[48]

The trials dramatically demonstrated the distinction between Jew and Christian. The central involvement of such powerful bishops as Dembowski, Sołtyk, and Wołłowski illustrated how determined some members of the Church hierarchy were to demonize and marginalize Jews. In fact, the involvement of these bishops in the 1740s and 1750s stimulated the worst period of persecution of this kind in Polish Jewish history.

Waldemar Kowalski has stressed that the frustration of Christian urban competitors and concomitant economic decline may well have played a key role in the two ritual murder accusations fomented by the priest Stefan Żuchowski (1666–1716) in Sandomierz (1698 and 1710–13).[49] In 1698, when the body of a female child was found in a church, the Sandomierz municipal court found that the death was a result of natural causes. The mother, who said she had placed the body in the church because she could not afford a burial, was sentenced to three days in the pillory. At the insistence of the bishop of Kraków, the matter was reconsidered, however, and, under torture, the mother accused a Jew named Berek and his wife, first, of taking blood from the corpse, and later of actually murdering her daughter. The latter accusation arose only after the matter had been transferred to the crown tribunal at Lublin. Both the mother and Berek were sentenced to death. Berek's wife apparently fled and was not caught. The second case arose after the corpse of a boy was found near the rabbi's house. Father Żuchowski sent the coffin to Lublin, and legal proceedings against nine Jews were instituted in the crown tribunal. The Jews were all tortured. There were also hearings in a district court, where the provincial governor attempted to defend the Jews. Eventually,

46. This is recorded in Stanisław Poniatowski's diary. Among the people whom he met was "stary Żyd portugalski Svasso szczególne okazywał mi przywiązanie, widząc jaki miałem wstręt do wszelkiego prześladowania i do tych zasad, które spowodowały wyrok Sołtyka wówczas kijowskiego a dziś krakowskiego biskupa, skazujący na stos jedenastur Żydów w Polsce." Stanisław Poniatowski, *Pamiętniki Króla Stanisława Augusta*, ed. Władysław Konopczynski and Stanisław Ptaszycki, vol. 1, pt. 1 (Warsaw, 1915), 81.

47. See Guldon and Wijaczka, "Accusation of Ritual Murder in Poland," 132–33, and the references there. Cf. id., *Procesy o mordy rytualne w Polsce w XVI–XVIII wieku* (Kielce, 1995).

48. *VL*, 8: 882–83. Hillel ben Ze'ev Wolf, *Heilel ben shahar* (Warsaw, 1804), 16a.

49. Waldemar Kowalski, "W obronie wiary," 221–33; cf. Weinryb, *Jews of Poland*, 153: "One can thus see a connection between false accusations plus pogroms and the competitive struggle for livelihood between the burghers and the Jews." And see also Tollet, *Accuser pour convertir*, 150–82.

four Jews died as a result of torture, the rabbi died in prison, his young son, Abraham, was baptized, and three Jews were executed.[50]

Stefan Żuchowski (1666–1716), a leading clergyman in Sandomierz has been described as "the leading antisemite in the history of the Polish Commonwealth."[51] He was born into a middle gentry family and held a doctorate from the university in Kraków. In 1700, King Augustus II appointed him secretary of the Crown (*sekretarz krolewski*), and in 1711, the synod of the Kraków diocese elected him commissioner for Jewish affairs.[52] He published two very influential books describing the accusations and trials in Sandomierz and elsewhere. His works were quoted not only in the subsequent literature defaming Jews but at later trials as well.[53] His first book opened with a lament over the recent decline of his town. The Jews had taken over and not only controlled commerce and trade but ruled the Christians. Moreover, "these kikes hold the breweries, the distilleries, and the taverns and the measures in the mills."[54] From his comments, it is clear that economic rivalry played a role in creating a climate conducive to libelous accusations against Jews. Although the provincial governor of Sandomierz strongly condemned Żuchowski, the bishop of Kraków and the primate of Poland stood by him.[55] Even the king, Augustus II, spurred by the accusation of ritual murder in 1710–13, issued an edict (never carried out) ordering the expulsion of the Jews from Sandomierz and the conversion of the synagogue there into a Christian chapel.[56] Thus, both the

---

50. See Guldon and Wijaczka, "Accusation of Ritual Murder in Poland," 122–28.

51. Kowalski, "W obronie wiary," 233.

52. Ibid., 103. For a more nuanced depiction of the Polish monarch's attitude to Jews and for new information on an inquiry on the question of the blood libel that he directed to the Faculty of Theology of the University of Leipzig, see Jacob Goldberg, "August II wobec polskich Żydów," *Rzeczpospolita wielu narodów i jej tradycje,* ed. A. Link-Lenczowski and M. Markiewicz (Kraków, 1999), 95–104; Tollet, *Accuser pour convertir,* 28, 257, citing F. Frank, *Mord rytualnej wobec trybunalu prawdy i sprawiedliwości,* vol. 1 (Warsaw, 1904), 133–34.

53. *Ogłos procesów kryminalnych na Żydach o różne ekscesy, także morderstwo dzieci osobliwie w Sandomierza w roku 1698 przeświadczone w preświentem Trybunale Koronnym przewiedzionych, dla dobra pospolitego wydany (1700); Proces kryminalny o niewinne dziecie Jerzego Krasnowskiego już to trzecie roku 1710 dnia sierpnia w Sendomirzu okrutnie od żydów zamordowane* (ca. 1720). The first of these was in the library of Anna Radziwiłłowa. Wanda Karkucinska, *Anna z Sanguszków Radziwiłłowa* (Warsaw, 2000), 97.

54. "Te parchy browary, / Garce, szynki trzymają i we młynach miary." As quoted by Kowalski, "W obronie wiary," 225. A series of paintings commissioned by Żuchowski that depict various threats to the city including Jews engaging in ritual murder still hangs in the cathedral and in the church of St. Paul in Sandomierz at this writing.

55. Guldon and Wijaczka, "Accusation of Ritual Murder in Poland," 127; id., *Procesy o mordy rytualne w Polsce w XVI–XVIII wieku,* 15–33.

56. Mathias Bersohn, *Dyplomataryusz dotyczący Żydów w dawnej Polsce na źródłach archiwalnych osnuty (1388–1782)* (Warsaw, 1910), no. 377, 214–16.

crown and the highest reaches of the Church hierarchy supported the procedure that led to the judicial murder of seven Jews.

During the second trial of Jews in Sandomierz, Father Żuchowski testified that "Jews murder Christian children and they do need their blood." Jan Serafinowicz, an apostate, supported his charges.[57] Serafinowicz was apparently the author of a long manuscript full of "evidence" supporting the libel against his former brethren, which became a sort of handbook for prosecutors of Jews. It eventually was summarized in a book, *Złość żydowska* ("Jewish Malice"), published in 1758 and in a revised version twice in 1760 by Gaudenty Pikulski, a priest.[58]

Pikulski's book was one of a number published in the eighteenth century containing anti-Jewish propaganda in various forms.[59] The popularity of the work in its revised version probably derived from its transcription of the 1759 Shabbatean (Frankist) disputation, which is presented together with some other documents pertaining to the Frankists. Even in the first edition, however, there is a fanciful chapter devoted to "The Sects of the Jews and the Contemporary Shabbateans" *(Sabsa Cwinników).*[60]

In the section of the book that is derived from Serafinowicz, "anthropological" observations of Jews are presented side by side with fantastic descriptions of the necessity for Christian blood for Jewish ceremonies.[61] There is an account of the supposed talmudic requirement that Jews acquire a sanctified Host twice annually, together with several pages on what Jews do with it.[62] Pikulski's massive book included a terrible illustration purportedly showing the corpse of the infant stabbed hundreds of times with needles by the Jews of Żytomierz "who kidnapped the child on Good Friday and murdered him on Saturday" *(poszabasie).*[63]

One of the most popular books in Poland in the middle of the eighteenth century was an encyclopedic work, *Nowe Ateny,* by Benedykt Chmielow-

57. On Serafinowicz, see Bałaban, *Letoledot,* 1: 55–59.

58. Pikulski, *Złość żydowska* 1st ed., 350ff.; 2d ed., 700ff.

59. See Bogdan Rok, "Z dziejów literatury antyżydowskiej w dawnej Rzeczypospolitej w XVIII w.," in *Studia historyczno-demograficzne,* ed. Tadeusz Jurek and Krystyn Matwijowski [*PRAWO,* vol. 251] (Wrocław, 1996), 55–64; Bałaban, *Letoledot,* 1: 92–95.

60. "These were most numerous in Volhynian lands among the Turks." Pikulski, *Złość żydowska,* 37.

61. On the blood libel in this section, see ibid., 701 (Serafinowicz says that he twice killed Christian children); Pikulski, *Złość żydowska,* 749–52 ; 763–87 (the use of blood for Passover; the requirement of Jews for Christian blood). Cf. R. Po-chia Hsia, "Christian Ethnographies of Jews in Early Modern Germany," in *The Expulsion of the Jews: 1492 and After,* ed. R. B. Waddington and A. Williamson (New York, 1994), 223–35.

62. Pikulski, *Złość żydowska,* 754–58.

63. Ibid., following 763.

ski, published in two volumes in 1745 and in a larger, four-volume format in 1755.[64] The book included a number of references to the desecration of the Host and to the use of Christian blood by Jews.[65] Earlier works such as the writings of Jan Achacy Kmita (early seventeenth century) and Canon Jacob Radlinski (early eighteenth century) are cited.[66] One article in *Nowe Ateny* advocated the expulsion of the Jews from Poland because they, together with the Dissidents, had caused the ruin of the country.[67]

In the first half of the eighteenth century, the Church was well organized, triumphant, and wealthy. Confronted with a large and growing Jewish population, which in the eastern half of the Commonwealth seemed to dominate urban life, the Church responded. The missionary campaigns, the literary attacks on Jews, and the involvement of Church officials, including bishops, in fomenting of accusations of ritual murder and in spreading the blood libel against Jews constituted a murderous public and symbolic theological attack on Jews. Catholics were taught that God had turned his back on the Jewish people, who were thus condemned to eternal punishment and degradation. Yet in the lands of the Polish Commonwealth there were hundreds of thousands of Jews who frequently did not appear to be suffering on the scale that the teachings of the Church suggested. The missionizing sermons of Kobielski, the hate-filled literature written by churchmen, and the trials for ritual murder and desecration of the Host can all be understood, in part, as attempts by the Church to validate its theological teachings on the Jews and Judaism. It sought to narrow the distance between theological principle and historical reality.

The Church's "intended audience" in its efforts to assert its theologically necessary superiority to Judaism and to Jews was the mass of

64. Benedykt Chmielowski, *Nowe Ateny albo Wszelkiej Scyencyi Pełna, na Różne Tytuły iak na Classes Podzielona*, 4 vols. (Lwów: JKMci Collegii S.J., 1755). Cf. Bałaban, *Letoledot*, 1: 94. Chmielowski's knowledge of Judaism and Jewish practices was inconsistent. In one place, he confuses what he called *"tfylym"* with *mezuzah*, depicting it as a talisman to protect the house from evil (3: 263). In another, he mentions a fast day on June 17 "in memory of the several thousand Jews killed in Ukraine by Chmielnicki, Hetman of the Cossacks"; and in still another, he describes the use of an amulet by Jews against the demon "Lilis albo Lilith," which is to be written to protect women in childbirth and children as follows: "Adam Chava, chye Lilis machszayf ło sechaie" (1: 1072).

65. Chmielowski, *Nowe Ateny*, 1: 1070; 3: 244; 4: 384–90.

66. Jan Achacy Kmita, *Talmud albo Wiara Żydowska* (Lublin, 1610, 1642); J. Radliński, *Prawda Chrześciańska od nieprzyiaciela swego zeznana* (Lublin, 1733).

67. Chmielowski, *Nowe Ateny*, 4: 383.

Catholic believers in the Commonwealth and particularly priests, who were most likely to read the published sermons, synodal enactments, and anti-Jewish literature. Pikulski, for example, announced simply that his purpose was to ensure "that every Catholic, seeing clearly the errors of the Jews, will be strengthened in his faith." By widening the distance between Jews and Christians, the actions of the Church complemented a deeper process that had already begun. Increasingly, Jewish and Christian Poles would be separated, "the Jew" would be seen as the other, and a modern, mono-ethnic Polish national consciousness would develop. The effect of the Church's onslaught against Jews was to exclude them from Polish national identity as it was crystallizing, and Jews would respond by widening the psychological distance between themselves and their Christian countrymen.

In the eighteenth century, however, the affairs of Jews and Christians were deeply entangled. This entanglement was primarily, but not exclusively, economic. Even the Church, as noted above, had deep ties to Jewish communal institutions in the form of massive credits or loans to Jewish communities, as well as contracts with individual Jews to manage Church estates. Perhaps ethnocentric self-definition became more urgent precisely because of physical and economic proximity. While disentanglement of Christian from Jew and the emergence of the duality "Pole and Jew" had begun, this certainly was not achieved in the eighteenth century.[68]

Just as Jews were crucial to and deeply integrated into the economy of the state in general, their multiple economic links to churchmen and to Church institutions served to moderate ideological hostility. This meant that while the Church nurtured Jewish separatism through libelous accusations and judicial murders, it simultaneously enhanced the degree of Jewish integration into the economy of the state, thereby contributing

---

68. The impact of the activities of the Church and churchmen on the thinking of Polish and Lithuanian Jews in the eighteenth century is easier to imagine than to document. Much is known about Jewish institutional responses to particular threats. The most dramatic of these was a series of three Jewish missions to the Vatican in 1754, 1758, and 1761. The Council of the Lands sponsored all three. The 1758 mission resulted in the publication of an extensive rejection of the libel of ritual murder by the future Pope Clement XIV, Cardinal Ganganelli. Hanna Węgrzynek, "Deputacje Żydów polskich do Stolicy Apostolskiej w drugiej połowie XVIII wieku," *Kwartalnik historii Żydów* 3 (2001): 319–26. The leader of the 1754 mission, Yisra'el Isser ben Yosef, was *shtadlan miPodolia* and is to be identified, following Israel Halpern's suggestion, with Israel of Międzyboż who participated in the debate with the Frankists. *PVAA*, p. 423, no 768. Cecil Roth, *The Ritual Murder Libel and the Jew: The Report by Cardinal Lorenzo Ganganelli (Pope Clement XIV)* (London, 1935).

to Jews' security. There is room to claim that just as the eighteenth century witnessed the intertwining of Catholicism and Polish national identity, the same developments fostered the beginnings of an incipient Jewish national consciousness in East Central Europe. Jewish "national" identity has been linked by some to the communal and intercommunal institutions of Polish-Lithuanian Jewry, which were more highly developed than any in European Jewish history.

CHAPTER 4

The Community

Kahal is the term used to designate the institutional leadership of the Jewish community, or *kehillah*. Since the Middle Ages, communal institutions had been integrated into the system of Ashkenazic halakhah. Thus, among members of the Jewish community, there was no distinction made between civil offenses and sins. Members of a limited number of prosperous and prominent families in each community held the offices of leadership. That is, the system is best described as oligarchic. The superiority of the wealthy and learned was taken for granted in Jewish society and was part of the order of things. Moreover, state authorities and the owners of private towns formally recognized the Jewish institutions, the *kahal*, its officers, and its courts. Just as Christian municipalities enjoyed legal autonomy based on their royal founding charters, so too royal charters and privileges from town owners assured Jews of corporate autonomy.[1]

The earliest charters dating to 1264 and regulating the status of Jews

---

1. Royal charters to cities were generally based on the model of the constitution of the city of Magdeburg and are often referred to as Magdeburg Law. Only a small number of communal minute books of Jewish communities in Poland-Lithuania in the eighteenth century have survived. Among those that have been published are Mordechai Nadav [Markiel Katzykovich], ed., *Pinkas kehal Tiktin [5]381–[5]566: Haskamot, hahelatot vetakanot kefi shehe'etikan min hapinkas hamekori she'avad basho'ah Yisra'el Halperin*, vol. 1: *Pinkas kehal Tiktin* (Jerusalem, 1996); Dov Avron, *Pinkas hakesherim shel kehillat Pozna (5)381–(5)595*, Acta Electorum Communitatis Judaeorum Posnaniensium (1621–1835) (Jerusalem, 1966); H. Z. Margoliot, *Dubno rabbati* (Warsaw, 1910); Salomon Buber, *Kiryah nisgavah, hi ir Zolkva* (Kraków, 1903); Anna Michałowska, "Pinkas gminy żydowskiej w Bockach," *BZIH* 190 (1999): 55–97. See below, and for further references, see Nahum Rakover, *Hakehillah*, A Bibliography of Jewish History, no. 4 (Jerusalem, 1977), 108–30, and Gershon Hundert and Gershon Bacon, *The Jews in Poland and Russia: Bibliographical Essays* (Bloomington, Ind., 1984), 17–22.

in Poland and Lithuania followed central and western European precedents in guaranteeing the juridical autonomy of Jews and subjecting them
exclusively to royal jurisdiction.[2] The steady expansion of the power of
the nobility, however, led to a law, promulgated by the Sejm in 1539, granting the owners of private towns the exclusive right to tax Jewish residents,
and transferring juridical authority over Jews residing in such towns from
royal officials to the town owners.[3] In both royal and private towns, Jews
had the legal right to try cases between Jews according to their own laws,
and to choose their own leaders without outside interference. Appeals of
cases heard in Jewish courts, however, were frequently heard in magnate
or royal courts. This procedure of appeal reflected one of the limits on
the self-government of Jews in Polish lands.

Particularly in the larger crown cities, Jews tended to live on a particular street or streets. Certain of these cities—Lwów, Poznan, Lublin—legally
restricted Jews to certain areas. Still, what divided Jews from Christians,
beyond the psychological distance, was not residence but jurisdiction. Jews
were exempt from the jurisdiction of the municipality except in matters
of real estate that belonged to the town. In this sense, Jews were in the
town but not of it. Indeed, the *kahal* and the municipality were similar
in structure and function. This institutional similarity dated back to the
Middle Ages and originated in central and western Europe.

For all their similarities, it is important to bear in mind certain fundamental and distinguishing characteristics of the *kahal*. The enactments of
the *kahal* had the force of Jewish law, which derived its authority from
the Torah, from divine revelation. Disobedience of a communal enactment was thus simultaneously a civil offense and a sin. Furthermore, the
kahal operated on the principle that the interests of the collective outweighed those of the individual. There was no public or social domain in
which individuals were not subject to the jurisdiction of the elders. In particular, any contacts with Gentiles, especially those related to business or
finance, required the prior approval of the communal government. And
while the stipulations of the sumptuary laws in the Jewish community
were not so different from those of the Christians, they were distinguished
by this concern for collective interests.

The *kahal*'s responsibilities were wide-ranging, fulfilling all of the functions of a municipal administration and more. It acted variously as a fiscal

2. Jacob Goldberg, *Jewish Privileges in the Polish Commonwealth* (Jerusalem, 1985), 2–8,
and the references there. See also S. Artur Cygielman, "The Basic Privileges of the Jews of
Great Poland as Reflected in Polish Historiography," *POLIN* 2 (1987): 117–49. In Hebrew:
Zion 48 (1983): 281–314.

3. *VL*, 1: 550.

administration collecting local and national taxes. There was a judiciary system with both lay and rabbinical courts and a board of education supervising schooling from the elementary to the most advanced levels. It also administered matters related to housing, health and welfare, utilities and safety, public morality, commerce, and defense. The *kahal* was also similar to the municipal government in its organization. A municipal government was generally three-tiered. It consisted of three to five consuls *(rajcowie),* three to five magistrates *(ławnicy),* and an assembly whose name may once have reflected the number of members (i.e., "the forty men"). The office of mayor *(burmistrz)* rotated among the consuls. Elections, when they were held at all, were generally held in the spring. Franchise was limited to those with the rights of municipal citizenship, and, despite concessions gained by guild artisans, especially in the sixteenth century, the municipality tended to be dominated by an oligarchic group of merchants and some wealthy guild masters.[4]

Like the municipality, the *kahal* had a three-tiered structure, consisting of *roshim* ("heads" or "seniors"), *tovim* (lit., "good men"), and a group variously called *alufim* ("outstanding men") or *kahal,* the term in this instance connoting a council. Like the office of mayor in the municipality, the position of *parnas* ("warden" or "leader") rotated monthly among the *roshim.* It was the *roshim* who took an oath to king and country after their election, which was held in the spring, generally on the first of the intermediate days of the Passover holiday. Franchise was strictly limited. Most communities followed some variation of the procedures described in the 1595 "constitution" of the Jewish community of Kraków-Kazimierz.[5] In it, the oligarchic character of the institution is abundantly clear:

Neither the *roshim* nor the *tovim,* nor the rabbi nor the *kahal,* may their Rock and Redeemer protect them, nor any other official will be chosen anywhere except on the street of the Jews. They will be chosen with the agreement of the [incumbent] *roshim, tovim,* and *kahal* and according to the prescriptions of our Torah, [and] as in the statutes we have from kings and other princes and rulers. Further, we are bound by oath to follow these procedures by the authority of Mount Sinai, and we have renewed this vow. . . .

4. Adam Przyboś, ed., *Akta radzieckie rzeszowskie* (Wrocław, 1957), xxxviii; Jan Riabinin, *Rada miejska lubelska* (Lublin, 1931), 2, 7–8; Jan Ptaśnik, *Miasta i mieszczaństwo w dawnej Polsce* (Kraków, 1934), 77–85; Janina Bieniarzówna, *Mieszczaństwo krakowskie XVII wieku* (Kraków, 1969), 23; Maria Bogucka and Henryk Samsonowicz, *Dzieje miasta i mieszczaństwa w Polsce przedrozbiorowej* (Wrocław, 1986), 454–88.
5. Shlomoh Eidelberg, "Pinkas Śniadowo," *Gal-Ed* 3 (1976): 295–314. Cf. S. Buber, *Kiryah nisgavah,* 93–94, 97, 100, 102, 106–7; S. Assaf, "Mipinkas Zablodovah," *Kiryat Sefer* 1 (1924–25): 314.

The time for the annual election of four *roshim,* five *tovim,* fourteen *kahal,* . . .
the three groups of [three] judges in their three degrees, and the three assessor-
treasurers who assist the *tovim* will be during the intermediate days of Passover. . . .

This will be the order of the election:

The *roshim, tovim,* and *kahal* sitting together will swear by their belief in Heaven
before God and man without reservation that no one . . . has made a secret agreement with his fellow or has wished to make one with individuals or groups, with
regard to the elections. Rather each will express his opinion for the sake of heaven
and for the good of the community in the way that heaven shows him, not for
his own benefit or that of another and not out of spite. They must choose the
men who seem most worthy and best suited to the good of the community. . . .
Each of the *roshim, tovim,* and *kahal,* may their Rock and Redeemer protect them,
may suggest [in writing on a slip of paper] the name of one elector [*borer*] with
whom he has no relationship [exclusion of blood relatives and business part-
ners]. . . . It is permissible to suggest the names either of members of the *kahal*
or of nonmembers. . . . The attendants will draw nine names from the ballot box.
No relationships as defined by Torah law [blood relationship close enough to eliminate them as witnesses] among the nine will be permitted. The second name to
be drawn will be eliminated.

As soon as the nine names have been drawn from the ballot box, those men
shall swear before the open holy ark in the presence of the attendants, may the
Rock and Redeemer protect them, to choose five men of understanding and wisdom who are familiar with the demands of communal leadership, and who are
worthy and suited to choose, for the good of the community, *roshim,* and
tovim. . . . They must swear also that there exist no secret agreements among
them . . . and to choose with wisdom the five [electors] not to please any particular individual but for the benefit of the whole community. . . . Only two of the
original nine may be included among the five electors.

[In addition to the *roshim, tovim,* and *kahal,* the judges and the assessor-
treasurers,] they will also select five superintendents [*gabba'im umemunim*], the
overseers of the orphans, and the overseers of the beverage tax [*czopowe*] from
among the old *kahal,* or the nine electors, people not in the *kahal,* or from among
themselves, as they are shown by heaven. If one of them [the five] or a relative or
partner of one of them is being discussed, he must arise [and leave].

They will make their choices in a locked room and all will sign and seal the
final results. As soon as it is sealed, [the document] will be given to one of the attendants. . . . As soon as this has been done, the group of five will be dissolved,
and they can make no changes in what they have done. But they should not be
hasty in their choices; the deliberations should last at least one night until the
light of morning.[6]

---

6. Majer Bałaban, "Die Krakauer Judengemeinde-Ordnung von 1595 und ihre Nachträge," *Jahrbuch der jüdisch-literarischen Gesellschaft* 10 (1912): 309, 314–317 (my translations).
Cf. Buber, *Kirya nisgavah,* 93–94, 97, 100; 102, 106–7; S. Assaf, "Mipinkas Zablodovah,"
314; Gershon Hundert, *The Jews in a Polish Private Town* (Baltimore, 1992), 85–87; Majer

In other communities, the names placed in the "ballot box" would also include those of the highest taxpayers. The proportion of "enfranchised" members of the community seldom exceeded 10 or 15 percent of the adult males, and was often much lower. Generally, the highest officers of the community were required to have the title *moreinu* ("our teacher"). That is, the level of their learning, in theory at least, was required to be roughly equivalent to that of a rabbi. While it is clear that only a limited number of families controlled communal offices, there was often some rotation, and it was relatively uncommon for the same person to hold the same office year after year.

In addition to the *kahal* officers, there was a broader council, referred to variously as "the twenty-one men," *yehidei segulah* (outstanding people), *keru'ei 'edah* (leaders of the community), *the householders who pay high taxes,* or *those who belong to the assembly.* Polish documents refer to this group as the *pospólstwo* ("people"). These terms all designated (some or all of) those who paid sufficient taxes to qualify for the *kahal* but who themselves did not hold office. They were convened to consider matters of broad importance affecting the life of the community, such as appointing a rabbi, or to consider legislation of a general character *(takanot).* For this reason, such groups were sometimes called *ba'alei takanot:* those who issue edicts.

Committees of supervisors were chosen separately from among members of the council. Among the various positions were: synagogue overseers; overseers of funds for the land of Israel; overseers of funds for the redemption of captives; overseers of charity collection; overseers of education *(talmud torah);* overseers of the *hekdesh* (poorhouse/"hospital"); tax assessors; account keepers; overseers of visiting the sick *(bikur holim).* In certain communities, these tasks were undertaken by voluntary societies.

The communities employed *shamashim* (beadles or syndics) to perform various tasks, including maintenance of communal property, carrying messages, awakening individuals for prayer, and announcing the onset of the Sabbath. Jewish and/or Christian guards maintained order and prevented fires, and the community employed a communal chimney sweep to try to prevent the all-too-frequent outbreak of fire. Midwives, doctors, and pharmacists received allocations from the *kahal* for treating the poor. The *kahal* also paid the salaries of teachers.

Decisions and actions of the *kahal* and its subsidiary groups were recorded in official minute books. In addition to *the* minute book *(pinkas)*

Bałaban, "Ustrój kahału w Polsce XVI–XVII wieku," *Kwartalnik poświęcony historii Żydów w Polsce* 2 (1912): 31. And see Nadav, *Pinkas,* passim.

of the community, there were others. In Tykocin, for example, there were specialized record books. Among them were books of contracts, lists of officers, tax records, a rabbi's minute book, a judges' minute book, and one that recorded financial transactions between the municipality and the *kahal*.[7] Great circumspection was exercised regarding what was actually written down, and this was not only because these were official records. Actually recording a misdeed was itself considered a sanction.[8]

The keeping of the records was the task of the scribe *(sofer)* of the community, one of several salaried officials. The office was a prestigious one, sometimes combined with judicial duties. Judges, preachers, cantors, and the rabbi were among the other salaried professionals. A specially qualified official lobbyist, or *shtadlan,* was sometimes employed. His tasks included interceding with government officials or the town owner on behalf of the community and accompanying and assisting individuals who appeared in Christian courts. In the eighteenth century, communities were more likely to rely on lobbyists appointed by the regional councils or by the Council of the Lands.[9]

The Rabbi: Chief Judge

The rabbi was the authority in matters of *halakha.* His title was *av beit hadin* ("chief judge"), and his task was to head the rabbinical courts of the community.[10] The words *reish metivta* ("head of the academy") would be added to his title if, as was often the case, he was also the principal of the communal yeshiva.[11] He generally participated in meetings of the *kahal* and endorsed their decisions with his signature.

In larger communities, there would be several cohorts of judges, who would hear cases of varying degrees of seriousness. For the most part, these were civil cases, but in criminal matters, a number of sanctions were available to the courts. The most common of these was a fine, but the removal of the right of residence was available for the punishment of deviance or crime.[12] Other sanctions included lashes, imprisonment, and being

---

7. Nadav, *Pinkas,* 20–22.

8. See, e.g., ibid., 35, 69, 111, 196.

9. Cf. Margoliot, *Dubno rabbati,* 47.

10. For a convenient general description, see Jacob Katz, *Tradition and Crisis,* 2d ed. (New York, 1993), s.v. "Rabbinate," "Communal Rabbi."

11. S. Assaf, "Mipinkas Zablodovah," 313–14. Cf. Buber, *Kiryah nisgavah,* 109.

12. Nadav, *Pinkas,* nos. 65–66 (removed), 111, 184, 216, 286, 287, 300, 302, 333, 462, 473, 476, 524, 589 *(galil),* 595, 974; newcomer to pay at least 2 ducats: S. Assaf, "Mipinkas Zablodovah," 314; Hundert, *Jews in a Polish Private Town,* 69–71.

chained in the *kune,* or *kuna,* which consisted of an iron collar for the neck and leg irons, placed in the vestibule of the synagogue. This sort of shaming was deemed an extreme punishment, worse than lashes, which were often administered away from the public's gaze in the *kahal* offices.[13]

In addition to supervising the courts and overseeing the yeshiva, the rabbi oversaw the elections to the *kahal,* the Burial Society, and other societies and guilds. Acting as a sort of magistrate-notary, he added his seal and signature to contracts, wills, and deeds. In private towns, the administration of the town owner demanded that he keep careful records, making the "Minute Book of the Rabbi" a crucial responsibility. The rabbi administered oaths to slaughterers of animals and butchers, taxpayers and tax collectors. He formulated and pronounced bans of excommunication in the synagogue. He bestowed the prestigious title of *moreinu* and the lesser title of *haver* (lit. "fellow," another honorific designating scholarly achievement).[14] He officiated at weddings and supervised divorces. The rabbi delivered the traditional sermons on the Sabbath before Passover and the Sabbath between New Year and the Day of Atonement. He toured the villages surrounding the community on fixed occasions to offer his services. He saw to it that village residents paid their taxes and ensured that the slaughterers of animals were properly qualified.

The income of a rabbi in a large community was quite respectable, and rabbinical positions were sought after. Rabbinical salaries in large towns exceeded those of municipal officials and of all but the most important estate managers.[15] The particular fees he could charge for various tasks were sometimes fixed and often under the supervision of a government official or the administration of the town owner.[16] For officiating at weddings, the rabbi received a percentage of the dowry. Divorces were common enough that a sliding scale of fees according to the assets of the parties was established in some communities. When the rabbi toured the smaller settlements in the countryside, he received customary gifts.[17] In the eighteenth century, the appointment of a rabbi required the consent

13. Adam Kaźmierczyk, *Żydzi w dobrach prywatnych w świetle sądowniczej i administracyjnej prakyki dóbr magnackich w wiekach XVI–XVIII* (Kraków, 2002), 200–202; D. Dawidowicz, *Omanut ve'omanim bevatei keneset shel Polin* (Tel Aviv, 1982), 84; Nadav, *Pinkas,* nos. 113, 119, 225, 472, 596, 866, 974.

14. Communal elders sometimes had the right to approve such actions. Nadav, *Pinkas,* nos. 91, 253, 582, 659 (23), 908, 988.

15. Hundert, *Jews in a Polish Private Town,* 190, n. 47.

16. AGAD, ADO I/109 (Opatów); Kraków, AP, Teki Schneidera 262 (Zasław); and see Israel Halpern, *Takanot medinat Mehrin* (Jerusalem, 1952), nos. 158–60, 166, 167, 172, pp. 52, 54, 55; Nadav, *Pinkas,* no. 72, p. 38.

17. These gifts were called *kolęda* in Polish. See Isaac Levitats, *The Jewish Community in Russia 1772–1844* (New York, 1943), 155, n. 27; Jacob Josef of Połonne, *Sefer Toledot ya'akov*

(konsens or *rabinostwo)* of the town owner or the provincial governor.[18] This required a substantial payment. In Żółkiew, the payment expected for a six-year contract was 350 ducats (6,300 florins). "Rabbinic posts were transformed into a type of *arenda*," M. J. Rosman notes.[19]

The rabbi enjoyed the deference of the community. He and his household were exempt from sumptuary regulations. Members of the community would come to greet him on the Sabbath and holidays.[20] He was entitled to be "obliged" to be the third called up to the reading of the Torah.[21] A family celebrating a circumcision would honor the rabbi with a gift of mead or fish. On certain holidays, the community itself would present the rabbi with a gift of this sort.[22] Children would be brought to him to be blessed on Friday evening. Nevertheless, the rabbi was appointed, generally for a fixed term of three years, and paid by the *kahal.*

Kahal Income and Expenditure

Based on the communal minute books that survive, it would seem that the communal government's chief concern was the collection of taxes. The *kahal* used the revenues to fund its own activities and to pay taxes both to the Regional Council and to the Council of the Four Lands. Tax monies were also used for regular and occasional "gifts" to churchmen and officials for protective purposes; these sums often amounted to more than 10 percent of the community's income. About one-third of the communal income went to servicing debts; another third was used to pay taxes. The remaining sum covered salaries, building repairs, and welfare activities.

Communal income was based on direct taxes on assets and income and

yosef (Korzec, 1780), "tsav"; Berakhia Berakh of Klimontów, *Zera berakh shelishi,* pt. 2 (Frankfurt a/O, 1735), 24.

18. J. Goldberg, *Jewish Privileges,* no. 2, 62 (Bobrowniki, 1744); no. 23, 166 (Lubraniec, 1783); no. 27, 193 (Łask, 1714); no. 57, 357 (Wojsławice, 1780). Adam Kaźmierczyk, *Żydzi polscy, 1648–1772: Źródła* (Kraków, 2001), no. 40, 75 (Lubartów, 1769); no. 54, 99 (Rzeszów, 1737); no. 56, 103 (Żółkiew, 1752).

19. M. J. Rosman, *The Lords' Jews: Magnate-Jewish Relations in the Polish-Lithuanian Commonwealth during the Eighteenth Century* (Cambridge, Mass., 1990), 200, and the sources cited there, 198–204; Adam Kaźmierczyk, *Żydzi w dobrach,* esp. 137–42.

20. *PML,* nos. 962–63, 266 (1761).

21. The first one called had to be of priestly descent and the second of levitical descent and had thus to be chosen from among a rather small group, so that the third person was effectively the first who could be chosen according to merit.

22. See, e.g., S. B. Nisenbaum, *Lekorot hayehudim beLublin* (Lublin, 1920), 14.

indirect taxes on meat and commercial activities.[23] Income was also derived from taxes levied on dowries and funerals and from fees for use of the bathhouse and the use of official weights and measures. The sale of pews in the synagogue and annual payments by slaughterers of animals also provided additional income to support the *kahal*'s budget. Finally, newcomers to the community, like new arrivals seeking citizenship in the Christian town, had to pay a fee for the "right of settlement." The amount varied with the community but could be quite substantial.

Other concerns of the *kahal* included the attempt to limit competition within the community, the supervision of education, and providing for the poor, the sick, and itinerants who arrived in the town. It also attempted to limit conspicuous consumption.

Sumptuary and Alimentary Regulation

Clothing demonstrated and communicated standing and confirmed an individual's self-image.[24] In the case of Jews, such social performance had two disparate audiences: outsiders and insiders. In the first instance, the Jewish collectivity sought to present itself in a certain way to its neighbors; in the second, the powerful sought to protect and reinforce their claims to status within Jewish society. Reflecting this tension, regulations on dress were a matter of foreign policy, while alimentary regulation was largely an internal matter. Thus, sumptuary laws, with very few exceptions, specified their universal application. Alimentary legislation, on the other hand, consistently indicated a hierarchy of restrictions dependent on the income of the householders. The richer the family, the more guests it was entitled to entertain at its celebrations.

The degree to which the limitations on dress were observed is impos-

23. On the tax on commercial activities known as *korobka*, see Hundert, *Jews in a Polish Private Town*, 173, n. 18, and index, s.v. "taxes."

24. On sumptuary laws see Alan Hunt, *Governance of the Consuming Passions: A History of Sumptuary Law* (New York, 1996); Salo Wittmayer Baron, *The Jewish Community: Its History and Structure to the American Revolution* (Philadelphia, 1942), 2: 301–7; Robert Bonfil, *Jewish Life in Renaissance Italy*, trans. Anthony Oldcorn (Berkeley, 1994), 104–11, 138–39, 243, 262; Diane Owen Hughes, "Distinguishing Signs: Ear-Rings, Jews and Franciscan Rhetoric in the Italian Renaissance City," *Past & Present* 112 (1986): 3–59; Jay R. Berkovitz, "Social and Religious Controls in Pre-Revolutionary France: Rethinking the Beginnings of Modernity," *Jewish History* 15 (2001): 1–40. And see Giza Frankel, "Notes on the Costume of the Jewish Woman in Eastern Europe," *Journal of Jewish Art* 7 (1980): 50–57.

sible to determine, but it is conventionally believed that such laws were generally unenforceable. Certainly, the regulations themselves frequently make exceptions for special occasions, for example, the Sabbath, holidays, or weddings. The insistence in one resolution that restrictions on dress apply "even in the Women's Gallery of the synagogue on the last day of Passover" has an unmistakable ring of frustration.[25] Distinctions were sometimes drawn between unmarried and married women, with the former being permitted more latitude.[26] At other times, though, such distinctions were overridden. A prohibition of wearing gold or silver, ducats, or coral was followed by the pronouncement: "This applies to unmarried girls and even more to women; it is even forbidden for brides to ornament themselves."[27] In general, sumptuary laws should be read not as descriptions of the behavior of Jews but as the inscription of norms or ideals by an elite sector of Jewish society.

By the eighteenth century, in Poland as elsewhere, the general norm that "Jews should wear distinctive clothing" had long been established. Dark and inconspicuous clothing was seen as appropriate to Jews living in this long and bitter exile, and wearing "Gentile clothing" was explicitly equated with immodesty and immorality.[28] Implicitly, the accommodative choice of modest dress suggested that Jews would not seek power or position in the state.[29] It cannot be stressed enough that these were norms and are not descriptions of actual behavior. Both men and women were known to wear colorful, stylish clothing, the latter more often than the former.

Limitations on consumption were regularly enacted in European Jewish communities by the fifteenth century. The explanations attached to the regulations include a number of continually recurring motifs. Certainly, the most frequently cited reason was the fear of arousing the envy and ire of the Gentiles by costly display (*mar'it ayin*, "appearances") that might lead to taxes being raised or to demands for the repayment of outstanding loans. Moreover, ostentation might be viewed as a transgression of

25. Avron, *Pinkas hakesherim*, no. 1866, 334 (1705).

26. Margoliot, *Dubno*, 59; Avron, *Pinkas hakesherim*, no. 2251, 438 (1787).

27. Avron, *Pinkas hakesherim*, no. 2144, 395 (1734).

28. PVAA, no. 50, 17 (1607); PML, no. 321, 69 (1637), no. 339, 71 (1637), no. 468, 103 (1650). And see the implicit equation of black clothing for males with propriety. Nadav, *Pinkas*, no. 185, item 18, 117–21 (between 1700 and 1720).

29. Moreover, as Robert Bonfil suggested in his study of Jews in Renaissance Italy, the choice of placing oneself on an inferior level with respect to others was the only viable option for Jews. The sumptuary laws made a virtue of necessity by redefining inferiority as modesty, and thus as superiority of a moral and religious type. Bonfil, *Jewish Life*, 243.

the Jews' place in society. After all, elaborate legislation enacted by the Polish parliament limited various luxurious articles of attire to the *szlachta*.[30] The claim to power implicit in a Jew's dressing like a nobleman was a danger to the whole community. There were complaints in the Sandomierz *sejmik* in 1699 that Jews were dressing, not as Jews, but *po kawalersku,* that is, like the *szlachta*.[31] In Poznan, one of the Jewish communal resolutions, which was repeated almost annually, insisted that earlier restrictions on dress be enforced vigilantly, invoking all of these motifs. Among the forbidden items were silver buckles on fur coats and other outerwear; silver belts and gold rings; lace and chains and ornaments of gold and silver on hats; and bodices with silver ornaments. A further prohibition fell on silk clothing. Ostentatious displays were "bringing misfortune to our holy community, particularly dresses and jewellery of the new style, which are strictly forbidden by the laws of the Gentiles. Moreover, this causes endless grief to our community. Our creditors, seeing Jews parade in royal garments, ornamented with silver and gold, shout for justice in the *sejmiki* [regional assemblies] and in the courts, saying that obviously they [the Jews] can pay their debts to noblemen and to priests."[32]

The emphasis in this passage is on the need to conceal wealth rather than the prohibition of luxurious goods. During the Seven Years' War, when Prussian troops entered Poznan at the end of February 1759, a resolution was adopted stressing the particular urgency of enforcing regulations requiring Jews to refrain from display: "These should be carefully enforced nowadays because the state is confused with armed soldiers. . . . It should be understood that we must not be visible because of *mar'it ayin*. . . . Everyone must caution his wife and daughter about the danger."[33] Regulations adopted by the Lithuanian Council in 1761 specified

30. *VL,* s.v., "Lex sumptuarya."

31. Opatów, May 5, 1699: "już nie po żydowsku, ale po kawalersku chodzą." Kaźmierczyk, *Żydzi Polscy,* 105–6; Jerzy Topolski, ed., *Polska: Dzieje narodu, państwa i kultury,* vol. 2 (Poznan, 1994), 431.

32. "Uveyihud malbushim vekishutim mikarov ba'u asher lo she'arum avoteinu shehem mamash issur gamur mishum hukot hagoyyim . . . sheba'alei hovot notnin 'eineihem vetso'akim . . . bekhol haseimikim uvekhol sandis kesheyehudim holkhim bevigdei melukhah uvekhesef uvezahav merukamim bevadai yedeihem masigot leshalem hovot pritsim vegalahot." Avron, *Pinkas hakesherim,* no. 1965, 355–56 (1713). See there also no. 1760, 310–11 (1699); no. 1971, 358 (1714); no. 2038, 375 (1719); no. 2210, 420 (1763); "ve'al yedei godel hamar'it ayin mit'orerim aleinu kin'at ha'umot," no. 2227, 428; Margoliot, *Dubno,* 58; "lehasir me'aleinu nesi'ut avon veharikat shen," Nadav, *Pinkas,* no. 886, 590 (1728); YIVO Institute, New York, RG 223 (printed cat. no. 1039, p. 265), pt. 2: 9, Minute Book of the Community of Skuodas, unpaginated.

33. Avron, *Pinkas hakesherim,* no. 2196, 414–15 (1759).

explicitly that luxurious clothing could be worn on holidays by women, and that unmarried women were not limited in what they chose to wear. In neither case, however, were they to wear such things *in the marketplaces and the streets where Gentiles lived.*[34] In the case of regulation of dress, there was generally only one exception enshrined in the legislation itself, and this was for the rabbi and his household.[35]

Contemporary preachers deemed luxurious display and the pursuit of fashion to be causes of misfortune afflicting the Jewish people and singularly inappropriate in the aftermath of suffering such as the attacks in 1768.[36] Moreover, profligate spending was condemned both on moral grounds and because it led to debt and ruin and "wasting the money of Israel."[37] An ascetic preacher of the period condemned the pursuit of fashion: "They continually acquire new luxurious clothes and after using them for a day or two, do not wear them again. They acquire other clothing, and this they do repeatedly. Every time the style of clothing changes, new forms are adopted and the old clothes are abandoned. They refuse to wear them and discard them in heaps—four or five outfits and dresses that they no longer require."[38]

Most but not all eighteenth-century sumptuary legislation concerned women's clothing. Despite this gendering of the legislation, it is of interest that commentary disparaging or demeaning females only rarely accompanied Polish-Lithuanian Jewish sumptuary laws, whereas it frequently appeared in early modern European Christian regulations. In Polish and Lithuanian Jewish communities, the principle was "the law for men is the same as the law for women."[39] More elaborate legislation affecting women limited vicarious consumption, that is, it put limits on the dress of women, which was taken to reflect the status of the family as a whole. One might add, though, that the necessity of per-

34. *PML*, no. 1026, 272 (1761).

35. In Poznan, also "the doctor and his wife." Avron, *Pinkas hakesherim*, no. 2129, 393 (1732); no. 2136, 394 (1733); Margoliot, *Dubno*, 59. In Lithuania, in the first half of the seventeenth century, exemption from restrictions on dress was granted to very high taxpayers. *PML*, no. 184, 40 (1628); no. 313, 68 (1637); no. 339, 71 (1637). For the exemption of the rabbis and their households in the five leading communities, see *PML*, no. 1026, p. 272 [1761]. Cf. Bonfil, *Jewish Life*, 138–39.

36. Mendel Piekarz, *Biyemei tsemihat hahassidut: Megamot ra'ayaniyot besifrei derush umussar* (1978; rev. ed., Jerusalem, 5758 [1998]), 68.

37. "The loss of money on the clothing and ornaments of women and on festive meals continues to increase." Avron, *Pinkas hakesherim*, no. 1798, p. 319 [1701].

38. Samuel ben Eli'ezer of Kalwarija, *Darkhei no'am* (Königsberg, 1764), 66b–67a. On this Lithuanian preacher, see Piekarz, *Biyemei tsemihat hahassidut*, s.v.

39. In the case of the limits on wearing furs in Dubno in 1747. Margoliot, *Dubno*, 59.

forming this task simultaneously provided women with a claim on the financial resources of the household and socially important cultural capital.[40]

One exceptional case of explicit misogyny is the resolution adopted in Poznan in 1723 repeating the previous year's prohibition against the latest fashion in footwear. This time, however, the prohibition was accompanied by reference to the biblical locus classicus of laws condemning women's dress: "Because the daughters of Zion are haughty and walk with outstretched necks" (Isa. 3:16ff.).[41]

One intriguing but not surprising omission in the treatment of the issue of luxurious dress in the communal regulations is the absence of any sense that the *promotion* of the consumption of luxurious goods could have positive economic consequences.[42] After all, Jews substantially dominated the domestic textile and clothing trade. Changing fashions and styles are the engine of the textile industry, promoting continuing demand. The countervailing principles—the danger to collective well-being inherent in the flaunting of wealth and the sense of the impropriety of display—clearly outweighed this economic interest.

For all that the primary motivation for the regulation of clothing was outwardly directed, a matter of foreign policy, the "domestic" dimension was present as well. The display of wealth and status in the form of expensive clothing and jewellery, particularly on special occasions in the synagogue, undoubtedly served as a means of establishing and defending social status.[43] Seating arrangements—whose pew was in the most prominent and prestigious position; the names of donors inscribed on such key ritual objects as curtains for the ark, mantles for the Torah scrolls, paintings on the walls; the distribution of the honor of being called up to the reading of the Torah (s. 'aliyah, pl. 'aliyot)—all served a similar purpose.[44] In the latter case, however, as Jacob Katz stressed, "certain 'aliyot [were reserved] for those who represented other communal values: the

40. Hunt, *Governance*, 249.

41. "[P]antofliher . . . mit kletslikh vekhen im shpitslikh . . . ekev betsad agodel." Avron, *Pinkas hakesherim*, no. 2079, p. 384 (1723). Cf. no. 2079, p. 420 (1763). And see the similar enactment in Lithuania much earlier: *PML*, no. 322, p. 69 [1637].

42. E. J. Hundert, "Bernard Mandeville and the Enlightenment's Maxims of Modernity," *Journal of the History of Ideas* 56 (1995): 577–93.

43. Katz, *Tradition and Crisis*, 153–54; Hundert, *Jews in a Polish Private Town*, 116–18.

44. In Tykocin, e.g., see: Nadav, *Pinkas*, no. 243, pp. 153–54 (1700); no. 659, pp. 405–9 (1703); no. 180, items 13–22, 24, pp. 112–13 (after 1703?); no. 174, items 34, 36, p. 108 (after 1703?); no. 185, item 18, p. 120 (between 1700 and 1720); p. 313, no. 459, item 5 (1719); no. 1, p. 1 (1737); no. 87, item 2, p. 46 (1742).

local rabbi, the district rabbi, [and] other scholars."[45] Jews in East Central Europe in the eighteenth century were acutely concerned with matters of hierarchy and the establishment and protection of even minute social distinctions. The most dramatic and disputed occasions in which the communal hierarchy was displayed were the processions in synagogue on the holidays of Tabernacles and Rejoicing in the Torah. Disputes over place sometimes led to violence. Communities frequently attempted to regulate the distribution of these honors in order to avoid disagreements.[46] In Tykocin in 1718, for example, a certain Jew was denied what he thought was his rightful place in the procession at Simhat Torah. The communal minute book recorded what followed: "R. Jacob Makover desecrated the Name [of God] in the synagogue during the prayers of the eve of Simhat Torah. He unlawfully opened his mouth and shouted out, raised his hand to beat [others] and disrupted the service and the reading of the Torah. . . . Therefore immediate judgment has been made—he will not be entitled *haver* for two years, will lose his franchise among the leaders of the community, and may hold no office whatsoever from today for the period mentioned."[47] Although distinctions of rank were most contested among the elite, social tensions were alive within the middle ranks of Jewish society as well. When in Lublin, Etil, wife of Isser ben Yitshak, called the wife of Pinhas a pickpocket and a thief *(hotekhes keshenes vegoneves)*, the former was fined 30 marks for insulting "such an important woman."[48]

Alimentary regulations continued to be enacted through the first half of the eighteenth century. Festive meals celebrating circumcisions and weddings provided multiple opportunities for demonstrating one's place in the social hierarchy. Communal laws generally specified the number of

---

45. Katz, *Tradition and Crisis*, 154. See the item in the communal minute book of Tykocin assuring that the rabbi would be called up to the reading of the Torah on the second as well as the first day of festivals. Nadav, *Pinkas,* no. 245, p. 154 (1690 or 1694). For a typical example, see the enactment in Działoszyn in 1788 to the effect that when the rabbi was absent, the senior officeholder in the community was to be called up third to the reading of the Torah. Jacob Goldberg and Adam Wein, "Księga kahału w Działoszynie," *BZIH* 53 (1965): 90–91.

46. Avron, *Pinkas hakesherim,* no. 1672, p. 295 (1696); Nadav, *Pinkas,* no. 174, items 39–41, p. 108 (after 1703?); no. 538, p. 391 (1716); no. 435, p. 289 (1720); YIVO Institute, New York, RG 87: Elias Tcherikower Archive: Simon Dubnow Collection (printed cat. no. 236, p. 69) 918 (Stary Bychów), p. 4a, item 2 (1763); Elyakim Druianov, "Keta'im mipinkas yashan shel hahevrah kadisha beDruja pelakh Vilna," *Reshumot* 1 (1918): 438 [1734]; Jacob Emden, *Shevirat luhot ha'aven* (Żółkiew, 1756; Altona, 1759), 50a.

47. Nadav, *Pinkas,* no. 596, 422 (1718).

48. YIVO Institute, New York, RG 87: 923, Pinkesei Lublin, 80–81, folio 14 (latter decades of the eighteenth century).

guests who could be invited along a gradient related to the amount of taxes paid by the celebrant. The communal *shamash* delivered all invitations to such festivities. The following resolution adopted by the elders of the community of Tykocin in 1705 illustrates both the degree to which social occasions were regulated and the privileges accorded those of high status:

No more than forty [*arba'ah minyanim*] may be invited to a circumcision. One cantor, one syndic, and one servant and close relatives [*pesulei de'orayta*] are not included in the forty. However, the twenty who pay the highest taxes may invite as many as they wish. No one at all under any circumstances may attend a festive meal unless the syndic has invited him. No celebrant of a circumcision or of a wedding is permitted to purchase *mitsvot* to honor anyone at all, including [granting the title] *moreinu*, [being called] to read the Torah, to bind or lift the Torah, or to open the ark. . . . A woman who has given birth is forbidden to send a casserole or honey cake or liquor except to the wife of the rabbi and to the midwife on pain of fines and punishments.[49]

Sometimes the distinctions among taxpayers and the number of guests they were permitted to invite were more elaborate. In Żółkiew in 1704, there were five gradations of tax payment with the number of permitted invitations to weddings and circumcisions ranging from twenty to sixty. In Zabłudów in 1750, there were three gradations entitled to invite twenty, thirty, or fifty guests.[50]

Sumptuary legislation illustrates Jewish society's paradoxical combination of separateness and connectedness; Jews imitated the dress of their Christian neighbors, for example, but rejected its gaudy colors. The preoccupation, not to say obsession, with hierarchical distinctions on the part of the wealthier half of the Jewish community reflected not only their relative separateness from Polish Christian society but also their comparative political powerlessness. Within the Jewish community, the main venue for the display of status was the synagogue, and the occasions for such displays were holy days—the Sabbath and the festivals—or domestic rites—circumcisions and marriages.

It appears, certainly in the case of Jews, that the less power a group has, the more concerned it becomes with internal distinctions. Moreover, intense concern both with dress appropriate to one's station and with very fine hierarchical distinctions of rank was just as characteristic of the Polish

49. Nadav, *Pinkas,* no. 582, pp. 416–17, item 3 (1705).
50. Buber, *Kiryah nisgavah,* 96 (1704); S. Assaf, "Mipinkas Zablodovah," 314. Cf. Avron, *Pinkas hakesherim,* no. 1710, 302 (1697).

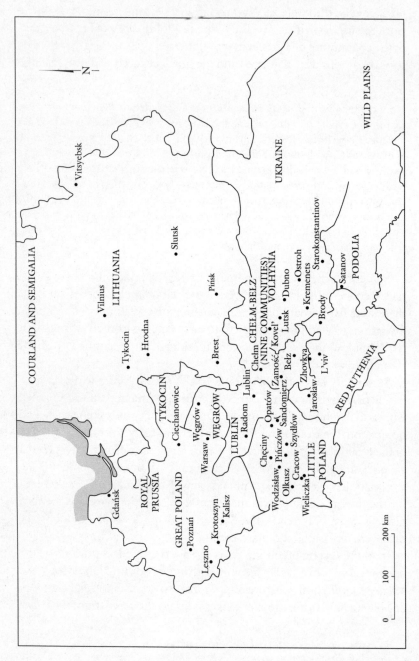

MAP 3. Leading communities and "lands"

nobility as it was of Jews. Thus, it is misleading to see Polish Jews as falling on one side or another of a simple binary opposition between insularity and integration.

Council of the Lands

The national council of Polish Jews, traditionally referred to as the Council of Four Lands, should perhaps be called the Council of the Lands, because by the eighteenth century the number of "Lands" far exceeded four (see map 3).[51] In addition to the delegates to the council who represented leading communities and regional councils, there were also rabbinical delegates, who formed a national tribunal to adjudicate matters related to *halakhah*. This second "chamber," however, created apparently in the 1670s, may have fallen into disuse after about 1720.[52] A warden or "chairman of the House of Israel of the Four Lands" was elected together with several trustees. In the eighteenth century, the officers served four-year terms, with the highest office rotating among the "lands."[53] The chief task of the council was to apportion the global and fixed tax owed the national Treasury. Originally established as a capitation tax on Jews, it was transformed to a global sum by 1580. From 1717 on, the amounts fixed were 220,000 florins for Poland and 60,000 for Lithuania.

By the eighteenth century, representatives of the crown Treasury regularly attended and supervised meetings of the council, thus significantly attenuating its independence. The council ceased meeting at the great fair in Jarosław and began to meet at the convenience of the crown treasurer, often in Stary Konstantynów and later, Pilica. The Treasury official, Działczyński, provided an apparently full report of the resolutions adopted at the meeting of the council in Jarosław between March 15 and July 8, 1739,

51. Jacob Goldberg and Adam Wein, "Ordynacja dla sejmu żydowskiego ziem koronnych z 1753r.," *BZIH* 52 (1964): 17–34; Jacob Goldberg, "The Jewish Sejm: Its Origins and Functions," in *The Jews in Old Poland 1000–1795,* ed. A. Polonsky, J. Basista, and A. Link-Lenczowski (London, 1993), 147–65; also published in Polish in *Żydzi w dawnej Rzeczypospolitej* (Kraków, 1991), 44–58, and in Hebrew in Jacob Goldberg, *Hahevrah hayehudit bemamlekhet Polin-Lita* (Jerusalem, 1999), 125–42. Shmuel Ettinger, "The Council of Four Lands," in *Jews in Old Poland,* 93–109; id., "Va'ad arba aratsot," in id., *Bein Polin leRussiyah* (Jerusalem, 1994), 174–85 (also appeared as the Introduction to *PVAA,* 2d. ed., vol. 1, rev. and ed. Israel Bartal [Jerusalem, 1990], 14–24).

52. Adam Teller, "Rabbis Without a Function? On the Relations between the Polish Rabbinate and the Council of Four Lands" (typescript).

53. *PVAA,* no. 659, 336 (1743).

to his superior. The following, in paraphrase, is a partial summary of this report. It reflects not only the concerns with status and power among Jewish officials but also the functioning of the council as a defensive lobby on behalf of Jews in Poland. The minutes include fourteen items. The lobbying activities of the council are referred to in candid fashion:

There are often disputes over primacy among the rabbis who attend our meetings. Since these arguments are often inordinately long and other delegates and officials become involved, wasteful and harmful actions often result. We have therefore determined and resolved that the rabbi of the "land" where the council is meeting will be seated first. This means only the following "lands": Kraków, Poznan, Lublin, and Ruś. The rabbi must hold the office of rabbi of the community and of the "land."

If the meeting is held in a place where no rabbi meets the condition of holding office both in the community and in the land, the rabbi of Kraków [both community and "land"] is authorized to be seated first. Failing this, the rabbi of the most important community will take primacy.[54]

Great harm is caused to the council by second-tier rabbis, that is, rabbis of communities, interfering in the economic concerns of the councils and the lands. They themselves have been elected to protect the customs of our religion and pay no taxes. Nevertheless, they try by various means to encroach on honors that properly belong to us householders, who must bear the full burden of taxes. They attempt to be chosen for appointment as delegate, assessor, trustee, or recorder [*deputactwa, symplarstwa, wiernikostwa, pisarstwa*]. Therefore, to eliminate such competition, which reflects no honor on the rabbis, we have resolved that no rabbi now or in the future will dare to seek any such office on pain of losing rabbinic office.[55] Any community or region that defies this injunction will be subject to a severe fine.

No one may hold both the office of trustee and the office of *parnas* simultaneously. [This rule was apparently directed against Heshel of Chełm who held both offices in 1739.]

Our *parnas* must closely supervise the trustees to see that the resolutions enacted at this meeting of the council are carried out in full and that accounts are provided annually to the Treasury.

In the resolution adopted previously, reference is made to the salary of trustees and the *shtadlan* [lobbyist] but not to their expenses for travel to Warsaw, Grodno, or Radom [that is, to meetings of the Sejm and the Treasury Commission]. The trustees shall be allowed 50 florins weekly out of which they must pay for transportation and meals. A further "entertainment" allowance of 200 florins will be permitted to the trustees and 100 florins for the *shtadlan*.

54. These quarrels over hierarchy were a continuing problem among the rabbis and the elders of the Council of the Lands. Indeed, in 1753, an official of the crown Treasury intervened and sought to impose a fixed order of precedence among the representatives of the communities and regions. Goldberg, "Jewish Sejm," 159–60.

55. This ruling was not observed; in 1753, rabbis held all of the positions outlawed in 1739. Ibid.

Trustees may not linger at meetings of apportionment committees for more than three or four days. Then the apportionments must be sent to the leaders of the lands and the regions who will forward them to the Treasury by the fifteenth of September.

Unauthorized reductions granted to village Jews by trustees are causing losses to the council. These are henceforth forbidden on pain of restitution of lost revenue and a fine.

Frequently, fires lead to ruin in particular Jewish communities. These are not to seek tax relief from trustees but must turn to the leaders and to the council of their region.

The sum apportioned by the council for the poor, 1,500 florins annually, is to be used by the trustees for no other purpose.

Some of the large expenditures by trustees on their own volition at meetings of the Sejm and of the Treasury Commission at Radom were not entirely necessary or useful, although such expenditures on such occasions cannot be avoided entirely. We have, therefore, decided to reduce the allotment for this purpose to no more than 334 ducats or 6,000 florins. If, God forbid, there are attacks on the council similar or worse than those heard last year at the Warsaw Sejm that was adjourned, then, in order to avoid in timely fashion the utter destruction of the council, our trustees are empowered to expend higher sums.[56] They shall first seek the protection of the honorable lord, the crown treasurer. (As we have asked this of him at the present meeting of the council.) He will indicate on the basis of his lordly wisdom and understanding, how they should comport themselves, which expenditures are necessary and to whom they should turn first. In this way, and through the wisdom and protection of this lord, the poor Jewish community of Poland will avoid unnecessary expenses. If the necessary expenditures indicated by his honor exceed the amount of cash in the possession of the trustees, they are hereby empowered to borrow the necessary sums.[57]

All five trustees are obliged to attend meetings of the apportionment committee. For the defense of interests at Sejm and commission meetings, in order to reduce costs, two trustees will suffice. The chief *shtadlan*, who understands the issues well, [and] is known and acceptable to the lords, will be a third attendee. The attendants must stay a short distance away from the meeting place, only the *shtadlan*, with some attendant [*szkulnik* = *shamash*], is actually to be continuously present at the meeting. He will report to the trustees about proposals related to the Jews of the country.

Taking into consideration the debt accumulated in 1739, which includes expenses related to the Warsaw Sejm, we shall have to set the assessment at 323,600

56. The Council of the Lands recorded an expenditure of 50,874 florins at the Warsaw Sejm where demanding an additional tax *(donatywa kupiecka)* of 450,000 florins from Jews was discussed. *PVAA,* no. 640, p. 322, n. 14.

57. Israel Halpern comments that "this lordly advice cost the Council of the Lands substantial sums. One of the delegates to the meeting of the Polish Sejm in 1748 thought the crown treasurer received 2,000 ducats (ca. 36,000 florins) from the Jews." Ibid., no. 642, p. 327, n. 2.

florins. If God wills it, the debt will be paid off over two years. If, with the protection of His Excellency the crown treasurer, there are no more extraordinary expenses leading to more debt, the tax for 1743 will be no more than 270,000 florins. This will make a reduction for everyone possible and will make the capitation tax burden easier to bear.

We know from experience that there has been a damaging tendency for trustees to take actions without consultation with their fellows. In serious matters, therefore, they must henceforth meet together and reach agreement calmly and with wisdom. No individual should oppose the majority needlessly on pain of loss of office and restoration of the damages caused by his stubbornness.

No decision regarding expenditures at Sejm meetings and other such occasions are valid without the knowledge and signature of the *parnas* of the council.[58]

As noted earlier, the crown treasurer sent representatives to the meetings. He also appointed Jewish trustees to oversee and to report on the activities of the council. These trustees, however, were explicitly made subject to the authority of the officers of the council.[59] What is important to note here is that the crown Treasury attempted to incorporate the council into its administrative apparatus, much as individual communal governments and rabbis began to be seen as forming part of the town owner's administration of his holdings.[60] Indeed, the close involvement of centers of state power in Jewish communal and intercommunal institutions was one of the elements that produced the so-called crisis in the functioning of those institutions in the eighteenth century.

58. Ibid., no. 57, pp. lv–lviii.

59. "[G]eneralności we wsystkiem szczerze służyli, exspens i długów żadnych bez wiadomości marszalka i Starszych czterech pryncypalnych powiatów nie czynili, dyspartamenta niezawodne w czasie wyznaczonym do skarbu odsylali, i to wszystko, cokolwiek do swego porządku należy, wypelnili." *PVAA,* no. 56, p. liv (no. 641, 323–24) (1739).

60. Ettinger, *Bein Polin leRussiyah,* 181, suggests that there were likely other gatherings of the Council of the Lands held without the knowledge of state officials.

CHAPTER 5

Was There a Communal "Crisis" in the Eighteenth Century?

The consensus of scholarly opinion since the beginning of the twentieth century has been that the institutions of Jewish autonomy experienced a profound crisis in the eighteenth century.[1] The interrelated ingredients in the explanation of this phenomenon have been variously emphasized. Some have stressed increasing oppression and persecution, rising fiscal exploitation, and economic decline. Others have pointed to the "interference" of magnate-aristocrats in the internal affairs of Jewish autonomous institutions. Benzion Dinur, who extensively analyzed the ethical literature and sermons of the period, concluded that the chief complaint was "that the Jewish community establishment was being overrun by strongmen, habitués of the nobles' courts and those with access to political influence."[2] These "new men" turned "Jewish self-government into a fiction, a caricature."[3]

Another stream of explanation focuses more on internal developments in the *kahals* of Poland-Lithuania and the strife and turmoil that characterized struggles for power. This view is depicted in the language of class conflict. Most often, stress is placed on the artisans, who, under conditions of economic decline, and reeling from exploitative regimes, demand representation in a more democratic *kahal*.

Although there were certainly stresses and strains on the institution of

---

1. Isaac Levitats, *The Jewish Community in Russia, 1772–1844* (New York, 1943).

2. Gershon Hundert, ed., *Essential Papers on Hasidism* (New York, 1991), 102. Benzion Dinur, *Bemifneh hadorot* (Jerusalem, 1972), 100.

3. Hundert, *Essential Papers,* 107; Dinur, *Bemifneh,* 105. Cf. Majer Bałaban, "Zalman, der rosh-hakohol fun Drohobitsh," in id., *Yidn in Poyln* (Vilna, 1930), 67–87.

the *kahal* in the eighteenth century, in fact it continued to function well into the nineteenth century in the overwhelming majority of towns and cities in eastern Europe. As noted earlier, the *kahal* was the institutional expression of the autonomy of Jews in the towns and cities where they lived. Its autonomy and relative detachment from outside influence did not mean, however, that it was separate from the general pattern of the distribution of power and authority of the state. Although there was indeed increased tension between autonomy and integration during the eighteenth century, these tensions did not constitute the "crisis" that some historians have seen.[4] It may be, in fact, that the very antinomy—autonomy/integration—conceals more than it reveals.

What follows below is an attempt to uncover some of the facets of the paradoxical nonseparateness of Polish Jews, as they relate to Jewish communal institutions. While the relationship between Jewish institutions and other centers of power became more complex and intertwined, this did not lead to equally strong trends toward acculturation and integration of individuals. The autonomous Jewish community remained one of the important crucibles in forging Jewish identity in eastern Europe.

The degree and extent of "interference" in Jewish communal institutions by town owners and royal officials increased during the eighteenth century. This same "interference" can also be seen as a sign of the progressive economic integration of Jews within the estates of the magnate-aristocrats or the local economies controlled by royal officials. The *kahal* was not the only vehicle for such mediation and interaction between individual Jews and the centers of power. Individual agents, factors, and lease-holders forged their own direct ties to aristocrats and their administrations. These ties to the possessors of power sometimes emboldened individuals to defy the authority of the communal elders. This did not necessarily, however, assure the individuals of immunity from communal

---

4. There is a substantial literature on this problem, including Benzion Dinur, "Reshitah shel hahasidut veyesodoteha hasotsiyaliyim vehameshihiyim," in id., *Bemifneh hadorot,* 92–139; Jacob Katz, *Tradition and Crisis: Jewish Society at the End of the Middle Ages,* trans. Bernard Dov Cooperman (1961; 2d ed., New York, 1993); Raphael Mahler, "Di Yidn in amolikn Poyln," in *Di Yidn in Poyln: Fun di eltste tsaytn biz der Tsveyter Velt-milkhome* (New York, 1946), cols. 2–402; Simon Dubnow, *Toledot hahassiduth* (Tel Aviv, 1967); Israel Halpern, *Yehudim veyahadut bemizrah Eiropah* (Jerusalem, 1968), 159–62, 313–39; Moshe J. Rosman, "An Exploitative Regime and the Opposition to It," in *Temurot bahistoriyah hayehudit hahadashah,* ed. S. Almog et al. (Jerusalem, 1988), xi–xxx. See also the contemporary criticisms of the Jewish communal organization by Jews influenced by Enlightenment thinking: *MDSC,* 6: 113–18 (Zalkind Hurwicz); 141–53 (Szymel Wolfowicz); 409–21 (Mendel Satanower); 421–33 (Salomon Polonus).

control. If the patron proved insufficiently intimidating, the community could retaliate by using or threatening to use its power to excommunicate.[5]

In Mścisław (Mstislav, Amtchislav) in 1731–32, the following denunciation was recorded in the communal minute book:

The evil one, Isaac the doctor, has defied the leaders of the *kahal,* and his wife, may her name be blotted out, has danced with gentrymen. Therefore, the elders of the *kahal* summoned Isaac. He spoke of the elders of the *kahal* with great disrespect. And he came to the *kahal* office together with his nobleman [*porets*]. Continuing in his ways, he insulted the elders to their faces in the presence of the gentryman. Therefore, he is banned and excommunicated together with his wife, may her name be blotted out, and cut off from all that is holy.

Simon Dubnow's depiction of these developments is representative of the general tone of the older historiography. He describes the situation of the communal government of Jews in Poland-Lithuania in the eighteenth century as one of progressive decay, decline, and weakness.[6] In support of this contention, Dubnow cites the "stinging" words of a Polish observer in 1744. Although Dubnow quotes this passage out of context, the content is important and suggestive. He fails to mention, however, that the words are drawn from the religious disputation in Brody initiated by Bishop Kobielski in 1743, described earlier (see chapter 3). The writer was replying to a Jewish response to Kobielski's conversionary sermon, which followed medieval models of Christian-Jewish disputation. The text below is part of the response to the spokesman for the Jews of Brody. Kobielski's text referred to a locus classicus in debates of this kind, namely Gen. 49:10 ("The scepter will not depart from Judah . . . until Shiloh comes . . .") purportedly indicating that Jesus [Shiloh] must have been the Messiah, since His coming coincided with the loss of sovereignty by Jews. The Jewish response maintained that since Jews had lost sovereignty centuries before the coming of Jesus, the word "scepter" must therefore be taken to connote administration, and Jews had autonomy and their own laws in the Polish Commonwealth itself.[7] Kobielski's unnamed associate replied to the Jewish position as follows:

How abject is this scepter—childish and comical—your [self-]rule and the freedom to observe the Jewish commandments are leased from Christian lords. Even

5. Simon Dubnow, "Fun mayn arkhiv," *Yivo bleter* 1 (1931): 406–7.
6. Dubnow, *Toledot hahassiduth,* 18–24.
7. Majer Bałaban, *Letoledot hatenu'ah haFrankit,* vol. 1 (Tel Aviv, 1934), 95–100.

the office of rabbi cannot be held except by someone who has purchased it, for life or for a fixed time, leasing the rabbinate from a Christian lord. The position of communal elder, for life or for a fixed time, also costs a goodly sum. It is only after you have paid the crown, the provincial governor *(wojewoda)*, the lieutenant governor *(podwojewoda)*, and various other officials and lords, that you are able to enjoy your synagogues and to live a Jewish life. . . . It is true that certain Christian lords hold you in greater esteem than poor Christians. This itself shows that both your living in accordance with the Jewish religion and the favor of these same lords for you have been purchased. These lords esteem you neither for your faith nor for your Jewish way of life, but for the income and payments they have from you.[8]

This passage helped cement a line of interpretation that characterizes the work of Dubnow, Raphael Mahler, Simhah Assaf, and Majer Bała-ban, all of whom emphasize the degree to which Jews were dependent on the whims of the *szlachta* in general and the magnate-aristocrats in particular. Indeed, Mahler begins his chapter on "Jewish Autonomy" in eighteenth-century Poland with the following sentence: "In the epoch of the unrestrained rule of the *szlachta* in Poland, Jewish communities and the intercommunal institutions of Jewish autonomy fell under the control of the ruling class and progressively lost their right to autonomy."[9] According to these historians, there was little distinction between royal and private towns in this regard. Reflecting the anti-noble bias of Polish historiography in the early decades of the twentieth century, Bałaban published a number of excerpts from the memoirs and diaries of Polish noblemen depicting capricious ill-treatment of Jews.[10] Elsewhere, he maintained that "the private towns were no better" than the royal cities.[11]

8. There is a partial Hebrew translation in ibid., 21. The translation here is based on the text cited in Mojżesz Schorr, *Organizacya Żydów w Polsce (od najdawniejszych czasów aż do r. 1772)* (Lwów, 1899), 43. The documents were published by N. M. Gelber in *Moriah*, vol. 5 and vol. 6 (1912 or 1918), *non vidi*. See also N. M. Gelber, "Die Taufbewegung unter den polnischen Juden im XVIII. Jahrhundert," *MGWJ* 68 (1924): 232–33; Jacob Goldberg, *Hamumarim bemamlekhet Polin-Lita* (Jerusalem, 1985), 32, 75, 76, 81.

9. Mahler, "Di Yidn in amolikn Poyln," col. 297.

10. Majer Bałaban, "Die polnischen Juden in den Memoiren des polnischen Adels," *Menorah* 5 (1927): 369–76; 6 (1928): 32–38.

11. Majer Bałaban, "Polskie Żydostwo w okresie Sejmu Wielkiego i Powstania Ko-ściuszki," in id., ed., *Księga pamiątkowa ku czci Berka Joselewicza pułkownika wojsk polskich w 125 letnią rocznice jego bohaterskiej śmierci (1809–1934)* (Warsaw, 1934), 9–10. Cf. Gershon Hundert, "Jews in Polish Private Towns: The Jewish Community in Opatów and the Town's Owners in the Eighteenth Century," in *Studies on Polish Jewry: Paul Glikson Memorial Volume* (Jerusalem, 1987), xx; id., "The Kehilla and the Municipality in Private Towns at the End of the Early Modern Period," in *The Jews in Old Poland, 1000–1795*, ed. A. Polonsky, J. Basista, and A. Link-Lenczowski (London, 1993), 174–75; Adam Kaźmierczyk, *Żydzi w*

More recently, Jacob Goldberg has written that, despite sometimes wide and far-reaching privileges in private towns, the social and legal status of Jews in royal towns was superior.[12] In some ways, this interpretation is defensible, but in the end, it distorts the picture and hampers a more nuanced understanding of the period. Formally, it is true that Jews were protected by extensive royal charters and that they could make use of the state juridical system to appeal all the way up to the crown. However, in the crown cities, the struggle with Christian competitors tended to be more intense and local legislation more restrictive than in private towns. Goldberg describes the *kahals* in private towns, without qualification, as integral parts of the administration of the magnates' domains. He refers to the "feudal dependence" of the *kahals* on the town owners, which, in the course of the seventeenth and eighteenth centuries, meant ever-greater involvement by the town owners in the internal affairs of Jewish communities.[13] Frequently, the lord or his agent had to approve rabbinical court judgments, *kahal* finances were closely supervised, and, as noted by the eighteenth-century cleric quoted above, rabbinical positions were obtained only after the payment of a fee to the town owner. For all that, the historical literature unanimously agrees that in the seventeenth and eighteenth centuries, Jews moved steadily out of royal cities to private towns. By the eighteenth century, a clear majority, and probably substantially more than that, lived on the estates and in the towns of the magnate-aristocrats. If the legal conditions and the degree of personal freedom were, in fact, worse in the private towns than the crown cities, how can the clear preference of tens of thousands of Jews for the former be explained?

Whether or not the term "feudal" properly describes the status of Jews, they were unquestionably legally dependent in private towns. Legislation adopted in 1539 transferred full jurisdiction over Jews in their towns

dobrach prywatnych w świetle sądowniczej i administracyjnej prakyki dóbr magnackich w wiekach XVI–XVIII (Kraków, 2002).

12. Jacob Goldberg, "Gminy żydowskie (kahały) w systemie władztwa dominialnego w szlacheckiej Rzeczypospolitej," in *Między historią a teorią: Refleksje nad problematyką dziejów i wiedzy historycznej,* ed. Marian Drozdowski (Warsaw and Poznan, 1988), 155; Hebrew version, *Hahevrah hayehudit bemamlekhet Polin-Lita* (Jerusalem, 1999), 144–58. Cf. id., "Bein hofesh lenetinut: sugei hatelut hafe'udalit shel hayehudim bePolin," in *Divrei hakongres ha'olami hahamishi lemada'ei hayahadut, 1969,* vol. 2 (Jerusalem, 1972): 107–13. More defensible is the position that the status of Christian townsmen "was incomparably better" in royal towns. Krystyna Zienkowska, "Reforms Relating to the Third Estate," in *Constitution and Reform in Eighteenth-Century Poland: The Constitution of 3 May 1791,* ed. Samuel Fiszman (Bloomington, Ind., 1997), 330.

13. Goldberg, "Gminy," 157.

from the crown to the aristocratic owners. Only rarely did a town owned by a cleric have a Jewish population.[14] It is true that town owners attempted to put limits on the freedom of movement of Jewish residents of their towns, even on occasion promulgating laws forbidding marriages to people not residing on their holdings, lest the married couple take up residence elsewhere. This placed Jews in the same category as the Christian residents of private towns, whose freedom of movement was also restricted.[15]

The lord of Rzeszów, Jerzy Ignacy Lubomirski, required that each adult male Jew sign a document to the effect that he would neither move out of the town nor marry his daughters to men of other towns without the town owner's permission.[16] An order of the same aristocrat in 1735 prescribed that Jewish bridegrooms could live with their in-laws outside of Rzeszów for a maximum of two years, and this only if their return was guaranteed by certain carefully specified citizens. Those who disobeyed not only endangered their guarantors but also would be forcibly returned and possibly even arrested for "escaping from serfdom."[17] Laws of this kind, which were occasionally only intended to prevent dowries from leaving the town, but more often were directed at the married couple, were

---

14. The law, adopted by the Sejm meeting in Kraków in 1539 was worded as follows:

Quod nobiles in oppidis aut in villis suis iudaeos habent: per Nos licet, ut soli ex eis fructus omnes, et emolumenta percipiant: iusque illis, arbitratu suo dicant: verum ex quibus iudaeis, nullum ad Nos commodum pervenit, eos uti judaeorum iure non permittimus, per Nos et Antecessores nostros concesso: neque de injurijs corum deferri ad Nos volumus. Ut ex quibus nullum commodum sentimus: hi etiam nullum in Nobis praesidium habeant collocatum.

Those nobles who have Jews in their towns and villages, are, from this day, permitted by us to receive all the income and emoluments from them. They shall administer the law for the Jews according to their own judgement. In fact, We do not permit these Jews, from whom We derive no benefit, to make use of the Jewry law conceded by Us and Our predecessors nor do We wish them to appeal to Us in cases of injustice. Those from whom we receive no benefit shall have none of Our protection. (VL, 1: 270 [550])

15. M. J. Rosman, The Lords' Jews: Magnate-Jewish Relations in the Polish-Lithuanian Commonwealth during the Eighteenth Century (Cambridge, Mass., 1990), esp. 185–205; Adam Teller, "The Legal Status of the Jews on the Magnate Estates of Poland-Lithuania in the Eighteenth Century," Gal-Ed 15–16 (1997): 47; Tomasz Opas, "Wolność osobista mieszczan miast szlacheckich województwa lubelskiego w drugiej połowie XVII i w XVIII wieku," Przegląd Historyczny 61 (1970): 609–29; Anatol Leszczynski, Żydzi ziemi bielskiej (Wrocław, 1980), 58.

16. Pęckowski, Dzieje miasta Rzeszowa, 357; Hebrew translation of a characteristic document of this kind in Bałaban, Letoledot hatenu'ah, 1: 84. Cf. Adam Kaźmierczyk, Żydzi polscy, 1648–1772: Źródła (Kraków, 2001), nos. 27–28, 48.

17. " . . . wysunięci się z poddaństwa." Jan Pęckowski, Dzieje miasta Rzeszowa, 70; A. Codello, "Zbiegostwo mieszczań rzeszowskich w pierwszej połowie XVIII w.," Małopolskie Studia Historyczne 1 (1958): 26–27. Cf. Goldberg, "Gminy," 159.

repeatedly issued in private towns.[18] The town owners wished to retain the wealthy and the gainfully employed.[19] The poor might very well be threatened with expulsion.[20]

It is evident that the town owners were concerned primarily with the economic prosperity of the towns. However, the frequent repetition of legislation attempting to restrict Jewish freedom of movement suggests that these laws were not always successfully enforced. Stanisław Poniatowski, the father of the future king, included the following passage in his privilege to the Podolian Jewish community of Jazłowiec (Iazlovets'): "Regarding the law still in force in other cities concerning those who give their children [in marriage] to foreign jurisdictions providing them with dowries and consequently the town declines significantly, I strictly order, therefore, that the Jews of Jazłowiec settle their children near them."[21] If legislation of this kind seems to highlight a "feudal" dependence, it can also be viewed along a different bias as illustrating the limits of the lords' power. Some owners had to resort to blandishments to maintain the Jewish populations of their towns. In 1762, Jan Klemens Branicki ordered 100 Polish florins paid to Wolf Moszkowicz of Tykocin, who had married a woman from Szkłów, to persuade him to live in Tykocin.[22]

Despite restrictions, the Jewish population of Poland-Lithuania was highly mobile. The threat of leaving constituted the most important limitation on the owner's power. Jews put their commercial, industrial, and managerial expertise directly or indirectly in the service of the aristocrat. In return, he provided peace, security, good order, and relative autonomy. The revenues Jews produced were their part of the bargain. If town owners did not fulfill their obligations, Jews would demand changes, threaten to leave, or actually do so.[23] That Jews might abandon a town

18. Cf. Hundert, *Jews in a Polish Private Town*, 152–53, and the references there.

19. For similar attempts to prevent Jews leaving in Boćki, Białystok, and Siemiatycze, see the references in Leszczynski, *Żydzi*, 58.

20. Ibid., 149; Hundert, "Jews in Polish Private Towns," xxxvi.

21. Goldberg, *Jewish Privileges*, 105; id., "Gminy," 159.

22. The original privilege granted to the Jewish community of Tykocin explicitly gave Jews freedom of movement ("jako dobrowolnie przyszedł tak też dobrowolnie precz iść może"). Leszczynski, *Żydzi*, 45, 57.

23. Hundert, *Jews in a Polish Private Town*, 153–54; Rosman, *Lords' Jews*, 73; Tomasz Opas, "Upadek i odrodzenie miasta," *Lubartów: Z dziejów miasta i regionu*, ed. S. Tworek (Lublin, 1977), 27–28, 32; id., "Wolność osobista mieszczań miast szlacheckich województwa lubelskiego w drugiej połowie XVII i w XVIII wieku." *Przegląd Historyczny* 61 (1970): 619; Jacob Goldberg, "Hamishar hakim'oni hayehudi bePolin bame'ah ha18," in *Studies on Polish Jewry: Paul Glikson Memorial Volume*, ed. E. Mendelsohn and C. Shmeruk (Jerusalem, 1987), 17.

for better conditions elsewhere must have shadowed the calculations and decisions of the town owners. Since the consequences of such actions were serious, a town owner would not be likely to act on mere whim.[24]

While it has been maintained that magnates endeavored to subject village Jews to the authority of their town *kahal,* insisting that they not be subject to a "foreign" *kahal,* the evidence for this is not extensive. There is apparently only one case in which such an explicit demand was made, and it is possible that in this instance the town owner was merely supporting the demand of the local *kahal.*[25] Throughout the eighteenth century, there were multiple jurisdictional disputes between large communities and smaller ones.

In 1749, the leaseholders and innkeepers of the villages near Tarłów demanded that the regional Jewish court authorize their freedom from the jurisdiction of the community there.[26] Representatives of both sides appeared before the elders of the region *(galil).* The *kahal* of Tarłów presented documents and records of the Council of the Lands indicating precisely which villages "belonged" to their jurisdiction. The judges found the documents to be authentic and binding and ruled that the villagers would continue to be subject to the Tarłów *kahal.* This meant not only that the villagers paid their taxes through the Tarłów *kahal,* but also that they had to bury their dead there; circumcise their sons there; have their cattle slaughtered by a *shohet* in Tarłów, and have their marriages performed by the rabbi of Tarłów. Appended to the decision was a list of the nineteen villages and one town that "belonged" to Tarłów. The document does not mention any intervention by the town owner. This is not to say that the magnate was disinterested; the document was, after all, preserved in a magnate archive. In the same archival file, another document shows that in 1788, the owner of Tarłów intervened on the side of the *kahal* in its claim that another community had usurped its jurisdiction over certain villages.[27] Occasionally, the town owner granted formal permission for his townlet's Jews to be subject to the jurisdiction of a *kahal* in a town owned by another noble.[28]

24. Hundert, *Jews in a Polish Private Town,* 154.

25. Goldberg, "Gminy," 163.

26. The following is based on a Polish translation of the lost Hebrew original. Warsaw, AGAD, Archiwum Zamoyskich 2808, 229–230. The document has been published by Adam Kaźmierczyk, *Żydzi polscy,* no. 105, p. 185.

27. AGAD, Archiwum Zamoyskich 2808, 227–28.

28. *Konsens . . . Jozefa Butlera starosty kwiecienskiego dziedzica Franopola inkorporujący Żydów franopolskich do kahału biłgorayskiego* (1741). AGAD, AGW, Anteriora 214, 10–11.

Disputes in the Lwów region continued for decades in the first half of the eighteenth century between the central community of Lwów itself and the smaller communities in its region. At various times, Adam Mikołaj Sieniawski and August Aleksander Czartoryski intervened attempting to settle matters after efforts by the Jewish regional councils and the Council of the Lands had failed.[29] On other occasions, there was no need for noble intervention. For example, contention between the community of Kraków and the towns of its region was resolved at a meeting of the Council of the Lands in 1717.[30]

The question of Jews appealing the decisions of their local courts to those of the region or the "land" is similar. Most often, Jews were explicitly permitted by the town owners to appeal cases from their own courts to the elders of the region or "land" in towns owned by other magnates, or in crown cities.[31] One case is known of the owner of a private town forbidding Jews to appeal decisions to the regional Jewish court, which was in a crown city. In 1682, Jan Franciszek Walewski, owner of the town of Dobra in the Sieradz region, forbade such appeals because they contradicted his prerogatives as owner of the town.[32]

The Jewish community's courts, perhaps even more than the communal government, embodied the legal and the cultural autonomy of the Jewish community. Jews had been permitted an independent judiciary conducted according to their ancestral custom by diverse states dating back to the Hellenistic era. Rabbinic literature stigmatized in the strongest possible terms the practice of "resorting to the courts of the Gentiles." In Poland-Lithuania, the practice, contrary to the rabbinic norm, of seeking redress in the courts of magnates or the crown certainly did not begin in the eighteenth century. Nevertheless, it did become more frequent at that time. For example, as the eighteenth century progressed, the number of cases between Jews that came directly before the court of the state-appointed judge in Lwów outnumbered those that came on appeal from rabbinical courts.[33]

In a few cases in Poland-Lithuania, there were attempts to limit the ju-

29. Rosman, *Lords' Jews*, 192, and the references there.
30. Majer Bałaban, *Historia Żydów w Krakowie i na Kazimierzu*, vol. 2 (Kraków, 1936), 258. Cf. *PVAA*, no. 563, 271.
31. Hundert, *Jews in a Polish Private Town*, 20 (Tarłów, Tarnobrzeg); Goldberg, *Jewish Privileges*, 234 (Olesko), 325 (Swarzędz).
32. Goldberg, "Gminy," 163.
33. Zbigniew Pazdro, *Organizacja i praktyka żydowskich sądów podwojewodzińskich, 1740–1772* (Lwów, 1903), 29–31.

risdiction of Jewish courts to ceremonial and ritual matters along the lines of contemporary developments in German territories.[34] In Leszno in 1707, an edict announced that Jews would be subject to municipal jurisdiction in all matters civil and criminal.[35] The owner of Szkłów, Sieniawski attempted to implement a similar policy there in 1725.[36] In neither case does it seem that these far-reaching directives were actually implemented.

During this period, the choice of the rabbi, the chief judge of the community, was increasingly subject to the approval of centers of power outside the community itself, from whom the office had to be purchased, or to whom a fee had to be paid.[37] Moreover, in private towns, the rabbi was treated as if he were part of the estate administration. His authority was enlisted to support the interests of the town owner; his fee scale was subject to approval by the administrators of the estate.[38] As a contemporary preacher put it, "The office of instruction [the rabbinate] has been so corrupted in some places that the rabbinate has become an agency for tax collection. In many places [control of] the rabbinate has been taken away from Jews and they have no say over it."[39] Another rabbi at the time found it necessary to insist that the householders "accepted me for the sake of heaven and there was no expenditure at all for the rabbinical office. They always support me before the authorities so that not even a single penny has been paid for these twelve years . . . unlike other communities in our land where in every town and city the rabbi is appointed for money, which is distributed in large amounts to the lord and to the *kahal*. Because of our many sins, this transgression is becoming increasingly common in our land."[40] The phenomenon of the purchase of rabbinical offices

34. Azriel Shohet, *Im hilufei tekufot: Reshit hahaskalah beyahadut Germaniyah* (Jerusalem, 1960), 72–88.

35. Zofia Kulejewska-Topolska, *Nowe lokacje miejskie w Wielkopolsce od XVI do końca XVIII wieku* (Poznan, 1964), 113, 130–31.

36. Rosman, *Lords' Jews,* 194–95. It may be that Sieniawski was insisting that appeals on matters other than religious questions be brought before him and not the regional Jewish authorities.

37. Stanisław Kutrzeba, *Zbiór aktów do historyi ustroju sądów prawa polskiego i kancelary i sądowych województwa krakowskiego z wieku XVI–XVIII* (Kraków, 1909), 209–10 (Wodzisław, 1740); 269–79 (Janów, 1782); Rosman, *Lords' Jews,* 198–204; Hundert, *Jews in a Polish Private Town,* 144–45. And see the incidents in Janów and Pacanów cited by Bałaban, *Letoledot hatenu'ah haFrankit,* 82–83.

38. Kaźmierczyk, *Żydzi w dobrach prywatnych,* 137–42.

39. "Oy la'einayim shekakh ro'ot shenithalal kise hahora'ah ad shebekamah medinot harabbanut kemokhsanut uveharbeh medinot netulah hi mehayehudim ve'ein lahem alav shum [shilton]." David ben Yitshak Hakaro, *Ohel Rahel* (Szkłów, 1790), 15a.

40. Sha'ul ben Moshe, *Sefer she'elot uteshuvot giv'at sha'ul* (Żółkiew, 1774), Introduction. And see Jacob Emden's criticism of Isaac Landau: "[H]e is one of the workers of

was not new. What was new in the eighteenth century was that now formal payments were made to the town owner, rather than primarily to the *kahal*. This was a fundamental change, marking the progressive, although still incomplete, integration of Jewish communities into the magnates' estates. The requirement to purchase the *rabinostwo* (or *konsens*), that is, the writ of appointment as rabbi, from the town owner or the governor was not an attempt on the part of the latter to gain some sort of cultural hegemony over "their" Jews. The approach of the authorities should be seen as strictly instrumental. They were interested in the smooth functioning of the Jewish communities, especially the prompt payment of fiscal obligations (which they understood depended on rabbinical enforcement), and in the financial returns from the purchase of the rabbinic license.

Contemporary preachers accused both rabbis and elders of purchasing their positions from noblemen.[41] Most commonly, they were charged with being frequenters of the palaces of the lords and with serving the lords' interests rather than those of the Jewish community. In fact, it was unusual for the town owner to appoint elders of the community, although this was not unknown. In Kutów, the privilege granted by Józef Potocki in 1715 specified that two of the elders would be elected and two appointed by the town owner.[42] On the other hand, the results of the annual elections were subject to the approval of the authorities, the provincial governor in crown cities, and the owner or administrator in private towns.[43] In the vast Sieniawski-Czartoryski holdings, where more than 30,000 Jews lived, "Jews with close ties to the owners enjoyed a dominant position in the Jewish community."[44]

Clearly, the independence of the *kahal* was tenuous. Town owners intervened in elections and closely watched tax collection and other functions. The real authority of the *kahal* was vitiated vis-à-vis the power of the aristocrats, who tended to ignore Jewish communal autonomy when

Caesar's house," and he is therefore suspect (Berakhot 27). Emden, *Shevirat luhot ha'aven* (Żółkiew), 1756, 50a.

41. Samuel ben Eli'ezer of Kalaveria, *Darkhei no'am* (Königsberg, 1764), 102a. See also Isaiah Shahar, *Bikoret hahevrah vehanhagat hatsibur besifrut hamusar vehaderush bePolin bame'ah ha18* (Jerusalem, 1992), 46; Rosman, *Lords' Jews,* 189–194.

42. Goldberg, *Jewish Privileges,* 142.

43. Majer Bałaban, "Die Krakauer Judengemeinde-Ordnung von 1595 und ihre Nachträge," *Jahrbuch der jüdisch-literarischen Gesellschaft* 10 (1912): 315; Pazdro, *Organizacja,* nos. 22, 63, 64; J. Bergerówna, *Księżna pani na Kocku i Siemiatyczach* (Lwów, 1936), 34; Rosman, *Lords' Jews,* 191; Hundert, *Jews in a Polish Private Town,* 156–57, 141–43.

44. Rosman, *Lords' Jews,* 191.

it suited their interests. While the *kahal* insisted on its right to control all activities within the community, the lord could blithely ignore their claim when it suited him. In 1732, for example, the town owner issued a privilege to the Jewish tailors' guild in Berdyczów that guaranteed that the lord would protect the guild against all interference in its internal affairs by the *kahal*.[45]

Some historians have seen the turmoil in larger Jewish communities as a form of class conflict in which artisans led the sometimes violent opposition to the oligarchic *kahal*.[46] Raphael Mahler presents these developments in a chapter entitled "The Struggle of the Jewish Masses against the Oppression of the *Kahal*."[47] Before evaluating Mahler's conclusions, some factors complicating this interpretation should be noted. Mahler, together with Mark Wischnitzer, among others, often confuses struggles for office among the wealthy with struggles between the lower and upper classes. In part, this may be explained by confusion about the terms *pospólstwo* (in Polish) and *hamon* (in Hebrew), which literally mean "the people" and "the masses." In the documents of the eighteenth century, however, they refer to those people who paid sufficient taxes to qualify for office but did not actually hold office. Adding to the confusion is the fact that while the lower classes and the artisans did indeed participate in the more dramatic and violent struggles, they did so as pawns, not as independent agents.

After referring to a series of seventeenth-century edicts of the Lithuanian Council that promised increasingly harsh punishment of plotters and conspirators against a *kahal* without specifying anything further about their identities, Mahler begins his discussion of eighteenth-century developments. In Poznan in 1752, the provincial governor annulled the election of three *kahal* officers, apparently at the behest of the established communal leaders. There is nothing in the documentation to indicate that

---

45. "[W] żadne sprawy do bractwa szczególne należące nie wdawał." Mark Wischnitzer, *A History of Jewish Crafts and Guilds* (New York, 1965), 260. Cf. Maurycy Horn, *Żydowskie bractwa rzemieślnicze na ziemiach polskich, białoruskich i ukraińskich w latach, 1613–1850* (Warsaw, 1998), 36.

46. Ibid., 258–60, and the sources cited there; [B.] D. Weinryb, "Al yahasan shel hakehillot bePolin leva'alei-melakhah ulepo'alim," *Yedi'ot ha'arkheiyon vehamuze'on shel tenu'at ha'avodah* 3–4 (1938): 9–22. Cf. Efraim Kupfer, "A tsushteyyer tsu der frage fun der batseyung fun kahal tsum yidishn ba'al mlokhe, meshares un oremshaft in amolikn Poyln," *Bleter far geshikhte* 2 (1949): 207–22.

47. Mahler, "Di Yidn in amolikn Poyln," cols. 335–56. See also Mahler's analysis of events in *Nowy Sącz:* "Z dziejów Żydów w Nowym Sączu w XVII I XVIII w.," *BZIH* 56 (1965): 43–48.

these three were representing the lower classes or artisans of the community. The next year, a council of twenty-one was added to the officers of the *kahal*. The creation of this new body was intended to allay suspicion of the elders among members of the community.[48] Again, nothing in the sources indicates anything about the social origin of the members of the new council. In Inowrocław, somewhat earlier, electors had to include representatives of the wealthy, the middle class, and the artisans. In that community, as Mahler stresses, the two wealthiest families had control of two of the four senior positions of the *kahal* administration.

In 1763, there was a rebellion in the largest Jewish community in western Poland—Leszno (Jews called it Lissa). Mahler cites the cause as the excessive rate of taxation in that community that eventually led to a violent rebellion by the "enraged masses": "[They] dragged the community elders to the synagogue and made them swear that they would resign. However, the feudal lord of Leszno, . . . Sułkowski, sided with the deposed heads of the community and had the leaders of the rebellion punished. Three of them were chained in the . . . [*kune*] for three consecutive Sabbaths, and the fourth was sentenced to four weeks of hard labor."[49] During the "rebellion" the most culpable of the *kahal* elders was subjected to what was referred to as "a living funeral." In 1792, an ordinance issued by the *kahal* of Leszno granted the artisans and others participation in community affairs. The ordinance provided that when matters of importance were to be decided, the elders were to summon a council that included representatives of dealers in fur, wool, grain, or leather, taverners, shopkeepers, agents, tailors, furriers, and goldsmiths. The members of the council were to have seven votes and the community elders three. The councilors were to have the right to examine the community's finances and expenditures. Mahler suggests that the relative strength of the artisans in western Poland and the partial reforms that were carried out indicate the more "progressive" nature of that part of the country, which was more closely linked to German lands and developments there. He notes, for example, that the elementary school curriculum in Leszno included the teaching of reading and writing German even before the partitions of Poland.

In Lublin, conflict over taxation led to the broadening of the *kahal* to

48. For the relevant texts, see Dov Avron, ed., *Pinkas hakesherim shel kehillat Pozna (5)381–(5)595*, Acta Electorum Communitatis Judaeorum Posnaniensium (1621–1835) (Jerusalem, 1966), 405–8.

49. Mahler, "Di Yidn in amolikn Poyln," cols. 330–52. Wischnitzer, *History of Jewish Crafts and Guilds*, 258–59, with some correction.

include members the Polish sources call the leaders of the people *(radcy pospólstwo).*[50] This probably referred to higher taxpayers who held no office. In the Volhynian town of Dubno, the *kahal* obtained an order from the town owner, Jabłonowski, disestablishing the Jewish artisan guilds of tailors, butchers, bakers, and others and forbidding their reestablishment on grounds that these guilds were oppressing the poor of the community.[51]

The Belorussian town of Mińsk was the scene of a struggle that became violent after petitions protesting corruption in the *kahal* leadership submitted to the local government authorities yielded no results.[52] Jews accompanied by soldiers invaded and occupied the offices of the *kahal.* The presence of the soldiers suggests that not only artisans and the poor were involved, and that this was essentially a dispute within the upper stratum of society. Communal records, documents, and ledgers were seized and submitted to the sheriff *(starosta),* the royal official in charge of the town. A boycott of communal direct taxes and of the *korobka* (indirect taxes, especially on meat) was organized. The elders were prevented from entering the synagogue. Eventually, the elders, with the support of the local officials, were able to reimpose their authority. Subsequent attempts by the opposition to turn to higher courts in Grodno and Wilno were equally unavailing. At one point, a leader of the "rebellion" was beaten and chained in the communal *kune.*

Even though further research is called for, these various disturbances and "rebellions" were not instances of class warfare or a struggle against taxation without representation on the part of lower-class Jews in eighteenth-century Poland-Lithuania. They were mainly struggles for power within the wealthier stratum of the population and involved the manipulation of the "masses" by both sides.

In Wilno, a simmering rivalry between the rabbi, Shmu'el ben Avigdor, and the *kahal* divided the community for decades.[53] The rabbi had gained the position when very young as a result of a very large payment to the *kahal* by his father-in-law, Yehuda ben Eli'ezer. The extended community council that assembled for the decision signed the formal writ of ap-

50. Ibid., 259.

51. See H. Z. Margoliot, *Dubno rabati* (Warsaw, 1910), 90.

52. Israel Klausner, "Hama'avak hapenimi bekehilot Rusiyah veLita vehatsa'at R. Shim'on ben Wolf letikunim," *He'avar* 19 (1972): 215–20.

53. Israel Klausner, *Vilna betekufat haga'on: Hamilhamah haruhanit vehahevratit bekehilat Vilna betekufat haGR'A* (Jerusalem, 1942); id., *Vilna: Yerushalayim deLita* (Tel Aviv, 1988); Israel Cohen, *Vilna* (Philadelphia, 1943), 490–501. And see below.

pointment (110 signatures).[54] Although the young man was qualified in a general way for the rabbinate, he was unqualified to be the spiritual leader of a community of scholars such as that in Wilno.[55] The first phase of the dispute between the rabbi and the community began after the death of the powerful Yehuda ben Eli'ezer and turned on attempts by the rabbi to extend his influence in *kahal* affairs by placing his supporters and relatives in key posts. The *kahal* establishment objected to this and also to the rabbi's far-flung commercial activities, which took him to Russia, Königsberg, and Gdańsk. A variety of levels of civil and Jewish jurisdiction were involved, and the dispute intensified and subsided as different cohorts of *kahal* leaders were elected, some sympathetic to the rabbi, others not. The dispute dragged on for fifteen years (1762–77), but eventually the rabbi triumphed, since the *kahal* undertook to pay him an indemnity to reimburse him for moneys lost while his powers were limited. Documents recording the declarations of both sides were deposited officially in the Wilno district *(grod)* court in 1777.[56]

Four years later, the rabbi precipitated a new and more furious outbreak by pressing his financial claims against the *kahal*. Opposition to the rabbi was led by Abba ben Ze'ev Wolf. The leading figure among the rabbi's supporters was Yosef ben Eliyahu Peseles, one of the wealthiest merchants in Wilno. At this point, a new group appeared, the *pospólstwo*: merchants and guild artisans who took the side of the rabbi, expecting his support in fighting against the heavy taxes of the *kahal*.[57] These alliances clearly indicate "an open war within the ruling groups" of the community and not a rebellion of the lower classes.[58]

A small group of intellectuals, some of those seeking to reform the situation of Jews in the Polish-Lithuanian state, also took the rabbi's side. Of these, the most prominent was Shim'on ben Ze'ev Wolf. The Ga'on of Vilna (Wilno, Vilnius), Elijah ben Solomon Zalman (1720–1797), did not play a visible role in the dispute, but he eventually sided with the opponents of the rabbi.

The rhetoric used by those on the side of Shmu'el ben Avigdor sug-

54. S. Fuenn, *Kiryah ne'emanah* (Vilna, 1915), 138–40.

55. Klausner, *Vilna betekufat*, 52; id., *Vilna: Yerushalayim deLita*, 89.

56. Klausner, *Vilna betekufat*, 82.

57. Israel Halpern objected, with justice, to Klausner's use of the Hebrew term *hamon* (the masses) to denote this group. Israel Halpern, "Mahloket harav beVilnah [5]522–[5]551," in id., *Yehudim veyahadut bemizrah Eiropah: Mehkarim betoledoteihem* (Jerusalem, 1968), 160.

58. Mahler, "Di Yidn in amolikn Poyln," col. 346f.

gests their identification with the cause of the poorer elements of the community. They accused the *kahal* establishment of extortionate taxation policies that favored the rich and oppressed the poor. "No one with a human heart," said a memorandum prepared by Yosef ben Eliyahu Pesseles, "can look with dry eyes on this oppression." Carried on in Jewish and civil law courts at various levels, and accompanied by polemical pamphlets published in Polish by both sides, the dispute also became one more battlefield in the struggle between the reformers and the conservatives among the Polish magnates. The rabbi had the support of Bishop Ignacy Massalski (1729–1794), the son of the grand hetman of Lithuania, who was a partisan of the reform-minded Czartoryski group and a member of the National Education Commission until he was removed for extortion. Massalski was something of a political opportunist and thought to be in the pay of the Russians. He was hanged by a furious Warsaw mob together with six others.[59] Massalski's enemy and rival was Karol Radziwiłł (1734–1790), a prominent member of the conservative magnate group who backed the *kahal*. Radziwiłł was enormously wealthy but uncouth and unstable. Indeed, he was as famous for his outlandish behavior as for his wealth.[60]

In the course of the dispute, each side accused the other of suborning perjured testimony.[61] Those testifying against the rabbi suggested that he had accepted bribes, made decisions contrary to *halakha,* and was frequently drunk. In early 1785, the *kahal* deposed the rabbi from his office, but without the consent of the provincial governor *(wojewoda)* who had ratified the original appointment. Shmu'el ben Avigdor refused to accept the validity of this action. The *wojewoda* agreed and supported the rabbi's demand that the dispute be brought before a rabbinical court in a "leading community" of Lithuania. When this rabbinical hearing failed to occur, the *kahal* petitioned the *wojewoda,* complaining that the rabbi's learning was insufficient to qualify him for his office and that he was transgressing divine commandments. A tribunal of three Polish Christian judges was appointed to hear the aspects of the case that did not pertain directly to religion.

Four groups made representations to this court: the newly elected *ka-*

---

59. Tadeusz Kasabula, *Ignacy Massalski, biskup wileński* (Lublin, 1998).

60. Many of the matters discussed here are taken up extensively and with great authority in the as-yet-unpublished doctoral dissertation by Adam Teller, "Tafkidam hakalkali uma'amadam hahevrati shel hayehudim be'ahuzot beit Radziwiłł beLita bame'ah ha18" (Ph.D. diss., Hebrew University, Jerusalem, 1997).

61. Klausner, *Vilna betekufat,* 89–91, 100–102, 107–10.

hal, consisting largely of supporters of the rabbi; the rabbi; the previous *kahal*; and the *pospólstwo*, consisting of artisan guilds and merchants. Both the previous *kahal* and the rabbi hired Polish Christian lawyers. Seven men were chosen to represent the groups that constituted the *pospólstwo*. Two represented 102 tailors, and one the haberdashers *(szmuklerzy)*. Shim'on ben Ze'ev Wolf was nominated by the tinsmiths. Other plenipotentiaries represented 65 furriers, 95 merchants, and 29 goldsmiths and copper engravers. A seventh representative was supported by 72 signatures, drawn mainly from the extended communal council. In sum, there were 447 signatures on these petitions, an impressive number even allowing for duplication. At the time, the extended communal council *(asefat rahash)* had about 180 members. A year earlier, 1,642 Jewish families had been counted in Wilno. There are good grounds to suspect that the 1785 petition did not represent the views of the 447 signatories authorizing representation in the original case before the *wojewoda*'s court.[62] It seems more likely that Shim'on ben Ze'ev Wolf was going well beyond his mandate in preparing this dossier, which "threatened the *kahal* itself as an autonomous institution."[63]

As the case progressed, the rabbi became dissatisfied and sought an alternative means of resolution. Radziwiłł agreed, annulled the new *kahal* elections that had been held at the behest of the tribunal and ordered the whole matter transferred to the jurisdiction of the Jewish communal court of Słuck, a town that he owned. This failed to occur because of interventions by various participants. Instead, Radziwiłł appointed a rabbinical court to hear the religious aspects of the case in Mir, also owned by him. All other claims would be adjudicated by the *wojewoda* himself. The rabbinical court decided against the rabbi. Radziwiłł's officials, dealing with the remaining matters, ordered that the rabbi's opponents substantiate their claims by taking an oath in the synagogue of Wilno. Radziwiłł accepted the judgment and removed the rabbi from his post. A writ [*rabinostwo*] from the *wojewoda* was prepared at the behest of the old *kahal*, permitting the appointment of a new rabbi and leaving a space to record the name. They appointed Abba (Abraham) ben Ze'ev Wolf, who paid 36,000 florins for the office.

The matter did not end there, however. In 1785, apparently guided by Bishop Massalski, an appeal was mounted to the royal court, while representatives of the *pospólstwo* submitted a petition formulated by Shim'on

62. Halpern, *Yehudim veyahadut*, 161.
63. Klausner, *Vilna betekufat*, 147.

ben Ze'ev Wolf to the Treasury with revelations of financial mismanagement by the *kahal*. The rabbi and his party were protected from the *wojewoda* by moving to the suburb of Antokol, which was under the bishop's jurisdiction. In the course of the dispute, Abba ben Ze'ev Wolf was accused of having apostatized some fifty years earlier and then reconverted to Judaism. This libel was intended to block him from assuming the office of rabbi in place of Shmu'el ben Avigdor.

On Radziwiłł's orders, twelve members of the old *kahal* solemnly swore an oath in the synagogue admitting that the rabbi was indeed guilty of the charges against him. The petition submitted to the Treasury by the *pospólstwo* presented serious problems for the *kahal* leadership. It revealed that the *kahal* had been systematically underreporting its income, borrowing new funds, and imposing unfair taxes. Specifically, in 1766, the *kahal* had reported income of 34,000 florins, when in fact it had collected 150,671 from the various sales and service taxes *(korobka)*. Moreover, there was additional income from the sale of offices and monopolies and from fines amounting to between 20,000 and 30,000 florins. The petition also attacked one Elijah, here called *hassid* and in Polish *patryarcha*, "who does nothing, who pays not one farthing to the *kahal*, and pays no *korobka*," but for whom the *kahal* was providing housing and 28 florins weekly. This was in addition to various gifts, such as fish. They demanded that this support *(donum gratuitum)* cease. The amount in question exceeded the remuneration of the communal rabbi. The reference is to Elijah ben Solomon Zalman (the "Vilna Ga'on," or "Elijah Ga'on"; acronym Ha-GRA = Ha-Ga'on Rabbi Eliyahu), the most distinguished and respected Jewish scholar of his age, who was identified with the "establishment" side of the struggle. Elijah held no rabbinical or other office and led no yeshiva; his vast influence was based on his enormous learning and his charismatic personality.

The *kahal*, with the backing of Radziwiłł's officials used every possible means to evade the threat embodied in the petition's claims. In an effort to undermine the case of the representatives of the *pospólstwo*, the *kahal* gathered signatures from as many community members as possible stating that they did not recognize the plenipotentiaries' right to file suit on their behalf. Of the 732 signatories, 117 stated that they could not write, and the community beadles signed their names.[64] Moreover, Shim'on ben Ze'ev Wolf was excommunicated and imprisoned for six weeks in 1786; in response, Bishop Massalski had Abba ben Wolf arrested and impris-

64. Ibid., 149–50.

oned for a month. The Lithuanian vice-chancellor, Joachim Chreptow-icz (1729–1812), who was closely linked to the king and to Massalski, with whom he had served on the National Education Commission, now in-tervened, obtaining a royal writ to protect the partisans of the rabbi and the *pospólstwo* while the case was before the courts. In October 1787, judi-cial proceedings began in Warsaw in the royal court, chaired by Chrep-towicz. Both sides published pamphlets in Polish defending their posi-tions. The court judgment accepted the Mir rabbinical court decision and removed Shmu'el ben Avigdor from his post. He was, though, to receive financial compensation and a pension.

The Treasury court found that the *kahal* had indeed underreported its income substantially and sentenced the elders to short terms of impris-onment, which they served, and to return the missing half-million florins to the Treasury so that it could be used for the payment of the *kahal*'s debts, which they did not do. Radziwiłł denied the validity of the Trea-sury court's ruling. Shim'on ben Ze'ev Wolf was arrested for the second time in July 1788 and imprisoned at Nieśwież (Nesvizh) by Radziwiłł. He and those imprisoned with him were not released until January 1790.

A final agreement was reached between the *kahal* and Shmu'el ben Avig-dor in late 1790. The *kahal* agreed to pay him damages and, on his death, to bury him with the same honors as all those who had held his office, al-though he would cease to hold it. Shmu'el ben Avigdor died just nine-teen days after the formal ratification of the agreement. The *kahal* of Wilno decided never again to elect a communal rabbi and symbolically placed a large stone on the rabbi's chair in the Great Synagogue. No meaningful changes were introduced in the conduct of the *kahal*.

As complex and local as this three-decade struggle was, there are ele-ments here that warrant further attention. First, the events in Wilno in many ways mirrored the larger political scene in the Polish Common-wealth in general. In both cases, the struggle was between conservative and liberal elements, involving, in fact, some of the same actors: Massal-ski on one side, Radziwiłł on the other. This suggests a form of integra-tion of the Jewish community into the web of political struggle in the Commonwealth. Its involvement, however, was primarily instrumental. Each side tried to enlist the community against the other. Secondly, in both cases, the struggle was conducted largely within a small group of powerful individuals. That is, the crisis in the *kahal* was the consequence of a struggle for power within the elite, each side bringing its magnate sponsors into play on its behalf. The rhetoric about the oppression of the poor, it seems, was mostly (although not entirely) empty sloganeering.

Indeed, one might say that this rhetoric marked the beginning of a "politics of the street" in the Jewish community in which the views of the masses were perceived as having political weight. The maturation of such politics, however, would take several decades.

In the Lithuanian town of Szawle (Siauliai), both the rabbi and the *kahal* were targeted by protest in 1790. The rabbi was accused, like the elders, of manipulating the tax system for his own benefit and of using the ban of excommunication in the service of his side of the dispute. As a result, the opposition could not bury their dead or purchase kosher meat. The opposition petitioned for the total abolition of the *kahal,* which was pictured as a vehicle of exploitation. In this case, as elsewhere, the two contending factions of the wealthy reached a compromise involving some broadening of the *kahal* council.

In Międzyboż, there were struggles across a number of different axes: between artisans and individuals aligned with the town owner, within the elite, between leaseholders and the *kahal* and so forth: "In addition to conflicts of elite versus plebeians, there were also different configurations of elite versus elite, as well as artisan versus artisan and poor versus poorer. The array of power relationships was not rigid, and alignments could shift."[65]

The occasional turmoil and conflicts that arose in these relatively larger centers must be understood without imposing an ideological template on them. The loosening of hierarchical distinctions and the weakening of the social sanctions that made the events described possible do not represent incipient and scattered instances of social revolution. There was no class warfare in the Jewish communities of Poland-Lithuania in the eighteenth century. There were competing interests and rival centers of power. There were instances of corruption and embezzlement, of exploitation and dishonesty. Rabbinical offices were indeed obtained by powerful men for members of their families. Most of the time, however, and in most places, the *kahal* continued to function and rabbis continued to be learned and qualified for their positions. After all, the rabbinate had always been in the hands of the relatively well born or, at least, well married. Still, there were profound changes afoot in this period, changes that would lead to a fundamental alteration of Jewish culture itself. Kabbalah entered the mainstream.

65. Moshe Rosman, *Founder of Hasidism: A Quest for the Historical Ba'al Shem Tov* (Berkeley, 1996), 93.

CHAPTER 6

The Popularization of Kabbalah

Beginning in the latter part of the seventeenth century, what some an-
thropologists call "the grammar" of Jewish culture was changed by the
addition of kabbalistic systems of meaning. Jacob Katz describes this as
"a general shift in religious values."[1] In a manuscript culture, the study
of kabbalistic texts had been an esoteric tradition restricted to a tiny elite.
The printing press facilitated the spread of knowledge of Kabbalah
among the learned. Simultaneously, beginning in the latter part of the
seventeenth century, works that popularized kabbalistic ideas in homiletic
and ethical treatises and in regimens of daily life appeared in substantial
numbers. Katz stresses that the impact of the growing literature popu-
larizing kabbalistic ideas led to a number of developments, including a
new understanding of the significance of observance of the commandments. Observance now had cosmic resonance, affecting the hidden divine realm and advancing or retarding progress toward redemption. Careful and proper observance became a fateful matter upon which the future
of the world hinged. This system of understanding erased the differences
in degree and weight between the fulfillment of one commandment and
that of another. It demanded full consciousness in the act of performing
a commandment or praying. This consciousness was ritualized by the
kabbalists in the form of *kavanot* ("intentions"; sing., *kavanah*), which
are intentional formulae preceding observance or recitation, intended to
focus the mind of the devotee on the symbolic significance of the act
about to be performed or the prayer about to be recited. For kabbalists,

---

1. Jacob Katz, *Tradition and Crisis: Jewish Society at the End of the Middle Ages,* trans.
Bernard Dov Cooperman, 2d ed. (New York, 1993), 190.

Katz observes, "performance of a commandment without *kavanah* virtually lost its religious significance."[2]

Many of the publications in question were essentially inexpensive pamphlets written in accessible language and guiding the reader through prayer services and rituals associated with the life cycle.[3] All these were imbued with mystical significance, and the individual, feeling privy to the esoteric realm, knew that his or her actions were in accordance with God's will. The spread of this popular literature had the additional effect of creating a constituency for the emerging kabbalistic elite. "Henceforth, traditional Jewish society contained not one elite but two," Jacob Katz notes.[4] Kabbalists took their place alongside talmudic scholars, equally worthy of respect and equally entitled to public support.

Individual mystics and small groups of kabbalists appeared in numerous communities. They were known by various names, including *benei aliyah* and *hassidim,* but are not to be confused with the later "Beshtian" Hasidim. The *hassidim* were eremitic, ascetic pietists who devoted themselves to the study of esoteric doctrine. In some towns, there were groups of *hassidim* who prayed separately in their own *kloyzen* (prayer "rooms"), or study halls, and were thought to benefit the community that supported them by their special ties to Heaven.[5] The most prominent of these groups was in Brody, but there were others in Ostróg, Wilno, Opatów, Brześć Litewski, Szkłów, Lwów, and elsewhere.[6] These ascetic mystics developed some characteristic customs and interests, including praying separately and following the liturgy prescribed by the so-called Lurianic prayer book (*nusah ha'ari*) instead of the conventional liturgy. On the Sabbath, they gathered for the third meal in the afternoon and wore white robes. They evinced a particular concern with all aspects of the slaughter of animals for food and sought to ensure that it be carried out with precise adherence to the prescriptions of *halakhah.*[7] Asceticism, including much fast-

---

2. Ibid., 191.

3. Ze'ev Gries, *Sifrut hahanhagot: Toledoteha umekomah behayei hassidei R. Yisra'el Ba'al Shem Tov* (Jerusalem, 1989), 45, 82–83, 90–92, 98–102. For discussion of resistance to this trend, see Moshe Rosman, "A Prolegomenon to the Study of Jewish Cultural History," *Jewish Studies, an Internet Journal* 1 (2002): 109–27. http://www.biu.ac.il/JS/JSIJ/1-2002/Rosman.doc.

4. Katz, *Tradition and Crisis,* 192.

5. Elchanan Reiner, "Hon, ma'amad hevrati vetalmud torah," *Zion* 58 (1993), 287–328. According to Reiner, a *kloiz* was privately supported; houses of study were usually but not always, more public institutions. Cf. Ya'akov Hisdai, " 'Eved HaShem'—Bedoram shel avot hahasidut," *Zion* 47 (1982): 287–88.

6. Reiner, "Hon," 298–99.

7. Ya'akov ben Yehezkel Segal, *Shem ya'akov* (Żółkiew, 1716), 8b (improper slaughter prolongs the Exile), 10b (slaughter with faulty knives leads to epidemic); Ya'akov Yisra'el ben Tsevi Hirsh, *Sefer shevet miyisra'el* (Żółkiew, 1772), pt. 2, 9b. And see Alexander Ziskind of

ing and sometimes mortification, characterized their way of life. Young men would "go into exile," wandering from town to town, depending on the goodwill of others for support, expressing in this way their total identification with the exile of the Divine Presence (*Shekhinah*). These phenomena persisted through the eighteenth century outside of [Beshtian] Hasidism. It is important to stress that the influence of Kabbalah was extraordinarily broad in scope and was not coextensive with or limited to the population that found its way to the Hasidic movement that appeared in the 1760s and 1770s.[8] (In an attempt to keep the distinction clear, I shall refer to old-style *hassidim* in lower-case italics, transliterated, and to the members of the new movement ostensibly founded by Israel Ba'al Shem Tov and still in existence as Hasidim [sing., Hasid].)

When Shabbetai Tsevi was proclaimed Messiah in 1665 by his prophet Nathan of Gaza (1643/4–1680), Jews responded with enthusiasm in virtually every country. The extent of the impact of Shabbateanism in 1665–66 in Poland-Lithuania has not been determined. The movement partially collapsed with the apostasy of Shabbetai Tsevi in 1666. Some adherents were unwilling to surrender the intoxicating conviction of living in a redeemed world, however, and developed a theological rationale to account for the conversion of Shabbetai Tsevi to Islam. These "believers" were forced to disguise their beliefs by the insistent opposition of and occasional bans of excommunication against them by normative Jewish leaders who wished to return to normalcy. During the years 1672–99, the southern Polish province of Podolia was annexed to the Ottoman Empire, and Jews there undoubtedly came into closer contact with Ottoman Jews, among whom were many "believers." Some of them had converted to Islam but continued to practice a messianic Judaism in secret. Other believers behaved in public as if they were normative Jews but persisted in their Shabbatean beliefs in secret. By the end of the seventeenth century, there were

---

Horodno, *Sefer yesod veshoresh ha'avodah,* as cited by Chone Shmeruk, "Mashma'utah ha-hevratit shel hashehitah hahassidit," in *Hakri'ah lenavi: Mehkerei historiyah vesifrut,* ed. Israel Bartal (Jerusalem, 1999), 37–38, 52 n. 66, first published in *Zion* 20 (1955): 47–72. Cf. Chone Shmeruk, "Hasidism and the *Kehilla,*" in *The Jews in Old Poland,* ed. Antony Polonsky, Jakub Basista, and Andrzej Link-Lenczowski (London, 1993), 186–95; Elijah ben Abraham Hakohen Itamari, *Shevet mussar* (Jerusalem, 1989), ch. 36; Mendel Piekarz, *Biyemei tsemihat hahassidut* (Jerusalem, 1998), 68, 161–62, 383–87, 391; Shaul Stampfer, "Lekorot mahloket hasakinim hamelutashot," in *Mehkerei hassiduth,* ed. Immanuel Etkes et al., Jerusalem Studies in Jewish Thought, 15 (Jerusalem, 1999), 197–210; cf. Mordekhai Wilensky, *Hassidim umitnaggedim: Letoledot hapulmus beineihem,* 2d ed. (Jerusalem, 1990), index s.v. *shehitah.*

8. A representative figure would be Alexander Susskind ben Moses of Grodno (d. 1793), who had no connection to Beshtian Hasidism. He was the author of the influential work *Yesod veshoresh ha'avodah,* which betrays considerable kabbalistic influence.

individuals and groups of Jews in Poland-Lithuania who followed this pattern. Many of these were among the "old-style" *hassidim*.

Some of these spiritually minded individuals, Shabbatean and non-Shabbatean, came to rather radical positions out of the intensity of their devotion to spiritual concerns. Most famously, a small number were attracted to the idea that a very pious person might sin for the sake of [fulfilling the commandment of] repentance. But for the most part, these groups and individuals followed a rigorously ascetic and reclusive regimen. On the whole, the spiritual elite remained aloof from the masses of Jews. The sometimes unusual or idiosyncratic ritual and liturgical practices of these *hassidim* were accepted as measures necessary for the achievement of mystical elevation possible only for distinctly qualified individuals.

The literature produced in these circles of *hassidim* demanded a rejection of frivolity and advocated constant mourning over the Exile and a continuous flight from sin. The appropriate countenance was dour, serious, and sober. Such demeanor was advocated, to take one example, in *Sha'ar hamelekh* ("The King's Gate") by Mordekhai ben Shemu'el of Wielkie Oczy. First published in 1762, it went through nine editions in the next thirty-five years.[9] The book is informed by an unsophisticated theology somewhat influenced by Lurianic ideas. The sort of spiritual life it advocates is one that venerates a perpetual pious asceticism characterized by much mournfulness, a certain precisionism in observance, and penitential behavior. Indeed, the author repeatedly claims that redemption depends fundamentally on repentance.

Katz stresses that the scholarly elite, which saw itself as separate from the masses because of its learning, was nevertheless involved in the community through teaching, judging, and preaching: "But the kabbalist elite saw itself as divided from the masses by a wide chasm even in the practical sphere. The only relationship possible between them and the masses was one of *shelihut* (agency or proxy). The few were transformed into exacting performers of the precepts on behalf of the many."[10] Because of this, the communities in which they lived sometimes supported certain *hassidim*, exempted them from the payment of taxes, or both. They were

9. Mordecai ben Samuel, *Sha'ar hamelekh* (Żółkiew, 1762). Cf. Avraham Ya'ari, *Ta'alumat sefer: Sefer Hemdat yamim: mi hibro umah haytah midat hashpa'ato* (Jerusalem, 1954), 123; Mendel Piekarz, "Hara'ayon hameshihi biyemei tsemihat hahassiduth," in *The Messianic Idea in Jewish Thought: A Study Conference in Honour of the Eightieth Birthday of Gershom Scholem* (Jerusalem, 1982), 238–44.

10. Katz, *Tradition and Crisis*, 194.

seen as precious, exceptional individuals *(yehidei segulah)* and "servants of God."[11]

The work of other scholars has substantiated Katz's observation that a broad popularization of aspects of Kabbalah and kabbalistic practice began to intensify in the last decades of the seventeenth century.[12] Evidence for this can be garnered by studying the history of publishing during the period to determine what literature was most in demand among Polish-Lithuanian Jews. This method of determining what the most popular books were, and by extension, what the important ingredients in popular literate culture were, is undeniably useful, but it must be qualified. The canonical works—the Bible, especially the Pentateuch, with the commentary of Rashi (Rabbi Solomon ben Isaac, 1040–1105), the Mishnah, the Talmud, and the *Shulhan arukh*—continued to be the basic texts of Jewish civilization. These, especially the Bible and the Mishnah, were unquestionably much more widely read by Polish Jews than any other religious writings, at least among the male population.[13] The history of publication nonetheless points clearly to the remarkable popularity of texts informed by kabbalistic-magical traditions.[14] The sermons of the time, drawn from materials found in the popular publications, evinced a growing preoccupation and concentration on esoteric matters broadly associated with Kabbalah.

Nonmystical texts were popular as well. The classical ethical treatise *Duties of the Heart* [*Hovot halevavot*] by Bahya ibn Paquda (second half of the eleventh century) went through twenty-seven editions between 1670 and 1797, including seven with Yiddish translations.[15] During that time,

11. The ascetic "old-style" *hassid* Alexander Ziskind ben Moshe of Grodno ordered that only the words *eved haShem* be inscribed on his gravestone. Ya'ari, *Ta'alumat sefer,* 124–25. Cf. Hisdai, "'Eved HaShem'."

12. Gries, *Sifrut;* Moshe Idel, "'One from a Town, Two from a Clan'—The Diffusion of Lurianic Kabbala and Sabbateanism: A Re-Examination," *Jewish History* 7 (1993): 79–104; Moshe Halamish, *Hakabalah batefilah, bahalakhah uvaminhag* (Ramat-Gan, Israel, 2000).

13. And among the elite, crucial changes in the way the Talmud was studied developed in the course of the eighteenth century. See Israel M. Ta-Shma, "HaGR'A uva'al *Sha'gat aryeh,* ha*Penei yehoshu'a* vesefer *Tsiyun lenefesh hayah:* Letoledoteihem shel hazeramim hahadashim besafrut harabbanit erev tenu'at hahaskalah," *Sidra* 15 (1999): 181–91, and the references there.

14. The list of "best-sellers" that emerges from the precious document published by Yehoshua Mondshine—an attempt to limit competition among publishers in Żółkiew and Lwów in 1801—includes the following: *Tikunim yesharim; Siddur sha'arei tsiyon; Nahlat ttsevi; Reshit hokhmah; Lev tov; Tikunei Zohar; Ets hayyim* (a condensation of SheLaH); and *Kav hayashar.* Mondshine, "Ma'amad shene'erakh bein hamadpisim beLevov veZolkiew," in *Sefer hazikkaron lerabbi Moshe Lifshits,* ed. R. Rozenbaum (New York, 1996), 898–916.

15. There was an additional edition in Ladino: Venice, 1713.

a number of commentaries on the work were published as well, an additional sign of its massive popularity.[16] The author of the book advocated a life of pious self-deprivation; in particular, the idea of *perishut,* or voluntary separation from the material world, came to be widely accepted. The anonymous *Orehot tsadikim,* an ethical work substantially in the ascetic-penitential spirit of *hassidei ashkenaz,* was published thirty-one times in the late seventeenth and early eighteenth centuries.

Still, many of the "best-sellers" of the eighteenth century were pervaded with kabbalistic ideas and approaches. No fewer than sixteen different editions of *Hemdat yamim* appeared between 1670 and 1770.[17] A homiletical-ethical work profoundly influenced by kabbalistic ideas, including those of the great charismatic mystic of Safed, Isaac Luria (1534–1572), it provides guidance along these lines for the observance of the holy days of the Jewish calendar. An eighteenth-century memoirist depicted the impact of the book on him and his fellow students when it arrived in the town where he was studying: "Students of Talmud were transformed into practical kabbalists fasting and mortifying themselves. In place of Torah scholars, there appeared 'masters of the name,' who blinded the eyes of the many with their enthusiasm. . . . The number of penitents multiplied, and they would afflict their bodies in strange ways: pounding their chests with rocks; falling to the ground during the reading of the Torah in the synagogues."[18]

One striking aspect of the popularity of *Hemdat yamim* is that this book taught a popular religiosity that was not only kabbalistic but also, to a limited extent, Shabbatean in origin. Jacob Emden (1697–1776), a promi-

---

16. A. L. Nadler, *The Faith of the Mithnagdim: Rabbinic Responses to Hasidic Rapture* (Baltimore, 1997), 78–79. Among the commentaries were Hayim Hayke ben Aaron of Zamość, *Derekh hakodesh,* published with Isaac ben Aaron of Zamość, *Pahad yitshak* (Frankfurt a/O, 1774), and Moses ben Reuben, *Ne'edar bakodesh* (Grodno, 1790). See the reminiscence of Yitshak ben Ben Zion—when he came to Opatów as *maggid,* a group requested that he teach them *Hovot halevavot,* "and I taught it beginning with *sha'ar habehinah.*" That is, he skipped the first Gate ("Of Unity"). *Sefer Mikhlal yofi* (Frankfort a/O, 1775). See Piekarz, *Biyemei,* 71–72. Among those who extolled asceticism was the same Hayyim Hayke ben Aaron of Zamość, *Tseror hahayim* (Lublin, 1908; Berlin, 1770). See also Mordecai ben Samuel of Wielkie Oczy, *Sha'ar hamelekh,* pt. 1, gate 5. For a moderate anti-ascetic view, see the citations in Piekarz, *Biyemei,* 38.

17. Cf., Ya'ari, *Ta'alumat sefer.*

18. As summarized by Abraham Ya'akov Brawer, *Galitsiyah viyehudeha: Mehkarim betoledot Galitsiyah bame'ah ha18* (Jerusalem, 1956), 203. Birkenthal and his colleagues saw the edition of *Hemdat yamim* published in Constantinople in 1735–37. Cf. "The Writer's [Dov Ber of Liniec's] Preface" to *In Praise of the Baal Shem Tov:* "[T]here were also mad people who injured themselves with stones during the reading of the Torah, and who used to reveal people's sins to them." Dan Ben-Amos and Jerome R. Mintz, *In Praise of the Baal Shem Tov: The Earliest Collection of Legends about the Founder of Hasidism* (Bloomington, Ind., 1970), 4.

nent rabbi and outstanding opponent of Shabbateanism in all forms, attributed its authorship to none other than Nathan of Gaza, the prophet-companion of Shabbetai Tsevi and ideologist of the Shabbatean movement. On the other hand, the Shabbateanism of *Hemdat yamim* was according to some scholars (astonishingly) not so obvious to its readers in the eighteenth century. At least one distinguished scholar of the mid twentieth century insisted that the book was not Shabbatean at all. At this writing, there is no agreement among scholars as to the Shabbateanism of its author.[19] Notwithstanding doubts as to whether contemporaries were universally aware of the origins of *Hemdat yamim,* it should be stressed that in *some* circles in East Central Europe, there was rather a benign attitude to the failed Shabbatean movement and its teachings. The popularity of *Hemdat yamim* is only one indication of this.

Note also the tolerant reference to (Joshua) Heshel Tsoref (1633–1700), the Shabbatean prophet, by Tsevi Hirsch Koidonover (d. 1712) in *Kav hayashar,* another very popular work of the period. Another eighteenth-century book commented that the Shabbatean movement failed "because the generation failed to achieved true penitence."[20] At the same time, in other circles, there was a rather ferocious atmosphere of heresy hunting. Much of this was generated by suspicions that various figures were adherents of Shabbatean doctrine. The controversies surrounding Jonathan Eybeschuetz (ca. 1690–1764), who was accused of being a Shabbatean, and Moshe Hayyim Luzzatto (1707–1746) of Padua, who had ties to eastern Europe and was suspected of various heresies, were followed by the Frankist phenomenon, which reached its greatest intensity in the late 1750s.[21]

19. Ya'ari, *Ta'alumat sefer.* See the review of Ya'ari's book by Gershom Scholem, "Vehata'alumah be'einah 'omedet," *Behinot* 8 (1955): 79–95, and the debate between Ya'ari and Scholem in *Behinot* 9 (1956), esp. 77–80, 83–84. Cf. also Isaiah Tishby, *Netivei emunah uminut: Massot umehkarim besifrut hakabbalah vehashabbeta'ut,* 2d ed. (Jerusalem, 1982), 108–68. Yehuda Liebes has asserted that "the Shabbateanism of the book [*Hemdat yamim*] is established." Liebes, *Sod ha'emunah hashabbeta'it: Kovets ma'amarim* (Jerusalem, 1995), 302, n. 15. The historiographical debate is summarized in detail by Moshe Fogel, "Shabbeta'uto shel sefer *Hemdat yamim:* Hitbonenut mehudeshet," in *The Shabbatean Movement and Its Aftermath: Messianism, Shabbateanism and Frankism,* Jerusalem Studies in Jewish Thought, 17, ed. Rachel Elior (Jerusalem, 2001), 377–94. Fogel takes the position that the Shabbatean element in the work is not very strong.

20. "Mah sheshama'ti mipeh kadosh, halo hu ha'ish ha'elohi mohr"r Heshel Tsoref z"al. She'amar beshem mekubal ehad." Tsevi Hirsch ben Aaron Samuel Koidonover, *Kav hayashar* (Frankfurt a/M, 1705), ch. 102. See references to Yehuda Hasid and Heshel Tsoref in Ya'akov ben Yehezkel Segal, *Shem ya'akov,* 15a, 22a, and see there 25a.

21. Rachel Elior, "Hasidism: Historical Continuity and Spiritual Change," in *Gershom Scholem's Major Trends in Jewish Mysticism, Fifty Years After,* ed. Peter Schäfer and Joseph Dan (Tübingen, 1993), 303–23.

Another book that enjoyed substantial popularity was *Sefer shevet mussar* by Elijah ben Abraham Hakohen Itamari. First published in Constantinople in 1712, it appeared in seventeen editions in Hebrew and eight editions in Yiddish (including two editions with both the Hebrew and the Yiddish texts) before 1800.[22] In fact, most if not all of the book's materials can be traced to Talmudic sources, medieval ethical literature, or to Luria and other mystic sages of sixteenth-century Safed. The author was a "moderate" Shabbatean, but this is not reflected in *Shevet mussar*.[23] It deals with topics such as punishment for sin, the importance of study, paths to repentance, proper conduct, and overcoming temptation. The graphic description of the punishments awaiting a sinner has been quoted often:

As for Hell below, it is large and occupies tens of thousands [of miles]. As the number of the wicked grows, it continually expands. In it are individual compartments by the thousands, one more terrible than the other. There all the wicked are punished, each according to his deeds. . . . The fire wherewith the wicked are burned is sixty times stronger than the fire in this world [BT, Berakhot 57b]. There are coals that are as large as mountains and valleys, and through hell flow rivers of pitch and sulfur springing out of the depths of the abyss. In it are all kinds of monstrous and ugly destroying spirits that inflict punishment on the wicked. And all these hosts of destroying spirits were, in fact, created by the sinful deeds of the wicked. As the sages declared [Mishnah, Avot 4:11]: "He who violates one commandment has obtained for himself one accuser." Besides these destroying spirits there are others that were appointed to punish sinners after hell was fashioned. The sufferings and afflictions wherewith the wicked are punished are diverse: some are strung up and they throttle them; . . . some have their eyes gouged out; some are hanged by the neck—each according to the magnitude of his sin.[24]

One feature of the book is its compilation of long lists to characterize, for example, "The Qualities of a Proper Female" (chapter 24). Chapter 39 includes a list of the forty-two holy names of the *tsaddik,* the perfectly righteous man, and their explanation.[25] The following is a paraphrased sampling and summary of that chapter with particular attention to one item:

22. According to Yitshak Isaac ben Ya'akov, *Otsar hasefarim* (Vilna, 1877–80), there was also an edition published in Amsterdam in 1712. No copy of this survives.

23. Shmu'el Werses, "Rabbi Eliyahu Hakohen me'Izmir," *Yavneh* 2 (1940): 156–73. Gershom Scholem, "R. Eliyahu hakohen ha'itamari vehashabbeta'ut," in *Sefer hayovel likhevod Alexander Marx* (New York, 1950), 451–70. *Shevet mussar* is quoted in *Hemdat yamim.*

24. Elijah ben Abraham Hakohen Itamari, *Shevet mussar* (Jerusalem, 1989), 26:9.

25. The term *tsaddik* was often a cipher for Shabbetai Tsevi in Shabbatean writings. This could be the case here too.

The Holy Names of the *Tsaddik*

1. *Or ne'erav:* he is the *light* of the Torah; the light hidden at the time of Creation.

3. *Gedulah:* he bestows *greatness* on others.

5. *Da'at tsalul:* he knows the esoteric secrets about the heavens, angels and other divine beings, and the dimensions of Divinity *(shi'ur komah).*

7. *Ziknah:* he controls his own *aging* and not the reverse. He knows what has been since creation and what will be until the end of the world.

8. *Hokhmah:* he knows the whole Torah in its seventy aspects more than angels or seraphs.

9. *Hayyim:* he controls his death; if he does not wish to, he will not die.

10. *Toharah:* he teaches distinctions between *pure* and impure. He himself is the purity that purifies others.

13. *Lohem:* he *wages the war* of Torah day and night. His study defends the people of Israel; because of his preoccupation with Torah, Israel does not fall in battle. His merit protects them.

14. *Mikdash:* everything in the *Temple* is in man. He is also called Temple because he atones for his generation like a Temple. For he takes the place of sacrifice that atones for a person.

15. *Makhriah malakhim: angels* are sent from heaven to *do the bidding of the righteous* as in the case of Abraham to whom angels were sent, and Jacob who dispatched angels ("messengers") to do his bidding.

17. *Mehapekh gezerah:* the Holy One decrees death for someone, the *tsaddik reverses the decree* from death to life.

19. *Memit umehayeh:* the *tsaddik* can *sentence to death or to life.* This is followed by examples of talmudic rabbis who resurrected people.

22. *Makhtir Torah:* the *tsaddik* can explain the Torah's difficult passages.

24. *Matsil nefashot:* the *tsaddik* by his Torah, the connectedness and skillfulness of his deeds and his making things integral [*vetikunav*] prevents epidemic, war, and famine from coming into the world.

26. *Madrikh shavim:* if he sees a sinner, he will teach him the proper penance for each sin--the number of fasts and mortifications. What he must do, how, and for how long.

27. *Mamshikh shefa:* according to what the kabbalists have written, the *tsaddik* is called "the one who *brings down the Divine plenty*" [*mamshikh shefa*].[26] God answers every petition, for He hears the prayer of every mouth, and immediately the *shefa* begins to descend toward this world. But it must pass the court that is on the "north" [*tsafon*] side. There they evaluate the worthiness of the petitioner. If he is found worthy, the *shefa* is permitted to pass onward. If not, they hold it up, storing it for gifts for the *tsaddikim* of the future. But if there is a *tsaddik* in the world, even if the petitioner is unworthy, the *shefa* is allowed to pass because of the *tsaddik*. Thus far what the kabbalists have said, see there for further elaboration. And he went on: this is the meaning of the verse (Ps. 31:20): "How great is Your goodness which You have stored up [*tsafantah*] for those who fear You; You acted for them that fear You against the mortals." If you wish I can say this means: "How great is the goodness that You stored up in the North [*tsafon*] for them that fear You, and You did good with it making it gifts for them." That is, the same *shefa* that was "against the mortals," that it was not fitting that it should descend and be held up there. For me, this explains the passage [Mishnah, Avot 3:15] "All is foreseen [*tsafui*] but free will is given [*vehareshut netunah*], and the world is judged for good" [*ubetov ha'olam nidon, vehakol lefi rov hama'asseh*]. All is *tsafui* ["foreseen"] that is, "stored up" in the Northern heavenly court, where the Divine plenty is delayed. [The author is playing on the similarity of the words for "north"—*tsafon*, "stored up"—*tsafun*, and "foreseen"—*tsafui*.] As mentioned, sometimes *hareshut netunah* literally [these words, translated as "free will is given," literally mean "permission is given"] permission is given for it to descend, even though the petitioner be unworthy because the world is judged *betov*, that is, because of the good [man]. Since there is this goodness and justice in the world personified by the *Tsaddik*, because of him the *shefa* is brought down. . . . The *tsaddik* causes the drawing down of the *shefa* from above to every petitioner, even if he be unworthy. Therefore the *tsaddik* is called *mamshikh shefa*.

29. *Sefer Torah:* just as one stands before *a scroll of the Torah,* one stands

26. The author cites Isaac ben Meir, *Siah yitshak* (Venice, 1664), referring to the second section of that book, entitled *"al perek shirah,"* ch. 2: *shirat haruah.* Isaac ben Meir there refers to Josef ben Abraham Gikatila, *Sha'arei orah,* sec. 6. In the 1883 Warsaw edition of *Sha'arei orah,* the reference is to folio 74.

before a scholar.[27] If one is precise, he is more than a *Sefer Torah,* since the *Sefer Torah* itself does not explain its words.

32. *Olam male:* all of creation is for one *tsaddik.*[28]

33. *Ezrah betsarah:* if there is some source of sorrow and suffering, the *tsaddik* goes before them [the heavenly court] and persuades them and cancels the evil decree. This is the nature of the *tsaddik* to benefit the whole world. Jew or Gentile, . . . and the Gentile he helps will reach high office and will be grateful to the *tsaddik* who in turn will be able to defend his people.

34. *Podeh nefashot:* the *tsaddik* is a *redeemer of souls.* Through his "acts of correction" [*tikunim*] and his devout intention [*kavanot*] he redeems the Divine sparks locked in the valleys of the *kelipot* ["shards"—the source of evil]. He can also save souls from Hell [*Gehinom*].

35. *Elohim:* the *tsaddik* by his study and his deeds attempts to repair the sin of Adam. He can do what the Holy One does like bring rain and resurrect the dead.

The question of the author's originality need not detain us. In general, he did not stray far from his literary predecessors. And it seems clear that the notion of the perfect man in *Shevet mussar* was a theoretical one. Still, while the concept of the *tsaddik* as described here in one of the most popular and influential Jewish books of the eighteenth century does not correspond precisely with the version actually institutionalized in Hasidism, enough is shared for this fact to be suggestive indeed.

Shenei luhot haberit [*Shelah*], a monumental work by Isaiah ben Abraham Halevi Horowitz (1565–1630), was first published in Amsterdam in 1649. Five more editions appeared before the end of the eighteenth century. Between 1681 and 1792, twenty-three editions of an abridgement by Yehiel Michal Epstein (ben Abraham Halevi, d. 1706) were published, in addition to fifteen editions of a Yiddish abridgment that appeared between 1743 and 1797.[29] The editor-translator added material of practical interest drawn from other books of kabbalistic preaching. The great popularity of the work is shown by an agreement among the publishers of Żółkiew and Lwów that included the Yiddish version in a list of those books that

27. TB Makkot 22b.
28. TB Yoma 38b; TB Hagigah 12b.
29. Yishayahu Vinograd, *Thesaurus of the Hebrew Book (Otsar hasefer ha'ivri),* pt. 2, "Places of Print" (Jerusalem, 1995).

were in demand and were continuously in print.[30] *Shenei luhot haberit* in its various forms was probably the single most important vehicle of mediation of the new kabbalistic ideas of the sixteenth century in the Ashkenazic world.[31] The work had a profound influence on all subsequent writing in genres including exegesis, ethical literature, and ritual practice. The indefatigable Rabbi Jacob Emden, the outstanding opponent of Shabbateanism in the eighteenth century, found Shabbatean hints both in Yehiel Michal Epstein's liturgical work and in his abbreviation of *Shenei luhot haberit*.[32] Epstein included material from the *Sha'arei tsiyon*, a kabbalistically informed prayer book by Nathan Neta Hannover (d. 1683), which went through more than forty editions during the eighteenth century, in his digest of *Shenei luhot haberit*.[33] *Sha'arei tsiyon* was by far the most popular specialized prayer book of the period.

The popularization of Kabbalah reflected in the wide diffusion of the works discussed here and others had social and cultural consequences including obsessive attention to one form of sinfulness, the appearance of shamanlike figures in Jewish society, mystical messianism, and finally, the Hasidic movement. These matters are taken up in the following chapters.

30. Yehoshua Mondshine, "Ma'amad shene'erakh bein hamadpisim beLevov veZolkiew," in *Sefer hazikkaron lerabbi Moshe Lifshits*, ed. R. Rozenbaum (New York, 1996), 898–916. About 75 percent of the list consisted of prayer books, psalms, elegies *(kinot)*, confessionals *(selihot)*, Yiddish prayers *(tehinot)*, and Pentateuchs.

31. Moshe Halamish singled out *Hemdat yamim* and *Shenei luhot haberit* as particularly important mediators of the influence of Lurianic Kabbalah on halakhah and practice. Halamish, *Hakabalah*, 186 and passim.

32. Hayyim Liberman, "Bamerkungen," *Yivobleter* 36 (1952): 310. Emden claimed there was a Shabbatean allusion in Epstein's liturgical book: the addition at the end of the service of Psalm 21, which Shabbateans recited three times daily, and which includes the phrase "HaShem be'ozekha yismah melekh uviyshu'atekha" ("O Lord, the king rejoices in Your strength and Your salvation"). Because the numerical value *(gematria)*, of the last word in this phrase was equivalent to the name Shabbetai Tsevi, this practice was also condemned by Ezekiel ben Judah Landau (1713–1793) in his *She'elot uteshuvot noda biyehudah* (Prague, 1811), "Hoshen mishpat": no. 16. Emden also said there was a Shabbatean allusion in the introduction to the digest of *Shenei luhot haberit* in the form of the phrase "veyizku lir'ot penei melekh hamashiah ha'amiti" ("they will merit seeing the face of the king, *the true messiah*"). The numerical value of the words *mashiah ha'amiti* is equivalent to that of the name Shabbetai Tsevi. See also Shneur Zalman Leiman, "Sefarim hahashudim beshabbeta'ut: Reshimato shel haga'on 'Y'abetz,'" in *Sefer hazikkaron lerabbi Moshe Lifshits*, ed. R. Rozenbaum (New York, 1996), 885–94. In a later comment, Hayyim Lieberman characterized Emden's condemnatory language as unusually mild and possibly uncertain. Lieberman, *Ohel Rahel*, vol. 2 (Brooklyn, 1984), 614–15.

33. First edition, Prague, 1662.

CHAPTER 7

Mystic Ascetics
and Religious Radicals

A late-eighteenth-century manuscript prayer book, clearly intended for use by the person conducting prayers in the relatively small Jewish community of Wschowa in western Poland, contains a prayer that at first sight is surprising.[1] Among the Sabbath prayers that follow the readings from Scripture, between the prayer for the government and the prayer for the new month, there is an instruction that the congregation should recite this prayer while the leader chants the prayer for the new month. On the festivals, at New Year and on the Day of Atonement, the allotted time for this same prayer was during the *Mussaf* ("additional" service) while the cantor was repeating the prayer *mipenei hata'einu* ("Because of our sins" we were exiled). The prayer they were to recite was "this awesome prayer for the *tikkun* [repair, correction] of *keri*." That is, they were to pray for the "correction" of the sin of *keri* (nocturnal seminal emission). The prayer ends with the invocation of two holy "Names" (of God) that had the power to effect the *tikkun*.

More than one scholar has noted that the problem of how to atone for *keri* attracted almost obsessive attention during the late seventeenth and eighteenth centuries, and later.[2] Here is a social or psychological conse-

---

1. YIVO Institute for Jewish Research, New York, RG 242, from the Personenstandes-Archiv Koblenz: RSAJ906.

2. Jacob Katz, *Tradition and Crisis: Jewish Society at the End of the Middle Ages,* trans. Bernard Dov Cooperman, 2d ed. (New York, 1993), 116, 121. A. J. Heschel, "R. Nahman miKossow, havero shel haBesht," in *Sefer hayovel likhevod Tsevi Wolfson,* ed. Saul Lieberman, Hebrew sec. (New York, 1965), 138; Joshua Trachtenberg, *Jewish Magic and Superstition* (New York, 1939), 282 n. 16; David M. Feldman, *Marital Relations, Birth Control and Abortion in Jewish Law* (New York, 1974), 118.

quence of the popularization of Kabbalah in this period. The subject it-self, as we shall see, had been discussed by kabbalists for centuries. What was novel was the concern of broad sections of the population. Entire books were devoted to the subject of *keri*,[3] and it is addressed in virtually every work of moral and ethical guidance published in that period.[4] Joseph Karo's *Shulhan arukh, the* authoritative sixteenth-century code, included the opinion that a person guilty of *hashhatat zera* ("slaughtering [his gen-erative] seed") is guilty of a sin more serious than all the sins of the Torah. This was a repetition of sentiments expressed in the (late-thirteenth-century) Zohar.[5] The word *zera* can mean "seed," or it can also mean "chil-dren" or "descendants." Hence, the following opinions in the Zohar: "Such a man's deed is worse than that of a murderer, he is a killer of his own children and therefore stands condemned as a criminal more repre-hensible than any other"; "even penitence will not avail him who is guilty of the sin of *hashhatat zera*"; by this sin, "one pollutes himself more so than through any other sin in this world or the next."[6]

The Mishnah and Talmud treat accidental seminal emission as a source of ritual pollution,[7] but sometimes the references are quite benign, as when

3. Heschel, "R. Nahman," notes the following works: Joseph ben Solomon Calahora [= Joseph Darshan] of Poznan, *Yesod Yosef: Mussar vetikkunim le'avon keri* (Frankfurt a/O, 1679); Moses Graff [Prager?], *Zera kodesh: tikkunei teshuvah al pegam ot haberit* (Fuerth, 1696); [Hananiah] Yom Tov [Lipmann] Deutsch, *Taharat yom tov,* in 9 vols.

4. *Shulhan arukh: Even ha'ezer* 23; Me'ir ben Gedaliah Lublin, *She'elot uteshuvot* (Venice, 1618), 116; Abraham ben Shabbetai Sheftel Halevi Horowitz, *Emek berakha* (Kraków, 1597), pt. 2, sec. 52, 60b, 61b; id., *Yesh nohalin* (Amsterdam, 1701), 18b, n. 17; Joel ben Uriah Heilperin, *Mif'alot Elohim* (Żółkiew, 1725), nos. 356, 357; Elijah ben Moses de Vidas, *Reshit hokhmah* (Venice, 1593), *"sha'ar hakedushah,"* ch. 17: 15; Isaiah Horowitz, *Shenei luhot haberit hashalem,* ed. Meir Katz (Haifa, 1997), Sha'ar ha'otiyot, nos. 342, 343, 349, 350–55, 360; Joseph Yuspa Hahn, *Yosif omets* (Frankfurt a/M, 1723), nos. 195, 196; Zelig ben Yitshak Isaac Margoliot, *Sefer hibburei likutim* (Venice, 1715), Introduction; Elijah ben Abraham Hako-hen Itamari, *Shevet musar,* ch. 19: 37; ch. 20; ch. 27: 45–49; ch. 30: 8–9; ch. 40; ch. 44; Mordecai ben Samuel, *Sha'ar hamelekh* (Żółkiew, 1762), pt. 2, sec. 2, ch. 3; Jehiel Mikhal Epstein, *Sefer kitsur shenei luhot haberit [im mahadura batra]* (Frankfurt a/M, 1724): *"Sefer toledot adam,"* 23a: *"Ot kof inyanei hotsa'at zera levatalah";* Alexander b. Moses Ziskind, *Yesod veshoresh ha'avodah* (Nowy Dwór, 1782), sec. 10, ch. 3; sect. 12, chap. 2; *sha'ar hakolel,* ch. 5; Tsevi Hirsch ben Aaron Samuel Koidonover [Kaidanover], *Kav hayashar,* 1st ed. (Frank-furt a/M, 1705), chs. 2, 11, 12, 22, 34, 45, 58, 61, 68, 70, 93; Perets ben Moshe, *Sefer beit Perets* (Żółkiew, 1759), 63b.

5. Isaiah Tishby, *The Wisdom of the Zohar,* trans. David Goldstein, vol. 3 (Oxford, 1989), 1364–67.

6. Zohar, *Vayehi,* 219b; *Vayeshev,* 188a. These citations are found in Feldman, *Marital Re-lations, Birth Control and Abortion in Jewish Law,* 115.

7. Mishnah, Berakhot 3:4; Kelim 1:5; BT Berakhot 21a; Baba Kamma 82a; Yebamot 7b, 76a; JT Sanhedrin 10: 2.

nocturnal emission is seen as one of six "good signs" for a person who is ill. Other passages in the Talmud enjoin vigilance in avoiding lascivious thinking during the day lest it lead to seminal emission at night.[8] On the other hand, emitting semen to no purpose was depicted in other, mainly midrashic, nonlegal passages in very grave and hyperbolic language. It was compared to murder and to idolatry and it had the consequence of delaying the Messiah. The guilty person was considered "an animal," had no share in the world to come, and was worthy of death. It was one of the sins of the generation of the flood in the time of Noah and thus had led to the destruction of the world.[9] In rabbinic times, furthermore, there were those who believed that nocturnal emission was caused by female demons who wished to be impregnated and give birth to more demons, but the man seduced in this way was not held responsible for his action.[10] Talmudic attitudes tended not to emphasize moral criticism of the person who had "seen keri."[11] It was the Zohar and the approach preserved in it that emphasized the negative and destructive consequences of the destruction of seed, displacing the more tolerant views in rabbinic literature in the enthusiastic embrace of Kabbalism in the seventeenth and eighteenth centuries.

Keri was a form of the more general sin of *pegam haberit,* that is, a sin against the covenant (of circumcision),[12] and thus against the root of one's identity as a part of the people of the covenant and indeed as a human being.[13] The human soul had three parts: *nefesh* (soul), *ruah* (spirit), and *neshamah* (divine breath of life), and all of these could be lost: "For the

---

8. BT Ketubot 46a; Avodah Zarah 20b; Hullin 37b.

9. Kallah Rabbati, ch. 2; Nidah 13a; Genesis Rabba 26: 6; Pirkei derabi Eliezer, ch. 22.

10. Tishby, *Wisdom,* 3: 1377, n. 119; Meir ben Gedaliah Lublin, *She'elot,* 116.

11. Feldman, *Marital Relations,* 116; Tishby, *Wisdom,* 3: 1366. Cf. the halakhic material adduced by Meir Havatselet, "Hishtalshelut minhag toharat ba'alei keri behashpa'at gormei zeman umakom," *Talpiot* 8 (1963): 531–37.

12. On kabbalistic interpretations of Abraham's circumcision and circumcision in general, see Elliot Wolfson, "Circumcision, Vision of God and Textual Interpretation: From Midrashic Trope to Mystical Symbol," in *Circle in the Square: Studies in the Use of Gender in Kabbalistic Symbolism* (Albany, N.Y., 1995), 29–49; id., "Circumcision and the Divine Name: A Study in the Transmission of Esoteric Doctrine," *Jewish Quarterly Review* 78 (1987): 77–112.

13. A sin against the covenant of circumcision was associated also with a sin against the covenant of speech. Both caused harm to the *sefirah* of *yesod.* See *Sefer Yetsirah,* ed. Yosef Kafah (Jerusalem, 1972), ch. 1, sec. 2. Yehuda Liebes, in his discussion of the prohibition of revealing secrets, has pointed to the way these associations are made explicit in the Zohar. Yehuda Liebes, "Hamashiah shel haZohar," in *The Messianic Idea in Jewish Thought: A Study Conference in Honour of the Eightieth Birthday of Gershom Scholem* (Jerusalem, 1982), 135–36.

first time [*keri* occurs], the 'other side' *(sitra ahra)* removes his *nefesh* from him, and the second time his *ruah,* and the third time his *neshamah,* which surrounds him, and gives them to the forces of evil [*kelipot*]."[14] A person guilty of this sin cannot receive the Divine Presence *(Shekhinah).* Such a sin would not befall a truly pious and holy person. "And it was because of this sin that our Holy City was destroyed and the Temple laid waste." Its continuing occurrence, therefore, prolongs the exile.[15] Perhaps most frightening of all, as Elijah ben Moses de Vidas put it in his influential ethical work *Reshit hokhmah* in the sixteenth century, echoing the Zohar, "for the sin of *keri* no repentance is possible" *(lehet keri ein teshuvah).*[16]

The author of the Zohar saw nocturnal emission as sexual contact with female demons and worthy of utter condemnation. The righteous were preserved from such defilement, but those who were weak were liable to seduction by Na'amah, the mother of demons.[17] The difficulty arose in part from the idea that penitence involved a compensatory good deed by the same part of the body that sinned. The destruction of seed involves more than one organ. The seed is formed initially in the brain, goes through the spinal cord and at its release, represents the whole person. Effective repentance therefore must involve the whole person in an extraordinary effort.[18] Yet even in the Zohar itself, an opinion exists that a truly penitent sinner could atone for this sin.[19]

14. Moses Hayyim Ephraim of Sudylków, *Degel mahaneh efrayim* (Zhytomyr, 1874), 70a–70b, *ekev.*

15. Mordecai ben Samuel, *Sha'ar hamelekh,* pt. 2, sec. 2, ch. 3: "[A] sin of monumental proportions that is delaying redemption." Heschel, "R. Nahman," 138; "because of this our city and Temple were destroyed and our precious ones were exiled." YIVO Institute for Jewish Research, New York, RG 242.

16. Elijah ben Moses de Vidas, *Reshit hokhmah,* "Sha'ar hakedushah," (Venice, 1593), ch. 17:15. See, in contrast, the ruling of Jacob ben Moses Moellin (Maharil, d. 1427) in the case of a person who "saw *keri* on the Day of Atonement." After requiring that the man mortify himself as far as possible, Moellin concluded that "he should not despair" but return to the Lord with his whole heart. Cited in Jacob Elbaum, *Teshuvat halev vekabalat yisurim: Iyunim beshitot hateshuvah shel hokhmei Ashkenaz uPolin, 1348–1648* (Jerusalem, 1992), 30. And see also Zelig ben Yitshak Isaac Margoliot, *Sefer hibburei likutim,* Introduction, where the author stresses that there is no one who is spared this sin.

17. Tishby, *Wisdom,* 3: 1366–67, and the references there.

18. Feldman, *Marital Relations,* 116. Cf. Perets ben Moshe, *Sefer beit Perets,* 63b: "the best penitential act for this sin [*motsi zera levatalah*] is to teach some new Torah [*lehadesh hidushei Torah*] through thought in the mind. Just as the essence of the sin of emitting seed for no purpose comes from the mind, since it is there that the drops of seed are formed in a man."

19. Zohar, Genesis 219b, 54b, 56b, 62b; Ruth 12. Yehuda Liebes has suggested that these, or some of these "milder" passages may have been later additions to the text. Liebes, *Studies in Jewish Myth and Jewish Messianism,* trans. Batya Stein (Albany, N.Y., 1993), 204, n. 110. See the rejoinder to this contention of Yehoshua Mondshine, "Al 'Hatikkun hakelali shel R. Nahman miBraslav veyahaso leshabbeta'ut,'" *Zion* 47 (1982): 199–201.

The Safed authorities and their European mediators, while accepting the gravity of the matter as expressed in the Zohar, generally maintained that forgiveness was possible if extraordinary acts of penitence were undertaken.[20] Isaiah Horowitz, in his *Shenei luhot haberit,* devoted considerable attention to the problem.[21] In characteristic fashion, he assembled relevant passages from the Talmud and the Zohar, together with references to *Sefer harokeah,* the pietist manual of repentance of Eleazer ben Judah of Worms (ca. 1165–1230), and extensive citations from *Reshit hokhmah.* While the latter work stressed the need for penitential acts affecting all the limbs of the body, Horowitz emphasized the requirement to repeat the acts of penitence according to the number of times the sin had been committed. In this case, the sinner's life would likely end before the penitence was complete. The Holy One, however, considers intention, and if the penitent died before achieving atonement, God would add the person's thoughts to his deeds and consider his intentions to have been fulfilled. The prescribed penance was ritual immersion and eighty-four fasts annually in accordance with a tradition attributed to Isaac Luria and "printed at the end of *Kitsur reshit hokhmah,* which everyone owns."[22]

Most of the popular works of the eighteenth century considered here did not accept the categorical denial of the possibility of penitence. The following passage in *Shevet mussar* adopts a characteristic position:

You, my sons, if the failing of spilling seed to no purpose is yours, even if it is absolutely involuntary and forced upon you [*be'ones gamur*], be sure to purify yourselves in the ritual bath immediately, God forbid that you should take this lightly. . . . Such a mating is with Lilith the temptress and other forces of uncleanness. She fastens herself to the sinner with plans to collect her due in the world to come. God save us. A person who dies without repenting and in such a state of impurity—such a soul is cut off.[23]

Yehiel Michal Epstein, in his *Kitsur shenei luhot haberit,* provided a summary of the seventeenth-century work *Yesod yosef* by Joseph ben Solomon

20. See the analysis of the treatment of this problem by Moses Cordovero (*Or yakar,* sha'ar 11, par. 3) in Elbaum, *Teshuvat halev,* 40, and the prescription of 84 fasts in the book, *Vayehal moshe,* ibid., 140, and see there 16, 30, 204. Cf. Vidas, *Reshit hokhmah,* sha'ar hakedushah, no. 17. For the relationship between Isaac Luria's teachings and those of Isaiah Horowitz, see Elliot Wolfson, "Hashpa'at Ha'Ar'i al haShelaH," in *Kabbalat ha'Ar'i,* ed. R. Elior and Y. Liebes, Jerusalem Studies in Jewish Thought, 10 (Jerusalem, 1992), 428–29.

21. Isaiah Horowitz, *Shenei luhot haberit hashalem,* Sha'ar ha'otiyot, nos. 342, 343, 349, 350–355, 360.

22. Ibid., no. 350, p. 362.

23. *Shevet mussar,* ch. 40:17.

Calahora, the Preacher of Poznan (1601–1696), a book devoted entirely to this problem. He listed the eleven actions that led a person to commit this sin, the eight punishments that await the sinner, and twenty-three *tikkunim* to atone for the sin.[24]

Any explanation of the eighteenth-century preoccupation with *keri* must consider the demographic history of Polish-Lithuanian Jewry. As the proportion of young people in the population grew, the possibility of early marriage diminished. That is, the number of young people with families who could not afford the practice of *kest*—housing, feeding, and supporting the newly married couple for a period of years—increased. The enormous popularity of the kabbalistic understanding of the commandments, the preoccupation with the demons of the *sitra ahra,* and the notion of almost inescapable sinfulness, together with the burgeoning number of young males, combined to make *keri* a central and urgent problem.

During the eighteenth century, in central and western Europe, physicians began to devote attention to masturbation and related topics in a new sort of language that found medical in addition to theological reasons for condemning the practice.[25] The best-known and most influential of these works was Samuel Auguste Tissot's *Onanisme* (1760). This coincidence in time with the preoccupations of eastern European Jewish males with the same subject is merely a coincidence. It may be, though, that researchers should attend to demographic as much as physiological changes in attempting to account for this development. The increasing proportion of young people among Jews in East Central Europe has been stressed here, but there was a similar demographic jump in western Europe.[26] The more

24. Epstein, *Sefer kitsur shenei luhot haberit,* "Sefer toledot adam," 23a: *"Ot kof inyanei hotsa'at zera levatalah."*

25. Dyan Elliott, *Fallen Bodies: Pollution, Sexuality, and Demonology in the Middle Ages* (Philadelphia, 1999); Pierre Hurteau, "Catholic Moral Discourse on Male Sodomy and Masturbation in the Seventeenth and Eighteenth Centuries," *Journal of the History of Sexuality* 4 (1993–94): 1–26; P. Bennett and V. Rosario, eds., *Solitary Pleasures: The Historical, Literary and Artistic Discourses of Autoeroticism* (New York, 1995); Michael Stolberg, "Self-Pollution, Moral Reform, and the Venereal Trade: Notes on the Sources and Historical Context of *Onania* (1716)," *Journal of the History of Sexuality* 9 (2000): 37–61.

26. What may be important is not a putative earlier onset of puberty but the relative increase in the number of pubescent young men. Cf. R. P. Neumann, "Masturbation, Madness, and Modern Concepts of Childhood and Adolescence," *Journal of Social History* 8 (1975), 1–27. On the other hand, we do not know enough about the median age at marriage to say whether it was changing among eastern European Jews at this time See, Jacob Goldberg, "Jewish Marriage in Eighteenth-Century Poland," *POLIN* 10 (1997): 3–39, and Lawrence Stone, *The Family, Sex and Marriage in England, 1500–1800* (London, 1979), 321–22.

traditional Christian literature is closer in tone to the material examined here. For example, a central European author of the late seventeenth century maintained that all of humanity would suffer the consequences of onanism—God's fire would destroy the whole universe.[27] In general, the case I am making is for a Jewish culture increasingly creating itself using elements drawn from its own palette, independent of broader European trends in its content.

Redeeming the Soul: *Pidyon*

The "Kabbalah" that informs the popular literature discussed here reflects no distinction between magic and mystical metaphysics. The esoteric knowledge that informs the prescribed prayers and ceremonies included both ancient Jewish traditions and folk ideas about averting danger and healing sickness that were by no means confined to Jews. Generally, the elaborate, abstruse and difficult speculations and systems of the Jewish mystical literature are absent in these writings. At times, it is as if that vast body of literature has been winnowed to elicit "practical" implications. At other times, what is being communicated is unrelated to the philosophical-mystical systems of the Zohar, Moses Cordovero, Isaac Luria, or anyone else. Rather, the prayer or ceremony turns on the belief that the infinite potency of the divine word as recorded in the Bible can be tapped by reciting particular verses in a particular order and/or a particular number of times. Very typical also was the use of *gematria*—finding words and names of God that can be assembled and found to correspond according to various manipulations of the numerical value of the Hebrew letters. The power of the letters helped to defend against the "other side" and the forces of impurity. The room of a sick person was a veritable battlefield between the holiness of life and the ultimate impurity in the form of death and its angel.[28] It was the scene for the ritual "redemption" (*pidyon*) of the soul of the ailing person.[29]

27. Stolberg, "Self-Pollution, Moral Reform, and the Venereal Trade," 45. And see Elliott, *Fallen Bodies,* ch. 1, on the succubus robbing men of their seed while they slept. The kabbalists, as we have seen, rejected this as an exculpatory rationale.

28. Avriel Bar-Levav, "Rabbi Aharon Berakhiah miModenah verabbi Naftali Hakohen Kats: Avot mehaberim sifrei holim umetim," *Assufot* 9 (1999): 207–8 (offprint).

29. Haviva Pedayah, "Lehitpathuto shel hadegem hahevrati-dati-kalkali bahassidut: Hapidyon, hahavurah veha'aliyah leregel," *Dat vekalkalah: Yahasei gomlin,* ed. Menahem Ben-Sasson (Jerusalem, 1995), 311–73, here esp. 329–38.

"The Ceremony of Redemption of the Soul for a Sick Person (May We Be Spared)" *(Seder pidyon nefesh al haholi b'm)* exemplifies this trend.[30] It appears both in Nathan Neta Hannover's seventeenth-century kabbalistic prayer book *Sefer sha'arei tsiyon* and in the condensed version of *Shenei luhot haberit*. The following is a paraphrase of the ritual:

The Ceremony of Redemption of the Soul for a Sick Person
(May We Be Spared)

Take coins, or the equivalent of coins, even nuts, as long as they are worth a penny, the rich according to their honor and the poor according to their position. Who gives a lot is the same as who gives a little as long as their intention is for the sake of heaven. The first step is to take something countable like pennies or other coins in the amount of 160 units, which corresponds to the numerical value of the word *ets* ["tree"]. *For man is a tree in the field* [Deut. 20:19] and the secret is that there is the Divine Name [the Tetragrammaton, four-letter name of God] in it if it is calculated according to the system of *gematria* known as *milui alpin*. That is, the calculation of the numerical value of a certain word by adding together the numerical value of the names of the letters of the word, spelled with alefs. Thus the value of *yod* [10] *heh* [5] *vav* [6] *heh* when the names of the letters are written out with *aleph* is 45, which equals the numerical value of *adam* ["man"]. And *ets* is also the numerical equivalent of the four-letter name of God if it is calculated according to another technique. This involves multiplying together the first two letters and the last two letters twice and adding up the total. Thus, *yod* times *heh* plus *heh* times *yod* equals 100 and then *vav* times *heh* plus *heh* times *vav* equals 60 for a total of 160, which is the numerical value of *ets*. It also equals the numerical value of the words *tselem* ["image"] and *kesef* [the word means both "silver" and "money"].[31] Because of the latter equivalence, it is better to redeem him with silver coins than anything else.

Then he should count the 160 coins one at a time but only in his mind without speaking, and he must do this with only a good [*tov*] intention. The numerical value of *tov* is 17, which is the same as the numerical value of the Divine Name Hvha. Then he should count out silently 80 of the coins, fixing his intention on the divine name Hyha, which is numerically 21. Next, he must silently count out a further 26, while concentrating on the Tetragrammaton, which has that numerical value. And he will keep the three groups of coins separate without mixing them. They number altogether 64, which is the numerical value of the word *din* ["judgment"]. And this is a hint that by these three divine names of mercy the judgment will be "sweetened," but the "sweetening" is still only in potential and not actualized. And this is why he must not yet count out loud, but only with his hands and in his thoughts, and why he must not yet mix the coins together, so that the word *din* will not yet be equaled. This is because the "sweetening" is still in potential and not actualized.

---

30. Epstein, *Sefer kitsur shenei luhot haberit*, 83a–84b.
31. Identified with the *sefira: hesed* in Kabbalah. See Pedayah, "Lehitpathuto," 331.

Then he must take these 160 and begin to count them out loud using his mouth in Hebrew numbers or letters up to 64. Then count out 65 and bring them together to join them with the 64. At the moment that he speaks the number, join the three first portions together, bringing the 65 to the 64, so that they are in combination and joined together. And they are thus transformed. And he should intend by the counted 65 the name ADONAI, which is equal to *aleph* plus *din* and the esoteric significance is in the letter *aleph*.

The letters of the name of the letter *aleph* can be made to spell *pele* ["marvel" or "wonder"], which is complete and simple mercy without any admixture of *din* at all. And it "sweetens" the judgment of *Adonai* and in this way these numbers transform the power from *potens* to actuality. And for this he should combine them and count them out loud. And he should include in them the three merciful names that were always in *potens* and are now actual with the number of the name *Adonai*. And the adding of the letter *aleph* to *din* is in order to "sweeten" the judgment. Together with the coming of the three merciful names to actuality, evil and Satan are no more. And wholeness and years of life will be added for him from Heaven.

After this ceremony of redemption, there are 129 of the original 160 coins. The *pidyon*, that is, the 129 used for the redemption of the soul of the sick person, should be distributed to the worthy poor in particular in a form useful to them, in cash or in valuables. There should be no delay. The money should be distributed quickly. And the 31 that are left over enter the realm of the profane [*yetsu lehulin*], and they are his. [After the *pidyon* ceremony, a prayer for its effectiveness is recited.][32]

The "his" mentioned near the end of the passage undoubtedly referred to the master of the esoteric who organizes the ceremony. The implied use of such a person is a phenomenon that is only apparently contradictory. That is, the use of a "professional" to conduct a ceremony described in detail in a popular book. The popularity of kabbalistic and kabbalistic-magical literature meant a growing appreciation of the power available to those who know the esoteric ways. And it was a consequence of what seems to have been a growing desire for spiritual enfranchisement on the part of more and more male Jews in East Central Europe. What was being forged was a multifarious popular religiosity suffused with kabbalistic forms and ideas.

There are indications that this widespread spiritual quest was also having an effect on the very architecture of the synagogue. The extraordinary

---

32. There follows a simple sort of *pidyon* that requires no kabbalistic expert: When praying for the sick person, the custom is that each and every individual gives charity for the sake of that person, and the charity is distributed to seven recipients. When it is distributed to the seven, another prayer is recited, which includes the following: "By these seven charitable gifts may he be spared the seven destructions mentioned in the Torah and the seven chambers of *Gehenom*."

genre of interior-domed wooden synagogues that appeared in the late seventeenth century and disappeared during the third quarter of the eighteenth century poses questions that still await answers.[33] These questions concern not only construction and patronage but also the appearance of remarkable paintings covering the interior walls. The paintings, especially, constitute a puzzling innovation, an enigmatic *novum,* in Polish synagogue decoration.

The new forms were concentrated mainly in the southeastern and eastern regions of the Polish Commonwealth. Their most distinctive external characteristic was a high, elaborate, multi-tiered roof, enclosing a wide dome with hidden sources of light. The walls were covered with rich, polychromatic paintings that drew on the iconography of folk and midrashic traditions and in forms that may have descended from those seen first in medieval Hebrew illuminated manuscripts. At almost precisely the same time, the form of the gravestones in Jewish cemeteries changed as well. These had previously been virtually unornamented, but at the beginning of the eighteenth century, they began to display a growing variety of symbols and other forms of decoration. The identity of the carvers of the gravestones, like that of the architects of the synagogues, is unknown. It seems likely that Jewish communities collaborated with architects employed by the magnate owners of the private towns where the synagogues were erected. On the other hand, the names of many of the artists who painted the interiors are known. They include Israel ben Mordekhai and Yitshak ben Yehuda Leib of Jaryczów, David Friedlander, Eliezer ben Shelomoh Zussman of Brody, and Hayyim ben Yitshak Segal of Słuck (Slutsk).[34] Their work was not restricted to wooden synagogues.

33. Rachel Wischnitzer, *The Architecture of the European Synagogue* (Philadelphia, 1964), 125–47; David Davidovitch, *Tsiyurei-kir bevattei kenesset bePolin* (Jerusalem, 1968); id., *Omanut ve'omanim bevattei keneset shel Polin: Mekorot, signonot, hashpa'ot* (Tel Aviv, 1982). Cf. Thomas Hubka, "Jewish Art and Architecture in the East European Context: The Gwoździec-Chodorów Group of Wooden Synagogues," *POLIN* 10 (1997): 141–82; id., "Beit hakenesset beGwoździec-Sha'ar hashomayim: Hashpa'at sefer haZohar al ha'omanut veha'adrikhalut," *Eshel Be'er Sheva* 4 (1996): 263–316; and id., "The 'Zohar' and the Polish Synagogue: The Practical Influence of a Sacred Text," *Journal of Jewish Thought and Philosophy* 9 (2000): 173–250. And see the literature cited in those articles.

34. Andrzej Trzciński and Marcin Wodziński, "Wystrój malarski synagogi w Pinczowie," *Studia Judaica: Biuletyn Polskiego Towarzystwa Studiów Żydowskich* 2 (1999): 87–102; 3 (2000): 91–98; Maria and Kazimierz Piechotkowie, "Polichromie polskich bóżnic drewnianych," *Polskie Sztuka Ludowa* 43 (1989): 65–87; Ignacy Schiper, "Malarstwo Żydowskie (1650–1795)," in I. Schiper, A. Tartakower, and A. Hafftek, eds., *Żydzi w Polsce odrodzonej* (Warsaw, n.d.), 324–28; Jozef Sandel, *Yidishe motivn in der poylisher kunst* (Warsaw, 1954); D. Dawidowicz, *Omanut ve'omanim bevatei keneset shel Polin: Mekorot, signonot, hashpa'ot* (Tel Aviv, 1982), 177.

An attempt has been made to link various aspects of the architecture, interior design, and decoration of the synagogue to prescriptions to be found in the Zohar.[35] Whatever the inspiration was, and surely it was not unitary, these synagogues must have been built in response to new feelings and ideas about the setting of prayer. The large expenditure required and the very novelty of the design and decoration unquestionably bespeak an effort to create a venue that would be responsive to a broader swath of the Jewish population. These synagogues were constructed near the end of the period when women reentered the synagogue proper; earlier they had had a separate structure known as a *vayber shul*. The possibility of a connection between women's presence and the new ornamentation awaits further investigation. In passages derived from the apostate Serafinowicz in Gaudenty Pikulski's book *Złość żydowska* ("Jewish Malice") (1760), there is a description of the manner of celebrating the holiday of *Shemini Atseret* that includes a reference to a custom otherwise unknown in Polish lands: "In the afternoon, women come to the synagogue and there they dance, eat and drink."[36]

The questions of the degree and motivation of architectural innovation in the design of the wooden synagogues aside, it is clear that they were vernacular structures.[37] The spatial setting for prayer created by these synagogues reflected a striking and strikingly novel concern with the visual on the part of Polish Jews. Previous to this period, mainly biblical

35. See the articles by Hubka listed in n. 34 above. On the Zohar influencing the design of eastern European synagogues see, Wischnitzer, *Architecture of the European Synagogue*, 121, 279, which notes that the prescription in the Zohar that calls for twelve windows in the hall of worship (Exodus, Pekudei) was codified in the *Shulhan arukh* (Orah Hayyim 90:4). And see the discussion of the theoretical issues in Moshe Halamish, *Hakabalah batefilah, bahalakhah uvaminhag* (Ramat-Gan, Israel, 2000), 106–13, 168 n. 43, 314.

36. Halamish, *Hakabalah batefilah, bahalakhah uvaminhag,* 743. The question of when the women's gallery moved from an attached or separate room to the balcony above the men's section is not resolved. Cf. Erich Zimmer, ed., *Minhagim dek'k Worms lerabbi Yuspa Shammes* (Jerusalem, 1988), 1: 220–21:

Between the Afternoon and the Evening [Prayers of the day of Simhat Torah, the women] come in their finest and most beautiful clothes to the outer courtyard of the synagogue. Outside the entrance of the Women's Synagogue, the young women join hands led by the wives of the Hatan Torah and the Hatan Bereishit, and dance round and round singing *Yigdal* and songs customarily sung in honor of a bride and groom, all for the honor of the Torah. Then they go to their synagogue, where there is a young man who calls out the commandments of women for the year and sells them. These include [preparing] the collation for the synagogue; distributing and folding wimples; preparing and lighting candles; drawing water in the courtyard of the synagogues of men and women for the [ritual] washing of hands.

37. Even the most passionate defender of their uniqueness has conceded that his position is based primarily on the interpretation of the interior design and the wall paintings. Hubka, "Beit hakenesset," 275, n. 48.

verses and the texts of various prayers were to be found on the walls of synagogues. A further point about wooden synagogues as well as the masonry houses of worship constructed during this period: although their exteriors generally lacked decoration, the size and distinctiveness of these buildings indicate a readiness on the part of Jews to have a vivid physical presence and to engage in a form of symbolic speech that projected considerable self-assurance and security. The disappearance of the special form of wooden synagogue with its elaborate decorative internal decoration by the end of the eighteenth century is puzzling. It is tempting to link it to the appearance of the Hasidic movement, which in its teachings was unconcerned with materiality and externality (*gashmiyut*). At this point, however, there is no evidence of such a link.

Manipulators of the Name

While most kabbalists chose the path of ascetic piety and separation (*hasidut uferishut*), the *ba'alei shem* linked the masses and the reclusive *hassidim*.[38] The authority of these figures probably owed its existence to the popularization of kabbalistic ideas and the belief that adepts, familiar with esoteric matters, could influence the celestial realms. These shamanlike figures traveled along a figurative cusp between mysticism and magic. In this sense, Kabbalah and magic are located along the same continuum.

Magic and magicians had never been entirely absent from Jewish society, and the eighteenth-century figures drew on long traditions and bodies of esoteric knowledge stretching back to the distant past. In the European context, both Sephardi sources, many of which were associated with Nahmanides (Moses ben Nahman, known as Ramban, 1194–1270), and traditions associated with the medieval Pietists known as *hassidei ashkenaz* were particularly important. In central and eastern Europe in earlier periods, most often particular rabbis were known to possess shamanlike skills. The use of the term *ba'al shem* extended back many centuries.[39]

38. This section depends substantially on the work of Moshe J. Rosman, *Founder of Hasidism: A Quest for the Historical Ba'al Shem Tov* (Berkeley, 1996); Immanuel Etkes, *Ba'al haShem: HaBesht: Magiyah, mistikah, hanhagah* (Jerusalem, 2000); and id., "Mekomam shel hamagiyah uva'alei hashem bahevrah ha'ashkenazit bemifneh hame'ot ha17-ha18," *Zion* 60 (1995): 69–104.

39. N. Brüll, "Beiträge zur jüdischen Sagen- und Spruchkunde im Mittelalter," *Jahrbücher für jüdische Geschichte und Literatur* 9 (1889), 23, 40. Gedaliah Nigal, *Magic, Mysticism and Hasidism: The Supernatural in Jewish Thought* (Northvale, N.J., 1994), 3, 13, and passim.

A *ba'al shem,* or *ba'al shem tov,*[40] was a person who knew the secret names of God and could manipulate them to serve his desires. He was familiar also with the "other side" and knew how to combat the demons and other evil forces resident there. He could see into the future and visualize what was happening far away. Often he was a healer who knew the power of certain herbs and other plants. He knew the magical arts of metoposcopy and chiromancy (reading the forehead or the palm to determine the state of a person's soul). He could prepare amulets and charms that would make a person invisible, ensure that a barren woman would conceive, protect a woman in childbirth, cure the sick, or safeguard a traveler on his journey. While these are universal human issues and problems, and the remedies and strategies for dealing with them used by Jews were often strikingly similar in form to those found among other groups, Jewish culture also produced its own forms of psychopathology, most notoriously the *dibbuk,* a form of possession in which a foreign spirit inhabits someone's body. It is worth noting that such pathologies were concentrated among the least powerful, often young women. The ability of the arsenal of Jewish tradition to cure such afflictions served to strengthen its hold and to further empower the healers, who were commonly *ba'alei shem.*[41]

Although demons and spirits could turn up in any place, they were generally held to inhabit abandoned and remote places, which tended to reduce their encounters and conflicts with mortals. Some forests and woods were to be avoided for this reason. At times, though, demons penetrated people's houses; new houses especially had to be protected. When the powerful Shmu'el Ickowicz, agent of the Radziwiłłs, built a new house in Słuck he, and/or his wife, invited Israel ben Eli'ezer, known to posterity as the Ba'al Shem Tov, to perform the rites necessary to ensure that the dwelling would be free of demons. That he apparently actually did travel the great distance between Międzybóż and Słuck to perform this service for the wealthy Jewish family is a reflection at once of Ickowicz's wealth and the Ba'al Shem Tov's fame.[42]

Sometimes demons might be found in houses that had long been in-

40. The terms *ba'al shem* and *ba'al shem tov* were used interchangeably. See, e.g., the reference to R. Ephraim Reischer as Ephraim Baal Shem Tov. Nigal, *Magic,* 13.

41. These ideas are based on the work of Yoram Bilu, "Dybbuk and Maggid: Two cultural patterns of altered consciousness in Judaism," *AJS Review* 21 (1996): 341–66; id., "'Dybbuk'-Possession as a Hysterical Symptom; Psychodynamic and Socio-Cultural Factors," *Israel Journal of Psychiatry and Related Sciences* 26 (1989): 138–49.

42. Adam Teller, "Masoret Słuck al reshit darko shel haBesht," in *Mehkerei hassiduth,* ed. Immanuel Etkes et al., Jerusalem Studies in Jewish Thought, 15 (Jerusalem, 1999), 15–38.

habited, as in the following remarkable story reported in *Sefer kav hayashar,* one of the most popular books of the period. It went through twenty-five editions in the course of the eighteenth century, including nine in Yiddish and six bilingual editions:

In the years 481 and 482 of the sixth millennium, there was a stone house on the broad street in the holy community of Poznan. The cellar of that house was closed and inaccessible. One day a young man entered the cellar, and after a quarter of an hour, the people living in the house found him lying at the entrance to the cellar dead. No one knew how he had died. About two years after the youth's death, demons arrived in the outer rooms [*fir hoyz*] of the house. When food was cooking on the fire, they would put dirt and ashes in the pot, so that the food would be inedible. They became even more active, entering the living quarters and throwing the implements and the lamps hanging on the wall in the room to the floor. They harmed no one physically but would confuse and torment those who lived in the house. The demons entered all the rooms of the house, striking such fear into its inhabitants that they were finally forced to abandon it and to go to live elsewhere. This became a cause célèbre in the holy community of Poznan. The communal elders discussed the matter and decided to seek the active aid of the priests called Jesuits. But the Jesuits were unable to drive the demons out of the house. Then they sent a special messenger to the famous *ba'al shem,* famous in his generation, known as R. Joel Ba'al Shem of Zamość. As soon as the rabbi, our teacher, Joel (may his memory be a blessing), arrived, he began to adjure the demons with holy names, demanding that they inform him why they had entered this house, which is the dwelling place of mortals. Demons have no right to live in a settled place, only in the wilderness or the desert. And they answered that this house belonged to them absolutely by the letter and law of the Torah and demanded that the matter come before the court of the holy community of Poznan.[43]

The matter came before the court, and the demons substantiated their claim by describing what had transpired a generation earlier. The court heard the voices but saw nothing. Apparently, the house had been inhabited by a smith and his wife and children. The smith had been seduced by a demon, who appeared to him in the form of a beautiful woman and she had conceived sons by him.

This smith "had too much love" [*hayah lo ahavah yeterah*] in him, and his soul was bound up with the soul of the demon. Sometimes, he would [feel] obliged

43. Koidonover, *Kav hayashar,* 1st ed. (Frankfurt a/M, 1705), ch. 69. The work was published again in Frankfurt a/M in 1706 (twice) and 1709. Subsequent places of publication included also Sulzbach (1714, 1724); Amsterdam (1722); Jessnitz (1725); Constantinople (1725, 1732); Furth (1738, 1743); Venice (1743, 1772); Żółkiew (1755, 1773, 1777); Frankfurt a/O (1786, 1791); Nowy Dwór (1788); Lemberg (1791); and Połonne (1794).

to interrupt his prayers and leave the synagogue to fulfill the wishes of the demon. One time, this smith was leading the Passover *seder* in the manner of all Jews in the dispersion of the people of Israel. In the midst of the meal he arose and went to the toilet. His wife followed . . . and looked through a hole in the door. She saw a palatial room there, with a table filled with silver and gold and a lavishly decorated bed. On the bed was a beautiful and naked woman together with the smith who was embracing her. In great fear . . . the woman returned to her place . . . and about a quarter of an hour later, the man also returned. His wife said nothing.[44]

The next day, the man's wife went to the rabbi, Shabbetai Sheftel Horowitz (ca. 1561–1619), and asked his help. The rabbi wrote an amulet that forced the smith to abandon his affair with the demon. Nevertheless, as the smith lay dying, the demon returned and seduced him into bequeathing the cellar of the house to her and her offspring. Therefore, the demons claimed, they inhabited the house legally. The inhabitants of the house answered with three claims: First, they had paid full price for the house to the heirs of the smith. Second, demons are not mortal and have no place in a human habitation. Finally, the demon had forced the smith into the affair. The court accepted the claim of the inhabitants of the house, and R. Joel adjured the demons to abandon the house forever, including the cellar (no *mezuzah* was required on a cellar or basement door, making such places accessible to demons).[45] He forced them to go to the forests and the desert where they belonged. In his analysis of this famous case, one scholar noted the following details from the story.[46] Demons follow the norms of the *halakhah*. Mortals therefore have to be very careful not to give them some basis for invading their presence. Demons and mortals can coexist in the same building keeping to separate areas. Only when their domain had been invaded by the youth, who had crossed the border, did the demons invade the mortals' sphere. If they are disturbed, the demons are liable to bring harm to human beings. The deeds of demons, spoiling food, breaking dishes, and knocking down lamps, are warnings

44. Ibid.
45. See Nigal, *Magic*, 88.
46. Immanuel Etkes, "Mekomam shel hamagiyah uva'alei hashem bahevrah ha'ashkenazit bemifneh hame'ot ha17–ha18," *Zion* 60 (1995): 69–104; id., *Ba'al haShem*, 19–21. Cf. Yisrael Zinberg, *Toledot sifrut yisra'el*, vol. 3 (Tel Aviv, 1958), 254–56; Joshua Trachtenberg, *Jewish Magic and Superstition: A Study in Folk Religion* (New York, 1939), 51–54; and particularly Sarah Tsfatman, *Nissu'ei adam veshedah* (Jerusalem, 1988), 82–102. See also Adam Teller, "Warunki życia i obyczajowość w żydowskiej dzielnicy Poznania w pierwszej połowie XVII wieku," in *Żydzi w Wielkopolsce na przestrzeni dziejów*, edited by J. Topolski and K. Modelski (Poznan, 1999), 64–67.

of what they are capable of. And this is enough to disturb the peace of the whole community. The community did not hesitate to resort first to Jesuit priests. No one doubted that Gentiles also had magical capabilities. And they were local and accessible. Only after they had failed was a special messenger sent to R. Joel Ba'al Shem, who demonstrated that the means at his disposal, holy names found in the Jewish tradition, were superior to the magical abilities of the Gentile priests. The preparation of an amulet is attributed to R. Sheftel Horowitz, a distinguished scholar and rabbi of the community. Most likely, such an action would not have been attributed to him without a historical basis in fact. Finally, the preachers' own moral was that a man must keep far from lasciviousness and lust so that no demon can approach him in the form of a beautiful woman and attach herself to him, God forbid, or his descendants, and cause him harm.

Going out at night, the time when demons are most active, is fraught with danger: "If a man is out on the road at night and he sees an image of candlelight skipping from place to place, called in Yiddish *parfir likhter,* these are spirits. It is their way to mislead a person causing him to go the wrong way. [To overcome this] he should say, three times: 'And God said to Satan.'"[47]

Newborns, the very embodiment of vulnerability, were particularly in need of protection from the female demons Mahlat and Lilith, who might steal the infant and substitute a clay and straw doll. The following is taken from *Sefer toledot adam,* first published in Żółkiew in 1720. It was probably written by the *ba'al shem tov* Joel Heilperin:

This came to pass in the days of the rabbi and kabbalist, our teacher and rabbi, Eliyahu, may the memory of a righteous man be a blessing, who was the rabbi of the holy community of Chelm. In a small town near Chelm, there was a man named Gabriel. His wife gave birth to a son and Gabriel sent word to the rabbi, the *ba'al shem,* that he should come to circumcise the child, since the rabbi was also a mohel. The name of the small town was Galinek, and the event took place on a Thursday in Sivan. In the late afternoon, R. Eliyahu left his town to go to Galinek, arriving at the outskirts of the town in the evening. He beheld more than a hundred thousand witches and warlocks, each emitting fire and flame, and there was also fire and flame around them. They were playing with the newborn child. When the rabbi saw this, he asked his attendant for water from his flask. He washed in the water, pronounced the Great and Terrible Name . . . and said: I hereby annul and cancel the witchery of these men and women without harm to the child [here a magical formula is reproduced including some magic words] . . . and

47. Ya'akov ben Moshe of Yanov, *Minhat ya'akov solet* (Wilhermsdorf, 1731), 2.

through this Name, our rabbi, Rabbi Eliyahu *Ba'al Shem,* slew all the witches. He took the child and brought him to his father and mother. And when he arrived, he [again] uttered the Holy Name. Immediately, all present there saw that what was lying next to the mother was straw and clay and only appeared to have the form of a human child. He gave the child that had been saved from the fire and the *kelipot* to his mother.[48]

Impotence and barrenness were understood as consequences of demonic activity. An impotent man was called "one who is prevented from having intercourse." What prevented him was witchcraft. Often the victim was a newly married groom, who was considered particularly vulnerable to demons. The multiplicity of magical solutions propounded in the literature of this period to solve the problem of impotence suggests that it was common indeed. Here is one prescription *(segulah)* for the combating of impotence: "If a person is prevented from having intercourse, he should take a sword with which a man has been killed in that very year and a red apple. He should cut the apple in two with the sword, giving half to her and half to himself. This should be done at dawn on a Tuesday or a Friday."[49]

The first fifteen entries in *Sefer toledot adam* deal with various charms for the problem of barrenness. Moreover, the whole variety of dangers related to childbirth could be combated in magical ways: ensuring a smooth and easy delivery, safeguarding the newborn, preventing miscarriage and protecting the mother. The following is from the memoir of Pinehas Katzenellenbogen, the scion of a distinguished eastern European rabbinical family, himself the rabbi of several communities. He writes of his having resorted to the services of a *ba'al shem* without self-consciousness and without apology:

Then the kabbalist, . . . Beinish [Binyamin Beinish of Krotoszyn] . . . came to me and I requested from him that he give me something as a charm for a woman having difficulty in childbirth. I had done several of the things mentioned in his *Amtahat binyamin* and none had helped. So he gave me two things: one, Names bound up in a white linen case, approximately five thumbs wide and seven fingers long. He wrote in his own handwriting on one side "inside," to say that that side should be placed inward toward the birthing woman's navel. On the other side, he wrote "outside," as a sign that it should face outward. At the two ends of the binding, he himself made two linen loops, so as to put a linen cord through them as ties. This binding with the Names was to be placed on the woman's navel and

48. *Sefer toledot adam* (Żółkiew, 1720), no. 86. Cf. nos. 39, 43, 49, 50, 80, and more.
49. Ibid., no. 38. See also nos. 20, 27, 28, 35, and more.

tightened with the cords by pulling them back and tying them there in order that the name binder be tied tightly to her body, so that it would not slip and fall from her belly. One must be very careful not to place the Name binder too early, only when the infant is ready to come out. The midwife who knows how to determine the time when it is necessary would know precisely.

One must also be very careful that the woman herself or the women standing there with her remove the binder immediately as the child emerges, since the woman herself is occupied with her pains and the midwife is busy with taking the child out. So the main responsibility falls on the women standing there with her that they be very, very careful to remove the name binder at the time when the child begins to emerge, for there is a danger, God forbid, that the woman's intestines will also come out after the child. Once this actually happened, the woman's intestines came out, and she died, God save us. So this must be watched very well, and there is a great warning to remove the binder in time and then the woman and child will be safe and sound with the help of God of awesome praise.[50]

Magical means could also be used to combat dangers posed by other mortals, such as thieves and robbers: "Here is a great secret for travel to become invisible [to see and not be seen] by any person who is an enemy, a thief or a violent man. It is tested and checked. I have myself tried it, with the help of God, in dangerous places several times, and it worked and is a great thing."[51] This charm, attributed to Nahmanides, is based on the recitation of certain verses in a fixed order.

The number of *ba'alei shem* began to increase at the end of the seventeenth century and continued to increase during the eighteenth century. Their appearance was concomitant with the rise in interest in popular kabbalistic teachings. *Ba'alei shem* were experts in the realm of the practical, popular Kabbalah. This expertise endowed them with high status in Jewish society. They had the respect of the scholars, even though they themselves often were not scholars. *Ba'alei shem* were very much part of normative communal existence and, at times, attained positions of spiritual leadership. This was probably because no sharp distinctions were drawn between esoteric knowledge in general and magical knowledge in particular. Magic was one dimension of esoterism, of Kabbalah. Thus, the author of *Yesh manhilin* did not distinguish between his father's knowledge of Lurianic Kabbalah and his familiarity with "names." At the same time, there were competing norms that arose from the sense that magical manipulation of divine names was dangerous and to be avoided. The at-

50. Pinehas Katzenellenbogen, *Yesh manhilin,* ed. Yitshak Dov Feld (Jerusalem, 1986), 99.
51. Binyamin Beinish Ba'al Shem Tov ben Yehuda Leib Hakohen of Krotoszyn [Krotoschin], *Sefer shem tov katan* (Żółkiew, 1781), 24a.

taching of taboos to such magic was characteristic of folk magic in general. Nevertheless, the desperation of people enmeshed by demons frequently overcame the prohibition. And precisely the dangerous quality of the magic was an integral part of its attractiveness.

Knowledge of magical techniques was concentrated among, although certainly not confined to, members of the learned elite. A man known as a learned rabbi *and* a *ba'al shem* was perceived as having more extensive powers than an unlearned *ba'al shem*. In fact, most of the *ba'alei shem* known to us from the eighteenth century were indeed learned. On the other hand, it must be recalled that these people are known principally because they themselves published books or are mentioned in the books of others. And books were written by the learned elite.

One of the outstanding figures of the day was the *ba'al shem* Binyamin Beinish Hakohen of Krotoszyn (ca. 1670–ca. 1725), whose published writings included *Sefer shem tov katan* and *Sefer imtahat binyamin*.[52] Binyamin Beinish was not a mystic but an itinerant scholar and kabbalist, and he held no communal office. This suggests that his knowledge of kabbalistic writings such as the Zohar and Lurianic doctrine was extensive. But the epithet—kabbalist—in his case seems most likely to have been connected to his magical skills. Katzenellenbogen calls him "the great *ba'al shem*."[53]

Binyamin Beinish's *Sefer shem tov katan* is informed by kabbalistic ideas and pays much attention to seminal emissions, supplying prayers both to prevent them and to allow those who had experienced them to atone for their sin. Considerable space is devoted to the necessity for sexual purity in marital relations as well. Another section treats the customs and prayers associated with the month of Ellul and the time of the New Year in the light of kabbalistic traditions. Only the last few pages are devoted to talismanic formulae and magic words and names. It is here that one finds the formula for invisibility attributed to Nahmanides, mentioned earlier, ways of protecting a house from fire, removing spells, and the like. The second book, *Imtahat binyamin*, is devoted mainly to magical means for combating illness, sexual dysfunction, and other dangers. Even what appear to be prayers turn out, on closer examination, to be more like magical formulae.

On the cover page of *Imtahat binyamin*, the author links his activities to the saving of lives by medical and magical means, equating this to the

---

52. Ibid.; id., *Sefer imtahat binyamin* (Wilhermsdorf, 1716).
53. *Yesh manhilin*, ch. 22, p. 95.

saving of souls by teaching the Fear of Heaven and repentance: "Just as it is a sacred obligation to arouse all of Israel to follow the path of the Fear of Heaven and of penitence . . . so too a person must save the souls of Israel through charms and cures." Binyamin Beinish was, as noted, an itinerant *ba'al shem*. It would seem that his published works served to enhance his reputation and to foster demand for his services. In his introduction, he explains that one reason he has written is because "expert doctors and pharmacists are to be found only in the larger cities." By "expert doctors," folk healers, practitioners of traditional medicine based on knowledge transmitted from one generation to the next, are meant. Pharmacists were those who knew the healing power of certain plants, flowers, and herbs. So it would seem that the book was intended for residents of small towns and villages who lacked access to expert healers and herbalists. Later though, Binyamin Beinish adds: "Moreover, I have recorded formulas and prayers and charms against enchantment and madness, the evil eye and the falling sickness and all sorts of demonic threats that cannot be treated successfully even by the expert doctors." He indicates that the sources of his knowledge and his talismanic formulae included teachings of Ramban and Isaac Luria. This magical knowledge was linked to the kabbalistic tradition, which served to legitimize it. It was because of this link that *ba'alei shem* were called kabbalists.

Joel ben Uri Heilperin of Zamość (1690–1755) was also known as Joel Ba'al Shem Tov and as Joel II, after his grandfather. Joel ben Yitshak Isaac Heilperin (d. Ostróg, 1713) became rabbi of the rather important community of Ostróg in 1692. He had a considerable reputation as a *ba'al shem* in Podolia and is reported to have saved a ship from sinking and to have driven out a *dibbuk*. His notes regarding charms and names were used by his grandson as the basis for his publications. Although Joel II held no rabbinical post, he was widely regarded as a scholar and as one who knew something of "external" wisdom. His reputation was widely known in Poland and Germany and even in Palestine. He is mentioned by Solomon Maimon (ca. 1753–1800) in the context in which he sought to exemplify the superstitious character of Jewish popular religion and the manipulation of the credulous by *ba'alei shem*. Maimon endeavors to provide a rational explanation for the "miraculous" cures effected by R. Joel. The latter is also mentioned in Katzenellenbogen's *Yesh manhilin* in the course of the author's warning to his sons about the dangers connected with the magical manipulation of "Names": "Even the *ba'al shem*, famous in all the countries in which I have lived, that is, the rabbi . . . master of all wisdoms, our teacher and rabbi Joel Ba'al Shem of the community of

Zamość, who worked his wonders for good, did not emerge unscathed, for two or three years he was struck by the Strict Judgment [a harsh divine decree] and became insane, dying before his time."[54] The respect accorded R. Joel by scholars is attested by his approbation of *Netsah yisra'el* by Israel Zamość (1700–1772).[55] According to the approbation, the two were friends of long standing. That a famous *ba'al shem* accorded such respect to a man generally thought of as a harbinger of the Haskalah, or Jewish Enlightenment, is no less surprising than that the fierce critic of Jewish society in the light of Reason accepted his approbation. It is striking in this context that another of the books approved by R. Joel is *Tavnit habayit* by Mordecai ben Meir of Lublin, whom one scholar has called a traditionalist enlightener *(maskil torani).*[56] Heilperin also gave his approval to two books of *segulot* signifying his authority in the field. Two other books to which he gave his approbation seem in fact to be largely his own work: *Sefer toledot adam*[57] and *Mif'alot elohim.*[58]

Sefer toledot adam is devoted to a relatively small number of problems for which magical solutions are proposed. For the most part, these are issues related to sexual function: inability to conceive; male impotence as a result of witchcraft; pregnancy; problematic births; miscarriages; protecting the birth mother and the infant from demons and witches (along the lines of "if a woman sees a woman suspected of being a witch and there is a basis for thinking she is a witch and eats children, then the woman should . . ."); and falling sickness.

The second book deals with a much broader range of issues, with substantial attention to what we might call first aid. Remedies are provided for the bites of dogs, spiders, and snakes, as well as for earaches, stomachache, and eye infections. Together with this sort of material, there are various incantations and *peules* ("actions"): one enables a person to see paradise; another improves the memory. There are amulets and formulae to ensure the success of a preacher's sermon as well. *Mifalot elokim* is arranged alphabetically in 452 entries for ease of consultation. Its publication, just five years after the earlier work, suggests that the first, more narrowly conceived book, had enjoyed commercial suc-

54. Ibid., p. 89.

55. Israel Zamość, *Netsah yisra'el* (Frankfurt a/O, 1741).

56. Mordecai ben Meir, *Tavnit habayit* (Frankfurt a/O, 1747). The heading of the approbation calls R. Joel "Ba'al Shem Tov." Mendel Piekarz, *Biyemei tsemihat hahassidut* (Jerusalem, 1998), 74, and index, s.v. Mordecai ben Meir.

57. Joel ben Uri Heilperin, *Sefer toledot adam* (Żółkiew, 1720).

58. Joel ben Uri Heilperin, *Mif'alot elohim* (Żółkiew, 1725).

cess sufficient to justify the publisher's investment in another work of the same kind.

The two books share some characteristics. Multiple suggestions are made for addressing one problem, implying that they might be employed simultaneously. Moreover, there is no distinction made between "natural" and magical remedies. They appear together one after the other. This did not mean that the reader could not distinguish between the two: it only meant that it was felt most effective to employ all available means of combating what had to be combated. Since the etiology of an affliction could not be determined, it was best to be comprehensive in fighting it.

The use of herbal medicines was not an essential part of the equipment of the *ba'al shem*, and there were differences among *ba'alei shem* in the degree of expertise that they claimed. Thus, herbal remedies are much more in evidence in the books attributed to R. Joel Ba'al Shem than they are in the books of Binyamin Beinish.

Although, it appears that many people came to Zamość to benefit from the skills of R. Joel Ba'al Shem, he also would travel from town to town. Part of his attraction lay in his lineage, since he was the grandson of a well-known kabbalist-healer. Like Binyamin Beinish and Israel ben Eli'ezer Ba'al Shem Tov, Joel Heilperin was a "professional" *ba'al shem*. He held no communal office and his income derived from his magical and healing activities.

In summary then, during the eighteenth century, kabbalistic ideas were incorporated into the very core of Jewish culture. They became part of the "grammar" of literary and religious and even folk expression. The spread of kabbalistic ideas and practices led to the appearance of a heterogeneous stratum of Pietists called *benei aliyah* and *hassidim,* among other names, who saw themselves and were seen by others as a spiritual elite. These Pietists prayed and studied separately from the rest of the community. Some were undoubtedly also adherents of Shabbateanism, but others were not. Their appearance was part of the same trend that led to a very substantial increase in the number of popular publications informed by Kabbalah. These books and booklets were often *sifrei hanhagot* devoted to detailing and explaining the daily regimen and the customs related to daily life in kabbalistic terms.

At the same time there was a noticeable increase in demand for the services of *ba'alei shem,* who often published books providing instructions based on their own esoteric knowledge and traditions and instructing the readers in the recitation of incantations and the preparation of talismans and amulets. These books themselves generated growing expectations and demands that could be met only by the experts, that is, the *ba'alei shem* themselves. They also raised the status of the authors, who were the self-same *ba'alei shem*.

The phenomenon described here may be termed the professionalization of the occupation of *ba'al shem*. Previous to the eighteenth century, the practices associated with them were carried out by rabbis, and, as in the case of Shabbetai Sheftel Horowitz, prestigious authorities. Although there continued to be such figures in the eighteenth century, most notably, Jonathan Eybeschuetz (d. 1764), a leading rabbinical scholar and probable Shabbatean, the trend was toward specialization and professionalization. The new professionals were itinerant, traveling from place to place to work their cures and simultaneously expanding their markets. That these developments occurred in the eighteenth century is not surprising, inasmuch as it was related to the popularization of Kabbalah.

Finally, the standing of the *ba'alei shem* in the cultural hierarchy was clearly not a lowly one. Certainly, the practitioners whose names are known were treated with respect analogous to that accorded a rabbi, which indeed, some of them were. It bears stressing though that *ba'alei shem* were consulted and honored by all sectors of Jewish society and were not particularly associated with the rustic and backward. It might be said that although their spheres often overlapped, there were three coexistent, different, but equally prestigious types who wielded forms of religious authority in Polish Jewish society in the mid eighteenth century. These were the kabbalist-*hassid*, the *ba'al shem*, and the rabbi.

Shabbateanism and Frankism

The question of how extensive a following Shabbetai Tsevi had in Poland-Lithuania during the brief period between the announcement of his claim to be the Messiah and his apostasy in September 1666 is unresolved.[59] There is no doubt, however, that from the last decades of the seventeenth century on, there were individuals and groups of Jews who maintained a more or less secret allegiance to the continuing Shabbatean movement.

59. Important evidence supporting the contention that from its beginning the movement found a large number of followers in Poland-Lithuania is assembled by Michał Galas, "Sabbatianism in the Seventeenth-Century Polish-Lithuanian Commonwealth: A Review of the Sources," in *The Sabbatian Movement and Its Aftermath: Messianism, Sabbatianism and Frankism,* Jerusalem Studies in Jewish Thought, 17, ed. Rachel Elior (Jerusalem, 2001), 51–63.

Many of them were old-style *hassidim*. Heshel Tsoref (Joshua Heschel ben Joseph, 1663–1700) of Wilno and later Kraków, was a Shabbatean prophet who apparently had a considerable number of followers. Another such figure was Zadok of Grodno, who appeared in the middle 1690s. One of his disciples, Moses ben Aaron HaCohen of Kraków, converted to Christianity out of a genuine belief in the Trinity, fostered by his study of the Zohar at the beginning of the eighteenth century, and subsequently became a professor at the University of Uppsala in Sweden.[60] Between 1696 and 1700, the Polish Shabbateans Hayyim ben Solomon of Kalisz, known as Hayyim Malakh, and Judah Hasid of Szydłowiec acquired a following of perhaps as many as several hundred pious ascetics. In the latter year, the group emigrated to Jerusalem to await the expected reappearance of Shabbetai Tsevi. Jacob Koppel Lifshitz of Międzyrzec composed a kabbalistic and Shabbatean theological work, *Sha'arei gan eden,* in the early years of the eighteenth century.[61] His brother, Hayyim Lifshitz of Ostróg, included clearly Shabbatean materials in a book published in 1703.[62] It seems that Shabbateans were particularly numerous in Podolia, which had been under Ottoman domination between 1672 and 1699. In consequence of this, Jews there likely had developed closer ties to the community of Salonika (Thessaloníki), where the largest group of Shabbateans was centered. Certain towns in Podolia and Volhynia were reputed to be particular focal points of Shabbatean activity.[63] Among these were Buczacz (Buchach), Busk, Gliniany (Glinyany), Horodenka, Żółkiew, Nadworna (Nadvirna), Podhajce, Rohatyn, and Satanów (Satanov). The eighteenth-century memoirist Ber Birkenthal of Bolechów (1722–1805) wrote the following about his youthful encounters with Polish Shabbateans:

Until the year 1742 . . . Moses Bressler and his son . . . of Nadwórna lived in my father's house. . . . My [older] brother told me that these men were members of the sect of the believers in Shabbetai Tsevi. Then we were told more about the

60. Yehuda Liebes, *Sod ha'emunah hashabbeta'it* (Jerusalem, 1995), 222.

61. He composed other works as well. See Isaiah Tishby, *Netivei emunah uminut: massot umehkarim besifrut hakabbalah vehashabbeta'ut* (Jerusalem, 1982), 204–26. On the basis of striking similarities between *Sha'arei gan eden* and the contemporary Shabbatean work by Jonathan Eybeschuetz (1690/95–1764), Tishby suggested cautiously that both might have been influenced by writings by Barukhya Russo, leader of the Doenmeh. Ibid., 222.

62. Ibid., 43–44.

63. A recent contention that there was messianic activity among Polish Shabbateans focused on the year 1740 (5500) is based entirely on the writings of a Pietist missionary and remains unconvincing in the absence of corroboration. Jan Doktór, "Ostatni rabin ziemski Wielkopolski," *Kwartalnik Historii Żydów* 1 (2002): 3–15.

members of the holy community of Nadwórna. On the ninth day of the month of Av [the traditional day of fasting and mourning in memory of the destruction of the Temple], several of them would go out into the fields and the mountains and steal a sheep or a lamb from the flock. They would slaughter it without any heed or knowledge of the halakhah of slaughtering animals and would eat it roasted on fire together with its fat *(helev)* [which is forbidden] on the ninth day of Av. [Because of disappointment at the failure of the messianic era to dawn,] in this time, many of the believers have drawn back and repented confessing the extent of their wickedness and the weight of the sinfulness that they permitted themselves. When I was in Tyśmienica [Tysmenitsa], I myself saw with my own eyes . . . the Zaddik, our teacher, Rabbi Solomon of Podhajce. All his life, he was a complete penitent, fasting daily, immersing himself and indulging in other mortifications until his legs were diseased [*nispehu*]. His only sin was to eat two currants on the Fast Day of the Ninth of Av. There was another man in Tyśmienica whose name was Ya'akov ben Leib. He was young, perhaps twenty years of age or somewhat more. . . . He finally joined the sect of Shabbetai Tsevi and in the year 1759 converted to Christianity with them. . . .

One heard also that they permitted the exchange of wives. If one of them visits the home of his fellow and finds the husband not at home, he tells the wife that he is a member of the sect. [To test him] she hands him a piece of fat that is used for lighting lamps. If he eats it without fear of the divine punishment for the sin of eating fat, she makes herself available to serve his every whim. It is said that they permit themselves all of the thirty-six sins punished by divine punishment [*keritot*] listed in the Torah. Barukhyah [Russo, the leader of the Shabbateans (Doenmeh = converts to Islam) in Thessaloníki] taught them that these thirty-six prohibitions are in fact positive commandments. *Most people do not believe this about them because most of them are learned, constantly studying the holy Zohar deriving from it divine secrets. Some of them hardly sleep at night, mourning the Destruction of the Temple* [emphasis added]. They call themselves kabbalists [*mekubbalim*]; some people are afraid to come in contact with them.[64]

In a general way, the Shabbateans in Poland-Lithuania were divided in two groups, one extreme and one moderate in their behavior. The extremists, perhaps under the influence of Hayyim Malakh, who had returned from Jerusalem, denied the conventional way of Torah entirely. Jacob Frank eventually gathered them together under his own leadership. The moderate group practiced a highly ascetic way of life and carefully obscured their Shabbatean beliefs.[65] This path was rejected ex-

64. Abraham Ya'akov Brawer, *Galitsiyah viyehudeha: Mehkarim betoledot Galitsiyah bame'ah ha18* (Jerusalem, 1956), 211–12.

65. "In my late father's generation, members of this sect were like wild pigs [and ungulates] falsely pretending to be pure. They would fast often and mortify their flesh presenting themselves as *hasidim uperushim*." R. Shelomoh Yitshak Heilperin, rabbi of Bar (1727–

plicitly by Frank, saying: "You who acted secretly, what have you achieved?"[66]

Jacob Leibowicz Frank (1726–1791) traveled as a young man to Thessaloníki, where he became a leader of the Doenmeh—Jews who had followed Shabbetai Tsevi into Islam.[67] In late 1755, Frank returned to Poland, where he claimed to be the reincarnation of the seventeenth-century Messiah. Traveling from town to town in the southeast, he met with underground Shabbatean groups and sought new "converts." Frank's message was antinomian and anarchistic. The rabbinic authorities excommunicated and hounded the Shabbateans because of rumors that their meetings included sexual orgies.

A rabbinical board of inquiry was formed in Satanów that heard testimony from a number of witnesses. As seen above, eating tallow seems to have been a sign of membership or a ritual of initiation in the group.[68] Those who testified confessed to many sins and confirmed the rumors of promiscuity among the Shabbateans. As a result, the regional assembly at Brody pronounced a ban of excommunication against the Shabbateans in June 1756. The ban was also announced in Lwów, Luck, and Dubno.

---

ca. 1784), as cited by Simon Dubnow, *Toledot hahassiduth* (Tel Aviv, 1967), 484–85. See also, as an example, the work by the Shabbatean Yaʿakov ben Yehezkel Segal, *Shem yaʿakov* (1716), 4b: *mah tov umah naʾim kesheyekayyem gilgul hasheleg.*

66. Alexander Kraushar, *Frank i Frankiści Polscy, 1726–1816: Monografia historyczna osnuta na źródłach archiwalnych i rękopismiennych* (Kraków, 1895), vol. 2 (no. 1312), 329–30: "W pierwszem przyjściu mojem do was, do Polski, widzieliście oczyma własnemi, że wszystkie czynności moje były wszem odkryte. Lubożeście mówili, iż macie przykaz, by chód wasz był ukryty, ja mówilem przeciwnie: niechaj koniecznie wie i widzi świat caly. . . . Wy zaś, coście skrycie czynnili, coż stąd wyszlo?" Cf. Jan Doktór, "Jakub Frank: A Jewish Heresiarch and His Messianic Doctrine," *Acta Poloniae Historica* 76 (1997): 58.

67. On Jacob Frank and his followers, see Majer Bałaban, *Letoledot hatenuʿah haFrankit* (Tel Aviv, 1934); Abraham Yaʿakov Brawer, *Galitsiyah viyhudeha;* Doktór, "Jakub Frank," 53–74; id., *Księga Słów Pańskich: Ezoteryczne wykłady Jakuba Franka,* 2 vols. (Warsaw, 1997); id., *Rozmaite adnotacje, przypadki, czynności i anekdoty Pańskie* (Warsaw, 1996); id., *Śladami Mesjasza-Apostaty: Żydowskie ruchy mesjańskie w XVII i XVIII wieku a problem konwersji* (Wrocław, 1998). N. M. Gelber, *Toledot yehudei Brody,* Arim veʿimahot beYisraʾel, vol. 6 (Jerusalem, 1955); Kraushar, *Frank i Frankiści Polscy;* Arthur Mandel, *The Militant Messiah: or, The Flight from the Ghetto: The Story of Jacob Frank and the Frankist Movement* (Atlantic Highlands, N.J., 1979); Bernard Dov Weinryb, *The Jews of Poland: A Social and Economic History of the Jewish Community in Poland from 1100 to 1800* (Philadelphia, 1973), 236–61.

68. Cf. Jacob Emden, *Sefer shimush* (reprint, Jerusalem, 1975), 20; Isaac Rivkind, "Verter mit yikhes," in *Judah H. Joffe Book,* ed. Yudel Mark (New York, 1958), 257–59: "kheylevne apikorsim." And see Moshe Fogel, "Shabbetaʾuto shel sefer *Hemdat yamim:* Hitbonenut mehudeshet," in *The Sabbatian Movement and Its Aftermath: Messianism, Sabbatianism and Frankism,* Jerusalem Studies in Jewish Thought, 17, edited by Rachel Elior, 356–422 (Jerusalem, 2001), 402.

The Council of Four Lands, meeting at Konstantynów in September, further confirmed the decree of excommunication. Jacob Emden published the contents of the bans in his *Sefer shimush*.[69] Those excommunicated were "everyone who believes in Shabbetai Tsevi, that he is the Messiah, and the believers in Barukhya." The ban applied to them and to anyone who knowingly had contact with them or with their books. The council forbade the study of the Zohar or any kabbalistic book, "in print or in manuscript," before the age of thirty. The specific prohibition of the Zohar is consonant with the fact that the Shabbatean followers of Jacob Frank were called "Zoharites" in some of the contemporary Polish sources. More generally, it seems clear that the elders understood that the Shabbateans were concentrated among the circles of students of Kabbalah.

In June 1757, Bishop Mikołaj Dembowski of Kamieniec-Podolski (Kam'yanets-Podil's'kyy) took the Shabbateans under his protection and organized a disputation between the Shabbateans, now labeled "anti-Talmudists," and the rabbis in June 1757. The Church declared the Shabbateans victors in the debate and ordered the burning of the Talmud (and perhaps other books) in Lwów and elsewhere.[70] However, Dembowski, who had meanwhile become archbishop of Lwów, died shortly thereafter, and having lost their powerful patron, the Shabbateans were pursued by their opponents with increased vigor.

Meanwhile, Jacob Frank had left Poland in the spring of 1756 for the Ottoman Empire, where he converted to Islam. In December 1758, he returned to Poland accompanied by a group of his followers. It was then that the archbishop of Lwów was given a letter by the Frankists in which the Jews were accused of using Christian blood for religious purposes. The messenger apparently explained that Frank and his followers were ready to adopt Christianity. This turn of events is usually explained as a case of the Frankists seeking protection in the face of persistent ostracism by the Jewish community. Frank's rationale for this action was his belief that one should adopt and reject every possible religion. In the summer of 1759, a second disputation was held. The Frankists supported the libel that Jews used Christian blood for religious purposes. With this, the Frankists cut themselves off entirely from the Jewish community. Frank and some hundreds of his followers were baptized. The authorities, feeling that Frank was a dangerous influence, incarcerated him in Często-

69. *PVAA*, nos. 751–53, pp. 415–18.
70. See Avraham Ya'ari, "Sereifat hatalmud beKamenets Podolsk," *Sinai* 42 (1958): 294–306.

chowa, where he remained for thirteen years. He was released in 1772 and eventually settled in Offenbach. The group retained its identity in secret, and the sect survived for several generations.

These events were referred to in a sermon delivered in Safed by Perets ben Moshe a little over a decade later. Perets ben Moshe was an itinerant preacher, a kabbalist-*hassid* and a member of the *kloiz* in Brody. Some of the ideas in his published sermons—*Beit Perets* (1759)—anticipate those emphasized in Beshtian Hasidism, such as opposition to asceticism and the duty to worship God in every deed, even such "material" actions as eating, drinking, and sleeping.[71] His sermon "On the Heretics and Shabbetai Tsevi" refers to his having preached against the Shabbateans in Poland in the year in which they apostatized. The earlier text apparently was not published or recorded. In this address, the preacher reviewed the events of 1759:

What happened in 1759 contains hints and portents of what is to befall us at the end of days. [In that year] the deviant heretics of Shabbetai Tsevi tried to destroy us in the presence of the nations. More than two hundred of these Shabbatean heretics had a great debate in Lwów with all the rabbis of Poland. They all became apostates, together with their wives and children. They had a debate with questions and answers before many princes and honorable people of the nations and before many priests and bishops. One of the leaders among them was a Sephardi, a great magician and [manipulator of] evil names. . . . These wicked transgressors of Israel, [believers in] Shabbetai Tsevi, may his name and memory be blotted out, wanted to annihilate the Oral Torah. Because of them, the nations and the priests have burned the whole Talmud, the Zohar, and Maimonides and the *Turim* in the center of the city before the whole people. They ordered . . . the burning of the Oral Torah in all the communities . . . as is well known in all the lands of Poland.

The preacher went on to say that the priest who ordered the burning of the books had a great fall just after this event and died a "strange death," crying out as he died that those books were burning him. Then "all the evil ones apostatized and left the community of Israel." He went on to offer a parable, apparently reproducing words he had uttered at the time of the events, in which he characterized the departure of the Shabbateans as a blessing for the people of Israel, because it purified their ranks.[72]

71. See Piekarz, *Biyemei*, 86–88, and see the other references there s.v. Perets ben Moshe.
72. Avraham Ya'ari, *Ta'alumat sefer: Sefer Hemdat yamim: Mi hibro umah haytah midat hashpa'ato* (Jerusalem, 1954), 129–30; id., "Shenei kuntrasim me'erets Yisra'el," *Kiryat sefer* 23 (1946–47): 155–59.

Another sermon delivered at the time also welcomed the apostasy of the Shabbatean heretics, saying that "now rest and quiet prevail in the land." The preacher blamed the spread of heresy and its consequences on the teaching of esoteric matters to people who were not sufficiently learned and to the young; worse, "they even reveal the secrets of Torah to females."[73] Because of this, they lost the basis of faith.[74]

The full story of the Shabbateans in East Central Europe who did not follow Jacob Frank into apostasy has not been recovered. Many questions remain unanswered and the sources, many of them produced by Christian missionaries, are difficult to evaluate. Finally, the attitudes of Jews who were not "believers" in Shabbateanism were not monolithic.

To summarize, the popularization of Kabbalah significantly altered the "grammar" of Jewish culture in eastern Europe, where Kabbalah was characteristically a mélange of mystical and magical teachings produced by mystics and masters of esoteric lore and included rabbinic, medieval, and sixteenth-century traditions. All these disparate elements, together with others, coexisted despite the inconsistencies among the particular doctrines. What emerged was an alteration of daily life and belief. Even more, we see a culture creating and recreating itself using paints drawn almost entirely from the palette of its own traditions.

73. See Ada Rapoport-Albert, "Al ma'amad hanashim bashabbeta'ut," in *The Sabbatian Movement and Its Aftermath: Messianism, Sabbatianism and Frankism,* Jerusalem Studies in Jewish Thought, 17, edited by Rachel Elior (Jerusalem, 2001), 143–327.

74. Ya'akov Yisra'el Halevi, *Shevet miyisra'el,* as cited by Piekarz, *Biyemei,* 334.

CHAPTER 8

The Contexts of Hasidism

Hasidism was one of many movements of religious enthusiasm that arose in the eighteenth century. It appeared among a population with particular and noteworthy demographic characteristics, namely, a continuously diminishing average age. The concentration of Jews in the eastern half of the Polish-Lithuanian Commonwealth, as I have emphasized, facilitated the production of spiritual, social, and theological innovations, using the palette of Jewish culture. When Hasidism began, Jewish society was still in the thrall of the messianic movement that arose in 1665 around Shabbetai Tsevi and engulfed large numbers of Jews in North Africa, Asia, and Europe. Of primary concern here is the role played by Israel son of Eliʿezer, *the* Baʿal Shem Tov, also known by acronym as the Besht (d. ca. 1760), whom the Hasidic movement treats as the founder and creator of Hasidism. Let us begin this chapter, then, by following the many scholars who have pursued the "historical" Baʿal Shem Tov.

Recent scholarship has changed the "story" of Hasidism's beginnings substantially.[1] Both the Hasidim and subsequent scholars constructed a

---

1. The most convenient bibliography of scholarship on Hasidism to about 1994 can be found in Ada Rapoport-Albert, ed., *Hasidism Reappraised* (London, 1996), 465–91. See also the following general studies: Rachel Elior, *Herut al haluhot: Hamahshavah hahasidit, mekoroteha hamistiyim veyesodoteha hakabbaliyim* (Tel Aviv, 1999); id., "Hasidism: Historical Continuity and Spiritual Change," in *Gershom Scholem's "Major Trends in Jewish Mysticism," Fifty Years After,* ed. Peter Schäfer and Joseph Dan (Tübingen, 1993), 303–23; Immanuel Etkes, *Tenuʿat hahassiduth bereshitah* (Tel Aviv, 1998); Immanuel Etkes et al., eds., *Bemaʿagalei hassidim: Kovets mehkarim lezikhro shel Professor Mordekhai Wilensky* (Jerusalem, 1999); Immanuel Etkes et al., eds., *Mehkerei hassiduth,* Jerusalem Studies in Jewish Thought, 15 (Jerusalem, 1999); Arthur Green, "The *Zaddiq* as *Axis Mundi* in Later Judaism," *Journal of the American Academy of Religion,* 45 (1997): 327–47; Gershon Hundert, "The Contexts of Hasidism,"

history of Hasidism as if it were a movement beginning with a founder, Israel ben Eliʿezer Baʿal Shem Tov, who was followed by an ideologue, Dov Ber, the *maggid* of Międzyrzecz (1704–1772). In this version of events, after the death of the Besht, Dov Ber "decentralized" the movement by sending disciples out to found various Hasidic communities of their own. Hasidic traditions, written and oral, harmonized the image of the beginnings of the movement in light of the more institutionalized forms of later decades, emphasizing the role of the Besht as "founder" of a new movement. Only fragments of this "narrative" have survived the critical analysis of scholars in recent decades.

The very concepts of "social movement" or "religious movement" would have been distinctly foreign to the worldview of the Baʿal Shem Tov.[2] There is no evidence that the Besht had any sort of "mass" following. The notion of "centralized" leadership distorts rather than clarifies what was actually the spontaneous emergence of various groups around charismatic leaders beginning in the decade following the death of the Baʿal Shem Tov. His immediate influence was on a limited circle of mystics and kabbalists, although he did have a considerable reputation as a *baʿal shem*. Ada Rapoport-Albert's introduction of variations of the word "spontaneous" into the discourse of analysis of the rise and spread of Hasidism effectively brought to an end the older approach that treated Hasidism as if it were an ideological movement founded and developed along the lines of those created in late-nineteenth-century eastern Europe.[3]

Israel ben Eliʿezer was first among equals in a group of *hassidim* and mystics. The "circle" was just that; it is anachronistic to describe the Baʿal Shem Tov as a leader *(tsaddik)* and the people around him as his followers (Hasidim). Some of these men, such as Pinehas of Korzec (Phinehas

in *Żydzi wśród Chrześcian w dobie szlacheckiej Rzeczypospolitej*, ed. Waldemar Kowalski and Jadwiga Muszynska (Kielce, 1996), 171–84. Moshe Idel, *Hasidism: Between Ecstasy and Magic* (Albany, N.Y., 1995); Mendel Piekarz, *Hahanhagah hahassidit: Samkhut veʾemunat tsaddikim baʾaspaklariyat sifrutah shel hahassiduth* (Jerusalem, 1999).

2. Two new books on the Besht have appeared in recent years: Moshe J. Rosman, *Founder of Hasidism: A Quest for the Historical Baʿal Shem Tov* (Berkeley, 1996), and Immanuel Etkes, *Baʿal haShem: HaBesht: Magiyah, mistikah, hanhagah* (Jerusalem, 2000). A third, by Rachel Elior, *R. Yisraʾel Baʿal Shem Tov: Bein magiyah lemistikah. Diyukan ruhani vehashpaʿot tarbutiyot baʿolam hayehudi bemizrah Eiropah bamahatsit harishonah shel hameʾah ha18*, is in press.

3. Ada Rapoport-Albert, "Hasidism after 1772: Structural Continuity and Change," in id., ed., *Hasidism Reappraised*, 76–140, and in Hebrew: "Hatenuʿah hahassidit ahar shenat 1772: Retsef miveni utemurah," *Zion* 55 (1990): 183–245.

ben Abraham Abba Shapiro, 1726–1791), Nahman of Kosów (d. 1746), and others, had their own circles of companions and followers.[4] It seems likely that, early in his life, Israel ben Eli'ezer, the Ba'al Shem Tov, was associated with the group around the distinguished rabbi and kabbalist Moses of Kutów (1688–1738).[5] Although the reliable historical evidence about him is thin, there are sufficient grounds to try to construct a "historical Ba'al Shem Tov" in such a way that his towering image in historical memory can be understood.[6]

Israel ben Eli'ezer Ba'al Shem Tov

Israel ben Eli'ezer was born around the turn of the eighteenth century and spent his childhood in Okopy, or Okop Góry Święty Trojcy, a town on the Polish side of the new frontier with Ottoman Turkey established by the Treaty of Karlowitz in 1699. He began his career as a *ba'al shem* in the nearby town of Tłuste, but around 1740, he moved to Międzyboż (Medzhybizh), where he remained until his death (ca. 1760).

Międzyboż, where the Ba'al Shem Tov spent the last two decades of his life, was a private town, owned by the Czartoryski family, and a thriving center of trade. It was home to one of the largest Jewish communities in Ukraine, and like many other such towns, it provided financial support in the form of housing and exemption from taxes to a small group of scholars and pietists, most probably five. One of these was Israel Ba'al

4. Rosman, *Founder,* especially ch. 11; Ada Rapoport-Albert, "Hasidism after 1772," 80–94, and in Hebrew: "Hatenu'yah hahassidit ahar shenat 1772," 187–201.

5. Rosman, *Founder,* 126.

6. The most extreme position on this matter has been taken by Moshe Rosman who rejects the reliability of virtually all traditions that date from the period after the Besht's death, such as the numerous quotations in the works of Ya'akov Yosef of Połonne and other companions and disciples of the Besht and the stories in the book *In Praise of the Baal Shem Tov.* Others have suggested that these traditions can be evaluated critically and used to reconstruct the teachings of the Besht. Most insistent in this regard is Immanuel Etkes, *Ba'al haShem.* Rachel Elior has maintained in effect that Hasidic memory is more important than historicity, because for subsequent generations all the traditions attributed to the Besht were bound together. Moreover, the differences among these various traditions are less important than what they have in common. Rachel Elior, "R. Yosef Karo veR. Yisra'el Ba'al Shem Tov: Metamorfozah mistit, hashra'ah kabbalit, vehafnamah ruhanit," *Tarbiz* 65 (1996): 671–708; id., *Herut al haluhot,* 87; Rosman, *Founder;* Immanuel Etkes, "HaBesht hahistori: Bein rekonstruktsiah ledekonstruktsiah," *Tarbiz* 66 (1997): 425–42; id., "HaBesht kemistikan uva'al besorah be'avodat HaShem," *Zion* 61 (1996): 421–54.Cf. Gershom Scholem, "Demuto hahistorit shel R. Yisra'el Ba'al Shem Tov," in id., *Devarim bego* (Tel Aviv, 1975), 287–324.

Shem Tov. This suggests that his reputation was already established when he came to Międzyboż. The Besht and his companions studied Torah and Kabbalah in a study hall, or *kloiz*. What made him worthy of communal support was probably the fact that he combined in himself a number of usually distinct roles.

He was, first, a *ba'al shem*, in all of the traditional ways discussed above. As the scholar Moshe Rosman discovered, Polish tax rolls from this period refer to him variously as "the Kabbalist," "the Ba'al Shem," and once as *Balszam Doktor*. Rosman translates the latter designation as "The Ba'al Shem, the doctor," taking it to reflect the Besht's healing skills, of which non-Jews were occasionally the beneficiaries.[7] The term *doktor*, however, according to a contemporary popular Polish encyclopedia, meant "teacher" or "rabbi" and not "doctor."[8] In any event, it is clear that the Besht was a healer of souls and bodies, as well as a teacher. He was, in addition, a mystic who had gained knowledge and insight through his experiences of "the ascent of the soul."

The activities of the Besht as a *ba'al shem* were characteristic. He wrote amulets, exorcised demons, could see across vast distances, and healed the sick. The Ba'al Shem Tov's clientele, therefore, included distinguished rabbis, scholars, wealthy merchants, and prosperous estate managers.[9]

On learning that his brother's child had fallen ill, Moses of Kutów wrote to the Besht, who was still at the time in Tłuste, and asked him to travel to Horodenka to treat the child. The Besht's response included a prescription for treatment, using what might be called "herbal medicine," and announced his immediate departure for Horodenka. Moses of Kutów was the leader of a fraternity of old-style *hassidim*, members of which had close links with the Besht. In about 1743 or 1744, the Besht was one of two signatories to a halakhic question addressed to Rabbi Me'ir of Konstantynów, the oldest son of Jacob Emden. The Besht signed his name, Israel Ba'al Shem of Tłuste. Among the rather hyperbolic epithets of praise for the Besht found in the letter answering the question is: "He provides remedy and healing to the person without strength." R. Me'ir also says

7. Rosman, *Founder*, 165.

8. A table of Polish equivalents and definitions of Latin terms: Latin: *doctor*; Polish: *doktor*; definition: *nauczyciel* (that is, "teacher"). Benedykt Chmielowski, *Nowe Ateny albo Wszelkiej scyencyi Pełna, na Rózne Tytuły iak na Classes Podźielona* (Lwów, 1755), vol. 4, 375. In 1715, a priest, testifying as to events leading to his being beaten by Jews, mentioned that he had gone to the house of the rabbi and asked whether he or his wife were in: "spytałem się jeżeli jest doktor albo doktorowa." Adam Kaźmierczyk, *Żydzi Polscy, 1648–1772: Źródła* (Kraków, 2001), no. 82, 144 (Oleszyce, 1715).

9. Etkes, *Tenu'at hahassiduth*, 24.

that the Besht is "famous for his good name."[10] The salutation of the response also referred to "all his [the Besht's] colleagues," but it named only "the great and eminent sage, our teacher Gershon"—that is, [Abraham] Gershon of Kutów (Kuty) (d. ca. 1760), the Besht's brother-in-law.[11] In 1748, two years after Gershon of Kutów had emigrated to Palestine, he wrote to the Besht from Hebron. In the course of the letter, he wrote, "How good it would be if you could send me an amulet for general purposes, and there would be no need for a new one every year."[12] As mentioned earlier, the Besht journeyed to Słuck in 1733 to bless the new house of the *arriviste* Ickowicz family and protect it from demons.[13]

Other sources confirm the association of the Besht with members of certain distinguished families, including David Heilperin ben Yisrael (d. 1765), a prosperous member of a very illustrious family, who from 1737 on was the rabbi of the important community of Ostróg.[14] Later, it is said, he left office and went to live in Zasław as a private citizen. Heilperin's published testament included bequests of quite substantial sums to many of the Besht's associates:

(a) *Mokhiah* of Połonne: 150 florins and my fur coat [*tuzlik*] [= Aryeh Judah Leib (The "Rebuker") of Połonne (d. 1770)]

(b) *Maggid* of Międzyrzecz: 150 florins [= Dov Ber (The "Preacher") of Międzyrzecz (d. 1772)]

(c) *Maggid* of Złoczów (Zolochiv), Jehiel Michael ben Isaac of Drohobycz (Drogobych): 150 florins [= Jehiel Michael ("Mikhl") of Złoczów (ca. 1731–1786)]

(d) Pinhas of Korzec: 150 florins and the hat that I recently acquired [= Phinehas ben Abraham Abba Shapiro (1726–1791)]

10. Gershom Scholem suggests that this may have been a pun alluding to his occupation as *ba'al shem tov*. On this source, see Rosman, *Founder,* 116–19, 127–28; Scholem, "Demuto," 291–92; Benzion Dinur, "Reshitah shel hahasidut veyesodoteha hasotsiyaliyim vehameshihiyim" (1955), reprinted in id., *Bemifneh hadorot* (Jerusalem, 1972), 83–227, esp. 205–6.
11. See "Rabbi Gershon Kutover: His Life and Immigration to the Land of Israel," in Abraham Joshua Heschel, *The Circle of the Baal Shem Tov: Studies in Hasidism,* ed. Samuel H. Dresner (Chicago, 1985), 44–112. The original Hebrew version can be found in *Hebrew Union College Annual* 23 (1950–51), pt. 2, 17–71.
12. Rosman, *Founder,* 129.
13. Adam Teller, "Masoret Sluck al reshit darko shel haBesht," in *Mehkerei hassiduth,* ed. Immanuel Etkes et al., Jerusalem Studies in Jewish Thought, 15 (Jerusalem, 1999), 15–38.
14. Abraham Hayyim Rubinstein, *Shivhei haBesht: Mahadurah mu'eret umevu'eret* (Jerusalem, 1991), s.vv. "Heilperin, David."

(e) Wolf Kuces: 100 florins [= Ze'ev Wolf Kuces, a scholar and *hassid* closely associated with the Besht][15]

(f) *Maggid* of Bar: 100 florins [= Menahem Mendel, the Preacher of Bar; probably an associate of the Besht][16]

(g) Zalman of Miédzyrzecz: 100 florins [= brother of Aryeh Leib Heilperin]

(h) Leib Heilperin: 100 florins [= Aryeh Leib Heilperin of Międzyrzecz, a leader of the Ostróg *hevrah kadisha* (d. 1775)][17]

(i) Nahman of Horodenka: 150 florins [student/disciple of the Besht (d. 1780); he emigrated to the Land of Israel in 1764]

(j) R. Fridl: 150 florins

(k) R. David son-in-law of the Rabbi of Stepań: 100 florins

(l) Tsevi son of "the Rabbi Ba'al Shem": 100 florins [= Tsevi Hirsh, son of the Besht]

(m) *Maggid* of Ostróg: 50 florins [= possibly the father [d. 1766] of Jacob Joseph (R. Yeivi) of Ostróg]

(n) And bequests to the poor of the holy land to be distributed by [Menahem] Mendel of Przemyślany (Peremyshlyany) [emigrated to the Land of Israel in 1764][18]

Immanuel Etkes has tentatively suggested that what distinguished those who received bequests of 150 florins from those who received only 100 was the esteem in which R. David held them. Aryeh Judah Leib (The "Rebuker") of Połonne, Dov Ber, the *maggid* of Międzyrzecz, Jehiel Michael ("Mikhl"), the *maggid* of Złoczów, Pinhas of Korzec, Nahman of Horodenka, and Menahem Mendel of Przemyślany were all charismatic individuals, many of whom led their own groups of Hasidim.[19] In fact, the only person prominently associated with the Ba'al Shem Tov not mentioned in the document was Jacob Josef of Połonne. His status, though, apparently depended on his being a disciple of the Besht. All

15. See Rosman, *Founder*, s.v. "Kuces."

16. See the references assembled by Idel, *Hasidism*, 260, n. 84.

17. See Dan Ben-Amos and Jerome R. Mintz, *In Praise of the Baal Shem Tov: The Earliest Collection of Legends about the Founder of Hasidism* (Bloomington, Ind., 1970), 116.

18. *Darkei tsiyon* (Połonne? 1796); also in *Sefer hayahas lemishpahat Heilperin* (Tel Aviv, 1982), 44. Details according to Heschel, *Circle*, 41, n. 202.

19. Etkes, *Ba'al haShem*, 214–15.

the others had independent standing as spiritual masters and their own followings.[20] The most influential among them was the scholar, kabbalist, and mystic Dov Ber, the *maggid* of Międzyrzecz, who, together with his disciples, developed not only new aspects of Hasidic teaching but the forms of organization and leadership that became *the* characteristics of Hasidism. Yet, in memory, not even Dov Ber had the stature of the Ba'al Shem Tov. One key to the Besht's stature was that he took on himself, and he did this without holding office and without communal sanction, the task of defending the whole people of Israel. According to traditions that date from a later time, he even intervened on behalf of Jewish leaseholders threatened by unfair competition or with imprisonment because they could not pay their debts to their lords.[21]

Another manifestation of the Besht's concern for the well-being of his people was his interest in supervising the slaughter of animals according to *halakhah*.[22] Concern with proper slaughter was characteristic also of the old-style *hassidim*, and, in this, he merely continued that tradition. He sought to ensure that the proper procedure was followed, particularly in the villages, where the *shohetim* might not be sufficiently learned in the laws of *kashrut*.[23] There was also the possibility that some of the slaughterers might be Shabbateans who would deliberately cause the meat to be ritually unacceptable.[24] The bans against the Hasidim in 1772 particularly objected to the Hasidic insistence on slaughter with special types of

20. Jehiel Michael ("Mikhl"), the *maggid* of Złoczów, established not only his own community of followers, which, in this case, was an elite brotherhood that was a continuation in many ways of old-style *hassidism*, but also a kind of school of thought that continued for another generation. In fact, this chain may have begun earlier, as the father of Jehiel Mikhl was Isaac of Drohobycz, a *ba'al shem* and preacher of considerable reputation, and possibly a rival of the Besht. See the claims advanced by Mor Altshuler, "Mishnato shel R. Mehullam Feibush Heller umekomah bereshit hatenu'ah hahassidit" (Ph.D. diss., Hebrew University, Jerusalem, 1994). Heschel, *Circle*, 152–74, 178–81. R. Isaac's father was known as R. Yosef Spravidliver. Heschel translates the name "Spravidliver" to mean "Truthful." In my opinion, however, *sprawiedliwy* is better translated as "just," i.e., the *tsaddik*. R. Isaac's mother was called Yente or Yentl the prophetess. We have, then, three generations of charismatic leaders, including at least one female.

21. Chone Shmeruk, "Hahassiduth ve'iskei hahakirot," in *Hakeriy'ah lenavi: Mehkerei historiyah vesifrut*, ed. Yisrael Bartal (Jerusalem, 1999), 64–77; Etkes, *Ba'al haShem*, 110–11.

22. Chone Shmeruk, "Mashma'utah hahevratit shel hashehitah hahassidit," in id., *Hakri'ah lenavi: Mehkerei historiyah vesifrut*, ed. Israel Bartal (Jerusalem, 1999), 33–63; first published in *Zion* 20 (1955): 47–72.

23. See e.g., Jacob Josef of Połonne, *Toledot ya'akov yosef* (Korzec, 1780; photo-offset reprint, Jerusalem, 1966), 78a, 123a.

24. Ben-Amos and Mintz, *In Praise of the Baal Shem Tov*, 32, 40, 45, 90–91, 192, 211–212; Etkes, *Ba'al haShem*, 111–15; id., *Tenu'at hahassiduth*, 31–33.

knives. The custom of using special knives "began apparently in the court of Dov Ber, the *maggid* of Międzyrzecz."[25] That is, sometime after the death of the Besht in 1760.[26]

The most famous and influential of the few texts attributed to the Besht himself is a letter written in about 1752 to his brother-in-law, (Abraham) Gershon of Kutów, who had emigrated to the Land of Israel in 1747, known as "the holy epistle" *(igeret hakodesh)*. The various versions of this have been analyzed carefully by scholars.[27] The following is from the text deemed to be the most authentic version:

On Rosh Hashanah 5510 [1749], I performed an ascent of the soul, as is known, and I saw a great accusation, until the Evil Side almost received permission to completely destroy regions and communities.[28] I put my life in jeopardy and I prayed: "Let us fall into the hand of God and not fall into the hands of man." And they gave me permission that instead of this [Haidamak (Cossack) attacks are probably meant here], there would be great epidemics and unprecedented plague in all of the regions of Poland and our neighboring areas. So it was that the epidemic spread so much that it could not be measured, and likewise the plague in the other areas. And I arranged with my group [*havurah*] to say *ketoret*[29] upon arising to cancel this decree. And they revealed to me in a night vision: "Did not you yourself choose 'Let us fall into God's hand' etc.? Why do you want to cancel? Is it not

25. Shaul Stampfer, "Lekorot mahloket hasakinim hamelutashot," in *Mehkerei hassidut*, ed. Immanuel Etkes et al., Jerusalem Studies in Jewish Thought, 15 (Jerusalem, 1999), 201. Shmeruk, "Mashma'utah hahevratit shel hashehitah hahassidit"; Mendel Piekarz, *Biyemei tsemihat hahassidut: Megamot ra'ayaniyot besifrei derush,* rev. ed. (Jerusalem, 1998), 383–87.

26. For all that the Besht was a *ba'al shem* and performed his healing and other services for individuals, including, according to legend, the family of R. David Heilperin, he also brought a unique dimension to those activities. He intervened in heaven not only on behalf of individuals but also in the name of the whole People of Israel. Here, we find ourselves at the cloudy and vague cusp between magic and mysticism. The integration of magic into our understanding of the core elements of Jewish life in eastern Europe in general and of Hasidism in particular is reflected in the use of the term in the titles of recent books (see nn. 1–2 above) such as Moshe Idel's *Hasidism: Between Ecstasy and Magic,* Immanuel Etkes's *Ba'al haShem: HaBesht: Magiyah, mistikah, hanhagah* ("Master of the Name: The Besht: Magic, Mysticism, Leadership"), and Rachel Elior's *R. Yisra'el Ba'al Shem Tov: Bein magiyah lemistikah* ("R. Israel Baal Shem Tov: Between Magic and Mysticism").

27. Rosman, *Founder,* 97–113; Etkes, *Ba'al haShem,* 88–109, 292–309. And see Abraham Rubinstein, "Igeret haBesht leR. Gershon miKutów," *Sinai* 67 (1970): 120–39, and the other scholarly literature cited by Rosman and Etkes.

28. The translations from the letter generally follow Rosman, but I have made some changes. I have also consulted translations of the published version by Norman Lamm, "The Letter of the Besht to R. Gershon of Kutov," *Tradition* 14 (1974): 110–25, and an unpublished translation by Zalman Schachter.

29. A Talmudic passage that is part of the standard liturgy but which, according to Lurianic traditions, was thought to be effective in sparing souls from plague. See Etkes, *Ba'al haShem,* 99, n. 28.

accepted that the prosecutor cannot [become the defender]?" From then on, I did not say *ketoret* and I did not pray about this except by means of several adjurations due to great fear on *Hoshanah Rabbah* [the last day of the holiday of Tabernacles (Sukkoth)]. I went then to the synagogue with the entire congregation. And I said *ketoret* one time so that the plague would not spread to our own environs. With the help of God, we succeeded.[30]

This passage is a description of the second of two such "soul ascents" in which the Besht learned why the Jewish people were experiencing persecution and suffering. In the other vision, he learned the reason for charges of ritual murder in Zasław, Szepietówka (Shepetivka), and Dunajów, or Dunajgród (Dunayev). That is, the Besht put his mystical and theurgical skills in the service of his people. Unlike earlier mystics who had sought to learn the secrets of the Divine in the course of their visionary experiences, the Besht used his powers to intervene in heaven on behalf of his fellows. He even debated with Sama'el (Satan) himself.

The other vision described in the letter to his brother-in-law includes one passage that has been the subject of much debate among scholars.[31] In the course of learning the explanation for the series of ritual murder accusations, the Besht met the Messiah:

On Rosh Hashanah 5507, I performed an adjuration for the ascent of the soul that is known to you,[32] and I saw wondrous things in a vision[33] [which I had not seen from the day that I became conscious until now. And what I saw and learned when ascending there is impossible to tell about and to speak of even face-to-face. But when I returned to lower paradise, I saw certain souls of the living and the dead, both familiar and unfamiliar to me, without measure or number, running back and forth[34] to ascend from world to world via the pillar known to mystical initiates.[35] The mouth could not describe the great joy that was there, nor could the physical ear ever hear it [Isa. 59:1]. Many sinners also repented and their sins were

30. Rosman, *Founder,* 107.

31. Dinur, "Reshitah shel hahasidut veyesodoteha hasotsiyaliyim vehameshihiyim"; Idel, *Hasidism,* 79; Rubinstein, "Igeret haBesht leR. Gershon miKutów"; Scholem, "Demuto," 287–324; id., *The Messianic Idea in Judaism* (New York, 1971), 178–84; Isaiah Tishby, "Hara'ayon hameshihi vehamegamot hameshihiyot bitsmihat hahasiduth," *Zion* 32 (1967): 1–45.

32. The last phrase can also be read "as is known to you." I follow Idel's interpretation here.

33. The following passage in square brackets appeared only in the later, printed version of the letter (Jacob Josef of Połonne, *Ben porat yosef* [Korzec, 1781]), but may be a homoteleuton, according to Rosman, because this section and the one following begin with the same word, *bemar'eh.*

34. Ezek. 1:14. See Idel, *Hasidism,* 319, n. 138, 328, n. 246, and the references there.

35. The spinal column of the Primordial Adam which is also the ladder of the angels.

forgiven them, since it was a time of grace. In my eyes also it was most surprising that certain ones who are known to you were accepted as penitents. They too were exceedingly happy and were able to ascend. All of them as one asked me and pleaded with me saying, "O exalted and honored teacher, God has granted you exceeding understanding to know about these matters. Go up with us to be a help and support to us." And because of the great joy that I saw among them, I agreed to go up with them. And I saw in a vision:] The Evil Side ascended to accuse with great, unparalleled joy and executed his deeds—persecutions entailing forced conversion—on several souls so that they would meet violent deaths. I was horrified and I literally put my life in jeopardy and asked my teacher and rabbi[36] to go with me because it is very dangerous to go and ascend to the upper worlds. For from the day I attained my position, I had not ascended such lofty ascents.

I went up step by step until I entered the messianic palace where the Messiah studies Torah with all of the *Tanna'im*[37] and the righteous [*tsaddikim*] and also with the Seven Shepherds.[38] And there I saw exceedingly great joy and I do not know the reason for this joy. I thought this joy was—God forbid—over my decease from this world [in this ecstasy][39] but they informed me afterward that I was not yet to die, because in the upper spheres they derive pleasure when I perform unifications [*yihudim*] down below by meditating on their holy teachings. The reason for the joy I still do not know. And I asked the Messiah, "When will the master come?" And he answered me, "Once your teaching [*Torah*] will have spread throughout the world," etc.

And I prayed there [in the palace of the Messiah] over why God did this—what was the reason for the great wrath that led to some souls of Israel being given over to the Evil Side for killing and, of them, several souls apostatized and afterward were killed. And they gave me permission to ask the Evil Side himself directly. I asked the Evil Side why he did this, and how he viewed their converting and then being killed. He replied to me that his intention was for the sake of heaven. For if they were to remain alive after apostatizing, then when some other persecution or libel occurred, they would not sanctify the name of heaven; rather everyone would just convert to save themselves. Therefore he acted; those who converted were later killed so that no son of Israel would convert and they would sanctify the name of heaven. Thus it was that afterward, because of our many sins, in the community of Zasław there was a libel against several souls [in 1747] and

36. According to Jacob Josef of Połonne, *Sefer toledot ya'akov yosef,* Balak, 156a: "Ahijah the Shilonite . . . who was the teacher of Elijah the Prophet and the teacher [*rabbo*] of my teacher." Mystical tradition numbers him among the seven whose life spans include all of time. The others are: Adam, Methusaleh, Shem, Jacob, Terah or Amram, and Elijah. See Etkes, *Ba'al haShem,* 103, n. 32, and Rosman, *Founder,* 249, n. 59, and the references there.

37. The term that designates rabbis mentioned in the Mishnah edited at the beginning of the third century.

38. Adam, Methusaleh, Seth, Abraham, Jacob, Moses, David [TB Sukkah 52b] *or* Abraham, Isaac, Jacob, Joseph, Moses, Aaron, David.

39. Zalman Schachter has suggested reading "my decease from this world" as equivalent to the Yiddish *nifter vern,* that is, being rid of the world.

two of them converted and later they killed them.[40] The rest sanctified the name of heaven in great holiness and died violent deaths. And then there were libels in the communities of Szepietówka (Shepetivka) and Dunajów, or Dunajgród, in 1748, and they did not convert after they saw what happened in Zasław, but all of them gave their souls for the sanctification of God's Name and sanctified the name of heaven and withstood the test.[41] And by virtue of this act may our Messiah come and take our vengeance. And God will conciliate His land and His people.[42]

The Besht returned from his ascent having failed to "avert the evil decree" but with knowledge about the etiology of the persecutions of his day. Sentence was pronounced against the accused Jews in Zasław in April 1747. The Dunajgród trial began a year later (the mother of the child allegedly offered to sell her son to Jews in Dunajgród on April 17, 1748) and the prosecution invoked the sentence in Zasław.[43] Since Rosh Hashanah 5507 occurred on September 15–16, 1746, the dates of the ritual murder trials cast doubt on the dating of the visionary experience as reported by the Besht. Presumably, the Besht's vision was a case of *vaticinium ex post eventu*.

Among his small circle of colleagues and disciples, to whom he revealed his extraordinary visions,[44] the Besht arrogated to himself the position of leader of Israel in his generation *(rosh hador; gedol hador)*. His willingness to share not only what he had beheld during his "soul ascents" but his mystical techniques themselves ("adjuration for the ascent of the soul that is known to you"), at least with those of his intimate circle *(anshei gilo)*, contributed to his attractiveness as a leader.[45]

The other versions of the letter provide more detail about the meeting with the Messiah. These longer versions can be taken to reflect either the views of the Besht or those of Hasidic leaders, and especially the *maggid* of Międzyrzecz, around 1780. In no version is the meeting charged with eschatological urgency. Nor is there any indication in the passage it-

---

40. According to other sources, only one Jew apostatized, and he was later executed. Zenon Guldon and Jacek Wijaczka, "The Accusation of Ritual Murder in Poland, 1500–1800," *POLIN* 10 (1997): 130.

41. According to I. Galant, cited in ibid., 130–31, three Jews were convicted in the Dunajgród case and sentenced to terms of one year and six weeks in prison. In Szepietówka, two Jews were executed.

42. Rosman, *Founder,* 106–7.

43. Guldon and Wijaczka, "Accusation," 130–31.

44. A third visionary experience is recounted in Ben-Amos and Mintz, *In Praise of the Baal Shem Tov,* 54–58. All three occurred during the Days of Awe, when the gates of heaven are open wide.

45. Idel, *Hasidism,* 291, n. 200.

self or in any other tradition attributed to the Besht or his associates that they sought "to bring the Messiah." The following is the passage as it appears in a manuscript dated 1776 (the translation is not strictly literal):

I came and entered the actual palace of the King Messiah. And I actually saw face-to-face what I had not seen from the day that I became conscious until now. They revealed to me, "this [joy] is not for your sake." They also revealed to me wonderful and awesome things in the depths of the Torah that I had not seen or heard and that no ear has heard for many years. And I decided to ask him if possibly this joy and happiness was related to the preparation of his coming, and "when will my master come?" His Highness answered: "It cannot be revealed, but by this will you know it [Exod. 7:17]: when your teaching [or 'what you have learned' *limudekha*] will become renowned and revealed throughout the world, when your springs are dispersed abroad [Prov. 5:16], [enlightening others with] what I have taught you and you have understood. Then they too will be able to perform unifications [*yihudim*] and ascents like you. Then all the *kelipot*[46] will perish and it will be a time of goodwill and salvation." I was astonished and exceedingly unhappy at the very long time [this would take]. When could this possibly occur? From what I heard, however—three things that are remedies [*segulot*] and three holy names that are easy to learn and to explain—I was assuaged. I thought that it was possible in this manner for distinguished people [*anshei segulah;* in the printed version, *anshei gili,* "my colleagues"] to attain this level and category as I do. That is, they would be able to perform ascents to heaven of the soul and to study and become like me. But I was not given permission to reveal this as long as I live. I asked on your behalf [for permission] to teach you, but they forbade it. On this, I remain bound by oath from there.[47]

The reference to the "teaching" that, when universally known, would bring about redemption is ambiguous. Does it refer to "unifications" and "ascents of the soul," that is, contemplative techniques and modes of ecstatic mysticism? Or does it refer to remedies and holy names that are the province of *ba'alei shem?* Since the Besht combined in himself the roles of leader, magician, and mystic, the distinction seems artificial. Surely, if everyone had the remarkable talents of the Besht, it would indeed be a messianic time. *However, he is forbidden to reveal what he has learned.* Not even his learned brother-in-law is exempt from this prohibition. If the Messiah's coming depends on the spreading of the special knowledge of the Besht so that everyone will be an adept like him, and if, further, he is

46. Lit., "shells." This is a reference to Lurianic teaching. The *kelipot* are the shards of the shattered vessels that contained the divine light emanated in the act of creation. They are the source of evil in the world.

47. Etkes, *Ba'al haShem,* appendix 2, 292–99, presents the three versions of the letter[s] in parallel columns.

forbidden to reveal his special knowledge gained in the actual palace of the Messiah, then redemption depends on an act of divine grace, which is precisely the traditional view. Immanuel Etkes has suggested that what the Messiah might have meant was that if there actually were others at the Besht's high level who were worthy of rising to the highest chambers of heaven, then it would be possible to destroy the *kelipot* and redemption would come to the world.[48]

The Message of the Besht and His Colleagues

The concern of the Besht in his teachings and the concern of most subsequent Hasidic masters was not the redemption of the nation but the redemption of the individual. In the pithy, aphoristic style characteristic of most of the sayings attributed to him, the Besht is said to have interpreted the passage in the prayer for welcoming the Sabbath, *Lekha dodi* ("Come My Beloved"), that reads: "Draw near to my soul to redeem it" *(karvah el nafshi ge'alah)* to emphasize that it is in the first person singular. It does not say "Draw near to *our* souls to redeem us"; each soul must find its own redemption. "Just as there is a general redemption of the community of Israel, so also is there a redemption of the individual, of each soul of Israel."[49]

Although he was not permitted to reveal the secrets he had learned from the Messiah, the Ba'al Shem Tov offered the following instruction to his brother-in-law as a kind of compensation:

During the time of your prayer and of your study, with every single utterance and all vocality, intend [in the MS version, "know how"] to unify [a Name]. For in every single letter, there are worlds and souls and divinity. And these ascend and link with each other and unite with each other. After that the letters link up with each other and unite together with each other and a word is formed. And they unite in a total unity in the Divine. Let your soul be a part of them in each and every stage of this. All the worlds will unite as one and ascend [so that there will be] great joy and happiness without limit. You understand the joy of the uniting of bride and groom in a normal state of consciousness [*katnut*] and corporeality, how much more so on a high level such as this.[50]

48. Etkes, *Ba'al haShem*, 95.

49. Abraham ben Alexander Katz [Kalisker], *Hesed le'avraham* (Lemberg [Lwów], 1851), 44b. And see there 46b, where this possibility is reserved for the *tsaddik:* "As it will be in the days of the Messiah [for every person] . . . it can be for the *tsaddik* who worships God in truth . . . that the words 'Draw near to my soul to redeem it' will be fulfilled, that is, individual redemption."

50. Ibid., 297–98.

Since the Torah is divine, so too is its language, and likewise each and every letter of the Hebrew alphabet. The infinity of divinity is in each one. The divinity enclosed in each letter is the focus of meditation, not the meaning of the words.[51] Although he mentions both study and prayer, the latter was at the center of the concerns of the Ba'al Shem Tov. The quest for continuous attachment to the Divine expressed itself in techniques of ecstatic prayer. The letters were to be pronounced individually and drawn out so that one could "enter" them, as if they were palaces.

The Besht was the leader of a group of mystics and scholars in Międzybóż,[52] and it was to members of his *havurah* (fellowship/fraternity) and to other scholars that he revealed and preached his message. The central idea in the Besht's message turned on the Divine Presence in the world. "There is nothing devoid of Him" ("Leit atar panui minei"). God fills all the worlds and surrounds all the worlds. Everything is divine. This was a joyful insight that implicitly rejected dualism, and formed the basis for many of his teachings. The Hasidic masters, including the Besht, were not systematic theologians. Attempts to identify or extract a Hasidic theology and to characterize Hasidism as if it taught a consistent set of doctrines miss its essence. Not only were there differences among various groups, but individual teachers seem to have been inconsistent in the ideas they taught. It is true that the general weight of the traditions ascribed to the Besht indicates monistic, panentheistic, and immanentist views. These indeed, seem to be characteristic of much Hasidic teaching in the latter half of the eighteenth century. Nevertheless, it is important not to demand philosophical consistency of insights gained in mystical ecstasy and spiritual intensity.

The personal charisma of the man and his descriptions of his own mystical experiences lent authority to his preaching. In a letter to his disciple Rabbi Jacob Josef of Połonne, the Besht could invoke "the decrees of the angels [Dan. 4:14] and . . . the Holy One, Blessed be He and His Presence [*Shekhinah*]" in adjuring Jacob Josef to change his behavior and take up a superior spiritual path.[53] The letter orders Jacob Josef not to place himself in danger by frequent fasting and mortification, because "this is the way of melancholy and sadness." It is a futile path, because "the Divine Presence [*Shekhinah*] does not inspire out of sorrow, but only out

51. For an extended discussion of the roots of these ideas see Idel, *Hasidism*, ch. 4.
52. Rosman, *Founder,* 107: "And I arranged with my group to say [*ketoret*]," 174–75 and passim.
53. Ben-Amos and Mintz, *In Praise of the Baal Shem Tov,* 65; Rosman, *Founder,* 115.

of the joy of performing the commandments [*simhah shel mitsvah*]." Jacob Josef knew, the Besht went on, that he had taught these things several times. The way of melancholy was to be rejected and replaced with the way of "joy of performing the commandments." This was to be achieved in the following way: "Every single morning when you study,[54] attach yourself to the letters with total devotion [*bidevekut gamur*] to the service of your Creator, blessed be He and blessed be His Name. . . . Do not deny your flesh [Isa. 58:7], God forbid, more than is obligatory or necessary. If you heed my voice, God will be with you."[55]

This message—the rejection of asceticism—constituted an overturning of the practice of the old-style *hassidim*, for whom the soul lay imprisoned in the body.[56] For the Besht, there was no need to declare war on the body and its instincts, because these too are rooted in the Divine and not the demonic. Moreover, sadness is itself an obstacle to true worship. This-worldly joy in the performance of the will of God frees the soul to rise to the upper worlds. And this was to be achieved through a contemplative technique that focused on the letters of the words of prayer or study. The historical importance of this practice is not its novelty—in fact, it was not a new teaching—but that in the case of Hasidism, the idea had social consequences.

Teachings attributed to the Besht indicate that he sought to free his contemporaries from the terrible burden of sinfulness attached to *keri*:

One should not worry over an impure accident, an involuntary seminal emission, but rather over the impure thought and not the seminal emission. Without it [the emission], he could have died. [The emission, in this view, expels an evil "spark" that must be extinguished.] "Precious [*yakar*] in the eyes of the Lord is the death of the pious [*hassidav*]" (Ps. 115:15). *Yakar* [*ykr*] is made up of the same letters as *keri* [*kry*] and is good for His pious ones [*tov lehassidav*]. That is, if it happens to him without his having had a lustful thought, it is good. For otherwise he might have died. Therefore, he should not worry except about purifying his thoughts. And when, heaven forbid, an evil thought comes to a person, he should see to its purification by raising it to join with the Creator, may He be blessed.[57]

54. There are differing opinions as to whether the Besht advocated mystical contemplation of the letters only during study or also during prayer. See Idel, *Hasidism*, 176–77.

55. Rubinstein, *Shivhei haBesht*, 105. Idel, *Hasidism*, 56ff.

56. See Immanuel Etkes, "HaBesht kemistikan uva'al besorah be'avodat HaShem," 443–46 and passim. See, e.g., the citation of an anti-ascetic sermon of Perets ben Moshe, an eighteenth-century preacher (*Sefer beit Perets*, 58b) by Avraham Ya'ari, *Ta'alumat sefer: Sefer Hemdat yamim: mi hibro umah haytah midat hashpa'ato* (Jerusalem, 1954), 128–29.

57. Translation of the passage, attributed to the Besht in Dov Ber of Międzyrzecz, *Or Torah* (Korzec, 1804), *re'eh*, and id., *Maggid devarav leya'akov* (Korzec, 1784), 38b; ed. Rivka

Although not all later Hasidic leaders followed the Besht in this remarkable reversal of the trends of thought among old-style *hassidim,* some certainly did.[58] Elijah, Ga'on of Vilna, rejected this Hasidic teaching in a letter written in 1796 to the communities of Mińsk, Mohylew, Połock, Żytomierz, Winnica, and Kamieniec-Podolski, saying, "and they distort the meaning of the Torah saying 'Precious [*ykr*] in the eyes of the Lord' are their ways, because of this 'the stone will cry out from the wall' [Hab. 2:11; wall = *kir* = *ykr* = *kry* = *keri*]."[59]

The most innovative element in the behavior of the Besht was his anti-asceticism.[60] He clearly did not believe that physicality threatened the spirit, or that it was potentially or actually demonic. Spirit and matter were one. Even base thoughts could be elevated, since there was divinity in them, as in all things. And since there is divinity in everything, worship is possible at all times and in the course of even the worldliest actions. The antinomian potential of this idea made it the object of criticism by the opponents of Hasidism in subsequent generations. Hasidic leaders later limited the practice of "worship through corporeality" *(avodah bagashmiyut)* to themselves alone.[61]

The teachings of the Besht contributed substantially to the forging of a Hasidic message that offered a positive and optimistic understanding of the spiritual capacities of every person. Life offered a joyous possibility of fulfilling God's will. This possibility was available to all, whatever the level of their learning. When the Ba'al Shem Tov died in the late spring of 1760, his message, combined with those of his colleagues, had reached

Schatz (Jerusalem, 1976), no. 160, 256, follows Heschel, *Circle,* 148; see also there 189–91. Cf. the more traditional view in *Maggid devarav leya'akov* (Jerusalem, 1976), no. 42, 64; no. 151, 250–52; no. 207, 331–33. See also Ben-Amos and Mintz, *In Praise of the Baal Shem Tov,* 210; Rubinstein, *Shivhei,* 266.

58. See the sources cited by Heschel, *Circle,* 189–91. And see Elimelekh of Leżajsk, *No'am Elimelekh,* ed. Gedaliah Nigal (Jerusalem, 1978), 1: 76 (14d), where a different, but still positive, interpretation is given to *keri.* See also Jacob Josef of Połonne, *Sefer toledot ya'akov yosef,* 179c–d, 194a, 194d. Heschel cites the nineteenth-century Hasidic master Yitshak Isaac Jehiel of Komarno (d. 1874), *Otsar hahayyim* to Deut. 21:22, who in this and in other matters revived or retained ideas associated with the Besht. Cf. Louis Jacobs, *Hasidic Prayer* (New York, 1973), 118–19.

59. Mordekhai Wilensky, *Hasidim umitnaggedim: Letoledot hapulmus beineihem* (Jerusalem, 1990), 1: 188; and see also ibid., 2: 108.

60. Rosman, *Founder,* 115; Etkes, "HaBesht," 443–46.

61. Gershom Scholem, *On the Mystical Shape of the Godhead: Basic Concepts in the Kabbalah* (New York, 1991), 291, n. 84. See also Rachel Elior *The Paradoxical Ascent to God: The Kabbalistic Theosophy of Habad Hasidism* (Albany, N.Y., 1993); id., *Herut al haluhot; Moshe Idel, Hasidism: Between Ecstasy and Magic;* Yoram Yakobson, *Hasidic Thought* (Tel Aviv, 1998).

only limited numbers of *hassidim*. That message, as mediated in the writings of the Besht's disciple, Jacob Josef of Połonne, however, clearly distinguished between the elite, the "men of form," and the rest of the community, the "men of matter."

The European Context

Alongside the eruptions in the general European context that have remained in popular memory such as the Enlightenment and the American and French revolutions, another powerful phenomenon emerged that is less well remembered. Johannes Kelpius, an eighteenth-century Pennsylvania German pietist mystic called it "[t]his late Revolution in Europe . . . which in the Roman Church goes under the Name of Quietism, in the Protestant Church under the Name of Pietism, Chiliasm and Philadelphianism."[62] The various spiritual movements of the eighteenth century, including the Great Awakening in the American church, Wesleyan Methodism, Shakerism, the prophetic movement, and certain forms of Jansenism in France, along with Catholic Quietism, the Pietists in mainly German-speaking lands, and the Old Believers in Russia,[63] constituted a fundamental part of the eighteenth-century European context. All of these mystical and enthusiastic movements criticized the orthodox establishment for presenting hard, dry teachings. Catholic Quietists taught that if one conducted everyday life with true inward concentration and devotion to the divine will, it would constitute "virtual prayer." The goal verged on psychical self-annihilation; the consequent absorption of the soul into the divine essence was likened to a river entering the ocean.

62. *The Diarium of Magister Johannes Kelpius,* trans. Julius F. Sachse (Lancaster, Pa., 1917), 47; Clarke Garrett, *Spirit Possession and Popular Religion: From the Camisards to the Shakers* (Baltimore, 1987), 13. There was evidently considerable interest in Kabbalah in Pennsylvania, where Kelpius lived in the eighteenth century. See, e.g., Elizabeth W. Fisher, "'Prophecies and Revelations': German Cabbalists in Early Pennsylvania," *Pennsylvania Magazine of History and Biography* 109 (1985): 319–21.

63. Although they first appeared in the second half of the seventeenth century, it was only early in the eighteenth century that the Old Believers became a religious movement of some import. Recent studies have also revised the notion that the movement was limited to peasants and have suggested that there were a considerable number of town dwellers among its adherents. Like the Quietists and the Pietists, there were groups or conventicles of adherents in various places and the different groups had varying teachings. See, e.g., Robert Crummey, "Old Belief as Popular Religion: New Approaches," *Slavic Review* 52 (1993): 700–712. See also Léon Poliakov, *L'Épopée des Vieux-Croyants: Une Histoire de la Russie authentique* (Paris, 1991).

There is no evidence of influence or imitation of Christian movements by Hasidim. There is rather what historians of an earlier generation liked to call the zeitgeist, nothing more, but nothing less either. Just as no direct link between the earlier Hasidim of medieval Ashkenaz and contemporary Christian trends, such as Franciscan spiritualism, has been established, despite some striking similarities, so too here one can point to the suggestiveness of the appearance of a similar *Geist* at a similar *Zeit* among both Jews and Christians.[64] This is particularly striking and paradoxical inasmuch as historians of the Catholic Church in Poland itself have reported that these spiritual movements in the Christian churches of Europe had no impact in Polish lands. Perry Miller's analysis of the success of Jonathan Edwards, the central figure in the so-called Great Awakening in America, shows how Hasidism was continuous with a number of elements of contemporary European culture:[65] "By 1740, the leader had to get down amongst [his followers] and bring them by actual participation into an experience that was no longer private and privileged but social and communal."[66]

None of these movements, including Hasidism, should be seen ab initio as a reaction to the Enlightenment. Rather, they were coextensive with the Enlightenment. What the spiritual movements and the Enlightenment shared was, most particularly, the emboldening of the individual to independence in matters of thought and spirit.[67]

Pietist churches, like the Old Believers, evoked considerable popular response. The church in Teschen, for example, had 40,000 congregants, three-quarters of whom were Poles or people from Poland who regularly crossed the Saxon border. Sermons were preached in Polish and Czech.[68] The Gymnasium at Breslau was an important outpost of Protestant Pietism from the end of the seventeenth century on.[69] Pietism, then, had

---

64. A recent general treatment of eighteenth-century Europe grouped Hasidism together with Evangelical groups and "those accused of 'Enthusiasm' all having a claim to a personal, private revelation." Jeremy Black, *Eighteenth-Century Europe, 1700–1789* (New York, 1990), 189.

65. See the remarks on a more particular parallel by Ze'ev Gries, "Mimitos le'etos: Kavvim ledemuto shel R. Abraham miKalisk," in *Umah vetoledoteha*, pt. 2 (Jerusalem, 1983), 126, n. 31.

66. Perry Miller, *Errand into the Wilderness* (1956; Cambridge, Mass., 1964), 154.

67. See Horst Weigelt, "Interpretations of Pietism in the Research of Contemporary German Church Historians," *Church History* 39 (1970): 236–41.

68. W. R. Ward, "Power and Piety: The Origins of Religious Revival in the Early Eighteenth Century," *Bulletin of the John Rylands Library of Manchester* 63 (1980): 231–52. Stanisław Salmonowicz, "Pietyzm na Pomorzu Polskim oraz w Wielkopolsce w pierwszej połowie XVIII wieku," *Roczniki humanistyczne* 27 (1979): 95–105.

69. W. R. Ward, "The Relations of Enlightenment and Religious Revival in Central Europe and in the English-Speaking World," in *Reform and Reformation: England and the Continent c1500–c1750*, ed. Derek Baker (Oxford, 1979), 287.

a considerable effect on the population in the western border regions of Poland and even among residents of western Poland itself. Moreover, there was a significant movement of German-speaking Protestant Pietists from the area around Teschen (Tešin) in Saxony, to Volhynia, particularly to the holdings of the Czartoryski family, in the eighteenth century.[70] About one thousand people began to arrive in the 1770s. But with the exception of Protestants along the western border and these late-century German migrants, the movement was greatly overshadowed by the overwhelmingly Catholic Polish context, and Quietism had virtually no impact on the Catholic Church in Poland.[71] Still, it may be that Polish Jews had contact with Protestant Pietists in their travels.

Seventy years ago, Torsten Ysander raised the possibility of a connection between Jews and members of the Russian Orthodox Church.[72] In the 1820s and 1830s, a large number of Old Believers settled in the southeastern regions of the Polish Commonwealth, mainly on the holdings of the Czartoryski and Lubomirski families. Some were fleeing persecution in Russia, others were attracted by the economic conditions across the border. Despite violent attacks by Russian troops in 1735 and again in 1764, their numbers in Polish lands approached 100,000 in 1772.[73] It is much to be regretted that virtually all aspects of the relationship between the Russian Orthodox Church and Jews have remained uninvestigated by modern scholarship. Consequently, this particular question about the possibility of contact between Russian Orthodox schismatics and Jews in precisely the areas where both were densely settled has not benefited from serious attention by scholars. Nevertheless, despite some striking similarities between Old Believers and Hasidim, the possibility of actual contact and influence on this level seems remote. Although there were significant numbers of them in regions where some of the early Hasidic figures lived, Old Believers kept themselves apart, considering all outsiders unclean. They did not shave, smoke, or drink alcohol. The contiguity in time and, to a certain extent, in space of these movements of religious

70. Z. Cichocka-Petrazycka, *Żywioł niemiecki na Wołyniu* (Warsaw, 1933), 9–14. On the Dutch Mennonite colony established in Zofiowka in Volhynia in the middle of the eighteenth century, see M. Szulmiecki, "Zofiowka," *Rocznik Wołynski* 4 (1935): 137–56.

71. Karol Górski, "Kwietizm w Polsce," *Kierownictwo duchowe w klasztorach żenskich w Polsce, XVI–XVIII w.: Teksty i komentarze* Textus et Studia, 11 (Lublin, 1980), 347–60.

72. Torsten Ysander, "Zur Frage der religionsgeschichtlichen Stellung des Hasidismus," in *Studien zum b'estschen Hasidismus in seiner religionsgeschichtlichen Sonderart* (Uppsala, 1933), 327–413.

73. Eugeniusz Iwaniec, *Z dziejów staroobrzędowców na ziemiach polskich* (Warsaw, 1977).

awakening to Hasidism may be merely an accident of history; the subject awaits further exploration.[74]

The Demographic Context

One motif that is discernible in Hasidic sources and very prominent in anti-Hasidic sources is the particular appeal that Hasidism had for the young. As noted earlier, the proportion of young people in the population was constantly expanding, with Jewish society as a whole becoming younger rather than older.[75] The first Hasidic book to be printed twice cited a teaching attributed to Nahman of Kossów (Kosiv) (d. 1746), a companion of the Ba'al Shem Tov. It is a play on the biblical injunction "Pay no heed to the witches" *(al tifnu el ha'ovot)* (Lev. 19:31), reading "fathers" *(ha'avot)* instead of "witches" *(ha'ovot)*: "I have heard in the name of the *hasid* . . . Rabbi Nahman Kossover: 'Pay no heed to the fathers.' When they say, 'Why did my father and my father's father not do this *hassidut?*' [You must] answer: 'Did he bring the Messiah?'"[76] Note that this passage reflects not only the youthfulness of the intended audience but also a consciousness of the innovation inherent in Hasidic teaching. Solomon Maimon, describing what he beheld in the late 1760s, wrote: "Young people forsook parents, wives and children and went *en masse* to visit the exalted 'rebbes' and to hear from their lips the new doctrine."[77]

The texts produced by the opponents of Hasidism unanimously con-

74. B. D. Weinryb has also raised "the possibility of some mutual copying" between the Hasidim and the Russian sects. See Weinryb, *The Jews of Poland: A Social and Economic History of the Jewish Community in Poland from 1100 to 1800* (Philadelphia, 1973), 237–38, and the notes there. Whether the close association of a former leader of the Filipowcy sect of the Khlysty, Antoni Kossakowski Moliwda, and the circle of Jacob Frank had consequences in Frank's teachings cannot be taken up here. Note of these contacts was taken by Jacob Emden and they have been discussed by various scholars. See Jacob Emden, *Sefer shimush* (Amsterdam, 1758–62; reprint. Jerusalem, 1975), 84b; Alexander Kraushar, *Frank i Frankiści Polscy, 1726–1816: Monografia historyczna osnuta na źródłach archiwalnych i rękopismiennych*, 2 vols. (Kraków, 1895), 1: 129–30; 2: 45; Rosman, *Founder,* 58–60; Jan Doktór, *Śladami Mesjasza-Apostaty: Żydowskie ruchy mesjańskie w XVII i XVIII wieku a problem konwersji* (Wrocław, 1998), 145–56, 167.

75. See chapter 1 above.

76. Jacob Josef of Połonne, *Sefer toledot ya'akov yosef,* 44a; 156b. Heschel, *Circle,* 133, n. 87, points out that this interpretation was not original with Nahman Kossover.

77. *The Autobiography of Solomon Maimon,* trans. J. Clark Murray (Oxford, 1954), 168. See Rapoport-Albert, "Hasidism after 1772," 96.

demn the consequences of a movement made up substantially of the young. "They hunt innocent souls . . . removing the yoke of Torah from their own necks and those of the precious young men." "It is a sin of the youth [who dare to study Kabbalah without prior knowledge of Talmud]." "They act crazily [in prayer] . . . and constantly insult the angels of God [= the rabbis]," "turning head over heels, as the clowns do." In Mińsk, the leaders of the community complained of the Hasidim that "they have spread their nets to hunt delicate and young souls, the children in school." The ban against the Hasidim proclaimed in Kraków in the fall of 1785 referred to them as "young in days . . . and soft in years." Mendel Lefin of Satanów's pamphlet also remarked that the new movement recruited "toujours des jeunes gens."[78] A complaint to the Russian government in 1800 asserted that "they seduce children, bringing them to disobey their parents and steal their property."[79] In the second part of his anti-Hasidic pamphlet *Shever posh'im,* Israel Loebel wrote: "The vast majority [*rubam kekhulam*] are young men. . . . There is no seniority [*ziknah*] here. . . . In general, they seduce only the young men of the Jewish people, those who have not yet reached the age of twenty. . . . It is truly a case of stealing souls."[80] Loebel used a striking analogy in describing how a young man was seduced by the Hasidim:

When the naïf arrives, he hears their tunes and their pleasant voices, for the majority of them have fine voices and know how to sing. This melodious sweetness leads him to attach himself to them with great love. He follows them like an ox to the slaughter or a stag caught fast [Prov. 7:22]. He does not know that he imperils his soul and that this will cause his death. His fate in this is like that of an inexperienced sailor. There is a certain creature that lives in the sea; its upper half has the appearance of a female human being, while below it is fishlike. It sometimes appears to those who sail the seas, showing only its upper half. It sings to them in a sweet and seductive voice. The foolish and inexperienced sea captain will be drawn closer to her to hear her better and to enjoy her singing. The sweetness of the singing will be fatal because it is oversweet [*mahmat rov hametikut*].[81]

78. *MDSC* 6: 411.

79. Wilensky, *Hasidim umitnaggedim,* 1: 38–39, 52, 59–60, 63, 68, 137–41, 185, 282, and numerous other places. Gershon Hundert, "The Contexts of Hasidism," in *Żydzi wśród Chrześcian w dobie szlacheckiej Rzeczypospolitej,* ed. Waldemar Kowalski and Jadwiga Muszyńska (Kielce, 1996), 177. Cf. Dinur, *Bemifneh hadorot,* 160; Louis Jacobs, "Honour Thy Father: A Study of the Psychology of the Hasidic Movement," in *Hagut ivrit be'Eiropah* (Tel Aviv, 1969), 136–43.

80. Wilensky, *Hasidim,* 2: 158–59, 172–73.

81. Ibid., 173–74. Wilensky notes that sirens are mentioned in the exegetical *midrash* on Leviticus: Sifra, Shemini, ch. 4, and in other rabbinic sources.

Note that in this version, the victims of the siren's song die from too much sweetness, not—as in the original tale—from being smashed against the rocks. The erotic attraction of the Hasidic community and its leader could hardly be more explicit.[82]

In times of relative security, the natural tension between generations is channeled in a way that does not threaten the stability of the family and the community. When there are elements of uncertainty in the social, economic, and political spheres, however, generational tensions are more likely to threaten individual families and society at large. Moreover, the relatively rapid growth of the population was itself a destabilizing element.

Turning head over heels is not something people advanced in years tend to do. That many of the early adherents of Hasidism, and its leaders, were young may have been the result of demographic and social conditions in which generational conflict was expressed by rejecting norms of behavior, religious practice, and traditional institutional authority. Despite serious methodological problems with the term "generation" (there's "one born every minute"), the image of the Hasidim that emerges from the sources unmistakably reflects their youthfulness.

THE GEOGRAPHY OF HASIDISM

Virtually every treatment of the early generations of Hasidism has suggested that it was restricted to the southeastern regions of the Polish Commonwealth. This convention requires qualification. The successful quest to popularize the new ideas and to seek adherents for its charismatic leaders began in the latter half of the 1760s. By 1772, certain elements in the Jewish communities of Wilno, Szkłów, Brody, and elsewhere had banned and excommunicated the Hasidim, referring to them as Karliners and "Mezritchers." Wilno is in Lithuania, Szkłów is in Belorussia, and Karlin is a suburb of Pińsk, also in Belorussia. We know from the autobiography of Solomon Maimon that, as a young man, he was recruited to visit a Hasidic rabbi. He traveled from Lithuania to Volhynia to the court of the *maggid* of Międzyrzecz. Menahem Mendel, later of Witebsk, began his career in Mińsk. The first attack on Hasidism in Wilno was mounted because of their *minyan* (lit., "quorum": small place of prayer)

82. In the paragraph following the one quoted, David of Maków wrote suggestively, "They all gather together at night sleeping in one room and who knows what ugly deeds transpire." See Haviva Pedayah, "Lehitpathuto shel hadegem hahevrati-dati-kalkali bahassidut: Hapidyon, hahavurah, veha'aliyah leregel," in *Dat vekalkalah: Yahasei gomlin,* ed Menahem Ben-Sasson, 311–73 (Jerusalem, 1995), 340–44; Gries, "Mimitos le'etos," 117–46.

in the city. Levi Yitshak, later of Berdyczów, was first the rabbi of Żelechów and then served in Pińsk from 1775 to 1785. Moreover, there were other Hasidic groups in the region, notably in Polotsk (Polatsk), Indura, Lubavitch (Lyubavichi), and Lyady. It is quite true that Israel ben Eli'ezer Ba'al Shem Tov lived in Międzyboż in Podolia, and the *maggid* Dov Ber lived in Korzec, Równo (Rivne), and Międzyrzecz, near Ostróg in Volhynia, but, as we have seen, the reputation of Israel Ba'al Shem Tov extended to Lithuania as early as the 1730s.[83] Clearly, there was a significant Hasidic presence from the 1760s on in all of the territories of the eastern half of Poland-Lithuania.[84]

SHABBATEANISM AND HASIDISM

Historians studying central and eastern European Jewish society during the middle and later decades of the eighteenth century see this period as one of "heresy hunting."[85] The examples cited include the bans against Nehemiah ben Moses Hayon (ca. 1655–ca. 1730); the condemnation of the writings and activities of Moses Hayyim Luzzatto (1707–1746); the bans promulgated against the Shabbateans; the case of Nathan Adler (1741–1800) and his followers in Frankfurt; the controversy over Jonathan Eybeschuetz (d. 1764) and his circle; and finally, the bans against the Hasidim in 1772 and thereafter.[86] This "heresy hunting" was accompanied

83. Teller, "Masoret Sluck al reshit darko shel haBesht," 15–38.

84. Wolf Zeev Rabinowitsch, *Lithuanian Hasidism from Its Beginnings to the Present Day*, trans. M. B. Dagut (London, 1970).

85. Weinryb, *Jews of Poland*, 238–40. Mendel Lefin noted of the Hasidim in about 1792: "Ils on pris un pied ferme en Podolie qui est leur patrie, de même qu'en Volhynie et Lituanie." He added, however, "Cependant il y a un bon nombre de villes, surtout en Lituanie, qui s'opposent aux conquêtes de ces zélateurs et ne veulent rien entendre de toutes leurs innovations." *MDSC* 6: 412.

86. Gershom Scholem, *Mehkarim umekorot letoledot haShabbeta'ut vegilguleha* (Jerusalem, 1974); id., *Mehkere shabbeta'ut*, ed. Yehudah Liebes (Tel Aviv, 1991); Isaiah Tishby, *Netivei emunah uminut: Massot umehkarim besifrut hakabbalah vehashabbeta'ut*, 2d ed. (Jerusalem, 1982); Yehuda Liebes, *Sod ha'emunah hashabbeta'it: Kovets ma'amarim* (Jerusalem, 1995); Elisheva Carlebach, *The Pursuit of Heresy: Rabbi Moses Hagiz and the Sabbatian Controversies* (New York, 1990); Rachel Elior, "R. Nathan Adler and the Frankfurt Pietists; Pietist Groups in Eastern and Central Europe during the Eighteenth Century," in *Jüdische Kultur in Frankfurt am Main von den anfangen bis zur Gegenwart*, ed. Karl E. Grözinger (Wiesbaden, 1997), 135–77; id., "Rabbi Nathan Adler of Frankfurt and the Controversy Surrounding Him," in *Mysticism, Magic and Kabbalah in Ashkenazi Judaism*, ed. Karl Grozinger and Joseph Dan (Berlin, 1995), 223–42; Yehuda Liebes, "Hatikkun hakelali of R. Nahman of Bratslav and Its Sabbatean Links," in id., *Studies in Jewish Myth and Jewish Messianism*, trans. Batya Stein (Albany, N.Y., 1993), 115–50, 184–210.

by book-burning and bans of excommunication. These actions signal a certain instability in traditional Jewish society and the perceived need to draw and redraw the boundaries of that society. It also indicated failure of the diurnal means of social control to limit behavior that challenged social and religious norms. The historian Chimen Abramsky sees the controversy between the renowned halakhic authority Jonathan Eybeschuetz (1690/95–1764) and his rival Jacob Emden (1697–1776) as a prime example of what he terms "the crisis of authority within European Jewry in the Eighteenth Century."[87] Emden branded Eybeschuetz a Shabbatean in a momentous and prolonged dispute that eventually involved most of the European rabbinate.

Coexisting with the trend of "heresy hunting" were other, more benign or indulgent responses, especially to Shabbateanism. There were those who attributed the failure of messianism to the unworthiness of the generation. Still others were saddened by the apostasy of the Shabbateans who followed Jacob Frank. Israel Ba'al Shem Tov himself is said to have expressed regret over the loss of those Jews who apostatized following the Lwów Disputation.[88] In this regard, there is a fascinating legend in the collection *In Praise of the Baal Shem Tov*, originally published in the early nineteenth century, about the Ba'al Shem Tov and Shabbetai Tsevi. The "authenticity" of the tale, that is, the question of whether it actually reflects opinions that were the Besht's and not those of the generation that published it, has been debated. Yehuda Liebes has maintained that it must be authentic or it would have been censored by the later Hasidic editors.

Rabbi Joel [of Niemirów (Nemyriv)] told me that Shabbetai Tsevi came to the Besht to ask for redemption [*takanah*]. Rabbi Joel said in these words: The redemption [*tikkun*] is [performed] through the connecting of soul to soul, spirit to spirit, breath to breath [the terms refer to three parts of the soul: *nefesh . . . ruah . . . neshamah*]. He [the Besht] began to connect with him moderately for he [Shabbetai Tsevi] was steeped in evil. One time, while the Besht slept, Shabbetai Tsevi (may his name be blotted out) came and tempted him, God forbid. With a mighty thrust, he hurled him so that he fell into the bottom of Hell. The

---

87. Chimen Abramsky, "The Crisis of Authority within European Jewry in the Eighteenth Century," in *Studies in Jewish Religious and Intellectual History Presented to Alexander Altmann on the Occasion of His Seventieth Birthday,* ed. Siegfried Stein and Raphael Loewe, (University, Ala., 1979), 13–28.

88. Ben-Amos and Mintz, *In Praise of the Baal Shem Tov,* 59. See also the tradition noted by Yehoshua Mondshine, "Al 'Hatikkun hakelali shel R. Nahman miBraslav veyahaso le-shabbeta'ut,'" *Zion* 47 (1982): 202, n. 12.

Besht looked around at where he had landed and saw that he was with Jesus on the same pallet called a *tavil*. And he [R. Joel] said that the Besht had declared that there was a spark of holiness in him [Shabbetai Tsevi], but Sama'el [Satan] caught him in his snare, God forbid. The Besht had heard an account that his downfall came about because of pride and anger.

There has been some disagreement as to who threw whom down to "the bottom of Hell." It seems reasonable to adopt the reading advocated by Yehuda Liebes to the effect that Shabbetai Tsevi threw the Besht down, but the sentence itself is open to interpretation. The manuscript version of *In Praise of the Baal Shem Tov* includes important variations that suggest that the text was censored at its publication. In the manuscript, after the statement that Shabbetai Tsevi "came and tempted him," we find the words *"to apostatize";* again, instead of "the Besht declared that there was a spark of holiness in him [Shabbetai Tsevi]," we read that "there was a spark of *messiah* in him [Shabbetai Tsevi]."[89]

Isaiah Tishby adopted perhaps the most extreme position on the relationship between Shabbateanism and Hasidism. First, he noted a possible close personal connection between Dov Ber, the great *maggid* of Międzyrzecz, and the Shabbatean Ya'akov Koppel Lifshits of Międzyrzecz (d. 1740). Then, in remarking on the purported veneration of Shabbatean works by the Besht, he concluded: "It may well become clear that Hasidism arose not outside of the realm of the failing Shabbatean movement and in opposition to it. Rather, [Hasidism arose] as an inner development within Shabbateanism itself when the great schism developed between the branches of the messianic movement. [That is, there ensued] a complete separation between those who followed the antinomian path and those who advocated the spread of pietistic teachings as ways of bringing about redemption."[90]

Tishby's position has not been adopted by other scholars, although Yehuda Liebes has pointed to numerous possible connections between

---

89. Yehuda Liebes, "Hatikkun hakelali shel R. Nahman miBraslav veyahaso leshabbeta'ut," *Zion* 45 (1980), 201–45, reprinted in id., *Sod ha'emunah hashabbeta'it: Kovets ma'amarim* (Jerusalem, 1995), 238–61; Mondshine, "Al 'Hatikkun hakelali shel R. Nahman miBraslav'"; Yehuda Liebes, "Megamot beheker hassiduth Braslav," *Zion* 47 (1982): 224–31; id., "Hadashot le'inyan haBesht veShabbetai Tsevi," *Mehkerei Yerushalayim bemahshevet yisra'el* 2 (1983): 564–69, reprinted in id., *Sod ha'emunah hashabbeta'it*, 262–65; Abraham Rubinstein, "Al sheloshah sippurim besefer *Shivhei haBesht*," *Sinai* 90 (1982): 277–79; Tzvi Mark, "Dibbuk udevekut be*Shivhei HaBesht*: He'arot lefenomenologiyah shel hashiga'on bereshit hahassiduth," in *Bema'agalei hassidim: Kovets mehkarim lezikhro shel Professor Mordekhai Wilensky*, ed. Immanuel Etkes et al. (Jerusalem, 1999), 282–84.
90. Tishby, *Netivei emunah uminut*, 226.

Shabbatean and Hasidic teachings. Still, the complexities of the question of the interrelationship between Shabbatean and Hasidic *ideas* remain without complete resolution. The issue of the general connection between the two movements is clearer. First, Hasidism was not a Shabbatean phenomenon; it did not proclaim either the presence of the Messiah or the imminent arrival of redemption. Still, the generation of the Baʿal Shem Tov and the one following lived amid the fallout of the Shabbatean movement, and it is important not to rigidify boundaries that, in life, did not exist. Many of the companions and the disciples of the Baʿal Shem Tov and his teachings were old-style *hassidim*. And since in those circles there was considerable sympathy for Shabbatean doctrine, it is likely that, for example, Jacob Emden's accusation that Nahman of Kossów was a Shabbatean had some basis in fact. The interpretation of the tale of the Baʿal Shem Tov and Shabbetai Tsevi quoted above as reflecting a "flirtation" with Shabbateanism on the part of the Besht may also be correct. Nevertheless, *as Hasidism developed,* whatever personal links with Shabbateanism may have existed in its generative phase disappeared. The teachings of the Hasidic masters, as stated, never strayed from the normative foundations of Torah and commandments.

Structurally, the Shabbatean groups contributed to the complication of the patterns of leadership and provided an avenue for individual choice in matters of the spirit. Despite condemnation and bans of excommunication, and the clandestine quality of the contacts among the believers, they were still often seen in a positive light as *hassidim* or *mekubbalim*. In the words of Ber Birkenthal, "Most people do not believe this about them [that they engage in antinomian behavior,] because most of them are learned, constantly studying the holy Zohar deriving from it divine secrets. Some of them hardly sleep at night, mourning the Destruction of the Temple."[91]

A new thirst for individual spiritual satisfaction in the eighteenth century stimulated the popularization of Kabbalah, the construction of new spatial forms of worship, the interest in Shabbatean teachings, and the popularity of *baʿalei shem*. The intense desires that expressed themselves in these ways empowered a new type of leader, one whose spiritual talents made it possible for him to satisfy the yearnings of his followers.

91. Abraham Yaʿakov Brawer, *Galitsiyah viyehudeha: Mehkarim betoledot Galitsiyah bameʾah ha18* (Jerusalem, 1956), 211–12.

CHAPTER 9

Hasidism, a New Path

Hasidism was a spiritual awakening led by charismatic masters. It transformed the configuration of the religious life of Jews in East Central Europe in the last decades of the eighteenth century. Although some saw Hasidism as a challenge to the status quo, its innovations never actually threatened the normative foundations of Torah and commandments. Hasidism was the culmination of earlier trends that had popularized kabbalistic ideas and practices and sought to accommodate devotional life to individual, personal religious experience.

The appearance of kabbalists—old-style *hassidim*—and *ba'alei shem* contributed to the emergence of the leadership form that characterized Hasidism. In the last decades of the eighteenth century (and thereafter), spiritual enthusiasm struck a responsive chord among Jews in East Central Europe. A galaxy of charismatic mystics led the "awakening," which was accompanied by remarkable literary and spiritual creativity.

One way to picture the emergence of Hasidism is as a series of nonconcentric circles that became ever wider in the course of the later decades of the eighteenth century. Its beginnings can be located among the retiring circles of kabbalists and mystics. Powerful, remarkable, innovative spiritual insights began to emerge from the teachings of charismatic individuals. The dissemination of these ideas was limited at first to the old-style *hassidim*. Some of these old-style *hassidim* began to recruit outstanding young students to their centers. Finally, with the institutionalization of the new form of leadership—the *rebbe* or *tsaddik*—broader and broader strata of people began to identify themselves at first as Hasidim per se and then as the Hasidim (in the sense of followers) of one or another of the new leaders.

By the end of the eighteenth century, the term *hassid* had been transformed. Until the last third of the eighteenth century, it designated a person who was part of the kabbalistic elite, an ascetic individual who might be associated in a fellowship with a small like-minded group. The earliest publications associated with the new Hasidism used the term *hassid* interchangeably with *tsaddik*. Early Hasidic writings referred to the followers of these individuals in a general way as the masses or as "people of matter" *(anshei homer)* as opposed to the "men of form" *(anshei tsurah)* who were the leaders. All were following the ways of *hassidut*. Gradually, the term "Hasid" came to designate anyone who followed those ways. Their leaders were no longer known as *hassidim* but as *rebbes*. In the last stage of its migration, the term "Hasid" came to be understood as if it were in the genitive case. That is, one did not become a Hasid in general; one became the Hasid of a particular *rebbe*. To a significant extent, it was opposition to the movement that forged the consciousness among the Hasidim that there was an "inside" and an "outside" of Hasidism. Simultaneously, a sense of the particularity of each Hasidic group or *'edah* emerged.

Hasidism

When the Besht died, there was no issue of succession, because he held no office or position, formal or informal.[1] He had been a charismatic innovator of a new spiritual path and had had a substantial impact among the limited circles of *hassidim* with whom he had come into contact. His fame as a *ba'al shem*, however, had reached well beyond the region of his birth, and one presumes that stories were told about him that began the construction of a mythic hero.

Some time during the 1760s, Dov Ber, the *maggid* of Międzyrzecz (d. 1772) began to be referred to as a source of authority by other Hasidic leaders. He recruited a group of disciples and students among them: Aaron of Karlin (1736–1772), Elimelekh of Leżajsk (1717–1786),[2] Abraham Kalisker (d. 1810), and Menahem Mendel of Mińsk and later Witebsk (1730–1788). When Aaron of Karlin added his signature of approval to a

---

1. This is argued most convincingly by Ada Rapoport-Albert, "Hatenu'ah hahassidit aharei shenat 1772: Retsef miveni utemurah," *Zion* 55 (1990): 196–199.

2. Elimelekh acted as a rebbe beginning in 1764 according to Mendel Piekarz, "R. Elimelekh miLezajsk umamshikhei darko," *Gal-Ed* 15–16 (1997): 46.

set of communal enactments in Nieśwież (Nesvizh), he added that he was acting on the authority of "our teacher [*admor*] . . . the learned sage of the whole Diaspora, the *maggid* of the holy community of Międzyrzecz." Each of these had his own disciples in his own place of residence. Simultaneously, there were other groups of Hasidim around, for example, Pinehas of Korzec and Jehiel Mikhl of Zloczów. The latter, however, may also have deferred to the authority of Dov Ber. In a document from the late 1760s, Jehiel Mikhl of Zloczów added his support to a decree by Dov Ber in a matter of unfair competition.[3]

Solomon Maimon (ca. 1753–1800) was a Lithuanian rabbinic prodigy who took up philosophy and lived a vagabond life. Maimon also published an autobiography in German during his own lifetime. He devoted an appendix of this book to the "New Hasidim," entitling it: "On a Secret Society and Therefore a Long Chapter." In the passage below, Maimon accounts for the rapid spread of the movement. He also described how he himself came to visit the group around "B——" of "M——," that is, Dov Ber, the *maggid* of Międzyrzecz.

The heads of the sect sent emissaries everywhere, whose duty it was to preach the new doctrine and procure adherents. . . . [T]his new doctrine was to make the way to blessedness easier, since it declared that fasts and vigils and the constant study of Talmud are not only useless but even prejudicial to that cheerfulness of spirit that is essential to genuine piety. It was therefore natural that adherence to the doctrine became widespread in a short time. They used to go to K—— [Karlin] and M—— [Międzyrzecz] and other holy places where the teachers and luminaries of this sect lived. Young people forsook parents, wives and children and went *en masse* to visit the exalted "rebbes" and to hear from their lips the new doctrine.[4]

3. Wolf Zeev Rabinowitsch, *Lithuanian Hasidism from Its Beginnings to the Present Day* (London, 1970), 12; Shmuel Ettinger, "Hasidism and the Kahal in Eastern Europe," in *Hasidism Reappraised*, ed. Ada Rapoport-Albert (London, 1996), 66–68; Israel Halpern, *Yehudim veyahadut bemizrah Eiropah* (Jerusalem, 1968), 333–39. Chone Shmeruk, "Hahassiduth ve'iskei hahakirot," *Hakeriyah lenavi: Mehkerei historiyah vesifrut*, ed. Israel Bartal (Jerusalem, 1999), 70. And see the implied account of the Hasidic succession in a letter written ca. 1777 by Meshullam Feibush Heller: "the wonder men, possessors of the holy spirit in this generation whom my eyes have seen . . . all drank from one spring, that is, the divine R. Israel Besht . . . I was privileged only to see the face of his disciple, the divine R. Dov Ber . . . after this . . . I visited R. Menahem Mendel of Przemyslany. . . . I heard even more . . . from the mouth of . . . the *tsaddik*, the son of a *tsaddik*, the great and divine rabbi, our teacher, Yehiel Mikhl of Zloczów." *Likutim yekarim*, 110a, as quoted by Mor Altshuler, "Mishnato shel R. Mehullam Feibush Heller umekomah bereshit hatenu'ah hahassidit" (Ph.D. diss., Hebrew University, Jerusalem, 1994), 30.

4. *Salomon Maimon's Lebensgeschichte von ihm selbst geschrieben*, ed. K. P. Moritz, 2 vols. (Berlin, 1792–93); *The Autobiography of Solomon Maimon*, trans. J. Clark Murray (Oxford, 1954), 166–79 (slightly modified). The references to "K——" and "M——" are omitted in

Maimon described one of the "emissaries" as follows:

He was a young man of twenty-two, of very weak bodily constitution, lean and pale. He traveled in Poland as a missionary. In his gaze there was something so terrible, so commanding, that he ruled men by means of it quite despotically. Wherever he came he inquired about the constitution of the congregation, rejected whatever displeased him, and made new regulations that were punctiliously followed. The elders of the congregation, for the most part old, respectable men, who far excelled him in learning, trembled before his face.

Maimon met another itinerant young Hasid "of the lowest grade of membership," whose revelations of some Hasidic teachings so entranced him that he "resolved therefore to undertake a journey to M—— where the exalted leader [*hohe Obere*] B—— resided. . . . The journey extended over some weeks." The young man had explained to Maimon that joining the group was "the simplest thing in the world." If this were so, it would seem that in around 1770, there was no strong opposition to the "new Hasidism."[5] On his arrival in M——, Maimon was not permitted to meet the leader at once, rather

I was invited to his table on Sabbath along with the other strangers who had come to visit him; that I should then have the happiness of seeing the saintly man face to face, and of hearing the sublime teachings from his own mouth; that although this was a public audience, yet, on account of the individual references which I should find made to myself, I might regard it as a special interview.

Accordingly, on Sabbath I went to this solemn meal, and found there a large number of respectable men who had gathered from various quarters. At length the awe-inspiring great man appeared, clothed in white satin. Even his shoes and snuffbox were white, this being among the Kabbalists the colour of grace. He gave every newcomer his greeting. We sat down to table and during the meal a solemn silence reigned. After the meal was over, the superior struck up a solemn inspiring melody, held his hand for some time upon his brow, and then began to call out. . . . Every newcomer was thus called by his own name and the name of his residence, which excited no little astonishment. Each recited, as he was called,

---

the English translation. See Ada Rapoport-Albert, "Hasidism after 1772: Structural Continuity and Change," in *Hasidism Reappraised,* ed. id. (London, 1996), 96, nn. 61, 62. Documents of opposition dating from 1772 also routinely refer to Hasidic centers in Międzyrzecz, Karlin, and Mińsk without distinction and without any sense of hierarchy. The last sentence here is reminiscent of a passage in the ban against the Hasidim pronounced in Vilna in 1781: "ad asher azvu kol heilam venesheihem verekhusham vayelkhu lanu'a ahar lo yo'il." Mordekhai Wilensky, *Hasidim umitnaggedim: Letoledot hapulmus beineihem,* rev. ed. (Jerusalem, 1990), 1: 103. See also ibid., 1: 187, for the Vilna Ga'on's charge that the Hasidim transgress the commandment "Honor thy father and thy mother."

5. Rapoport-Albert, "Hasidism," 132–33.

some verse of the Holy Scriptures. Thereupon the superior began to deliver a sermon for which the verses recited served as a text, so that although they were disconnected verses taken from different parts of the Holy Scriptures, they were combined with as much skill as if they had formed a single whole. What was still more extraordinary, every one of the newcomers believed that he discovered, in that part of the sermon that was founded on his verse, something that had special reference to the facts of his own spiritual life. At this, they were of course greatly astonished.[6]

Maimon was about sixteen years old at this time. The passages above reveal a number of the practices of Dov Ber, his disciples, and other Hasidic leaders in the 1760s and later. Promising young men were recruited as candidates to visit and to join the Hasidic leaders. His description of his own enthusiasm, which led him to undertake a journey of "some weeks," is an indication of his generation's thirst for spiritual guidance. The anticipation of the meeting, the dramatic choreography, the costume, the melodious singing, and the rhetorical sleight of hand displayed in, one can assume, the numinous darkness of the third meal on the Sabbath, all intensified the astonishment and awe that being in the presence of a spiritual master evoked. The intense propagandizing and recruiting activities at the behest of the *maggid* and the gradual evolution of ritualized behaviors around the master at Międzyrzecz, can be viewed as "the essential element in the transformation of Hasidism to a movement."[7]

At the center of concern of the early Hasidic masters was the presence of God. It is in prayer that one focuses one's attention on divinity, and prayer "occupied a central place in early Hasidic life and has continued to do so down to the present."[8] The following is a tale about the Ba'al Shem Tov, first published in 1795.[9] The Besht is speaking to his own soul: "The soul declared to the Rabbi . . . that the reason why supernal mat-

6. *Autobiography of Solomon Maimon,* 167–68, 177, 175–76. And see the striking parallels pointed out by Haviva Pedayah between this account and the description, apparently of the "court" of Hayyim Hayke of Indura, in a contemporary anti-Hasidic pamphlet: Pedayah, "Lehitpathuto shel hadegem hahevrati-dati-kalkali bahassiduth: Hapidyon, hahavurah veha'aliyah leregel," in *Dat vekalkalah: Yahasei gomlin: kovets ma'amarim,* ed. Menahem Ben-Sasson (Jerusalem, 1995), 350–51, and the notes there.

7. Seeking one "essential" *(ha'ikari)* element in such complex questions is futile. Nevertheless, the teasing of this particular element out of the complex of developments at the time is a valuable contribution. Pedayah, "Lehitpathuto," 323.

8. Louis Jacobs, *Hasidic Prayer* (New York, 1973), 17.

9. On this book, Aaron ben Tsevi Hirsh, *Keter shem tov,* see Gedaliah Nigal, "Makor rishoni lesifrut hasippurim hahasidit: Al sefer 'keter shem tov' umekorotav," *Sinai* 79 (1976): 132–46. See also Moshe J. Rosman, *Founder of Hasidism: A Quest for the Historical Ba'al Shem Tov* (Berkeley, 1996), 260, n. 69.

ters were revealed to him was not because he had studied many Talmudic tractates and Codes of Law but because of his prayer. For at all times he recited his prayers with great concentration. It was because of this that he attained an elevated state."[10] Study, and particularly study for its own sake, is important, but, as Meshullam Feivish Heller (d. 1795) taught, "the prior, essential condition is prayer with attachment to the divine [*devekuth*], with burning enthusiasm of the heart [*hitlahavut*]." Mere accumulation of knowledge is without spiritual significance:

In fact, many of those from among our people who think of themselves and are thought of as great, wise men of the Torah—revealed and esoteric—and who think of themselves as God-fearing. . . . [I]n fact, the truth is that they possess not the slightest amount of knowledge of the divine Torah . . . because they study only its external side. They do not seek to be attached to God and to be His Chariot, to fear Him and to love Him through the Torah. . . . They understand nothing of attachment to God [*devekuth*] or the love or the fear of God. They think these are identical with study itself. . . . This cannot be because it is well known that, because of our many sins, certain of those who study are adulterers, God save us, and sinners. There are even Gentiles who study our Torah. How, then, can this be considered attachment to God? A person truly attached to God in love and fear cannot possibly commit even a minor transgression not to mention a serious sin or, God forbid, become lustful. . . . The matter of the love and fear of God is [determined] in a person's heart.[11]

The contemporary of the Besht, Menahem Mendel of Przemyślany expressed much the same sentiment: "The rule is not to engage overly much in study. . . . If we remove our thoughts from attachment to God . . . and study excessively, we will, Heaven forbid, forget the fear of God. . . . Therefore one needs to study less . . . and not to think many thoughts, but only one thought."[12] Passages in the so-called *Tsava'at haRiv'ash* ("Testament of the Ba'al Shem Tov"), first published in the early 1790s, but actually a collection of materials found in publications attributed to Dov Ber, also draw a clear distinction between attachment to God *(devekuth)* and study: "When you study, pause briefly every hour to attach yourself to God. . . . Even so, you must study. In the midst of study, it is impossible to cleave to God . . . Nevertheless, one must study."[13] The collec-

10. *Keter shem tov,* 22b, as quoted by Jacobs, *Hasidic Prayer,* 17. Cf. *Tzava'at Harivash,* ed. and trans. Jacob I. Schochet (Brooklyn, 1998), 29.

11. Jacobs, *Hasidic Prayer,* 21.

12. Menahem Mendel of Przemyslany, *Darkhei yesharim,* as quoted by Yoram Jacobson, *Hasidic Thought,* trans. J. Chipman (Tel Aviv, 1998), 77.

13. Ze'ev Gries, *Sifrut hahanhagot* (Jerusalem, 1989), 149–230.

tion *In Praise of the Baal Shem Tov* preserves traditions in which the *maggid* of Międzyrzecz described his encounter with the Ba'al Shem Tov.[14] In one version, we find the Ba'al Shem Tov demonstrating the proper way to study, one that rested on vocal performance and spiritual experience:

He asked me whether I had studied Kabbalah. I answered that I had. A book was lying in front of him on the table and he instructed me to read aloud from the book. The book was written in short paragraphs, each of which began, "Rabbi Ishmael said, 'Metatron, the Prince of Presence, told me.'"[15] I recited a page or a half a page to him. The Besht said to me: "It is not correct. I will read it to you." He began and read, and while he read he trembled. He rose and said: "We are dealing with *ma'assei merkavah* [the vision of Ezekiel] and I am sitting down." He stood up and continued to read. As he was talking he lay me down in the shape of a circle on the bed [in another version: he ordered me to lie myself down on the bed and made a circle around me].[16] I was not able to see him any more. I only heard voices and saw frightening flashes and torches.[17]

In interpreting this passage, Moshe Idel pointed out that what distinguished the Besht was not his knowledge of Kabbalah—the *maggid* asserts his knowledge of Kabbalah too—but the special vocal performance or recitation of the text. The text is not only a source of esoteric knowledge but also an inducement to spiritual experience. In fact, "according to this story, what concerned the Besht was the revelation that he experienced by performing the text rather than the gnosis inherent in it."[18]

Jacob Josef of Połonne set out his view of the contrast between the new path and the old rather starkly:

It used to be thought that the proper service of God was nothing but study as well as prayer with fasting and crying etc. When [ordinary] people saw that they [could] not take up this path, they were angered and disappointed thinking that they had thus lost eternal life . . . and this brought anger and disappointment into the world. . . . Until [the Hasidim] realized that this [understanding of the proper

14. There are several different traditions describing how the *maggid* first "came to" the Besht. See Immanuel Etkes, *Ba'al haShem: HaBesht: Magiyah, mistikah, hanhagah* (Jerusalem, 2000), 195–198; Abraham Hayyim Rubinstein, *Shivhei haBesht: Mahadurah mu'eret umevu'eret* (Jerusalem, 1991), 126–29, 339–45.

15. The reference is to the so-called Hebrew Book of Enoch, an ancient book of Jewish mysticism. See Dan Ben-Amos and Jerome R. Mintz, *In Praise of the Baal Shem Tov: The Earliest Collection of Legends about the Founder of Hasidism* (Bloomington, Ind., 1970), 322, n. 3. And see the references in Moshe Idel, *Hasidism: Between Ecstasy and Magic* (Albany, N.Y., 1995), 353, n. 3; and id., "Enoch is Metatron," *Immanuel* 24–25 (1990): 220–40.

16. Rubinstein, *Shivhei*, 341 from the Yiddish version of *Shivhei Habesht*.

17. Ben-Amos and Mintz, *In Praise of the Baal Shem Tov*, 83.

18. Idel, *Hasidism*, 172.

service of God] was in fact wrong and taught a more correct path, a path of compassion. One need not devote all one's time to the study of Torah, but one should also become involved with other human beings. In that too he can experience the fear of God and the fulfillment of the commandment of being aware constantly of God's presence.[19]

In this way, in Hasidism, the pursuit of the experience of the presence of God, including in human community, joined study, traditionally the central obligation of every [male] Jew, as an equal if not preeminent duty.

The Tsaddik: Intermediary between Heaven and Earth

The paradigm of the perfect man, the idea of the *tsaddik,* was not an innovation of Hasidism.[20] The long passage from *Shevet mussar,* one of the most popular books in the category of ethical mystical literature, quoted in chapter 6 is but one instance among many.[21] Moses Cordovero, an influential mystic in Safed in the sixteenth century, wrote in his *Pardes rimmonim:* "When a *tsaddik* and a *hassid* are present in this world, the entire world is nourished, as it is written [TB Berakhot 17a]: the entire world is nourished for the sake of [*bishevil*] R. Hanina, My son."[22] The novelty

19. Jacob Josef of Połonne, *Sefer toledot ya'akov yosef* (1780; photo-offset reprint, Jerusalem, 1966), 23b, 24d. Cf. Wilensky, *Hasidim,* 2: 145.

20. Wilensky, *Hasidim,* 2: 189–207. And see the survey of the literature there, 365, n. 1. To these may be added: Mendel Piekarz, *Hahanhagah hahassidit: Samkhut ve'emunat tsaddikim be'aspaklariyat sifrutah shel hahassiduth* (Jerusalem, 1999).

21. Mendel Piekarz, *Biyemei tsemihat hahassidut: Megamot ra'ayaniyot besifrei derush umussar* (1978: rev. ed. Jerusalem, 5758 [1998]), 299–302.

22. *Pardes rimmonim,* 32 as cited by Idel, *Hasidism,* 201. Mendel Piekarz stresses the influence of Isaiah Horowitz on this and many other central themes in Hasidic writing. He cites Horowitz's *SheLaH,* 299b, where we find the following: "It is similar to the case of 'all the world is nourished for the sake of my son Hanina' . . . the point is that R. Hanina was a great *tsaddik* in his generation, the one pillar on which the world stood. This is the meaning of 'for the sake of my son Hanina.' And the meaning of the term *bishevil* is 'pathway' and 'pipeline.'" Piekarz, *Biyemei,* 17. See also the citation from *Zohar hadash, vayera* 33a, where Simeon ben Yohai is described as preventing a divine plan to destroy the world because there are too few righteous men [*tsaddikim*]. The biblical negotiation over Sodom between God and Abraham over how many righteous would be required to avert the plan is echoed until Simeon is made to say: "'If there are not two, there is one, and I am he, as it is written: *tsaddik* is the foundation of the world.' In that hour a voice went forth from heaven saying: 'Blessed is your lot, Rabbi Simeon, *for God issues a decree above and you nullify it below!* [emphasis added] Surely of you it was written: He does the will of them that fear Him.'" Arthur Green, "The Zaddiq as *Axis Mundi* in Later Judaism," *Journal of the American Academy of Religion* 45 (1997): 334.

in Hasidism was that it was organized around the existence of actual *tsad-dikim* in the world; the body of theoretical literature, such as the passages cited, served as an explanation and justification for their claims to lead-ership. This new kind of leader, these spiritual supermen,[23] were prepared to put their spiritual skills in the service of the people. The retiring, iso-lated mystic was replaced by the *tsaddik* who announced his readiness to enter the life of the community. He took on the obligation to elevate the common people to a higher level of existence. In the 1750s and 1760s, to judge by later Hasidic literary sources, there were no individual *tsaddikim* who led their own communities of followers. The chief contrast in those decades was between the generalized elite, called variously men of form, or *hassidim,* and everyone else, referred to as people of matter, or the masses. There was also the idea that there was one *tsaddik* whose presence on earth sustained the entire world. Thus, Jacob Josef of Połonne wrote:

The entire world is nourished for the sake of [*bishevil*] R. Hanina, My son. . . . In the name of my teacher [the Besht] I heard the following: "Hanina made a pathway and channel [= *shevil*] that draws the divine plenitude [*shef'a*] into the world. This explains the passage, 'the entire world is nourished for the sake of [*bi-shevil*] Hanina My son.'" . . . To me it seems that he not only made a pathway and channel, etc., but that he actually was himself the pathway and channel through which the *shef'a* passed.[24]

The *maggid* of Międzyrzecz proclaimed a similar interpretation, though in more kabbalistic language:

We begin with the Zohar's interpretation of "One generation passes and another comes" [Eccles. 1:4]. There is no generation that does not have a *tsaddik* like Moses (Zohar I:25a; Genesis Rabba 56:7). This means that Moses included the entire six hundred thousand of the generation [of the Exodus]. . . . This is why "One gen-eration passes and another comes" is said in the singular and not the plural: it refers to the *tsaddik* of the generation. . . . *Tsaddik* is the foundation [*yesod*] of the world. Now it is known that *yesod* has the power to ascend and draw abundance from above, because it includes everything.[25] The same is true of the earthly *tsad-*

23. Various scholars have used this term. See, e.g., Norman Lamm, *The Religious Thought of Hasidism: Text and Commentary* (New York, 1999), 287 (to characterize the teach-ings on the subject of Elimelekh of Leżajsk).

24. Jacob Josef of Połonne, *Ben porat yosef,* 63b, in G. Nigal, *Torot ba'al hatoledot: De-rashot R. Ya'akov Yosef miPolenoye lefie nos'ei yesod* (Jerusalem, 1974), 7–8.

25. "The ninth of the ten emanations (*sefirot*): the same word thus designates an aspect of the divine Self and a particular group of humans. This ninth level of divinity is otherwise commonly referred to as *yesod* ('foundation'), as Joseph, as the phallus of *Adam Qadmon* [the primordial Adam], or, in better Kabbalistic language, as 'the sign of the holy covenant.'"

dik: he is the channel that allows the abundance to flow down for his entire generation. Thus, the rabbis said: "The entire world is nourished for the sake of Hanina, My son." This means that Hanina brought the divine flow forth for all of them, like a pathway through which all can pass; R. Hanina himself became the channel for that overflow. In the same way, he [the *tsaddik*] was the ladder of which it is said, "They go up and down on it" (Gen. 28:12). Just as he has the power to cause the downward flow of divine bounty [*shefʿa*], so can his entire generation rise upward through him.[26]

The many, the people of matter, could turn to God through the *tsaddik,* who was the channel or the pathway between heaven and earth. While the Besht may have seen himself as the singular *tsaddik hador—the* righteous person for whose sake his entire generation is sustained, later Hasidic masters allowed for a multiplicity of *tsaddikim.* Each of them was in a category quite different from that of ordinary Jews. As these ideas developed later in the century, there were variations of emphasis on the precise role of the *tsaddik.* The earliest Hasidic texts published in the 1780s did not use this term consistently to designate a particular position of leadership.[27] Some of the leaders in the previous decade tended to emphasize their obligations as teachers, seeking to be the pathway upward. Others stressed their ability to provide blessings from heaven for their followers, serving as a channel for divine plenty as it came down to earth. Nevertheless, it was only "the concept of the Tsaddik and his role as a religious and social leader, his relationship with his community on the one hand and to God on the other" that was "characteristic of the Hasidic movement as a whole and only to it."[28]

Opposition and Crystallization

It seems that in the 1760s and 1770s, Hasidim moved easily from one master to another, and there were groups of men who followed the Hasidic path in their own places of prayer without being attached to any particular teacher. At the same time, differences in emphasis and in patterns of leadership developed among the various masters. At the same time, there

---

Yesod is called *kol* ("all") because it includes the flow of all eight upper *sefirot.* Green, "Zaddiq as *Axis Mundi,*" 332–33, 344, n. 16.

26. *Or Torah, Noah,* 12, as translated by Idel, *Hasidism,* 203, and Green, "Zaddiq as *Axis Mundi,*" 338.

27. Rapoport-Albert, "Hasidism," 130.

28. Joseph Dan, "A Bow to Frumkinian Hasidism," *Modern Judaism* 11 (1991): 175–93.

was growing alarm among some rabbis and in several communities. By 1772, largely at the instigation of the Vilna Ga'on, bans of excommunication were pronounced against these "newly arrived" Hasidim.[29]

Successive bans of excommunication were issued in Vilna in 1772, 1781 (1785), and 1797.[30] Each ban was more severe than the last. In addition to Vilna, there were bans against the Hasidim by the communal elders of Brody in 1772, by the elders of the community of Pińsk, and by the rabbi and elders of Grodno, Słuck, and Brześć Litewski in 1781, and Kraków in 1785. In 1798, the reading of Hasidic texts was banned in Kraków. Other communities, while not excommunicating the Hasidim, adopted rules intended to make them conform to communal and traditional norms. Such *takanot* (edicts) were adopted in Lesznów (Leshnuv, in the region of Brody) around 1772, in Mińsk in 1786 (renewed in 1796), in Mohylew (Mahilyow) in 1786 or early 1787, and in the region of Szkłów in 1787. There were debates in writing and in person between representatives of the two sides, the Hasidim and their "opponents" *(mitnaggedim)*. In addition, there were polemical literary attacks against the Hasidim, especially in the last decade of the eighteenth century. Of these, the most important were the writings of two preachers, David of Maków and Israel Loebel.[31] Hasidic books were burned on several occasions, and Hasidic leaders were sometimes driven out of their communities. The most notorious cases were the expulsion of Menahem Mendel from Mińsk and of Levi Yitshak, who was removed from his position as *av beit hadin* (communal rabbi) of Pińsk at the behest, apparently, of the Vilna Ga'on in 1785.[32]

Scholars have explained this opposition to Hasidism in a variety of ways and have proposed diverse answers to such related questions as why the opposition should have arisen primarily in Lithuania and not in Galicia or Ukraine and how widespread the opposition to Hasidism actually was.

---

29. Much of the material on the opposition to Hasidism between 1772 and 1815 was collected and edited by Wilensky, *Hasidim umitnaggedim*. See also, id., "Hasidic-Mitnaggedic Polemics in the Jewish Communities of Eastern Europe: The Hostile Phase," in *Essential Papers on Hasidism*, ed. Gershon Hundert (New York, 1991), 244–71.

30. "Without the position and the initiative of the GR'A [the Gaon Rabbi Elijah], the establishment would not have been led to a war of excommunication against Hasidism." Immanuel Etkes, *Yahid bedoro: Haga'on miVilnah — demut vedimui* (Jerusalem, 1998), 104, 84–163. Ettinger, "Hasidism," 68.

31. Their writings are collected, edited, introduced, and annotated in Wilensky, *Hasidim*, vol. 2.

32. Wilensky, *Hasidim*, 1: 132–36. There remain, as Wilensky noted, some problems with the dating of the letter (1784) and the identity of the rabbi who is unnamed in the text. Cf. Rabinowitsch, *Lithuanian Hasidism*, 25, 36–40.

The tenor and content of the accusations remains fairly constant from the 1770s to the 1790s. They were charged with separatism, rejecting normative Torah study, defying traditional morality, exploiting the naïve, and being Shabbatean sympathizers.

Hasidic Separatism: Separate Places of Prayer

The insistence of the Hasidim on praying separately was itself objectionable.[33] The ban proclaimed against them in Brody, for example, contained no fewer than five references to their having "built 'high places' [bamot] for themselves, separating themselves from the holy community, gathering separate quorums for prayer, not praying with the congregation in the established synagogues and study halls."[34] This separatistic tendency not only threatened to reduce communal revenues from the sale of honors and pews but threatened good order in the community. Established places of prayer were where communal proclamations and the distribution of honors took place. The inscriptions bearing the names of donors on the various objects in the synagogue reflected hierarchical distinctions that served the interests of the communal establishment.[35] By removing themselves from this locus, they were removing themselves from communal influence.

THE LURIANIC PRAYER BOOK

Jews in Poland-Lithuania traditionally followed a version of the Ashkenazic prayer book. The Hasidim followed a form of the rite named for the famous Safed kabbalist Isaac Luria. This form of the prayer book is sometimes referred to, without precision, as Sephardic.[36] Although Jewish society in eastern Europe was prepared to make an exception for small groups of elite kabbalists who also used this liturgy,[37] its use by the masses,

33. See the interpolation by the anonymous editor of the collection of anti-Hasidic materials published in 1772, *Zemir aritsim*, in Wilensky, *Hasidim*, 1: 55–57, esp. p. 56, where the Hasidim are called *kat haperushim*—a sect of separatists.

34. Wilensky, *Hasidim*, 1: 45.

35. Yekutiel Kamelhar, *Sefer mofet hador* (Piotrków and Warsaw, 1934), 1: dedication of *parokhet* and *kaporet* by members of a powerful family.

36. For a more detailed explanation see Jacobs, *Hasidic Prayer*, 38–39.

37. Thus the ban in Brody exempted from this prohibition the Pietists who prayed in the "*kloiz* of our community, for it is definitely clear that [they] . . . are filled with [knowledge] of the revealed Torah, Gemara, and Codes and have also mastered the secrets of the

as advocated by the Hasidim, was an act of defiant arrogance and was seen as a rejection of the ways of previous generations.

STRANGE MOVEMENTS, GESTURES, AND SOUNDS DURING PRAYER

One reason why the Hasidim preferred to have their own place of prayer was precisely the ecstatic intensity with which they prayed. Clapping, shouting,[38] using words in languages other than Hebrew, gyrating in ugly ways,[39] and even dancing were part of their ecstatic reveries. Numerous anti-Hasidic texts recount with disgust that Hasidim "turn over before the Ark . . . heads down and legs up."[40] Turning somersaults was indeed associated with a number of Hasidic leaders, including Shne'ur Zalman of Lyady (1745–1813), Hayyim Hayke of Indura (Amdur, d. 1787), and Abraham Kalisker (d. 1810).[41] Hasidim understood the practice as a way of overcoming pride. In general, gesticulation and movement during prayer were explained in a parable ascribed to the Besht. A person who is drowning in a river gesticulates and makes wild movements in order to draw attention so that someone will save him. He is not to be laughed at, because he is fighting for his life. Similarly, a Hasid while praying is fighting for his soul against the forces of evil trying to drown him in a river of impurity. He thus gesticulates and makes wild movements.[42]

NOT PRAYING AT THE CORRECT TIME

Some of the anti-Hasidic writings refer to Hasidic neglect of the proper hour of prayer. This was not a major motif; its importance is that it was

---

Kabbalah. They have been reading their prayers from the prayer book of the ARI [Isaac Luria] for many years." Wilensky, *Hasidim*, 1: 47. And see also there 1: 67, where one R. Yo'el is permitted to lead a separate prayer quorum in Lesznów.

38. Wilensky, *Hasidim*, 1: 41 n. 27.

39. On prayer in *la'az*, see ibid., 59, n. 15, 65. "Prayer is *zivug* [copulation] with the *Shekhinah* [the Divine Presence understood as female]." *Tzava'at Harivash*, 54–55, and see the reference to two parallel passages in *Keter shem tov* there, n. 1.

40. Wilensky, *Hasidim*, 1: 18, 39–40 (n. 24), 60, 65, 68, 75–77, 82, 83, 108, 139; 2: 33, 41, 44–45, 140, 172; id., "Hasidic-Mitnaggedic Polemics," 257–58.

41. H. M. Heilman, *Beit rabbi* (Berdyczów, 1903), 90. Cf. A. Wertheim, *Halakhot vehalikhot bahassiduth* (Jerusalem, 1960), 17; Wilensky, *Hasidim,* 1: 39–40, 76. Wilensky's contention (ibid., 39, n. 24), on the basis of a letter written in the midst of a dispute, and forty-four years after the fact, that the practice "originated among the Hasidim of Abraham Kalisker" is unpersuasive.

42. Cited by Wilensky, "Hasidic-Mitnaggedic Polemics," 252.

the only genuinely *halakhic* objection to Hasidic practice, and a relatively minor one at that. While the Mitnaggedim attributed this to willfulness and lack of seriousness, some Hasidim maintained that the hour of prayer was less important than being properly prepared for it.[43]

SPECIAL KNIVES FOR SLAUGHTERING ANIMALS

Given the concern of the old-style *hassidim* for proper *halakhic* slaughter and their eventual adoption of specially sharpened (*geshlifine*) knives for this purpose, the preoccupation of the Hasidim with this matter, like their use of the so-called Lurianic prayer book, amounted to popularization of an existing practice among the kabbalistic elite.[44] There seem to have been three main elements behind Hasidic preoccupation with slaughter of animals. Two of the Hasidic concerns have been mentioned—that there were untrained slaughterers in the villages and that some of the slaughterers might be Shabbateans.[45] The historian Chone Shmeruk explains the third concern as follows:

In Hasidism . . . [a] belief in reincarnation and the transmigration of souls closely connected with ritual slaughter gained great importance. If a Jewish soul . . . was reincarnated into a "clean" animal fit for kosher consumption, then the ritual slaughter and pious consumption, together with the necessary blessings and intentions, enabled that soul to be "liberated" into another human embodiment. Making meat *terefa* ["torn" and therefore unfit for consumption] was seen as the equivalent of another "killing" of the soul, thus sentencing it to further non-human wandering.[46]

Transmigration/reincarnation was a motif in the writings of some influential mystics in sixteenth-century Safed. Scholars have stressed that Jewish law was not the basis of the objection to the Hasidic method of slaughtering animals, since the practice was acceptable in those terms,

43. Ibid., 250.

44. See chapter 6 above, around and in n. 7.

45. See the possible allusion to this in Jacob Josef of Połonne, *Sefer toledot ya'akov yosef,* 123a.

46. Chone Shmeruk, "Hasidism and the Kehilla," in *The Jews in Old Poland, 1000–1795,* ed. Antony Polonsky et al. (London, 1993), 186, 189. And see, too, Shmeruk, "Mashma'utah hahevratit shel hashehitah hahassidit" (1955), in id., *Hakri'ah lenavi: Mehkerei historiyah vesifrut,* ed. Israel Bartal, 33–63 (Jerusalem, 1999), 51–52, around n. 65, on the fact that the link between slaughtering animals properly and the belief in reincarnation did not originate with the Hasidim. See also Wilensky, *Hasidim,* 1: 79–80, and Shaul Stampfer, "Lekorot mahloket hasakinim hamelutashot," in *Mehkerei hassidut,* ed. Immanuel Etkes et al., Jerusalem Studies in Jewish Thought, 15 (Jerusalem, 1999), 197–210.

and that none of the anti-Hasidic documents emanating from Vilna mention it.[47] The objections accordingly were political and economic. The Hasidic slaughterers did not see themselves as subject to the authority of the *kahal*. Moreover, the institution of a separate type of slaughter diminished income from the tax on meat, which formed a significant part of the community's budget. The social consequences resulted from the fact that Hasidim would not eat meat slaughtered in the usual way.

Rejection of the Normative Place of Torah and Torah Scholars

REVERSAL OF THE TRADITIONAL PRIORITY OF STUDY OVER PRAYER

The bans and other oppositionist writings return again and again in various ways to the issues of the centrality of prayer and the diminution of the importance of study in the teachings of early Hasidic masters. The Hasidim were guilty of *bitul Torah,* of wasting time that should be used in study. "They do away with the study of Torah." "They say God forbid that we should spend our days in the study of Torah." They trapped young students in their nets by telling them that Torah study was unimportant, contradicting the central norm of the community.[48] Indeed, "in all the Mitnaggedic writings, from 1772 on, the argument that the Hasidim are fostering neglect of Torah study and denigrating scholars is raised repeatedly."[49] "This is what most angered the Mitnaggedim of Vilna and particularly Elijah Ga'on."[50] For the Ga'on, nothing, including the performance of the commandments, was more important than the study of Torah. Every word a person learns, he taught, is equal in value to all of the commandments.[51]

47. Wilensky, "Hasidic-Mitnaggedic Polemics," 253–57. See Wilensky, *Hasidim,* index, s.v. *shehitah.* Even Avraham Katzenellenbogen who fiercely opposed Hasidism, including its use of special knives, declared: "their slaughter is *very close* [emphasis added] to being unacceptable." Ibid., 1: 126.

48. Wilensky, *Hasidim,* 1: 38, 43 n. 47, 60, 63, 138, 322–23.

49. Ibid., 263. See also ibid., index, s.v. *bitul Torah uvizayon lomdeha,* and also 1: 38 n. 13.

50. Ibid., 1: 18.

51. Etkes, *Yahid bedoro,* 257–60.

STUDY OF KABBALAH BY THE UNINITIATED

The opponents further objected to the fact that, despite the traditional limitations on the study of Kabbalah to those of mature years and great knowledge, Hasidim "spend all their time [studying] esoteric texts"; they "enter the [dangerous] rose garden of Kabbalah." "They separate themselves from the community, refusing to take hold of the revealed Torah . . . their entire concern is with the hidden [Torah]." Moreover, they tried to study the esoteric, "to which they have no claim and which is reserved for a small elite—one or two in each generation."[52] They even wore white robes, which had been reserved for the elite kabbalists.[53]

Defiance of Acceptable Comportment and Traditional Morality

"ALL THEIR DAYS ARE LIKE HOLIDAYS"

The visage that a dignified Jewish scholar presented to the world was dour and serious, as was appropriate in the "long and bitter exile" of the Jewish people. The Mitnaggedim took it as self-evident that to say of the Hasidim, "all their days are like holidays," and "they waste the time of study all the day in matters of silliness and laughter," was to condemn them. They further accused the Hasidim of only loving "celebration, spending all their time in song." Just as bad, "they waste time spending all their days smoking tobacco."[54]

THEIR FOLLOWERS ARE TAUGHT
NOT TO REGRET THEIR SINS

"They say, 'God forbid that one should regret a sin one has committed lest it lead to sadness.'" This complaint at once echoed and distorted a teaching ascribed to the Besht and published in *The Testament of Rivash*: "Sometimes the Evil Inclination deceives a person telling him that he has

---

52. Wilensky, *Hasidim*, 1: 50, 51, 52. See Alan Lawrence Nadler, *The Faith of the Mitnaggedim: Rabbinic Responses to Hasidic Rapture* (Baltimore, 1997), 29–33.

53. Wilensky, *Hasidim*, 1: 54, 56.

54. Ibid., 1: 39 and n. 20, 54, 57; 2: 60, 75. See Louis Jacobs, "The Uplifting of Sparks in Later Jewish Mysticism," in *Jewish Spirituality: From the Sixteenth-Century Revival to the Present,* ed. Arthur Green (New York, 1989), 121–22; id., "Tobacco and the Hasidim," *POLIN* 11 (1998): 25–30.

committed a grave sin even though it was only a simple stringency [*humra be'alma*], or not a sin at all. His purpose is to make the person un-happy . . . and unhappiness is a great obstacle to the service of the Cre-ator Blessed Be He."[55]

Several allusions hint at homosexual activity among the Hasidim. "They all gather at night sleeping in one room, and who knows what ugly deeds transpire." One Hasid is supposed to have received forgiveness for this sin from Menahem Mendel of Mińsk (later in Witebsk).[56] References to homosexuality are rare in this culture and period, but not completely unknown, and there is no way to evaluate the veracity of these claims. Nevertheless, it is striking that none of the descriptions of lewd and or-giastic behavior among the Shabbatean Frankists raise the issue of ho-mosexuality.[57]

The Tsaddik as Confidence Man and Exploiter of Women and the Young

The anti-Hasidic documents depict the rebbes as shameless exploiters of the naïve for the sake of their own material profit. To cover expenses in-volved in providing for the followers who visit him, the leader turns to the rich and prophesies disaster that can be averted only by a substantial contribution *(pidyon)*. They pretend to be wonder-workers: "this one heals the sick; that one expels ghosts; this one frees *agunot;* that one finds what is lost; this one cures barren women; that one reads minds; this one pre-dicts the future." "And they say of their leader, 'He will pray for us.'"[58]

Only in one anti-Hasidic pamphlet, *Shever posh'im* by David of Maków, are women referred to as an element in the new movement. There is no reference to women in the bans of excommunication or other documents of opposition. In *Shever posh'im*, rebbes are accused of claiming to be able to cure barrenness. In one passage, the author addresses women with words to the following effect (his ornate style defies direct translation): For naught you bring gifts and donations seeking healing. You will be

55. Wilensky, *Hasidim*, 1: 38 and n. 17, 59; 2: 74.

56. Ibid., 1: 41, 65; 2: 174.

57. The *Book of Visions* by Hayyim Vital, perhaps reflecting realities in late-sixteenth-cen-tury Safed, includes a number of references to homosexuality. Morris M. Faierstein, trans., *Jewish Mystical Autobiographies: Book of Visions and Book of Secrets,* "Book of Visions," II, 24, pp. 70, 71; IV, 31, p. 187.

58. Ibid., I, 53, 54, 59, 63; II, 62–67, 84, 137, 321.

disappointed; you will not be spared accident and disaster, your broken heart will not be mended, your sick will not be healed, your barrenness will not be ended. The rebbe wants only your money.[59] There is no indication in Hasidic literature that women had any role or importance as actors in this new spiritual path.[60] The most frequent reference to women in the anti-Hasidic literature was to their men abandoning them and going off to visit the rebbe.[61]

SHABBATEANISM SUSPECTED

It is difficult to distinguish between actual accusations that the Hasidim were Shabbateans, on the one hand, and attempts to malign them by "tarring them with the same brush" as the almost contemporary Shabbatean heretics, on the other.[62] The appearance of a new group that rejected or neglected Torah study and its authoritative representatives certainly must have called to mind the Shabbatean-Frankist heretics. Moreover, Hasidism must have aroused fears, even among those who were not necessarily opponents of the movement, that the fire of heresy had not been extinguished. This was expressed most eloquently by R. Shelomoh Yitshak Heilperin, rabbi of Bar (1727–ca. 1784), in Podolia, in the second half of the eighteenth century, in a comment on one of his father's responsa. He began by recalling a prediction by his father, Ya'akov, rabbi of Zwaniec (d. 1738), in the first half of the century:

In the responsum of my lord, father, and teacher, rest in peace [on the question of reading the prayers in the Sephardic manner of pronunciation], the rabbinic dictum that a scholar is better than a prophet was fulfilled. For he saw from the outset [the fate] of the believers in Shabbetai Tsevi, may the name of the evil ones rot. . . . In my late father's generation, members of this sect were like wild pigs [and ungulates] falsely pretending to be pure. They would fast often and mortify their flesh, presenting themselves as *hassidim uperushim*. . . . They began to effect changes in our liturgy . . . then they ate on the four fast days, saying that they had become days of celebration. Hearing of this, my lord, father, teacher, and rabbi,

59. Ibid., II, 60, 67, 76, 77, 84, 136–37.

60. Ada Rapoport-Albert, "On Women in Hasidism: S. A. Horodecky and the Maid of Ludmir Tradition," in *Jewish History: Essays in Honour of Chimen Abramsky*, ed. id. and S. Zipperstein (London, 1988), 495–525.

61. Ibid., 497, and the references cited there.

62. See Avraham Rubinstein, "Hakuntras *zimrat am ha'arets*," *Areshet* 3 (1961): 211, where he suggests such a distinction, and Wilensky, *Hasidim*, 2: 45–46, where he responds that the attempt is "artificial." And see the texts in Wilensky, *Hasidim*, 1: 46, 60, 63, 67 n. 32; 2: 45–46 nn. 105–6, 75, 77.

the *ga'on*, prophesied of them that in the end, they would leave, free of all of the commandments. And indeed after several years, and after my father's death, I my self saw that as he had prophesied, so it was. Everyone knows about the apostasy in the holy community of Lwów in the presence of all of the rabbis of the region at the disputation in the church with those evil sectarians. I myself was obliged to be [there] since I was rabbi of Roczyn [Rohatyn?]. . . . How much we suffered when this sect, which numbered several hundred, came out against us in their in solence, trying to destroy us with false accusations and slander. . . . They permitted themselves everything, some became Muslims and some became Christians. They all left the community, together with their wives and their sons and daughters — young and old. They forced them to convert against their will, for they did not wish to do so. They wept before their families, as I saw with my own eyes when I was in Lwów at that time. They called themselves *mitnaggedim* [opponents], that is, opponents of the Talmud. . . .

And now, in our own generation also, because of our many sins, a malignant sore is spreading. They despise the Oral Torah, the Talmud, and the Codes and with undue haste study the books of Kabbalah. They call themselves Hasidim be cause they pray using the Sephardic rite. Some of them . . . wrap themselves in white robes. . . . They waste their time, filling their days smoking tobacco. They have appointed animal slaughterers who use specially sharpened knives. [The doc ument goes on to describe how the author has seen Hasidim who are ignora muses.] If there are [any] among my sons and descendants who wish to be Ha sidim, may it be God's will that they follow [instead] the sacred traditions of their ancestors, or at the very least, first fill themselves with the study of Talmud and Codes.[63]

The author does not totally condemn this new Hasidism and seems to realize that it is not a transient phenomenon.

THEOLOGICAL OBJECTIONS

Anti-Hasidic literature seldom mentioned strictly theological matters. The only important document in this context is a letter written by the Vilna Ga'on in the autumn of 1796. After accusing the Hasidim of having brought forth a generation that rejects its parents, and after a direct allu sion to Hasidic teaching on *keri,* he declared that it was "an abomination" that they called themselves *hassidim.* The letter then makes a laconic but hostile reference to what might be termed Hasidic immanentism — that

---

63. Published on the basis of a manuscript by Simon Dubnow, *Toledot hahassiduth* (Tel Aviv, 1967), 484–85. Dubnow suggests that since the bans of excommunication are not men tioned in the passage, it was likely written before 1772. His argument is unconvincing. Cf. Rosman, *Founder,* 133–34.

there is no place where God is absent—equating this doctrine with idolatry: "How they have deceived this generation, uttering these words on high: 'These are your gods O Israel': every stick and stone' [see Exod. 32:8]. They interpret the Torah incorrectly regarding the verse 'Blessed be the name of the glory of God from His dwelling place' [Ezek. 3:12] and also regarding the verse, 'You enliven everything' [Neh. 9:6]."[64] It is possible to attempt to identify the precise allusions in Hasidic literature to which the Ga'on might have been reacting. Thus, for example, in Tsava'at haRiv'ash and Keter shem tov: "Everything in the universe contains holy sparks. Nothing lacks these sparks, even wood and stones." "One must always bear in mind about the Creator that 'the whole earth is full of his glory' and His Shekhina [presence; providence] is constantly with one. . . . And one should consider that when he looks at physical things, it is as if he is beholding the Shekhina that is within him. This is a form of divine worship on the level of katnut ["smallness," lowered consciousness]." In the second section of Shne'ur Zalman of Lyady's magnum opus, Tanya, a book published some months after the composition of the Ga'on's letter, we find a direct reference to the verse from Ezekiel: "The verse, 'Blessed be the name [of the glory of God from His dwelling place]' teaches the lower-level . . . unity, namely, that His very essence and being . . . which is called Eyn Sof [Infinite], completely fills the earth both in space and in time . . . everything is filled with the light of the Eyn Sof . . . and all . . . is completely nullified in the light of the Eyn Sof." The verse from Nehemiah was reread in the same text in a punning reinterpretation to mean, not "You enliven everything," but "You are [mehaveh instead of mehayeh] everything."[65] In other words, the Ga'on feared that the ascription of divinity to everything, "even wood and stones," would obscure the distinction between good and evil.

The Importance of the Bans against the Hasidim

It must be stressed that the efforts to ostracize and eventually eradicate this new phenomenon failed entirely. Even in Lithuania-Belorussia, where it is usually said that Hasidism was absent, there were Hasidic courts with

64. Wilensky, Hasidim, 1: 187–88. On this issue, see Nadler, Faith, 11–28, where he maintains that the issue was not immanentism per se (on which Hasidim and Mitnaggedim did not really disagree) but the way this idea should be understood and its implications for the religious worldview.

65. Wilensky, Hasidim, 1: 188–89; Nadler, Faith, 11–13.

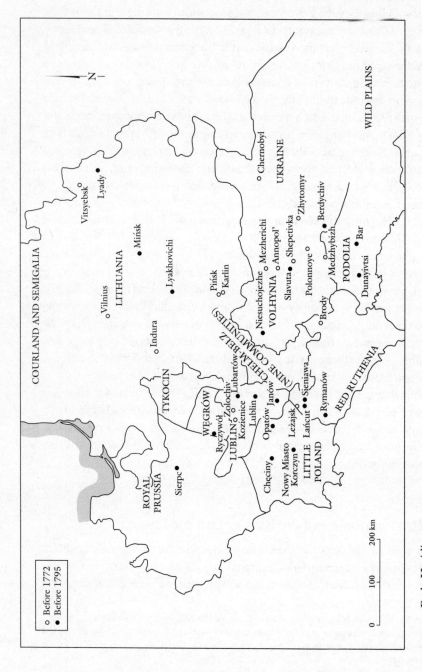

MAP 4. Early Hasidic centers

COURLAND AND SEMIGALIA

ROYAL PRUSSIA

LITHUANIA

UKRAINE

WILD PLAINS

VOLHYNIA

PODOLIA

RED RUTHENIA

LITTLE POLAND

CHEŁM-BEŁZ
(NINE COMMUNITIES)

LUBLIN

WĘGRÓW

TYKOCIN

-N-

Before 1772
Before 1795

Vitsyebsk
Lyady
Mińsk
Vilnius
Lyakhovichi
Indura
Pińsk
Karlin
Niesuchojeże
Mezherichi
Annopol'
Slavuta
Shepetivka
Zhytomyr
Polonnoye
Berdychiv
Medzhybizh
Bar
Dunayivtsi
Brody
Sieniawa
Rymanów
Lańcut
Leżajsk
Janów
Lubartów
Opatów
Zolochiv
Ryczywół
Lublin
Kozienice
Korczyn
Nowy Miasto
Checiny
Sierpc

Chernobyl

0   100   200 km

considerable followings.[66] The number of Hasidic centers grew continuously throughout the thirty-five-year period of bans and polemics against them. The response to the attacks was apparently formulated by Dov Ber, the *maggid* of Międzyrzecz. His policy was to seek peace, answer calmly, and never to counter attack with attack or excommunication with excommunication. Even before the first bans were pronounced in 1772, a senior disciple of Dov Ber and leader of his own Hasidic community, Menahem Mendel of Mińsk, attempted to visit the Vilna Ga'on to allay his doubts about the new-style Hasidim. The Ga'on refused to see him and would refuse again when Menahem Mendel made a second such attempt in 1777.[67] In a letter of 1797, a Hasidic leader reflected on the success of this policy of restraint, "since . . . thousands have become ten thousands."[68] The main exception to this policy of nonretaliation was the widespread destruction of copies of the first anti-Hasidic pamphlet of 1772.

Just what was the extent of Hasidic communities in 1772? On the basis of existing sources, no complete answer can be given. (See map 4.) There were certainly Hasidic communities in Międzyrzecz and Karlin (near Pińsk), as well as Mińsk, Vilna, and Brody, since these are mentioned in the 1772 pamphlet. R. Abraham Kalisker led a community, probably in Kolszki near Witebsk. Israel ben Shabbetai Hapstein (1733–1814) of Kozienice may have established a community in that town by 1772. Levi Yitshak, later of Berdyczów, may have been in Żelechów by 1772; he moved to Pińsk in 1775–76 and to Berdyczów in 1785. Hayyim Haykl ben Samuel (d. 1787) of Indura (near Grodno) established a Hasidic community there in or shortly after 1772. Elimelekh of Leżajsk may have established himself there as early as 1764. It is difficult to establish the precise identities of "the famous *tsaddikim* of Volhynia" who suffered greatly as a result of the publication of the anti-Hasidic pamphlet in 1772.[69] Most likely, they included Menahem Nahum Twersky of Czarnobyl (Chornobyl, or Chernobyl) (1730–1787); Jacob Samson of Szepietówka (d. 1801); and Ze'ev Wolf of Żytomierz (Zhytomyr) (d. 1800). Even this undoubtedly very partial list should make it clear that the appearance of Hasidism in the generation following the death of the Besht was not at all restricted

66. Rabinowitsch, *Lithuanian Hasidism*.

67. In both cases, he may have been accompanied by Shne'ur Zalman of Liady.

68. See the important letter of Shne'ur Zalman of Liady to his Hasidim in Vilna (!) published by Yehoshua Mondshine in *Kerem HaBaD* 4 (1992): 111–13, as cited by Etkes, *Yahid bedoro*, 118–20.

69. Letter of 1797 by Shne'ur Zalman of Liady quoted in Etkes, *Yahid*, 118.

to the southeastern regions of the Polish Commonwealth but encompassed its entire eastern half. For the close of the eighteenth century, an anti-Hasidic document written in about 1798 included a list of sixteen rebbes located in Lithuania, Belorussia, Mazovia, Little Poland, Galicia, Volhynia, and Ukraine.[70] Despite the vast increase in the number of Hasidim in the last three decades of the eighteenth century, it is important to remember that even in 1800, most Jews in Poland-Lithuania were neither Hasidim nor Mitnaggedim. It should also be stressed that those who were not Hasidim were not at all necessarily Mitnaggedim. Finally, while some Mitnaggedim were extreme and active, others were moderate and simply pursued their own paths.[71]

Numerous scholars have attempted to account for the opposition to Hasidism. Some have sought to find social, political, and even economic and class-related causes. Others suggested that the heart of the matter turned on the claims to authority made by the Hasidic leaders based on spiritual charisma as opposed to the great learning underlying the vast authority and charisma of the Vilna Ga'on.[72] This movement of spiritual awakening numbered members of all social classes and descendants of both distinguished and unknown families among its adherents and leaders. The Hasidic masters did not preach rebellion against the communal establishment, so this cannot be the explanation for the steps taken by some communities to restrict or ban Hasidic activity. Moreover, a number of Hasidic leaders were identified with or actually were part of the *kahal* administration. Levi Yitshak was the communal rabbi of Berdyczów, just as earlier Jacob Josef had been rabbi of the important community of Połonne, and even earlier the Ba'al Shem Tov himself had had the support

70. Wilensky, *Hasidim*, 2: 101–2. In Lithuania: Shmu'el Amdurer (son and successor of Hayyim Hayke of Indura). In Belarus: Zalman Lozner (Shne'ur Zalman of Lyady) and Mordekhai Lahovitser (Mordecai of Lachowicze [Lyakhovichi], 1742–1810). In Mazovia: Me'ir Shepser (Yosef Me'ir Horovits of Sierpc). In Little Poland: the *maggid* of Koznits (Israel ben Shabbetai of Kozienice), Mordecai Yanover (Mordecai of Janów), Itsik Lantsut (Jacob Isaac of Lańcut and later "The Seer" of Lublin). In Ruthenia or Galicia: Mendel Pshitiker (Menahem Mendel of Rymanów, d. 1815) and Melekh Lizhensker (Elimelekh of Leżajsk). In Volhynia: Zishe Napoler (Zusya of Annopol) and the Rabbi of Shoiz (Mordecai of Neskhiz [Niesuchojeze], 1752–1800). In Ukraine: Levi (Yitshak) of Berdyczów, Wolf Zitomir (Ze'ev Wolf of Żytomierz), Nahum Charnoblir (Menahem Nahum of Czarnobył), and his son, Motl Tsarnobler (Mordecai of Czarnobył), as well as probably Yeshayah Dunatser (Isaiah of Dunajewcy [Dunayivtsi]?). Rabinowitsch, *Lithuanian Hasidism*, 236–38.

71. For examples, see Mordecai Nadav, "Kehilot Pinsk-Karlin bein hassiduth lehit-naggedut," *Zion* 34 (1969): 98–108.

72. H. H. Ben-Sasson, "Ishiyuto shel haGra vehashpa'ato hahistorit," *Zion* 31 (1966): 39–86, 197–216.

of the community of Międzyboż. In fact, "the Hasidic movement did not aspire to create new frameworks of Jewish self-governing institutions or to promote any new model of communal leadership." It operated quite effectively within "the existing institutional framework."[73] Hasidism ultimately involved the masses, but it had no agenda of political or social revolution, or even dramatic reform of any kind. It taught a particular way to worship God, and it was on that level that the Vilna Ga'on responded to it with such ferocity.

The Ga'on's conviction that these "newly arrived" Hasidim were heretics stimulated and maintained the opposition to them as long as he lived. In this regard, the key passage in the quotation from his letter of 1797 is his declaration that it was an "abomination" that they dared to call themselves Hasidim. The Ga'on himself was referred to frequently as a *hassid*, but he was an old-style *hassid*. The changes in *hassidism* introduced by "the new ones, recently arrived" amounted to nothing less than heresy, as indicated by their disparagement of scholars, their repulsive custom of somersaulting during prayer, and their perversions of the meaning of mystical texts. The Ga'on's decision to declare them heretics was influenced also by his consciousness of the almost contemporary phenomenon of Shabbatean Frankism. He pursued the Hasidim because they "have sin in their hearts and are like a sore on the body of Israel." The opposition of communal authorities to the Hasidim, at least at the outset, was a confirmation of the judgment of the Ga'on, or a sign of their obedience to his vast authority.[74]

The efforts of the Mitnaggedim failed to put an end to Hasidism. This raises the question of exactly how widespread active opposition to Hasidism was. There continued to be more than one Hasidic prayer quorum even in Vilna itself throughout the eighteenth century, and it apparently enjoyed the support of some influential members of the community. Certain of the bans against the Hasidim were not signed and perhaps not endorsed by communal rabbis, most notably in the case of Brody in 1772.

If eastern European Jewish society was dramatically different in 1800 from what it had been in 1750, perhaps the outstanding element of change was the appearance of Hasidism in all its variegated styles and emphases. It introduced a sense of spiritual possibility available to every man. A positive and optimistic orientation to the real world, which, Hasidim

73. Ettinger, "Hasidism," 72.
74. Etkes, *Yahid*, 106–7.

believed, hid the divine reality behind the world of appearance, was made available when a person attached himself to his *tsaddik*. The appearance of *tsaddikim* viewed as nearly divine figures who mediated between heaven and earth was an utter *novum*. The communities of Hasidim that formed around these leaders were not limited to one city or town and, in consequence, a new form of socioreligious community arose alongside the existing institutions of Jewish autonomy. Moreover, unlike Jewish communal institutions, the Hasidic community was beyond the sphere of influence of the state.

Jewish society had been transformed by a spiritual revolution that drew its sources from the vast palette of Jewish culture itself and resulted in an explosion of spiritual insight and creativity, leaving an enormous, enduring library of texts and a social and religious movement that has yet to run its course. While the traditional framework of *halakha* and Torah remained, Hasidism provided new answers to questions of meaning that affected the lives of hundreds of thousands of Jews, and the movement was still growing at the end of the eighteenth century.

Hasidism as Resistance

Menahem Mendel of Witebsk expressed the fear that government actions were "making Jews equal to the Gentiles in custom and manner." There is little question that there were many Jews in Poland-Lithuania who were well aware of the profound changes afoot in European culture and of the changed thinking of certain Jewish intellectuals influenced by those changes. Menahem Mendel's advice went on to invoke the Zohar's interpretation of the Egyptian exile. "They did not mix with the Gentiles and did not learn their ways. For this they were redeemed from Egypt: because they did not change their names or their language, and in their hearts they never accepted the government of the ruler of Egypt."[75] Menahem Mendel understood precisely how dangerous the possibility of the integration of Jews into the general population was to traditional beliefs and values. These fears, born of awareness, may be part of the reason why Hasidism enjoyed such an enormous and *continuing* success among eastern European Jews.

75. *Likkutei amarim* (Lwów, 1811), pt. 2, letter 6, pp. 9b–12b; Yaakov Barnai, *Igerot hasidim me'erets Yisra'el* (Jerusalem, 1980), 117–24; Isaac Levitats, *The Jewish Community in Russia 1772–1844* (New York, 1943), 45.

CHAPTER 10

Jews and the Sejm

If the Hasidic movement can be seen as a social configuration of Jews outside of the reach of the state, there were Jews and Christians associated with the Enlightenment who deplored it as a corrupting influence and sought to use the authority of the government to break down the barriers and to have them enter a putative civil society.

In the course of the eighteenth century, the Polish parliament (Sejm) rarely enacted legislation that singled out Jews.[1] Legislation against non-Catholics exempted Jews.[2] When Jews were discussed in the regional assemblies *(sejmiki)* and in the Sejm, it was because it was felt that their fiscal contributions were inadequate or that their commercial activities were causing hardship for Christians. Occasionally, a voice would be raised demanding that old laws forbidding Christians to serve Jews be reenacted.

Speakers who demanded an increase in the amount of taxes paid by Jews often claimed that the Jews themselves collected much more than they paid into the state's coffers. In 1746, one deputy asserted that Jews in Little Poland alone collected 900,000 florins, but gave the Treasury only "a hundred and some tens of thousands."[3] In 1752, it was claimed that in their district assemblies, Jews collected 1.2 million, of which only

---

1. In 1699, when the Treaty of Karlowitz returned Kamieniec-Podolski to Polish jurisdiction, the Sejm reenacted the prohibition of Jewish residence in the city. *VL,* 6: 62–63.

2. *VL,* 6: 119, 124–25, 286 (1717, 1733, 1736): Non-Catholics forbidden to build new churches; to recruit foreign teachers or preachers; to hold public worship or to sing during private worship; to hold public office except in the army.

3. Władysław Konopczyński, *Dyaryusze Sejmowe z wieku XVIII,* vol. 2: *Dyaryusz Sejmu z r. 1746* (Warsaw, 1912), 122–23.

200,000 reached the Treasury.[4] Speakers often stressed that if there were more taxes paid by Jews, there would be more funds to support the army. They believed that there were far more Jews than the number reflected in what was supposed to be a capitation tax. In addition to advocating a higher tax, speakers demanded that Jews pay directly and individually and not through the agency of their "parliament," which some members of the Polish Sejm wanted closed down.[5] Taxes on Jews were raised, in fact doubled, in 1716 but were not raised again until the Council of the Lands was finally abolished in the context of a more general fiscal reform in 1764.[6] This stability may be attributable, at least in part, to the combination of successful Jewish lobbying and the protection of Jews by certain magnates. It is likely, though, that the general disarray of the Sejm in that period, when very little legislation was enacted at all, was as important in the explanation of the failure to raise taxes on Jews between 1716 and 1764. Taxes on Jews were raised again in 1775.

Conventional wisdom held that those who spoke in the Jews' favor at meetings of the Sejm had received something from them, while those who spoke against them hoped to get something.[7] The memoirist and priest Jędrzej Kitowicz thought that Sejm delegates from Lithuania and from Ukraine were particularly likely to be lackeys of the Jews: "[They], being educated among Jews, not knowing any other burghers but Jews, used to being supplied by Jews with goods and other necessities of life, from school days fed on Jewish bread and matzo, made drunk by Jewish drinks. . . . [O]thers bribed with protection money [kozubalec] by the Jews, shout with all their might in their defence."[8] Nevertheless, several delegates advocated restricting Jewish movement, tying them to the land to ensure the proper payment of their taxes. In 1746, a deputy responded to this proposal by asserting that if that were the case, noblemen would be unable to find leaseholders and Jews would fall into penury. His ar-

---

4. Ibid., vol. 3: *Diarjusze Sejmów z lat 1750, 1752, 1754 i 1758* (Warsaw, 1937), 69–70.

5. "O zniesienie Sejmu żydowskiego instabat," ibid., 2: 76, 78, 127, 160, 175–77, 180, 251; 3: 69–70, 81.

6. *PVAA*, no. 43, p. xli. It is puzzling that in the Hebrew text, no. 561, p. 271, Halpern translates "Dwakroć Sto Dziesięc Tysięcy" as *"pa'amayim* 105,000 zł'." Cf. *VL*, 7: 44.

7. "Kto mówi za Żydem, musiał coś wziąć, kto przeciwko niemu, spodziewa się co wziąć," Konopczyński, *Dyaryusze Sejmowe z wieku XVIII*, 2: 176.

8. Jędrzej Kitowicz, *Pamiętnik czyli Historia Polski* (Warsaw, 1971), 442. Translation mainly follows Jacob Goldberg, "Poles and Jews in the Seventeenth and Eighteenth Centuries: Rejection or Acceptance," *Jahrbücher für Geschichte Osteuropas*, n.s., 22 (1974): 258.

9. Konopczyński, *Dyaryusze Sejmowe z wieku XVIII*, 2: 175, 78, 251.

gument prevented debate on the matter.[9] Despite occasional complaints, magnates, in their own interests, tended to protect Jewish commercial activities.[10]

Sejm legislation affected the status of Jews in the jurisdiction of the crown. In private towns, owned and controlled by magnates or churchmen, the legal situation was controlled by the town owner. While it might be true that in crown towns, "the status of Christian residents was incomparably better than in private towns,"[11] the same cannot be said about Jews. It is true that in accordance with royal privileges that granted them the right to judge themselves, Jews were not subject to municipal jurisdiction in crown towns, but when it involved municipal land, transfers of real estate were subject to the city's magistrate even when Jews were party to the transaction. Jews frequently lived in jurisdictional enclaves (*jurydyki*), properties owned by noblemen, in crown towns, however, and thus were exempt from all municipal jurisdiction. The best-known cases were Lublin, Przemyśl, and Warsaw.[12] In the case of Lublin, where the area of Jewish residence was restricted, there were protracted struggles. The protectors of the Jews were identified in a royal decree of 1737, one of many responses to the continuing battles between Lublin Christian burghers, on the one hand, and Jews and their patrons, on the other. The list included some of the most powerful noblemen in the country as well as churchmen. Among them were the Lwów canon, Władisław Zolewski; the crown hetman, Józef Potocki; the Lithuanian marshal, Paweł Sanguszko; the Lubomirskis, and the Trinitarian, Piarist, and Bernardine churches. All these were ordered to stop harboring Jews in their palaces and houses and desist from leasing breweries and taverns to them.[13]

Still, the distinction between private and crown cities should not be overstressed. Frequently, the crown-appointed officials with jurisdiction over these cities treated them as if they were their own property. The ap-

10. Yehudit Kalik, "Hayahas shel hashlakhta lemishar hayehudi," *Gal-Ed* 13 (1993): 43–57.

11. Krystyna Zienkowska, "Reforms Relating to the Third Estate," in *Constitution and Reform in Eighteenth-Century Poland: The Constitution of 3 May 1791,* ed. Samuel Fiszman (Bloomington, Ind., 1997), 330.

12. Jacob Shatzky, *Di geshikhte fun Yidn in Varshe,* vol. 1 (New York: 1947); Józef Mazurkiewicz, *Jurydyki lubelskie* (Wrocław, 1956); Mojżesz Schorr, *Żydzi w Przemyślu do końca XVIII wieku* (Lwów, 1903), no. 101, 182; no. 124, 202, no. 139, 232–33.

13. Isaiah Trunk, *Shtudies in yidishe geshikhte in Poyln* (Buenos Aires, 1963), 119; Majer Bałaban, *Die Judenstadt von Lublin* (Berlin, 1919), 57.

pointees were often themselves magnates who also owned vast estates. Nevertheless, in older, long-established cities such as Lublin, Kraków, and Lwów, competition between Jews and Christians tended to be more intense and the municipality more effective in limiting commercial activities and handicrafts pursued by Jews. Legislation enacted by the Sejm governed royal towns, and, at least occasionally, did respond to the demands of townspeople and of the petty gentry. Both groups had interests that sometimes clashed with those of Jews.

The matter of forbidding Christians to serve Jews was an ancient convention of canon law. Such laws had been enacted repeatedly and to little effect by the Polish parliament until as late as 1690. After that time, they were not repeated.[14] An exception to the lack of attention to this matter in the Sejm and the *sejmiki* was in Halicz, where virtually every set of instructions to its delegates included a point prohibiting Christians from serving Jews. One scholar has suggested that although it is possible that this was a rote repetition or an example of entrenched conservatism, it is more likely that their concerns stemmed from the Jews' raising the standard level of remuneration for hired servants. The same explanation could account for attention to this matter in Lithuania.[15] More representative is the fact that some communal privileges specifically permitted the practice of Jews having Christian servants.[16]

The Reign of Stanisław August Poniatowski (1764–1795)

After Stanisław Poniatowski was elected king and crowned as Stanisław II in 1764, public discussion of matters relating to Jews grew more frequent in the intense debates over the reform of the Polish state. These debates reflected the ideas current in Europe in general during the second half of the eighteenth century. Neither smashing the corporations on the French revolutionary model nor the absolutist centralism of Prussia and Austria could be accepted in Poland because of the immense power of the great magnate-aristocrats, who wished to retain their privileged status.

14. Jacob Goldberg, "Poles and Jews," 253. The matter of Christian servants did remain a concern of the Church. See chapter 4 above.

15. Adam Kaźmierczyk, "The Problem of Christian Servants as Reflected in the Legal Codes of the Polish-Lithuanian Commonwealth during the Second Half of the Seventeenth Century and in the Saxon Period," *Gal-Ed* 15–16 (1997): 34–35, 39.

16. Jacob Goldberg, *Jewish Privileges in the Polish Commonwealth* (Jerusalem, 1985), no. 6, 87 (Dobromil, 1612); no. 51, 324 (Swarzędz, 1621).

Moreover, whatever form Polish reform might have taken, neither Russia nor the other neighboring states would have long tolerated a resurgent Poland. Despite the ultimate failure of the reform movement, the debates and the legislation of the period of Stanisław August are examined here because of the light they shed on political thinking about and by Jews.

In the course of what Emanuel Ringelblum called the "Jewish Debate in the Polish Sejm" on February 7, 1775, a number of subjects arose that became central to discussions during subsequent decades.[17] The poll tax on Jews was raised to three florins from two; a proposal to raise it to four florins was rejected. Jews and Karaites who agreed to take up agriculture and actually work the land themselves were promised tax exemptions. The intention was that Jewish agriculturists would begin to work uncultivated fields in Ukraine. They would not be allowed ownership of the land but would pay money rents. Jews did not take up this offer, perhaps partly because they feared they would be tied to the land as the peasants were. The physiocratic proposal to channel Jews to productive and healthy occupations like agriculture was a leitmotif of Enlightenment-informed discussions of the Jewish question in Europe. In the Polish case, however, there was no willingness on the part of the gentry to give up its exclusive right to landownership. Even when, in 1791, burghers were finally permitted to acquire land, it was stipulated that factories would be built on it.

Jews who did live in rural settlements for the most part managed taverns and inns. Artur Eisenbach notes that it was in this period that they began to be seen as responsible for the dissolute way of life of the peasants: "During the second half of the eighteenth century the idea arose that Jews in the countryside acting as innkeepers, publicans and leaseholders were the main cause of the misery, drunkenness and ignorance of the peasants and were economically harmful because they took over the commodity surpluses of the peasantry. The issue was taken up by the *Sejm* itself in 1775 and later . . . was an oft-repeated motif in political writings and reform plans of the period."[18] A Hasidic leader, writing in the 1780s,

17. Emanuel Ringelblum, "A yidishe debate in Poylishn Sejm fun yor 1775," in id., *Kapitlen geshikhte fun amolikn yidishn lebn in Poyln* (Buenos Aires, 1953), 118–25.

18. Artur Eisenbach, *The Emancipation of the Jews in Poland, 1780–1870,* ed. A. Polonsky, trans. Janina Dorosz (Oxford, 1991), 45; cf. Emanuel Ringelblum, "Projekty i próby przewarstwowienia Żydów w epoce stanisławowskiej," *Sprawy Narodowościowe* 1 (1934): 3–9. Apparently, in 1776, legislation was adopted barring Jews from leasing distilleries or taverns, but only in the towns, not the villages. N. M. Gelber, "Korot hayehudim bePolin mireshit halukatah ve'ad milhemet ha'olam hasheniyah," in *Beit Yisra'el bePolin,* ed. Israel Halpern, 1: 110n. Cf. *VL,* 8: 917 (p. 562).

recalled that in Podolia in earlier decades, Jews had been forced out of the liquor trade. In its place, they had turned to commerce. The result was prosperity, "and the land, which earlier had been poor and impoverished, was filled with money." In fact, between 1765 and 1784, as many as half of all Ukrainian inns and taverns may have passed from Jewish into Christian hands.[19]

It was decided in the Sejm in 1775 that Jews without a known means of support would be forbidden to marry.[20] A similar clause was included in the stillborn Zamoyski revision of Polish law that was prepared for the Sejm of 1778. The preacher Hillel ben Ze'ev Wolf and others depicted "the absence of marriage" as one of the aspects of Jewish suffering during this period.[21] This attempt at social engineering may have reflected the increasing size of a stratum of vocationless, homeless, itinerant Jews, displaced by economic change. It was also a motif of European Enlightenment literature on Jews, which consistently overestimated their number. Similar legislation had been enacted in Prussia and was adopted in Galicia after the first partition. The complaints of the Jewish preachers may well have referred to the Austrian-Galician limitations on marriage.

Jews and the Discussion of Jews during the Four-Year Sejm, 1788–1792

European-wide Enlightenment-inspired discussions of how or whether Jews could be integrated into the emerging nation-state were one influence on debates over similar issues in Poland during the last years of the existence of the state before it was partitioned.[22] Another was the paradoxi-

19. Daniel Stone, *The Polish-Lithuanian State, 1386–1795* (Seattle, 2001), 304–5; *Likkutei amarim* (Lwów, 1811), pt. 2, letter 6, pp. 9b–12b (Menahem Mendel of Witebsk); Ya'akov Barnai, *Igerot hasidim me'erets-Yisra'el* (Jerusalem, 1980), 117–24. See chapter 3 above.

20. Gelber, "Korot hayehudim bePolin," 110. Cf. Israel Halpern, *Yehudim veyahadut bemizrah Eiropah* (Jerusalem, 1968), 289–309.

21. Hillel ben Ze'ev Wolf, *Hileil ben shahar* (Warsaw, 1804), 16a, 22b.

22. On the issue of Jews at the time of the Four-Year Sejm, see *MDSC*, vol. 2, ed. Janusz Woliński, Jerzy Michalski, and Emanuel Rostworowski (Wrocław, 1959); vol. 6, ed. Jerzy Michalski, Emanuel Rostwowrowski, Janusz Wolinski, and Artur Eisenbach (Wrocław, 1969). And see Artur Eisenbach, "Prawo obywatelskie i honorowe Żydów (1790–1861)," in *Społeczeństwo Królestwa Polskiego: Studia o uwarstwieniu i ruchliwości społecznej*, ed. W. Kula and J. Leskiewicz (Warsaw, 1965), 237–300; id., "Wokół świadomość i roli politycznej mieszczaństwa polskiego na przełomie XVIII i XIX w.," *KH* 95 (1988): 173–196; id., *Z dziejów ludności żydowskiej w Polsce w XVIII i XIX wieku* (Warsaw, 1983), 281; and id., *Emancipation of the Jews in Poland*. Nathan Michael Gelber, "Żydzi a zagadnienie reformy Żydów na

cal wish of some aristocrats to reform their polity and maintain their special privileged status at the same time. Jews should be treated like all other burghers but remain a distinct group providing extra revenues to the state.[23] The burghers themselves wanted an end to jurisdictional enclaves within their municipalities, so that everyone resident in a town would be equally subject to the city government, but they also wished to limit Jewish commercial and artisanal competition by restricting their activities. During the reign of Stanisław Poniatowski, a tiny but influential group of Jewish banking and commercial families achieved some importance in Warsaw. These also included some recent migrants from German lands and elsewhere. Probably the best known and perhaps the wealthiest Jew in Warsaw was Samuel Zbytkower (d. 1800), an army supplier and banker. Judyta, or Gitl, Levy of Frankfurt a/M, Zbytkower's third wife, used to attend the famous Thursday dinners presided over by the monarch, where the most current affairs were discussed, which were purportedly meetings of the enlightened of all classes. In truth, however, members of the bourgeoisie were rarely found at these meetings.

A number of other Jews participated in these debates as well, but in writing. Frequently the recipients of patronage from Catholic aristocrats or Jewish bankers, these Jewish intellectuals sometimes served as media-

Sejmie Czteroletnim," *Miesięcznik Żydowski,* year 1, vol. 2, no. 10 (1931): 326–44; no. 11 (1931): 429–40; Jacob Goldberg, "Pierwszy ruch polityczny wśród Żydów polskich: Plenipotenci żydowscy w dobie Sejmu Czteroletniego," in *Lud żydowski w narodzie polskim: Materiały sesji naukowej w Warszwie 15–16 wrzesień 1992,* ed. Jerzy Michalski (Warsaw, 1994), 45–63, in Hebrew, "Mishtadlanut lemedina'ut: Netsigei hakehillot bitekufat Seym Arba Hashanim," in Jacob Goldberg, *Hahevrah hayehudit bemamlekhet Polin-Lita* (Jerusalem, 1999), 217–31; Jerzy Michalski, "Sejmowe projekty reformy położenia ludności żydowskiej w Polsce w latach 1789–1792," in *Lud żydowski,* ed. id., 20–44; Emanuel Rostworowski, "Miasta i mieszczanie w ustroju Trzeciego Maja," in *Sejm Czteroletni i jego tradycje,* ed. Jerzy Kowecki (Warsaw, 1991), 138–51; Me'ir Verete, "Hatsa'ot polaniyot lepitaron teritoriyali shel 'she'elat hayehudim' 1788–1850," *Zion* 6 (1941): 148–55; 203–13; Z. Zielińska, *Walka 'familii' o reforme Rzeczypospolitej 1743–1752* (Warsaw, 1983); Krystyna Zienkowska, "Citizens or Inhabitants: The Attempt to Reform the Status of the Polish Jews during the Four Years' Sejm," *Acta Poloniae Historica* 76 (1997): 31–52; id., "The Jews Have Killed a Tailor," *POLIN* 3 (1988): 78–101, originally published as "Tumult w Warszawie w Maju 1790 roku," *KH* 95 (1988): 121–48; Krystyna Zienkowska, "Reforms Relating to the Third Estate," in *Constitution and Reform in Eighteenth-Century Poland: The Constitution of 3 May 1791,* ed. Samuel Fiszman (Bloomington, Ind., 1997), 329–55; id., *Sławetni i urodzeni: Ruch polityczny mieszczaństwa w dobie Sejmu Czteroletniego* (Warsaw, 1976); id., "Spór o Nowa Jerozolime," *KH* 93 (1986): 351–76; id., "W odpowiedzi profesorowi Arturowi Eisenbachowi," *KH* 95 (1988): 197–201.

23. Azriel Shohet has noted the same contradiction in the Jewish policies of absolutist Central European states. Shohet, *Im hilufei tekufot: Reshit hahaskalah beyahadut Germaniyah* (Jerusalem, 1960). Cf. Michalski, "Sejmowy projekte," 40; Zienkowska, "Reforms," 343.

tors of western European opinions for the Polish reading public. Salomon Polonus translated more than a hundred pages of material related to Jews and the French Revolution. Zalkind Hourwitz participated in debates about the status of Jews both in France and in Poland.[24]

An abbreviated loose Polish translation of Hourwitz's *Apologie des juifs* appeared in Warsaw in late 1789.[25] A summary of the pamphlet by Christian Wilhelm von Dohm, *Über die bürgerliche Verbesserung der Juden*, first published in Berlin in 1781, and probably the most influential discussion of the place of Jews in the modernizing state, was presented in a positive light in the Polish press in early 1783. Among the tiny group of Jewish intellectuals in the Polish Commonwealth influenced by Enlightenment ideas was the Vilna-born, German-trained physician Eliasz Ackord, who lived in Warsaw. He translated the anonymous pamphlet *Żydzi, czyli konieczna potrzeba reformowania Żydów w krajach Rzeczypospolitej Polskiej* ("Jews, or the Necessary Requirements for Reform of the Jews in the Lands of the Polish Commonwealth, by an Anonymous Citizen") into German (Warsaw, 1786) and dedicated it to the king. Jacob Kalmansohn, another physician, produced a plan for reforming Jewish life in Poland, which was published in 1796 in French and in 1797 in Polish.[26] Mendel Lefin of Satanów, Moshe Markuse,[27] and Szymel Wolfowicz among others, presented the interests of the emerging Jewish bourgeoisie to a larger public. Mendel Lefin (1749–1826) was a prolific author in the spirit of the Enlightenment and a protégé of Adam Kazimierz Czartoryski (1734–1823). He published *Essai d'un plan de reforme ayant pur objet d'éclairer la nation juive en Pologne et de redresser par là ses moeurs* anony-

24. Czartoryski Library, Kraków, MS II 1408: "Zbiór prozb Żydów francuskich do Narodowego Zgromadzenia; Mowa J. X. Grzegorza plebana embermenilskiego, deputata nantskiego, za Żydami, z francuskiego na polski ięzyk przelozony, z dodatkiem projektu reformy żydów polskich i potrzebnemi Notami obiasniona przez JMPana Salomona Polonus, doktora medycyny, konsyliarza JKMci w Wilnie roku 1792," *MDSC*, 6: 421–33. Frances Malino, *A Jew in the French Revolution: The Life of Zalkind Hourwitz* (Cambridge, Mass., 1996), 84–85.

25. Zalkind Hourwitz, *Apologie des juifs en réponse à la question: Est-il des moyens de rendre les juifs plus heureux et plus utiles en France?* (Paris, 1789), cited in *MDSC* 6: 113–18.

26. In 1783, a certain Ya'akov Hirsh submitted a memorandum to the Russian government proposing the establishment of a network of schools in Mogilev Province that would train students in the sciences, useful crafts and ethics so that they could take their place in "human society." He promised to find some teachers locally and to find the rest in German lands through the good agency of "the learned Moses Mendelssohn." Yehuda Slutsky and M. Bobe, "Letoledot yehudei Russiyah besof hame'ah ha18," *He'avar* 19 (1972): 78–80. Cf. *Regesty i nadpisi*, vol. 3 (St. Petersburg, 1913), 240–43. See above, p. 35.

27. Alexander Guterman, "'Sefer refues' leDr. markuze vehatsa'otav letikunim behayyei hayehudim," *Gal-Ed* 4–5 (1978): 35–53.

mously in 1791.[28] It was addressed to the National Education Commission of Poland. Salomon Polonus, mentioned above, and known in Vilna as the "Amsterdam doctor," also translated the long defense of Jewish rights by the abbé Henri Grégoire, a member of the French Constituent Assembly of 1789 and an advocate of Jewish emancipation. Polonus's collection ends with his own proposals for the Reform of Polish Jews.[29] His proposals, covering eighteen pages, begin with a reference to events in France: "If 50,000 Jews have convinced the French nation, today the most refined and enlightened in Europe, that they can be useful to the country . . . that they will put their property and lives in the service of their country, if these Jews have been granted the right of citizenship and have been put on an equal footing with all Frenchmen, there can be no doubt that the nearly one million Jews found in the land of Poland will, with the help of Enlightenment, become happy and useful to the[ir] country."[30] Jewish officials, including rabbis, were to be elected by the whole community, but Jewish courts would be confined to matters of religion. Rabbis were to be educated in general disciplines and sciences in addition to rabbinic literature and must know the language of the country well. In fact the language of the country must be taught in Jewish schools. Among Polonus's other proposals were the following:

—freedom of religion

—freedom of occupation, with poor Jews directed to agriculture

—liability to military conscription like Christians

—rights of citizenship for enlightened Jews immediately and for the rest after twelve years

—government to appoint one official each for Poland and Lithuania to supervise the enforcement of these policies

—marriage before the age of sixteen for females and eighteen for males should be forbidden

28. *MDSC*, 6: 409–421. See Nancy Sinkoff, "Strategy and Ruse in the Haskalah of Mendel Lefin of Satanow," in *New Perspectives on the Haskalah,* ed. Shmuel Feiner and David Sorkin (London, 2001), 86–102; and id., "Benjamin Franklin in Jewish Eastern Europe: Cultural Appropriation in the Age of the Enlightenment," *Journal of the History of Ideas* 61 (2000): 133–52.

29. Henri Grégoire, *Essai sur la régénération physique, morale et politique des juifs: Ouvrage couronné par la Société royale des sciences et des arts de Metz, le 23 août 1788* (Metz, 1789); Czartoryski Library, Kraków, MS 1408a II, 223–42; *MDSC*, 6: 421–33.

30. *MDSC*, 6: 421.

Polonus also asked for the enhancement of the conditions in which Jews lived.

—the young must respect their elders without distinction (Polonus cited Matt. 5:5, 9 and 22:21 in the New Testament as his authority)

—the clergy must persuade the population of the baselessness of the claim that Jews required Christian blood

—the clergy must be forbidden to convert any Jew who was under the age of fourteen

—Jews were not to be referred to as infidels *(niewierni)*, but as Old Believers or Hebrews

—Jews should be eligible for membership and for office in guilds and for appointment as professors in the universities

The Sejm convened in October 1788, and almost immediately, circumventing the city government, some three hundred Warsaw Jews petitioned it asking for the legalization of their residence and for occupational freedom in the city. As an inducement, they asserted that three hundred Jewish merchants were ready collectively to pay an extra tax of 3,000 ducats annually and to make a one-time payment of 180,000 florins to the Treasury to benefit the army.[31] Very shortly thereafter, the Warsaw city magistrate published a venomous pamphlet rejecting the Jews' demands.[32] A Jewish response appeared in pamphlet form before another month had passed.[33] The Jewish community of Warsaw, it said, needed "more consideration from the state authorities, not expulsion but an inevitable reform, which, if it includes them in a definite estate, and in this way secures the fate of their offspring, does not forbid them to engage in trade, arts and crafts, and in this way includes them in society. . . . [They] having become citizens, will kiss the soil that has become their motherland, will respect the paternal government, and, the better they see their happiness, the greater will be their love for this country and the greater their courage in its defense." The example of Holland was cited, and the financial inducements mentioned above were repeated.[34]

31. *MDSC*, 2: 23, n. 1.
32. *Ekspozycja praw miasta Warszawy względem Żydów oraz odpowiedź na żadaną przez nich w tymże mieście lokacyą, MDSC*, 2: 23–31.
33. Wyłuszczenie praw wolnego mieszkania i handlu Żydom w Warszawie pozwalają cych, z odpowiedzią na pismo magistratu warszawskiego preciw Żydom r. 1789 wydane, *MDSC*, 6: 27–42.
34. Eisenbach, *Emancipation*, 83–84. *MDSC*, 6: 38.

In this period, the city government of Warsaw acted energetically to publish pamphlets, brochures, and other forms of political propaganda that served its interests. A pamphlet published anonymously by Michał Świnarski maintained, for example, that it was the foreigners and the Jews who had gained control of trade and artisanry in Poland and who were responsible for the decline of the cities. Warsaw and other large cities should be freed of their Jews.[35] The attitude of the municipal authorities in Warsaw to Jews and to Jewish competition was consistently negative and had been for decades, if not for centuries. For this reason, the contention that it was a tactical error on the part of Jews and their advocates to circumvent the municipal authorities and address their concerns directly to the estates and the crown is mistaken.[36] There was simply no hope of a sympathetic hearing from the municipal authorities. (There was, in fact, one such Jewish appeal for support addressed directly to the bourgeoisie in Warsaw, which was published immediately following anti-Jewish riots in that city in May of 1790.)

The symbolic birth of the Polish bourgeoisie took place on the occasion of the so-called black procession on November 25, 1789, with the unofficial support of Stanisław Małachowski (1736–1809), the marshal of the Sejm. The representatives of the royal cities were called to Warsaw in November 1789 by Hugo Kołłątaj (1750–1812) and other noble reformers, together with Jan Dekert, president of the Old Warsaw magistracy.[37] Their purpose was to present their petition to the Polish parliament. The 294 representatives of 141 crown cities, wearing their black robes of office, marched through the streets to bring their demands before the Sejm. Their petition had been formulated in large measure by Hugo Kołłątaj and other members of the gentry. It was obvious to all concerned that any attempt to interfere with private towns as part of the proposed reforms would end in failure, since it challenged the interests of the most powerful magnates.

The burghers' main demands included representation in the Sejm; the right to acquire landed estates, which, they maintained, were needed for the establishment of manufactures; abolition of the jurisdictional enclaves (*jurydyki*) and full municipal jurisdiction over all city residents, including Jews; and the abolition of supervision of municipal governments by royal governors. In response, a parliamentary commission was established

35. *Wiadomość o pierwiastkowej miast zasadzić w Polsce* (1789), *MDSC*, 2: 32–57 (esp. 43–47). Cf. Emanuel Rostworowski, *Ostatni rok król Rzeczpospolitej* (Warsaw, 1966).
36. Krystyna Zienkowska, "Citizens or Inhabitants," 38–39.
37. Kołłątaj (1750–1812) was a priest of noble descent and rector of the Jagiellonian University in Kraków. He was one of the main authors of the Constitution of the 3rd of May 1791.

on December 18, 1789, and several hundred burghers were ennobled. At precisely the same time that the representatives of the royal cities were arriving in the Polish capital, "plenipotentiaries" of Jewish communities in Poland-Lithuania were gathering in Warsaw at the order or request of the monarch himself.[38]

The early result of these meetings was the first submission of the Jewish delegates, an extremely modest petition entitled "A Humble Request to the Honorable Members of the Sejm from the Jews of Warsaw and the Provinces of the Crown," which can be seen as reflecting either the urgent interest of Warsaw Jews in establishing their residence in the capital on a legal footing or an extremely conservative stance by representatives of the Jewish communities.[39]

The humble request was essentially for freedom of residence in any town. The petitioners claimed that, as mentioned earlier, in addition to Warsaw, 200 of 301 royal and ecclesiastical towns forbade Jewish residence. In return for the granting of their wishes, the authors offered unspecified financial aid for the state. They also offered to conclude agreements with factory owners to help them sell their products and thus help in the development of domestic manufacturing.

In February 1789, Mateusz Butrymowicz (1745–1814), a parliamentary delegate from Pińsk, published a pamphlet including the contents of an anonymous brochure that had first appeared in 1785, together with his own comments. The original document was entitled "Jews, or the Necessary Requirements for Reform of the Jews in the Lands of the Polish Commonwealth, by an Anonymous Citizen."[40] Butrymowicz added little besides a few words of introduction and at one or two places noted his disagreement with the original author. Some scholars argue that Butrymowicz was the author of the original pamphlet. Butrymowicz's patron was M. Ogiński, hetman of the Grand Duchy of Lithuania.

---

38. The delegates came at the "request" of the king, according to a letter of Avigdor, rabbi of Pińsk, and Moshe Elhanan of Tulczyn to the community of Pińsk, *MDSC*, 6: 381, or "at his order," *MDSC*, 6: 356. On the subject of Jewish delegates at this period, see Goldberg, "Mishtadlanut lemedina'ut," in id., *Hahevrah*, 217–31, and id., "Pierwszy ruch polityczny wśród Żydów polskich," 45–63.

39. *Pokorna prosba od Żydów warszawskich i prowincyj koronnych do Najjasniejszych Sejmujących Stanów* ("A Humble Request to the Honorable Members of the Sejm from the Jews of Warsaw and the Provinces of the Crown"), in *MDSC*, 6: 129–32.

40. Anon., *Żydzi, czyli konieczna potrzeba reformowania Żydów w krajach Rzeczypospolitej Polskiej* ("Jews, or the Necessary Requirements for Reform of the Jews in the Lands of the Polish Commonwealth, by an Anonymous Citizen") trans. into German by Eliasz Ackord (Warsaw, 1786), in *MDSC* 6: 78–93.

Butrymowicz had leased substantial estates in Pińsk from Ogiński and invested in a complex, large-scale project to improve water transport there. Butrymowicz took other steps to promote and develop his leased holdings, including founding a school for the children of artisans and peasants. He was an active participant in the Four-Year Sejm, taking a particular interest in fiscal matters, the development of Polish industry, and the question of the status of Orthodox and Uniate Christians. But he is best remembered for his involvement in the debates over the status of Jews. Given the demography of the Pińsk region, he probably had extensive contact with Jews.[41]

The pamphlet began with the premise that human beings were born neither evil nor good, neither wise nor foolish. Since Jews were human beings, they could become useful citizens. Nothing in the Jewish religion prevented this, as could be seen in Holland, England, and Prussia. However, a serious obstacle to their becoming good citizens was their dual loyalty to their own community and to the government. The *kahal* amounted to a state within a state.

Our laws regarding the Jews are wrong. Their situation, outside a class, is wrong. It is wrong to place the power over them in the hands of private individuals or special Jewish bureaucrats. It is wrong to consider them a bad nation and to offer them no fatherland. Worst of all is that we allow them to live with special laws and customs. Owing to this, they appear as a *corpus in corpore,* a state within a state; in view of the fact that Jewish laws and rites are different from ours, such a state of things gives rise to conflicts, confusion, mutual distrust, contempt, and hatred.

The heavy taxes Jews paid were another obstacle to their becoming good citizens. And the third impediment was the discriminatory legislation that prevented Jews from pursuing dignified occupations and that barred them from guilds and associations. As a result, they were forced to pursue dishonorable occupations like peddling and innkeeping. Finally, Jews did not become agriculturalists because the terrible conditions of the peasantry discouraged them and they were forbidden by law to bequeath land to their heirs. As a result, since being granted the right to do so in 1775, only fourteen Jewish families had taken up agriculture.

Jews should be integrated into urban populations and benefit from the same rights as the other residents of municipalities. "To assign Jews to the municipal estate is to grant them all the freedoms and prerogatives

41. *Polski Słównik Biograficzny* (Kraków, 1937), 3: 153–54.

that have been and are a source of pride to our towns. It is to remove Jews from any other authority and to make them subject to the government and rule of the municipal magistracy. In a word, it is to eliminate all of the distinctions heretofore existing between Jew and Christian."[42] He further argued that rabbinical courts should have jurisdiction only in strictly religious matters, and that the demeaning capitation tax be abolished. Noting that many Jews in Poland already knew how to read and write Polish, he advocated that all official documents be in Polish. This meant that the printing and the importing of books in Hebrew letters would be prohibited. Jewish books would be translated into Polish. He further proposed that the Jewish costume, which exposed them to ridicule, be abolished, and that the number of holidays celebrated by Jews be limited. The excessive number of these holidays, he said, kept many hands idle, leading to losses of revenue by the state. He argued that the abolition of the dietary laws would bring Poles and Jews closer together. Jews were to be expelled from rural taverns and inns to protect the peasants.[43] The liquor trade would be in the hands of Christians, even if this led to losses among the nobles. In the towns, however, Jews could continue to sell alcoholic beverages, since competition there prevented exploitation. On the last point, Butrymowicz dissented from the anonymous author who proposed that Jews be obliged to do four years of army service in units in which no more than one-third of the soldiers were Jewish. In this way, Jews would learn about order, cease to be idle, and acquire a dignified bearing, and the genius that had been obscured by the burden of discriminatory laws would be revived. The anonymous pamphleteer pointed out that while some, especially military men, maintained that nature had denied Jews bravery and courage, there was no basis for these reservations. After all, their religion had not prevented Jews from triumphing over many nations in the past. Moreover, if the Jew was a coward today, past Polish policy was responsible. Once the constitution and the education of Jews was changed, the Jews would become what we wished them to be.[44] Behind Butrymowicz's dissent was his feeling that Jews were unfit for combat and that military service was, in any case, an unimportant issue. At the end of his pamphlet, he undertook to bring an appropriate program before the Sejm.

---

42. "Słowem jest znieść wszelką różnicę, która była dotąd między Żydem a Chreścijaninem."

43. "Żeby nie wywysali majątku chłopów naszych."

44. "Żyd jeżeli jest lękliwym i niepożytecznym, nasze to dzieło. Odmieńmy prawo i edukacyją, a Żyd będzie takim, go uczynić zechcemy."

The proposals of Butrymowicz and the anonymous writer were fully compatible with those produced in France and Austria during the same decade, but the plan to abolish class distinctions was too radical for Poland. On November 30, 1789, Butrymowicz's resolution was nonetheless read before the Sejm, which asked that it be submitted in printed form.[45] And when the Sejm appointed a committee to discuss a plan for Jewish reform, on June 19, 1790, Butrymowicz was named a member.

The Jews' "humble" petition never reached the floor of the Sejm. Butrymowicz's pamphlet evoked a published response early in 1790. The author of the reply, published as an anonymous brochure, was the provincial governor of Lublin, Kajetan Hryniewiecki. The decision to adopt a policy of expelling Jews from the villages, he asserted, would have to rest with the lords themselves. Clearly, Hryniewiecki was concerned that the right of the magnates to govern their estates not be abridged, and, it seems clear, that Jews not be expelled.[46] Having said this, the author nevertheless outlined a series of practical objections to Butrymowicz's proposal. The expulsion of the Jews from the villages might spell the end of the distilling and brewing industries. To staff the inns in the villages, 50,000 taverners would be needed, and they were not available. Serfs would be unsuitable; as was well known from several disastrous experiments, they would simply drink the liquor themselves. An expulsion of the Jews would, moreover, reduce the income from leaseholdings so much that the *szlachta* would be unable to pay taxes to the state. In Wielkopolska and Mazowsze, German innkeepers had been brought in, but in eastern Little Poland and Ruthenia, Christian innkeepers were not to be found. To drive Jews out of the village taverns and inns on grounds that they caused the drunkenness of the serfs by selling them liquor on credit would be futile, since serfs would simply go to the towns. Finally, since Jews were unsuitable for any other occupation, to ban them from selling liquor would drive them to robbery and theft or make them dependent on charity in Jewish towns that were already poor.[47]

On March 22 and April 19, 1790, relatively minor anti-Jewish disturbances broke out in Warsaw. On May 16 of that year, however, a riot broke

45. *MDSC*, 6: 118–28.
46. See the memorandum, likely from Piattoli to Kołłątaj, of January 1792 that begins: "L'objet le plus important et en même temps, le plus difficile, dont il faut s'occuper dans le projet des Juifs, est la préservation des droits, que les seigneurs perçoivent sur les individus de cette nation, domiciliés dans leurs terres." *MDSC*, 6: 400.
47. *MDSC*, 6: 153–68.

out that led to widespread violence and destruction of property. Butrymowicz, together with Jacek Jezierski Kasztelan of Luków and the delegate from Bracław, Tomasz Wawrzecki, denounced the rioters in the Sejm.
Butrymowicz framed these attacks as attempts to eliminate opposition to
the program of the burghers, and he warned darkly, undoubtedly alluding to events in France, that other "obstacles to the burghers' proposal
will soon be attacked too."[48]

In 1790, one of a number of crude literary attacks on Jews appeared,
entitled: *A Mirror of Poland for the Public, Which Although Corrupt, It Truly
Represents; and One Can See in It Various People and Their Faults; and Especially the Jews, Who Are Harmful in General and in Particular.*[49] After a
long catalogue of the harmful activities of Jews, mixing prose and verse,
the author concluded:

> There can be no reform for this. Here is the solution:
> We have enough trees, but not enough hanging trees—
> Hang a hundred Jews every year.

Still, it was just after the attacks on Jews in the streets of Warsaw that
an open letter by an anonymous member of the Jewish bourgeoisie of
that city was addressed to the delegates representing the towns. It took
up the entire issue of the *Journal hebdomadaire de la Diète de Varsovie* on
May 30, 1790. Replete with references to the slogans of the French Revolution, and the principles of the Rights of Man, the author declared
Jews to be members of the Third Estate, since such membership was not
to be defined by religion but by occupation. Just as the burghers demanded that their natural rights be respected, those of the Jews ought
to be considered in the same way. This document is remarkable for having been addressed, not to the monarch or members of his court, but to
representatives of the bourgeoisie, with the claim that Jews, too, should
be regarded as belonging to it. The author was probably the originally

---

48. In the 1980s, a debate arose between the historians Artur Eisenbach and Krystyna
Zienkowska in which Zienkowska maintained that there had been a transformation of the
form of Jew-hatred during the last decades of the eighteenth century, especially in Warsaw.
The debate turned on whether the Warsaw burghers who attacked Jews in 1775 and in the
more serious anti-Jewish riots in the spring of 1790 were motivated by traditional animosities,
or, on the other hand, by "progressive" tendencies associated with the Enlightenment, such
as those described by Arthur Hertzberg and Jacob Katz. K. Zienkowska, "Citizens or Inhabitants," 40.
49. *MDSC*, 6: 235–68.

Silesian Jewish merchant David Koenigsberger, a leading member of the Warsaw Jewish bourgeoisie.[50] Koenigsberger was a highly visible figure, and anti-Jewish literature of the time frequently singled him out.[51]

At about the same time, a petition signed by a number of prosperous Warsaw Jews was submitted to the Sejm, asking that the rights of citizenship be extended immediately to 250 Jewish families in Warsaw. (This is as likely a figure as any to represent the numerical strength of the embryonic polonizing Jewish middle class in Warsaw.) Koenigsberger's letter and this petition were part of the struggle over Jewish residence rights in the capital that was being waged in tandem with the broader discussions of the place of burghers and of concerted attempts (sometimes temporarily successful) to expel the Jews from the city.[52] Among the main protectors of the interests of Warsaw's Jews were August Sułkowski, Adam Poniński, and Józef Potocki, who were known to be amenable to "gifts" and presumably received appropriate tokens of appreciation from members of the Jewish community.[53]

Perhaps spurred by the May riots, the Sejm appointed a commission to discuss a plan for Jewish reform (Deputacja do rozstrzygnięcia projektu reformy Żydów) on June 19, 1790. The committee had ten members, the most active of whom were Butrymowicz and Kasztelan Jacek Jezierski of Luków. In his motion for the establishment of the committee, Jezierski, a fierce opponent of municipal reform, had said: "[T]he Jews do not threaten us with rebellion, as the towns do, they are not impudently demanding a settlement but are humbly asking for it."[54] The bishop of Chełm, Maciej Garnysz, chaired the committee, which finished its assignment in August, although it took more than the four weeks allotted it.[55] Bishop Garnysz signed the report, but dissenting members of the committee blocked its coming to the floor of the Sejm. The stillborn proposal included tolerance of Judaism and regulations regarding the organization of Jewish communities and their tax obligations. Jews were to

50. *MDSC*, 6: 188–90. Eisenbach, *Emancipation*, 90–91; Raphael Mahler, *Toledot hayehudim bePolin: Kalkalah, hevrah, hamatsav hamishpati*, trans. Avigdor Hame'iri (Merhavia, Israel, 1946), 450–51; Ringelblum, "An opklang fun der frantsoyzisher revolutsiye," in id., *Kapitlen*, 173–79.

51. E.g., "Zwierciadło polskie dla publiczności," *MDSC*, 6: 249, and "Katechizm o żydach i neofitach," ibid., 479. Cf. Goldberg, "Mishtadlanut lemedina'ut," 227.

52. Marian Marek Drozdowski, "Żydzi Warszawy Stanisławowskiej," in *Żydzi w dawnej Rzeczpospolitej* (Wrocław, Warsaw, and Kraków, 1991), 192–200, and the literature cited there.

53. Ibid., 193.

54. Zienkowska, "Citizens or Inhabitants," 41.

55. *MDSC*, 6: 215–28.

be granted freedom of occupation, although barred from selling liquor in the villages. Jews were to be subject to municipal authorities and taxation. There was no reference to municipal citizenship or freedom of settlement.

There was only one tangible change made in the laws that affected Jews in the course of the entire Four-Year Sejm. This was a further limitation on Jews residing in the crown towns to which the new law on cities, adopted on April 18, 1791, applied. Municipal citizenship and freedom of occupation were the rights of any free Christian; Jews were to be subject to municipal authorities, who could exclude them or restrict their business activities. All towns were ordered to conclude agreements with their Jewish populations that would detail the limitations on Jewish commercial and artisanal activities and their rights of residence. The Constitution of May 3 incorporated the town law. Jews were left in an exposed legal position, and numerous towns took advantage of the situation by attempting to limit Jewish business, levying new taxes, threatening expulsion, and limiting or forbidding the construction of housing for Jews. The Police Commission or Department of the Interior intervened at times to forbid limitations on free trade.[56]

The Constitution of May 3 enshrined a constitutional monarchy but failed to address either the peasant question or the issue of Jewish status. It retained the privileges of the nobility while expanding, only slightly, the rights of burghers, who could now send observers, called plenipotentiaries, to the Sejm. The crown cities did, however, achieve much of what they desired in terms of jurisdiction over the Jews of their towns, who also lost the protection of the *jurydyki*.

A month after the adoption of the Constitution, Jewish delegates (the document is unsigned) presented not a "humble petition" but *demands*. Jews should have free rights of domicile, "in all towns, even those where they have not lived before." Jews with property in towns should be admitted to the same rights of citizenship as the other inhabitants. All royal and communal privileges should be reaffirmed. No creditor should be allowed to seize the children or wife of his Jewish debtor.[57] Jews were to continue to have their own courts to resolve disputes among themselves.[58]

In sum, the Jewish delegates sought the removal of restrictions on their

56. Eisenbach, *Emancipation,* 71–72. Cf. A. Zahorski, *Centralne instytucje policyjne w Polsce w dobie rozbiorów* (Warsaw, 1959), 159–60; 168–69.

57. Cf. *MDSC,* 6: 101–2 (Herszel Jozefowicz).

58. *MDSC,* 6: 272–76 (Pesah Haimowicz).

rights of residence and on their economic activities. Two of the demands in particular, to retain the Jewish court system and to have their privileges endorsed, reflected the absence of identification with the Enlightenment-inspired idea of a unitary society shorn of privilege and class. A similar view is seen in the *cahiers de doléance* of Jewish communities in Alsace that were submitted to the Estates General. Those communities also sought the removal of restrictions on their rights of residence and occupation and at the same time demanded the right to retain their corporate autonomy and identity.[59]

A new summons was issued for representatives of the Jewish communities in the early autumn of 1791.[60] According to one observer, as many as 120 Jewish representatives had arrived in Warsaw by the end of November 1791.[61] These delegates came with written instructions approved by their communal elders, much like the new Christian urban plenipotentiaries who arrived in Warsaw at the same time. The preparation of instructions mirrored the practice of the *sejmiki,* which sent their delegates to the Sejm with written instructions. The Jewish delegates successfully arranged meetings with the monarch, with senators, with Sejm delegates, and with representatives of various governmental institutions.[62]

The king and his advisors were eager to have legislation adopted that would bring order to the situation of Jews in Poland. The king's interest was as much venal and mercenary as it was legislative or ideological. He designated Scipio Piattoli, his secretary, together with Hugo Kołłątaj and Aleksander Linowski, to meet with the Jews' representatives. Piattoli held innumerable meetings, prepared memoranda, and drafted plans and proposals. On the king's behalf, he negotiated with Jewish delegates over the size of their "contribution" to help retire royal debts in return for legislation that would serve Jewish interests. At one point, in early January 1792, a promissory note for 5 million zlotys was actually handed to the king, contingent on the passage of a bill that at least guaranteed the Jews economic freedom and the integrity of their religion. At the same time,

59. Arthur Hertzberg, *The French Enlightenment and the Jews* (New York, 1970), 343–44.

60. *MDSC,* 6: 355–58, circular letter or proclamation from Jews, inhabitants of Warsaw, to their brother Israelites residing in the kingdom of Poland and in the grand duchy of Lithuania: "Przetłumaczenie listu cyrkularnego, czyli uniwersalu od Żydów bawiących się w Warszawie do braci w Israelu zamieszkanych w Polszcze i w Wielkim Ksiestwie Litewskim . . . przez Kalmansona, tlomacza JKMci i Komisyi Policyi." ("We have . . . an order signed by the king's hand and sealed with his seal [to assemble ten plenipotentiaries authorized by the synagogues from each province, thirty in all, in Warsaw on November 3].")

61. *MDSC,* 6: 328.

62. Ibid., 515–17.

the Christian town representatives lobbied and published broadsheets and pamphlets rejecting any concessions to Jews.

The participation of representatives of many Jewish communities was not recognized in law. Jews did not have the right to send observer-plenipotentiaries to the Sejm. Moreover, the Sejm never actually adopted a law to regularize the situation of Jews in the Commonwealth. The combination of the conservatism of most of the Jewish representatives, the opposition of the burgher plenipotentiaries and the refusal of the aristocrats to countenance any diminution of their authority over their own holdings, prevented the passage of a new law governing Jews.[63]

Krystyna Zienkowska describes the course of development in Poland as fundamentally different from the Habsburg reforms of the 1780s, which were "introduced from above using repressive decrees." She stresses that "the specific feature of the second stage of the debate on Jewish reform, prepared by Piattoli within Stanisław August's circle and by members of the 'Patriotic Party' after the Constitution of 3 May, was the inclusion in these debates of Jewish plenipotentiaries."[64] This reading should not be dismissed but needs the qualification of an alternative interpretation that might see the consultations, meetings, and correspondence as an elaborate charade disguising what was, at bottom, extortion on the part of the king and his representatives and traditional lobbying-bribery on the part of the Jewish representatives.

The debates, pamphlets, discussions, memoranda, and petitions ultimately had no effect. No new law on the status of Jews was adopted. A very small number of Jews, mainly in Warsaw, were, however, no less enchanted by the Enlightenment's vision of civil society than their brethren elsewhere in Europe. Among these were Berek Joselewicz and Józef Aronowicz, who, in the fall of 1794, sought to form a Jewish light cavalry unit to fight for Polish independence in the ranks of the forces led by Tadeusz Kościuszko against the Russians. (Kościuszko was a Polish soldier who had fought in the American War of Independence and returned to fight to restore Polish independence in the last decade of the eighteenth century.) Joselewicz had witnessed the revolutionary events in France together with his patron Bishop Ignacy Massalski in 1789 and returned to Poland inspired by what he had seen. He apparently organized the Jewish forces that participated in the defense of Warsaw in the spring of 1794. On September 17, he was appointed colonel, receiving permission from

63. Ibid., 400.
64. Zienkowska, "Reforms," 345.

Kościuszko himself to recruit a light cavalry unit from among the Jews of Warsaw, which was decimated in the Warsaw suburb of Praga by Suvorov's Russian army in November 1794. We do not know how many Jews fought under Joselewicz, and he himself apparently had to endure the dismissive attitudes of some superior officers.[65] Nevertheless, he went on to join the famed Polish legions of General Dąbrowski and ultimately fell in battle against the Austrians at Kock on May 5, 1809. For Polish Jews, the memory of Joselewicz and his participation in the armed struggle for a free Poland acquired a powerful symbolic importance beginning in the early years of the twentieth century.[66] This was, after all, the first Jewish fighting unit since the second century! And, as Jacob Goldberg stressed, "two hundred years ago, only in Poland were conditions created that made [this] possible."[67]

Near the marketplace in Kock there is a plaque marking the place where Berek Joselewicz fell in battle. Not far from the marketplace in Kock is another "monument" sacred to Jewish memory. It is the house that was the home of Menahem Mendel Morgensztern (1787–1859), the famous Kotsker Rebbe—a brooding iconoclast and theological radical. These two figures, a Jewish fighter for Polish independence and a man of the spirit, stand for the twin trends that animated Polish Jewry from the nineteenth century to the eve of World War II.

65. Krzysztof Bauer, *Wojsko koronne powstania kosciuśzkowskiego* (Warsaw, 1981), 233.

66. See Majer Bałaban, ed., *Księga pamiątkowa ku czci Berka Joselewicza pułkownika wojsk polskich w 125 letnią rocznice jego bohaterskiej śmierci (1809–1934)* (Warsaw, 1934); Emanuel Ringelblum, *Di poylishe Yidn in oifshtand fun Koshtsyushko—1794* (Vilna, 1937; Polish trans., Warsaw, 1938); Jerzy Tomaszewski, ed., *Żydzi w obronie Rzeczypospolitej* (Warsaw, 1996); Goldberg, *Hahevrah hayehudit*, 277–88; Józef Andrzej Gierowski, "The Jews in the Kościuszko Insurrection," in *Der letzte Ritter und erste Bürger im Osten Europas: Kościuszko, das aufständische Reformpolen und die Verbundenheit zwischen Polen und der Schweiz*, ed. Heiko Haumann and Jerzy Skowronek (Basel and Frankfurt a/M, 1996), 192–99; Bauer, *Wojsko*, 231–33.

67. Goldberg, *Hahevrah hayehudit*, 288; in Polish: "Żydzi wobec wrogów Rzeczypospolitej," in *Żydzi w obronie*, ed. Tomaszewski, 18.

Afterword

The view that there are fundamental distortions in the way modernity in Jewish history has been described lies at the heart of this book. As I argue in the Introduction, historians have placed too much emphasis on change and focused too much on ideology. They have assigned too much weight to religious behavior and belief as indications of change; they have concentrated too much on regions where few Jews lived and not enough on the areas where most Jews lived. History is not a train that moved progressively across Europe from west to east bringing the same developments to different countries as it traveled along. In writing the story of "modern" Jewish history, we cannot ignore the ancestors of about 80 percent of world Jewry who lived in eastern Europe in the eighteenth century and whose experience did not duplicate that of their fellow Jews living in regions to the west.

The experience of western European Jews has been the template for the story of modernization told by virtually every Jewish historian of the period. That narrative concerns only small Jewish communities comprising tiny proportions of the total populations of the countries in which they lived and of the total number of Jews in Europe. Economically, these communities were becoming progressively more integrated into the state. They chafed, however, under the contradiction between their economic integration and political rightlessness. These Jews found the culture of the majority attractive and persuaded themselves that the bourgeoisie was beckoning to Jews, bidding them join and take their place in civil society. That is, they persuaded themselves that the new nation-state included a place for Jews. They exchanged their values for those of the dominant culture in the hope of acceptance, politically and socially. This exchange involved varying degrees of self-rejection, however, and was at times traumatic. The configuration of this master narrative along geographical lines has been contested with some justice. After all, Königsberg (now Kaliningrad), an important center of the Enlightenment and its Jewish counterpart, the Haskalah, was in *East* Prussia, and there were Jews in Poland-Lithuania affected by the new thinking as early as Jews were further west. In any case, masses of Jews, overwhelmingly from the lands east of Germany, do not fit into the master narrative just described.

If we are to understand the developments of recent centuries properly, we have to investigate the experience of the *majority* of Jews in the context of their experience. In addition, we have to excavate more deeply and reach the magmatic level of Jewish experience so that we can identify what I see as elemental continuities persisting from the early modern period almost to the present. The ingredients of modernity have been grafted, often imperfectly, onto those elemental continuities through adaptation, appropriation, and negotiation. Multifarious changes have occurred among the masses of Jews over the past two centuries. They abandoned their homes, a minority of them adopted multiple and contradictory ideologies, and many more left behind, in varying degrees, the practices and beliefs associated with traditional Jewish society. Nevertheless, for all of these changes, there was also an irreducible continuity among the majority of these Jews. They continued to carry, at the core of their being, a sometimes painful, but invincible, prerational, and positive feeling about their Jewishness. The positive sense of Jewishness was not necessarily joyous, since pain often accompanied the abandonment of traditional beliefs and habits of thought. Persecution did not contradict but rather confirmed Jewish distinctiveness and led to various mechanisms of defense and adaptation. Moreover, among Jews themselves, the broad spectrum of deviance—those who rejected, in various ways, their very identities as Jews—generally served to validate and objectify these core values. The unsettling of Jews' representation of themselves as possessing a homogeneous and integral identity did not disturb the deepest reaches of that sense of self.

This positive sense of Jewish identity, the central ingredient of the eastern European Jewish *mentalité*, was tied to the theological idea of chosenness.[1] It constituted a kind of social-psychological translation, or trans-

---

1. Shmuel Ettinger, in a posthumously published paper, insisted that the consciousness of chosenness deepened in the period following 1648 in East Central Europe precisely at

mutation, of that concept. My suggestion is that despite ideological, geographical, economic, political, and even linguistic and cultural change, and despite the fact that the so-called western European template was far from unknown in eastern Europe, the vast majority of eastern European Jews and their descendants carried this core with them. What I have tried to do in this book is to explain how that *mentalité* was formed.

I began with a description of the most objective and the most important of the ingredients of this explanation, namely, demography. The proportion of Jews in the Polish Commonwealth in the eighteenth century was significant and increased throughout the century, exceeding 5 percent by its end. The more than three-quarters of a million Jews in the lands of Poland-Lithuania vastly exceeded in their numbers the 60,000 to 70,000 Jews within the borders of the future imperial Germany. The Jewish experience in German lands was thus, inevitably, that of a relatively small group overwhelmed numerically by the majority. In Poland-Lithuania, the situation was so different as to render the German and Polish-Lithuanian Jewish communities incomparable in many ways. Indeed, no other Jewish population in the world was comparable, in terms of absolute numbers or proportions, to the Jewish community of Poland-Lithuania in the eighteenth century.

The Jewish population there was unevenly distributed; it was concentrated substantially in the eastern half of the Polish Commonwealth. Slightly more than two-thirds of Jews lived in urban settlements. Indeed, from the last decades of the eighteenth century on, the number and proportion of Jews living in villages constantly diminished. The Jewish population, in general, was quite mobile, and this was particularly the case with those who were most prosperous, as well as those who were at the opposite side of the economic scale, the vocationless and itinerant poor. Not only were Jews essentially urban, but they lived in the midst of a society that was overwhelmingly rural and agricultural. Here is an indication of separateness, distinctiveness, and otherness that cannot be gainsaid. More to the point, the fact is that half of the urban population was Jewish, and in large parts of the country, more than half. This is one of the strongest arguments for the thesis that Jews in the eighteenth-century

---

the time when Jewish numbers were growing and social and cultural differences were widening. "Ra'ayon habehirah beyisra'el uva'amim," in *Ra'ayon habehirah beyisra'el uva'amim*, ed. Shmuel Almog and Michael Heyd (Jerusalem, 1991), 11–12. I think his implicit polemic there against Jacob Katz is based on a misunderstanding of Katz's position. Katz did not suggest that Polish Jews had a diminished sense of chosenness. Jacob Katz, "Bein Tatnu letah-tat," in *Sefer-yovel le Yitshak Baer,* ed. S. Ettinger et al. (Jerusalem, 1960), 318–37.

Polish Commonwealth cannot be characterized properly as a minority group.

The term "minority" is used to describe groups in modern nation-states where there is an imagined homogeneous citizenry. It has a set of connotations that are only misleadingly applied to Jews in the Polish Commonwealth. In Polish society, as in all societies, a multiplicity of loyalties and memberships defined identity. Polishness, however, was coterminous with the gentry. In the towns, local patriotism was the order of the day, and there was little sense of belonging to a nation. Moreover, many of the cities and towns were distinguished, even in the eighteenth century, by ethnic and religious diversity. There was no majority. It is singularly inappropriate to speak of Jews as a minority group when less than 20 percent of the population of the country was urban, and only 40 to no more than 60 percent was ethnically Polish. And in this connection, it is useful to recall again the general observation about the Jewish historical experience made by Salo W. Baron: "The status of Jews was most favourable in states of multiple nationality and most unfavourable in national states."[2]

A significant proportion of Jews lived in towns where there was a Jewish majority, and an even larger proportion can be said to have *experienced* living in towns where there appeared to be a Jewish majority, because so many of the Christian townsfolk had turned to agriculture. Thus, most of the shops and stalls on the marketplace, the inns, and the taverns would have belonged to Jews. Indeed, most of the people moving through the streets would have been Jews. In other words, most Jews lived in communities that were quite large enough to support the living of the dailiness of life in a Jewish cosmos. For all of these reasons, the term "minority group" seems misleading and inappropriate.

The distinctiveness of Polish-Lithuanian Jews as expressed in their economic activities lay in their indispensability to the national economy, chiefly because of their roles in domestic and foreign trade and in the alcohol industry. Jews contributed to the delay in the collapse of the manorial-serf economy. At least in the eastern half of the country, urban economic vitality depended on Jews. In a very substantial number of towns, Jews were the only economically active segment of the population. In much of the Commonwealth, Jews managed the manufacture, distribution, and sale of alcoholic beverages. The lion's share of the profits, however, went to the magnates. Still, as long as the old regime persisted, Jews

---

2. Salo Wittmayer Baron, *A Social and Religious History of the Jews*, vol. 11 (Philadelphia, 1976), 199.

had a certain security because they occupied important and integrated sectors of the economy of the state.

As I said in chapter 2, Jews can usefully and with some accuracy be described as having been a colonized economic group in the Polish Commonwealth during the eighteenth century. They performed indispensable services and played a crucial role in the economy, but the primary beneficiaries were their patrons, the magnate-aristocrats. Even the Church was profoundly tied both to Jewish communal institutions, through massive credits or loans, and to individual Jews, who performed the same tasks on many Church estates that they did on the estates of the magnates. This economic linkage between Jews and Church institutions, which functioned to a degree to protect Jews from harsh measures, was contradicted by another trend that tended to a disentanglement of Christians from Jews.

In the eighteenth century, the Catholic Church sought to consolidate its influence. Simultaneously, it became inextricably linked to the emerging Polish national identity. It was not unusual in Church documents of the eighteenth century for the term "Polak" to be used as a synonym for (Latin) Catholic. The Church created and supported moves to increase the pressure on marginals in a society that was working to achieve religious and national conformity. Synodal and other Church legislation often reinforced boundary-drawing and discriminatory enactments. More popular forms of identification such as catechisms, sermons, and lessons in the schools, as well as contemporary literature, brimmed with negative stereotypes of Jews. The constant repetition undoubtedly did have an effect on the shaping of Catholic attitudes to Jews. Most cruelly, trials based on the blood libel and the accusation of desecration of the Host dramatically demonstrated the distinction between Jew and Christian. The central involvement at midcentury of powerful bishops like Dembowski, Soltyk, and Wołłowski emphasized the determination of some in the Church hierarchy to demonize and marginalize Jews to the greatest extent possible. In fact, the involvement of these bishops in the 1740s and 1750s led to the worst period of persecution of this kind in Polish Jewish history.

The communal organization of Polish-Lithuanian Jewry was more ramified, extensive, and complex than any other in European Jewish history. This was a result, partly, of the particular complexion of the distribution of power in the Polish Commonwealth, which tolerated the autonomy of relatively powerless strata in society. And when, in the eighteenth century, these institutions were weakened in order to incorporate them into the administration of the state or an individual magnate's holdings, they continued to function nevertheless, expressing Jewish separatism in an institutional form.

Polish Jews were at once insular and integrated into the society in which they lived. There were varied and sometimes intense forms of contact between Jews and Christians, which were not by any means limited to instrumental commercial transactions, although these were the most common. People who sometimes lived cheek by jowl inevitably began to relate to one another in all the ways of which human beings are capable. They feuded, they discussed, they gossiped, they made love, they robbed, they loved and they hated one another. They became more or less familiar with the goings-on in each other's communities. The costumes of Jews mimicked those of their neighbors, Yiddish teemed with Polish words, and the architecture and decoration of synagogues betrayed their baroque origins. But this mirroring does not contradict my contention that there was little admiration on the part of Jews for much of what they saw among their Christian neighbors. The single exception here is the occasional appearance of opinions about the nobility that are not characterized by expressions of scorn. The nobility, however, was impenetrable to Jews as long as they were Jews. In the ideology of the magnates, Jews were perceived as inferior. Among Polish Jews, though, this did not lead to tortured compunctiousness, because Jews could not be noblemen in the Polish Commonwealth. In their general view of culture and morality in Poland-Lithuania, Jews held themselves to be superior and regarded their neighbors with disdain. Polish society held no attraction for Jews. Indeed, one of the hardships of the Exile was that Jews were thrust into the midst of the corrupt, immoral, and violent world of the Gentiles.

In the three chapters following the discussion of the Jewish community, I attempt to convey a sense of the cultural activity and preoccupations of Polish Jews in the eighteenth century by assembling a list of the "best-sellers" of the eighteenth century and summarizing their contents and concerns. This confirms that beginning in the latter decades of the seventeenth century, Kabbalah became part of the grammar of Jewish culture. In the chapters devoted to Hasidism, I argue that the Hasidic phenomenon was created substantially from the palette of Jewish culture, even if, on the surface, it seemed similar to other contemporary movements of spiritual awakening. I suggest that the movement might be considered a movement of resistance in two ways. First, it offered shelter from ways of thinking that threatened traditional beliefs, and, second, it created a form of social organization that, unlike Jewish communal institutions, was beyond the reach of the state.

The final piece in my argument rests on the general absence in Poland-Lithuania of what I call "the beckoning bourgeoisie." This absence is illustrated by a failure to disassemble the hierarchy of power in the Commonwealth even in the Constitution of May 3, 1791. The critical, indispensable framework for many, if not all, of the developments associated with conventional definitions of modernity was the rise of the bourgeoisie, and, in this context, the perception among Jews that it was permeable. The growth of the conviction, however illusory, that the middle class was permeable or penetrable—that there was a place in civil society and in the nation-state for Jews—was what led to the weakening of traditional Jewish society, memberships, and values. Even in terms of this "Germano-centric" definition of modernity, the rare cases of Jews who sought to find their place in the bourgeoisie in East Central Europe prove the rule that that bourgeoisie was weak and limited to a few cities. A few Jews did, in varying degrees, seek to find their place in the bourgeoisie of Szkłów, Vilna, and, especially, Warsaw. Sometimes, as in Berlin or Paris, this involved an exchange of values that led to a critique of Jewish life. Among the upper stratum of Jews in Warsaw, a process that was somewhat analogous to what was happening further west took hold. There were more than a few cases of what Jacob Shatzky called "total assimilation."[3] The three daughters of Judyta Levi Zbytkower, who was herself the daughter of a wealthy German Jewish family, eventually converted to Christianity for example.

There were also eastern European Jews who traveled to the west, figuratively or literally. The familiar paradigm is the story of the eastern European Jew who comes to Berlin and is enchanted by what he beholds and powerfully attracted by the promise of a place in civil society. My argument concerns the overwhelming majority who, with various levels of awareness, responded differently.

For the vast majority of Jews, the changes that were afoot were dangerous and frightening—"an empty void." The circumstances under which they lived, and that are described in this book, created a mentality that acted as a filter through which new cultural, political, and economic currents had to pass. That mentality both buffered Jews and buttressed their defenses. And when, in the nineteenth century, certain important aspects of this context broke down, the vast majority of these Jews were armored against trauma and splitting—psychological reversals of loyalty—

3. Jacob Shatzky, "Alexander Kraushar and His Road to Total Assimilation," *YIVO Annual* 7 (1953): 146–74.

by the mentality that had been formed earlier. Self-affirmation and a feeling of Jewish superiority and solidarity dominated the spectrum of self-evaluation of eastern European Jews. This irreducible sense of separateness forms a kind of resistance, a "red line" still characteristic of most Jews, despite their manifold and contradictory adaptations and acculturations. This refusal to be defined by others is, in my view, the defining, and heretofore neglected, element in the modern Jewish experience.

Select Bibliography

Archival Sources

ARCHIWUM GŁÓWNE AKT DAWNYCH, WARSAW (CITED AS AGAD)

Archiwum Gospodarcze Wilanowskie, Administracja dóbr opatowskich (cited as ADO) I/109; Anteriora 214
Archiwum Kameralne III
Archiwum Zamoyskich 2808

ARCHIWUM PAŃSTWOWE, KRAKÓW (CITED AS AP)

Akta Żydowskie III/11/8
Archiwum Dzikowskie Tarnowskich, sygn. 105
MS 2347/1
Teki Schneidera 262

BIBLIOTEKA CZARTORYSKICH, KRAKÓW

II 1408

V. STEFANYK SCIENTIFIC LIBRARY OF THE ACADEMY OF SCIENCES OF UKRAINE, LVIV

Fond 5, Opis 1, Dzial 310 [CAHJP HM 2/8111.9]

I. VERNADSKY LIBRARY OF THE ACADEMY OF SCIENCES OF UKRAINE, JEWISH DIVISION, KIEV

Opis 1, 33

YIVO INSTITUTE FOR JEWISH RESEARCH, NEW YORK

RG 87: 918, 923, 939

RG 223. Pt. 2: 9, Minute Book of the Community of Skuodas.

RG 242 [Personenstandes-Archiv, Koblenz: RSAJ906]

Published Materials

Abraham ben Alexander Katz [Kalisker]. *Hesed le'avraham.* Lemberg [Lwów], 1851.

Abramsky, Chimen. "The Crisis of Authority within European Jewry in the Eighteenth Century." In *Studies in Jewish Religious and Intellectual History Presented to Alexander Altmann on the Occasion of His Seventieth Birthday,* edited by Siegfried Stein and Raphael Loewe, 13–28. Alabama, 1979.

Ahat lamo'adim. Żółkiew, 1751.

Akta grodzkie i ziemskie z czasów Rzeczypospolitej polskiej z archiwum tak zwanego Bernardyńskiego we Lwowie. Edited by O. Pietruski, K. Liske, and A. Prochaska. 24 vols. Lwów, 1868–1931. Cited as *AGZ.*

Alexander b. Moses Ziskind. *Yesod veshoresh ha'avodah.* Nowy Dwór, 1782.

Altbauer, Moshe. "Zutot letoledot hatarbut shel yehudei Polin." *Gal-Ed* 7–8 (1985): 263–69.

Altshuler, Mor. "Mishnato shel R. Mehullam Feibush Heller umekomah bereshit hatenu'ah hahassidit." Ph.D. diss., Hebrew University, Jerusalem, 1994.

Aniszczenko, Eugeniusz. "Rządowa organizacja kahałów Białorusi Wschodniej na terytorium anektowanym przez Rosje w 1772 r." *Prawo* (Wrocław) 251, *Studia historyczno-demograficzne,* edited by Tadeusz Jurek and Krystyna Matwijowski (1996): 65–76.

Assaf, David. "'Money for Household Expenses': Economic Aspects of Hasidic Courts." In *Studies in the History of the Jews in Old Poland in Honor of Jacob Goldberg,* Scripta Hierosolymitana, 38, edited by Adam Teller, 14–50. Jerusalem, 1998.

Assaf, Simhah. "Mipinkas Zablodovah." *Kiryat Sefer* 1 (1924–25): 307–17.

Avron, Dov. *Pinkas hakesherim shel kehillat Pozna (5)381-(5)595. Acta Electorum Communitatis Judaeorum Posnaniensium* (1621–1835). Jerusalem, 1966.

Bałaban, Majer. *Die Judenstadt von Lublin.* Berlin, 1919.

———. "Die Krakauer Judengemeinde-Ordnung von 1595 und ihre Nachträge." *Jahrbuch der jüdisch-literarischen Gesellschaft in Frankfurt a/M* 10 (1912): 296–360; 11 (1916): 88–114.

———. "Die polnischen Juden in den Memoiren des polnischen Adels." *Menorah* 5 (1927): 369–76; 6 (1928): 32–38.

———. *Historia Żydów w Krakowie i na Kazimierzu.* 2 vols. Kraków, 1931–36.

———. *Letoledot hatenu'ah haFrankit.* 2 vols. Tel Aviv, 1934–35.

———. "Ustrój kahału w Polsce XVI–XVII wieku." *Kwartalnik poświęcony historii Żydów w Polsce* 2 (1912): 17–54.

——. *Zabytki Historyczne Żydów w Polsce.* Warsaw, 1920.

——. "Zalman, der rosh-hakohol fun Drohobitsh." In id., *Yidn in Poyln,* 67–87. Vilna, 1930.

——. *Żydzi lwowscy na przełomie XVIgo i XVIIgo wieku.* Lwów, 1907.

——, ed. *Księga pamiątkowa ku czci Berka Joselewicza pułkownika wojsk polskich w 125 letnią rocznice jego bohaterskiej śmierci (1809–1934).* Warsaw, 1934.

Baranowski, Andrzej J. "Oprawy uroczystości koronacyjnych wizerunków Marii na Rusi Koronnej w XVIII w." *Biuletyn Historii Sztuki* 57 (1995): 299–322.

Baranowski, Bohdan. *Życie codzienne małego miasteczka w XVII i XVIII wieku.* Warsaw, 1975.

Baranowski, Bohdan, and Władysław Lewandowski, eds. *Nietolerancja i zabobon w Polsce w XVII i XVIII wieku.* Warsaw, 1987.

Bar-Itzhak, Haya. *Jewish Poland: Legends of Origin. Ethnopoetics and Legendary Chronicles.* Detroit, 2001.

Bar-Levav, Avriel. "Rabbi Aharon Berakhiah miModenah verabbi Naftali Hakohen Kats: Avot mehaberim sifrei holim umetim." *Assufot* 9 (1999): 189–234. Offprint.

Barnai, Yaakov. *Igerot hasidim me'erets-Yisra'el.* Jerusalem, 1980.

Barnett, R. D. "The Correspondence of the Mahamad of the Spanish and Portuguese Congregation of London during the Seventeenth and Eighteenth Centuries." *Jewish Historical Society of England: Transactions* 20, sessions 1959–61 (1964): 1–50.

Baron, Salo Wittmayer. "Changing Patterns of Antisemitism." *Jewish Social Studies* 37 (1976): 5–38.

——. *The Jewish Community: Its History and Structure to the American Revolution.* 3 vols. Philadelphia, 1942.

——. *A Social and Religious History of the Jews.* Vols. 10, 11, and 16. Philadelphia, 1965–76.

Bauer, Krzysztof. *Wojsko koronne powstania kościuszkowskiego.* Warsaw, 1981.

Ben-Amos, Dan, and Jerome R. Mintz. *In Praise of the Baal Shem Tov: The Earliest Collection of Legends about the Founder of Hasidism.* Bloomington, Ind., 1970. Reprint, Northvale, N.J., 1993.

Benayahu, Me'ir. "Ha'hevrah kedoshah' shel rabbi Yehudah Hasid ve'aliyatah le'erets Yisra'el." *Sefunot* 3–4 (1960): 133–82.

Bennett, Paula, and Vernon A. Rosario II, eds. *Solitary Pleasures: The Historical, Literary and Artistic Discourse of Autoeroticism.* New York, 1995.

Ben-Sasson, Haim Hillel. *Hagut vehanhagah.* Jerusalem, 1959.

——. "Ishiyuto shel haGra vehashpa'ato hahistorit." *Zion* 31 (1966): 39–86; 197–216.

——. "Mekomah shel hakehillah-ha'ir betoledot Yisra'el." In *Hakehillah hayehudit bimei habeinayim,* edited by Haim Hillel Ben-Sasson, 7–24. Jerusalem, 1976.

Berekhiah Berakh of Klimontów. *Zera berakh shelishi.* Pt. 2. Frankfurt a/O, 1735.

Berger, David. *The Jewish-Christian Debate in the High Middle Ages: A Critical Edition of the Nizzahon Vetus.* Philadelphia, 1979.

Bergerówna, J. *Księżna pani na Kocku i Siemiatyczach.* Lwów, 1936.

Berkovitz, Jay R. "Social and Religious Controls in Pre-Revolutionary France: Rethinking the Beginnings of Modernity." *Jewish History* 15 (2001): 1–40.

Bernfeld, S. *Sefer hadema'ot.* Vol. 3. Berlin, 1926.

Bersohn, Mathias. *Dyplomataryusz dotyczący Żydów w dawnej Polsce: Naźródłach archiwalnych osnuty (1388–1782).* Warsaw, 1910.

Bieniarzówna, Janina. *Mieszczaństwo krakowskie XVII wieku.* Kraków, 1969.

Bilu, Yoram. "Dybbuk and Maggid: Two Cultural Patterns of Altered Consciousness in Judaism." *AJS Review* 21 (1996): 341–66.

———. "'Dybbuk'-Possession as a Hysterical Symptom: Psychodynamic and Socio-Cultural Factors." *Israel Journal of Psychiatry and Related Sciences* 26 (1989): 138–49.

Binyamin Beinish Ba'al Shem Tov ben Yehuda Leib Hakohen of Krotoszyn [Krotoschin]. *Sefer imtahat binyamin.* Wilhermsdorf, 1716.

———. *Sefer shem tov katan.* Żółkiew, 1781.

Birkenthal, Dov Ber, of Bolechów. *Zikhronot R. Dov me-Bolihov (483–565).* Edited by M. Vishnitzer [Mark Wischnitzer]. Berlin: Hotsa'at Kelal, 1922. Translated and edited by M. Vishnitzer [Mark Wischnitzer] under the title *The Memoirs of Ber of Bolechow (1723–1805).* London, 1922; reprint, New York, 1973.

Black, Jeremy. *Eighteenth-Century Europe, 1700–1789.* New York, 1990.

Bogucka, Maria. "Les Villes et le développement de la culture sur l'exemple de la Pologne au XVIe–XVIIIe siècles." In *La Pologne au XVe Congrès International des Sciences historiques à Bucarest,* 153–69. Warsaw, 1980.

Bogucka, Maria, and Henryk Samsonowicz. *Dzieje miasta i mieszczaństwa w Polsce przedrozbiorowej.* Wrocław, 1986.

Bonfil, Robert. *Jewish Life in Renaissance Italy.* Translated by Anthony Oldcorn. Berkeley, 1994.

Brawer, Abraham Ya'akov. *Galitsiyah viyehudeha: Mehkarim betoledot Galitsiyah bame'ah ha18.* Jerusalem, 1956.

Brill, Alan. "The Spiritual World of a Master of Awe: Divine Vitality, Theosis, and Healing in the *Degel mahaneh ephraim.*" *Jewish Studies Quarterly* 8 (2001): 27–65.

Brüll, N. "Beiträge zur jüdischen Sagen- und Spruchkunde im Mittelalter." *Jahrbücher für jüdische Geschichte und Literatur* 9 (1889): 1–71.

Buber, Salomon. *Anshei shem asher shimshu bekodesh be'ir Levuv.* Kraków, 1895.

———. *Kiryah nisgavah, hi ir Zolkvah.* Kraków, 1903.

Budzyński, Zdzisław. *Ludność pogranicza polsko-ruskiego w drugiej połowie XVIII wieku: Stan rozmieszczenie, struktura wyznaniowa i etniczna.* 2 vols. Przemyśl and Rzeszów, 1993.

Burnett, George. *View of the Present State of Poland.* London, 1807.

Burzyński, Andrzej. "Struktura dochodów wielkiej własności ziemskiej XVI–XVIII wieku (Próba analizy na przykładzie dóbr królewskich województwa sandomierskiego)." *Roczniki dziejów społecznych i gospodarczych* 34 (1973): 31–66.

Cackowski, Stefan. "Wiejscy Żydzi w województwie chelmińskim w 1772r." *Acta Universitatis Nicolai Copernici: Historia* 28 (1993): 61–72.

Carlebach, Elisheva. *Between History and Hope: Jewish Messianism in Ashkenaz and*

Sepharad. Third Annual Lecture of the Victor J. Selmanowitz Chair of Jewish History, May 17, 1998. New York, 1998.

——. *The Pursuit of Heresy: Rabbi Moses Hagiz and the Sabbatian Controversies.* New York, 1990.

Carlen, Claudia. *The Papal Encyclicals, 1740–1878.* Vol. 1. Wilmington, N.C., 1981.

Chazan, Robert. *Medieval Jewry in Northern France: A Political and Social History.* Baltimore, 1973.

Chmielowski, Benedykt. *Nowe Ateny albo Wszelkiej scyencyi Pełna, na Rózne Tytuły iak na Classes Podzielona.* 2 vols. Lwów, 1745. 4 vols. Lwów, 1755.

Chrościcki, J. A. "La Reconquête catholique dans l'architecture et la peinture religieuses." *XVIIe Siècle* 199 (1998): 345–57.

Cichocka-Petrazycka, Z. *Żywioł niemiecki na Wołyniu.* Warsaw, 1933.

Codello, A. "Zbiegostwo mieszczań rzeszowskich w pierwszej połowie XVIII w." *Małopolskie Studia Historyczne* 1 (1958): 37–49.

Cohen, Gerson D. "Messianic Postures of Ashkenazim and Sephardim." In *Studies of the Leo Baeck Institute,* edited by M. Kreutzberger, 115–56. New York, 1967.

Cohen, Israel. *Vilna.* Philadelphia, 1943.

Coxe, William. *Travels into Poland, Russia, Sweden and Denmark Interspersed with Historical Relations and Political Inquiries.* London, 1784.

Crummey, Robert. "Old Belief as Popular Religion: New Approaches." *Slavic Review* 52 (1993): 700–712.

Ćwik, Władysław. *Miasta królewskie lubelszczyzny w drugiej połowie XVIII wieku.* Lublin, 1968.

Cygielman, Shmuel Artur. "The Basic Privileges of the Jews of Great Poland as Reflected in Polish Historiography." *POLIN* 2 (1987): 117–49.

Czacki, Tadeusz. *Rozprawa o Żydach i Karaitach.* Edited by Kazimierz Józef Turowski. Kraków, 1860.

Czapliński, W. "Rządy oligarchii w Polsce nowożytnej." *Przegląd Historyczny* 52 (1961): 445–63.

Czapliński, W., and T. Ładogórski, eds. *Atlas historyczny Polski.* Warsaw, 1993.

Dan, Joseph. "A Bow to Frumkinian Hasidism." *Modern Judaism* 11 (1991): 175–93.

——. *Torat hasod shel hassiduth Ashkenaz.* Jerusalem, 1968.

David ben Yitshak Hakaro. *Ohel Rahel.* Szkłów, 1790.

Davies, Norman. *God's Playground: A History of Poland.* 2 vols. New York, 1982.

Dawidovitch, David. *Omanut ve'omanim bevatei kenesset shel Polin: Mekorot, signonot, hashpa'ot.* Tel Aviv, 1982.

——. *Tsiyurei-kir bevattei kenesset bePolin.* Jerusalem, 1968.

Diamant, Adolf. *Chronik der Juden in Leipzig.* Leipzig, 1993.

Dinur, Benzion. *Bemifneh hadorot.* Jerusalem, 1972.

——. *Dorot vereshumot.* Jerusalem, 1978.

——. "Hazemanim hahadashim betoledot yisra'el: Avhanatam mahutam udemutam." *Zion* 2 (1937). Reprinted in id., *Bemifneh hadorot,* 19–68.

——. "Reshitah shel hahasidut veyesodoteha hasotsiyaliyim vehameshihiyim." 1955. Reprinted in id., *Bemifneh hadorot,* 83–227.

Długosz, Jan [Ioannis Dlugossi]. *Annales seu cronicae incliti regni Poloniae.* Warsaw, 1978.

Doktór, Jan. "Jakub Frank: A Jewish Heresiarch and His Messianic Doctrine." *Acta Poloniae Historica* 76 (1997): 53–74.

———. *Księga Słów Pańskich: Ezoteryczne wykłady Jakuba Franka.* 2 vols. Warsaw, 1997.

———. "Ostatni rabin ziemski Wielkopolski." *Kwartalnik Historii Żydów* 1 (2002): 3–15.

———. *Śladami Mesjasza-Apostaty: Żydowskie ruchy mesjańskie w XVII i XVIII wieku a problem konwersji.* Wrocław, 1998.

Dov Ber of Międzyrzecz. *Maggid devarav leya'akov.* Korzec, 1784.

———. *Maggid devarav leya'akov.* Edited by Rivka Schatz. Jerusalem, 1976.

———. *Or Torah.* Korzec, 1804.

Drozdowski, Marian Marek. "Żydzi Warszawy Stanisławowskiej." In *Żydzi w dawnej Rzeczpospolitej,* edited by Andrzej Link-Lenczowski, 192–200. Kraków, 1991.

Druianov, Elyakim. "Keta'im mipinkas yashan shel hahevrah kadisha beDruja pelakh Vilna." *Reshumot* 1 (1918): 437–49.

Dubnow, Simon. "Fun mayn arkhiv." *Yivo bleter* 1 (1931): 404–7.

———. *History of the Jews in Russia and Poland from the Earliest Times until the Present Day.* Translated by Israel Friedlaender. 3 vols. Philadelphia, 1916–20.

———. *Toledot hahassiduth.* Tel Aviv, 1967.

———. "Der tsvayter khurbn fun Ukrayne (1768)." *Historishe shriftn* 1 (1929): 27–54.

———, ed. *Pinkas hamedinah, o pinkas va'ad hakehilot harashiyot bimedinat Lita.* Berlin, 1925. Cited as *PML.*

Eidelberg, Shlomoh. "Pinkas Śniadowo." *Gal-Ed* 3 (1976): 295–314.

Eisenbach, Artur. *The Emancipation of the Jews in Poland, 1780–1870.* Edited by A. Polonsky; translated by Janina Dorosz. Cambridge, Mass., 1991.

———. "Prawo obywatelskie i honorowe Żydów (1790–1861)." In *Społeczeństwo Królestwa Polskiego: Studia o uwarstwieniu i ruchliwości społecznej,* edited by W. Kula and J. Leskiewicz, 237–300. Warsaw, 1965.

———. "Wokół świadomość i roli politycznej mieszczaństwa polskiego na przełomie XVIII i XIX w." *Kwartalnik Historyczny* 95 (1988): 173–96.

———. *Z dziejów ludności żydowskiej w Polsce w XVIII i XIX wieku.* Warsaw, 1983.

Elbaum, Jacob. *Teshuvat halev vekabalat yisurim: Iyunim beshitot hateshuvah shel hokhmei Ashkenaz uPolin, 1348–1648.* Jerusalem, 1992.

Eliezer ben Tsevi Hirsh. *Sefer hahokhmah im peirush Asirei hativkvah.* Talmudische und sum Theil Cabbalistische Erklarung der Spruchworter Salomons. Neuwied, 1749.

Elijah ben Abraham Hakohen Itamari. *Shevet mussar.* Jerusalem, 1989.

Elimelekh of Leżajsk. *No'am Elimelekh.* Edited by Gedaliah Nigal. 2 vols. Jerusalem, 1978.

Elior, Rachel. "Hasidism: Historical Continuity and Spiritual Change." In *Gershom Scholem's "Major Trends in Jewish Mysticism," Fifty Years After,* edited by Peter Schäfer and Joseph Dan, 303–23. Tübingen, 1993.

——. *Herut al haluhot: Hamahshavah hahasidit, mekoroteha hamistiyim veye-sodoteha hakabbaliyim.* Tel Aviv, 1999.

——. *The Paradoxical Ascent to God: The Kabbalistic Theosophy of Habad Hasidism.* Albany, N.Y., 1993.

——. "Rabbi Nathan Adler of Frankfurt and the Controversy Surrounding Him." In *Mysticism, Magic and Kabbalah in Ashkenazi Judaism,* edited by Karl Grözinger and Joseph Dan, 223–42. Berlin, 1995.

——. "R. Nathan Adler and the Frankfurt Pietists; Pietist Groups in Eastern and Central Europe during the Eighteenth Century." In *Jüdische Kultur in Frankfurt am Main von den Anfängen bis zur Gegenwart,* edited by Karl E. Grözinger, 135–77. Wiesbaden, 1997.

——. "R. Yosef Karo veR. Yisra'el Ba'al Shem Tov: Metemorfozah mistit, hashra'ah kabbalit, vehafnamah ruhanit." *Tarbiz* 65 (1996): 671–709.

Eliyahu ben Yehezkel [Margaliyot of Biłgoraj]. *She'elot uteshuvot har hakarmel.* Frankfort a/O, 1782.

Elliott, Dyan. *Fallen Bodies: Pollution, Sexuality, and Demonology in the Middle Ages.* Philadelphia, 1999.

Emden, Jacob. *Megilat sefer.* Edited by David Kahana. New York, 1954 or 1955.

——. *Sefer shimush.* Amsterdam, 1758–62. Reprint, Jerusalem, 1975.

——. *Shevirat luhot ha'aven.* Żółkiew, 1756.

Epstein, Jehiel Mickal. *Sefer kitsur shenei luhot haberit [im mahadura batra].* Frankfurt a/M, 1724.

Etkes, Immanuel. *Ba'al haShem: HaBesht: Magiyah, mistikah, hanhagah.* Jerusalem, 2000.

——. "HaBesht hahistori: Bein rekonstruktsiah ledekonstruktsiah." *Tarbiz* 66 (1997): 425–42.

——. "HaBesht kemistikan uva'al besorah be'avodat HaShem." *Zion* 61 (1996): 421–454.

——. "Mekomam shel hamagiyah uva'alei hashem bahevrah ha'ashkenazit be-mifneh hame'ot ha17-ha18." *Zion* 60 (1995): 69–104.

——. *Tenu'at hahassidut bereshitah.* Tel Aviv, 1998.

——. *Yahid bedoro: Haga'on miVilnah—demut vedimui.* Jerusalem, 1998.

Etkes, Immanuel, David Assaf, Israel Bartal, and Elhanan Reiner, eds. *Bema'agalei hassidim: Kovets mehkarim lezikhro shel Professor Mordekhai Wilensky.* Jerusalem, 1999.

Etkes, Immanuel, David Assaf, and Yosef Dan, eds. *Mehkerei hassidut.* Jerusalem Studies in Jewish Thought, 15. Jerusalem, 1999.

Ettinger, Shmuel. *Bein Polin leRussiyah.* Jerusalem, 1994.

——. "The Council of Four Lands." In *The Jews in Old Poland, 1000–1795,* edited by Antony Polonsky, Jakub Basista, and Andrzej Link-Lenczowski, 93–109. London, 1993.

——. "Hasidism and the Kahal in Eastern Europe." In *Hasidism Reappraised,* edited by Ada Rapoport-Albert, 63–75. London, 1996.

——. "Ra'ayon habehirah beyisra'el uva'amim." In *Ra'ayon habehirah beyisra'el uva'amim,* edited by Shmuel Almog and Michael Heyd, 9–15. Jerusalem, 1991.

Faierstein, Morris M., trans. *Jewish Mystical Autobiographies: Book of Visions and Book of Secrets.* New York, 1999.

Feldman, David M. *Marital Relations, Birth Control and Abortion in Jewish Law.* New York, 1974.

Fijałkowski, Paweł. "Kultura Żydów pogranicza wielkopolsko-mazowieckiego w XVI–XVIII wieku." In *Żydowskie gminy wyznaniowe,* edited by Jerzy Woronczak, 25–33. Wrocław, 1995.

———. *Żydzi w województwach łęczyckim i rawskim w XV–XVIII wieku. Warsaw, 1999.*

Fisher, Elizabeth W. "'Prophecies and Revelations': German Cabbalists in Early Pennsylvania." *Pennsylvania Magazine of History and Biography* 109 (1985): 319–21.

Fishman, David E. *Russia's First Modern Jews: The Jews of Shklov.* New York, 1995.

Fogel, Moshe. "Shabbeta'uto shel sefer *Hemdat yamim:* Hitbonenut mehudeshet." In *The Sabbatian Movement and Its Aftermath: Messianism, Sabbatianism and Frankism,* Jerusalem Studies in Jewish Thought, 17, edited by Rachel Elior, 356–422. Jerusalem, 2001.

Frankel, Giza. "Notes on the Costume of the Jewish Woman in Eastern Europe." *Journal of Jewish Art* 7 (1980): 50–57.

Freudenthal, Max. *Leipziger messgaste: Die jüdischen besucher der Leipziger messen in den jahren 1675 bis 1764.* Frankfurt a/M, 1928.

Friedberg, H. D. *Toledot hadefus ha'ivri bePolanyah.* Tel Aviv, 1950.

Fuenn, S. *Kiryah ne'emanah: Korot edat Yisra'el be'ir Vilna.* Vilna, 1915.

Galas, Michał. "Sabbatianism in the Seventeenth-Century Polish-Lithuanian Commonwealth: A Review of the Sources." In *The Sabbatian Movement and Its Aftermath: Messianism, Sabbatianism and Frankism,* Jerusalem Studies in Jewish Thought, 17, edited by Rachel Elior, 51–63. Jerusalem, 2001.

Garrett, Clarke. *Spirit Possession and Popular Religion: From the Camisards to the Shakers.* Baltimore, 1987.

Gąsiorowska, Patrycja, and Stefan Gąsiorowski. "Inducta rzeczy spisanych po zabitym Gerszonie w roku 1746." *Studia Judaica: Biuletyn Polskiego Towarzystwa Studiów Żydowskich* 1 (1998): 88–94.

Gąsiorowski, Stefan. "Walka chrześcijańskich cechów z konkurencja żydowska w Żółkwi w świetle przywilejów z XVII i pierwszej połowy XVIII wieku." *Prawo* (Wrocław) 251, *Studia historyczno-demograficzne,* edited by Tadeusz Jurek and Krystyna Matwijowski (1996): 35–41.

Gelber, Nathan Michael. *Toledot yehudei Brody.* Arim ve'imahot beYisra'el, 6. Jerusalem, 1955.

———. "Korot hayehudim bePolin mireshit halukatah ve'ad milhemet ha'olam hasheniyah." In *Beit Yisra'el bePolin,* edited by Israel Halperin, 1: 110–27. Jerusalem, 1948.

———. "Die Taufbewegung unter den polnischen Juden im XVIII. Jahrhundert," *Monatsschrift für Geschichte und Wissenschaft des Judentums* 68 (1924): 225–41.

———. "Toledot yehudei Tarnopol," In *Tarnopol,* edited by P. Korngruen, 21–108. Jerusalem, 1955.

———. "Żydzi a zagadnienie reformy Żydów na Sejmie Czteroletnim." *Miesięcznik Żydowski,* year 1, vol. 2, no. 10 (1931): 326–44; no. 11 (1931): 429–40.

Gelber, Nathan Michael, and Y. Ben-Shem, eds. *Sefer Zolkvah.* Jerusalem, 1969.

Gierowski, Józef Andrzej. "The Jews in the Kościuszko Insurrection." In *Der letzte Ritter und erste Bürger im Osten Europas: Kościuszko, das aufständische Reformpolen und die Verbundenheit zwischen Polen und der Schweiz,* edited by Heiko Haumann and Jerzy Skowronek, 192–99. Basel, 1996.

Gieysztorowa, Irena. "Ludność." In *Encyklopedia historii gospodarczej Polski do 1945 r.* Warsaw, 1981.

———. "Remarks to Polish Historical Demography of the Recent Years." In *Changes in Two Baltic Countries: Poland and Sweden in the XVIII Century,* edited by Edmund Cieślak and Henryk Olszewski, 69–72. Poznan, 1990.

Gikatila, Abraham. *Sha'arei orah.* Warsaw, 1883.

Gmiterek, Henryk, ed. *Materiały źródłowe do dziejów Żydów w księgach grodzkich lubelskich z doby panowania Augusta II Sasa 1697–1733.* Judaica Lublinensia, 1. Lublin, 2001.

Goldberg, Jacob. "August II wobec polskich Żydów." In *Rzeczpospolita wielu narodów i jej tradycje,* edited by Andrzej Link-Lenczowski and Mariusz Markiewicz, 95–104. Kraków, 1999.

———. "Bein hofesh lenetinut: Sugei hatelut hafe'udalit shel hayehudim be-Polin." In *Divrei hakongres ha'olami hahamishi lemada'ei hayahadut, 1969,* 2 (1972): 107–13.

———. "De Non Tolerandis Iudaeis: On the Introduction of Anti-Jewish Laws into Polish Towns and the Struggle against Them." In *Studies in Jewish History Presented to Professor Raphael Mahler on His Seventy-Fifth Birthday,* edited by S. Yeivin, 39–52. Merhavia, Israel, 1974.

———. "Gminy żydowskie (kahały) w systemie władztwa dominialnego w szlacheckiej Rzeczypospolitej." In *Między historią a teorią: Refleksje nad problematyką dziejów i wiedzy historycznej,* edited by Marian Drozdowski, 152–71. Warsaw, 1988.

———. *Hahevrah hayehudit bemamlekhet Polin-Lita.* Jerusalem, 1999.

———. "Hamishar hakim'oni hayehudi bePolin bame'ah ha18: Takanot lahenvanim beZaslav uveBrody veshe'elat hamekorot ha'ivriyim-hapolaniyim letoledot hamishar vehahevrah hayehudiyim." In *Studies on Polish Jewry: Paul Glikson Memorial Volume,* edited by Ezra Mendelsohn and Chone Shmeruk, 11–64. Jerusalem, 1987.

———. *Hamumarim bemamlekhet Polin-Lita.* Jerusalem, 1985.

———. "Jewish Marriage in Eighteenth-Century Poland." *POLIN* 10 (1997): 3–39.

———. *Jewish Privileges in the Polish Commonwealth: Charters of Rights Granted to Jewish Communities in Poland-Lithuania in the Sixteenth to Eighteenth Centuries.* Jerusalem, 1985.

———. "The Jewish Sejm: Its Origins and Functions." In *The Jews in Old Poland 1000–1795,* edited by Antony Polonsky, Jakub Basista, and Andrzej Link-Lenczowski, 147–65. London, 1993.

———. "Manufaktura żelazna księdza infułata Kazimierza Lipskiego i Szlamy Efraimowicza w Choczu: Inicjatywy gospodarcze Żydów w XVIII wieku." In *Żydzi w Wielkopolsce na przestrzeni dziejów,* edited by J. Topolski and K. Modelski, 83–99. Poznan, 1999.

———. "O przywilejach biskupich dla gmin żydowskich w dawnej Rzeczypospolitej." In *Christianitas et cultura Europae: Księga jubileuszowa Profesora Jerzego Kłoczowskiego*, edited by H. Gapski, pt. 1, 625–29. Lublin, 1998.

———. "Pierwszy ruch polityczny wśród Żydów polskich: Plenipotenci żydowscy w dobie Sejmu Czteroletniego." In *Lud żydowski w narodzie polskim: Materiały sesji naukowej w Warszwie 15–16 wrzesien 1992*, edited by Jerzy Michalski, 45–63. Warsaw, 1994.

———. "Polacy-Żydzi-Niemcy w Polsce w XVII–XVIII wieku." In *Między Polityką a Kulturą*, 167–82. Warsaw, 1999.

———. "Poles and Jews in the Seventeenth and Eighteenth Centuries: Rejection or Acceptance." *Jahrbücher für Geschichte Osteuropas*, n.s., 22 (1974): 248–82.

———. "Posłowie miasta Lwowa na sejmy wobec Żydów lwowskich w XVII–XVIII wieku." *Rocznik Naukowo-Dydaktyczny WSP w Krakowie* 203 (1999): 85–94.

———. *Stosunki agrarne w miastach ziemi wieluńskiej w drugiej połowie XVII i w XVIII wieku*. Łódz, 1960.

———. "Władza dominialna Żydów-arendarzy dóbr ziemskich nad chłopami w XVII–XVIII wieku." *Przegląd Historyczny* 81 (1990): 189–98.

———. "Żyd i karczma miejska na Podlasiu w XVIII wieku." *Studia Podlaskie* 2 (1989): 27–38.

———. "Żydowski handel detaliczny w Polsce w XVIII wieku w świetle polsko-hebrajskiego 'Porządku kramarzów miasta Zasławia 1771 anno.'" *Przegląd humanistyczny* 37, no. 4 (1993): 45–56.

———. "Żydowski Sejm Czterech Ziem w społecznym i politycznym ustroju dawnej Rzeczypospolitej." In *Żydzi w dawnej Rzeczypospolitej*, edited by Andrzej Link-Lenczowski, 44–58. Wrocław, 1991.

Goldberg, Jacob, and Adam Wein. "Księga kahału w Działoszynie." *Biuletyn Żydowskiego Instytutu Historycznego* 53 (1965): 81–112.

———. "Ordynacja dla sejmu żydowskiego ziem koronnych z 1753r." *Biuletyn Żydowskiego Instytutu Historycznego* 52 (1964): 17–34.

Górski, Karol. *Kierownictwo duchowe w klasztorach żeńskich w Polsce, XVI–XVIII w.: Teksty i komentarze*. Textus et Studia, 11. Warsaw, 1980.

Grayzel, Solomon. *The Church and the Jews in the XIIIth Century: A Study of Their Relations during the Years 1198–1254, Based on the Papal Letters and Conciliar Decrees of the Period*. 1933. Rev. ed., New York, 1966.

Green, Arthur. "The *Zaddiq* as *Axis Mundi* in Later Judaism." *Journal of the American Academy of Religion* 45 (1997): 327–47.

Gries, Ze'ev. *Hasefer kesokhen tarbut bashanim [5]460-[5]660 (1700–1900)*. Tel Aviv, 2002.

———. "Hit'orerut ha'inteligentsiyah haredumah: Hadpasat sefarim bame'ah ha18 bikhlal velakahal hakor'im bemizrah Eiropah bifrat kevitui letalahilkhei temurah veshinui bahinukh yehudi." Typescript. Jerusalem, 1996.

———. "Mimitos le'etos: Kavvim ledemuto shel R. Abraham miKalisk." In *Umah vetoledoteha*, pt. 2, 117–46. Jerusalem, 1983.

———. *Sifrut hahanhagot: Toledoteha umekomah behayei hassidei R. Yisra'el Ba'al Shem Tov*. Jerusalem, 1989.

Grunwald, Max. *Samuel Oppenheimer und sein Kreis (ein Kapitel aus der Finanzgeschichte Österreichs).* Quellen und Forschungen zur Geschichte der Juden in Deutsch-Österreich, 5. Vienna and Leipzig, 1913.

Guldon, Zenon, and Waldemar Kowalski. *Żydzi i Szkoci w Polsce w XVI–XVII wieku: Studia i materialy.* Kielce, 1990.

Guldon, Zenon, and Jacek Wijaczka. "The Accusation of Ritual Murder in Poland, 1500–1800." *POLIN* 10 (1997): 99–140.

———. "Die zahlenmäßige Stärke der Juden in Polen-Litauen im 16.–18. Jahrhundert." *Trumah: Zeitschrift der Hochschule für Jüdische Studien, Heidelberg* 4 (1994): 91–101.

———. *Procesy o mordy rytualne w Polsce w XVI–XVIII wieku.* Kielce, 1995.

———. "Żydzi a Chrześcianie na Wołyniu w XVI–XVIII wieku." *Nasza Przeslość* 80 (1993): 227–48.

Gumplowicz, Ludwik. *Prawodawstwo Polskie względem Żydów.* Kraków, 1867.

Guterman, Alexander. "Hatsa'oteihem shel yehudei Polin letikunim bema'amadam hahuki hakalkali hahevrati vehatarbuti bitekufat hasejm hagadol." Master's Thesis, Hebrew University, 1975.

———. "'Sefer refues' leDr. Markuze vehatsa'otav letikunim behayyei hayehudim." *Gal-Ed* 4–5 (1978): 35–53.

Hahn (Nordlingen), Joseph Yuspa ben Phinehas Seligmann. *Yosif omets.* Frankfurt a/M, 1723.

Halamish, Moshe. *Hakabalah batefilah, bahalakhah uvaminhag.* Ramat-Gan, Israel, 2000.

Halper[i]n, Israel, ed. *Beit Yisrael bePolin miyamim rishonim ve'ad liyemot hahurban.* 2 vols. Jerusalem, 1948, 1950.

———. *Pinkas va'ad arba aratsot: Likkutei takkanot ketavim vereshumot.* 2d ed., vol. 1, revised and edited by Israel Bartal. Jerusalem, 1990. Cited as *PVAA.*

———. *Takanot medinat Mehrin.* Jerusalem, 1952.

———. *Yehudim veyahadut bemizrah Eiropah: Mehkarim betoledoteihem.* Jerusalem, 1968.

Hannover, Nathan Neta (d. 1683). *Sefer sha'arei tsiyon.* Jozefów, 1846.

Havatselet, Meir. "Hishtalshelut minhag toharat ba'alei keri behashpa'at gormei zeman umakom." *Talpiot* 8 (1963): 531–37.

Hayyim Hayke ben Aharon. *Tseror hahayyim.* Lublin, 1908.

Heilman, H. M. *Beit rabbi.* Berdyczów, 1903.

Heilperin, Joel ben Uriah. *Mif'alot Elohim.* Żółkiew, 1725.

Hertzberg, Arthur. *The French Enlightenment and the Jews: The Origins of Modern Anti-Semitism.* New York, 1968.

Heschel, Abraham J. *The Circle of the Baal Shem Tov: Studies in Hasidism.* Edited by Samuel H. Dresner. Chicago, 1985.

———. "R. Nahman miKossow, havero shel haBesht." In *Sefer hayovel likhevod Tsevi Wolfson,* edited by Saul Lieberman, Hebrew section, 113–42. New York, 1965.

Hillel ben Ze'ev Wolf. *Heilel ben shahar.* Warsaw, 1804.

Hisdai, Ya'akov. "'Eved HaShem'—Bedoram shel avot hahassiduth." *Zion* 47 (1982): 253–92.

Horn, Maurycy. *Regesty dokumentów i ekscerpty z Metryki Koronnej do historii Żydów w Polsce, 1697–1795.* Wrocław, 1984–88.

——. "Rola gospodarcza Żydów w Polsce do końca XVIII wieku." In *Żydzi wśród Chrześcijan w dobie szlacheckiej Rzeczypospolitej,* edited by Waldemar Kowalski and Jadwiga Muszyńska, 17–29. Kielce, 1996.

——. *Żydowskie bractwa rzemieślnicze na ziemiach polskich, białoruskich i ukraińskich w latach 1613–1850.* Warsaw, 1998.

——. *Żydzi na Rusi Czerwonej w XVI i pierwszej połowie XVII w.: Działalnosc gospodarcza na tle rozwoju demograficznego.* Warsaw, 1975.

Horowitz, Abraham ben Shabbetai Sheftel Halevi. *Emek berakha.* Kraków, 1597.

——. *Yesh Nohalin.* Amsterdam, 1701.

Horowitz, Isaiah ben Abraham Halevi. *Shenei luhot haberit hashalem.* Edited by Meir Katz. Haifa, 1997.

Horowitz, Tsevi Halevi Ish. *Letoledot hakehillot bePolin.* Jerusalem, 1978.

Hourwitz, Zalkind. *Apologie des juifs en réponse à la question: Est-il des moyens de rendre les juifs plus heureux et plus utiles en France?* Paris, 1789.

Hsia, R. Po-chia. "Christian Ethnographies of Jews in Early Modern Germany." In *The Expulsion of the Jews: 1492 and After,* edited by R. B. Waddington and A. Williamson, 223–35. New York, 1994.

Hubka, Thomas. "Beit hakenesset be Gwoździec-Sha'ar hashomayim: Hashpa'at sefer haZohar al ha'omanut veha'adrikhalut." *Eshel Be'er Sheva* 4 (1996): 263–316.

——. "Jewish Art and Architecture in the East European Context: The Gwoździec-Chodorów Group of Wooden Synagogues." *POLIN* 10 (1997): 141–82.

——. "The 'Zohar' and the Polish Synagogue: The Practical Influence of a Sacred Text." *Journal of Jewish Thought and Philosophy* 9 (2000): 173–250.

Hughes, Diane Owen. "Distinguishing Signs: Ear-Rings, Jews and Franciscan Rhetoric in the Italian Renaissance City." *Past & Present* 112 (1986): 3–59.

Hundert, E. J. "Bernard Mandeville and the Enlightenment's Maxims of Modernity." *Journal of the History of Ideas* 56 (1995): 577–93.

Hundert, Gershon David. "Approaches to the History of the Jewish Family in Early Modern Poland-Lithuania." In *The Jewish Family: Myths and Reality,* edited by Steven M. Cohen and Paula E. Hyman, 17–28. New York, 1986.

——. "The Conditions in Jewish Society in the Polish-Lithuanian Commonwealth in the Middle Decades of the Eighteenth Century." In *Hasidism Reappraised,* edited by Ada Rapoport-Albert, 45–50. London, 1996.

——. "The Contexts of Hasidism." In *Żydzi wsród Chrześcian w dobie szlacheckiej Rzeczypospolitej,* edited by Waldemar Kowalski and Jadwiga Muszyńska, 171–84. Kielce, 1996.

——. "The Implications of Jewish Economic Activities for Christian-Jewish Relations in the Polish Commonwealth." In *The Jews in Poland,* edited by Antony Polonsky, Chimen Abramsky, and Maciej Jachimczyk, 55–63; 226–31. Oxford, 1986.

——. "Jewish Urban Residence in the Polish Commonwealth in the Early Modern Period." *Jewish Journal of Sociology* 26 (1984): 25–34.

——. *The Jews in a Polish Private Town: The Case of Opatów in the Eighteenth Century.* Baltimore, 1992.

——. "Jews in Polish Private Towns: The Jewish Community in Opatów and the Town's Owners in the Eighteenth Century." In *Studies on Polish Jewry: Paul Glikson Memorial Volume,* edited by Ezra Mendelsohn and Chone Shmeruk, xvii–xxxviii. Jerusalem, 1987.

——. "The *Kehilla* and the Municipality in Private Towns at the End of the Early Modern Period." In *The Jews in Old Poland 1000–1795,* edited by Antony Polonsky, Jakub Basista, and Andrzej Link-Lenczowski, 174–85. London, 1993.

——. "No Messiahs in Paradise." *Viewpoints: The Canadian Jewish Quarterly* 2 (1980): 28–33.

——. "On the Jewish Community in Poland during the Seventeenth Century: Some Comparative Perspectives." *Revue des études juives* 142 (1983): 349–72.

——. "On the Problem of Agency in Eighteenth-Century Jewish Society." *Scripta Hierosolymitana* (Publications of the Hebrew University of Jerusalem) 38 (1998): 82–89.

——. "Reflections on the 'Whig' Interpretation of Jewish History: *Ma'assei banim siman le'avot.*" In *Truth and Compassion: Essays on Judaism and Religion in Memory of Rabbi Solomon Frank,* edited by Howard Joseph, Jack N. Lightstone, and Michael D. Oppenheim, 111–19. Waterloo, Ont., 1983.

——. "The Role of the Jews in Commerce in Early Modern Poland-Lithuania." *Journal of European Economic History* 16 (1987): 245–75.

——. "Some Basic Characteristics of the Jewish Experience in Poland." In *From Shtetl to Socialism: Studies from POLIN,* edited by Antony Polonsky, 19–25. London, 1993.

——, ed. *Essential Papers on Hasidism.* New York, 1991.

Hundert, Gershon, and Gershon Bacon. *The Jews in Poland and Russia: Bibliographical Essays.* Bloomington, Ind., 1984.

Hunt, Alan. *Governance of the Consuming Passions: A History of Sumptuary Law.* New York, 1996.

Hurteau, Pierre. "Catholic Moral Discourse on Male Sodomy and Masturbation in the Seventeenth and Eighteenth Centuries." *Journal of the History of Sexuality* 4 (1993–94): 1–26.

Idel, Moshe. "Enoch Is Metatron." *Immanuel* 24–25 (1990): 220–40.

——. *Hasidism: Between Ecstasy and Magic.* Albany, N.Y., 1995.

——. "'One from a Town, Two from a Clan'—The Diffusion of Lurianic Kabbala and Sabbateanism: A Re-Examination." *Jewish History* 7 (1993): 79–104.

Istoriko-iuridicheskie materialy, izvlechennye iz aktovykh knig gubernii Vitebskoi i Mogilevskoi, khraniaschchikhsia v tsentralnom arkhivie v Vitebskie. Vitebsk, 1871–1906.

Iwaniec, Eugeniusz. *Z dziejów staroobrzędowców na ziemiach polskich.* Warsaw, 1977.

Jacob Josef of Połonne. *Ben porat yosef.* Korzec, 1781.

——. *Sefer toledot ya'akov yosef.* Korzec, 1780. Photo-offset reprint, Jerusalem, 1966.

Jacobs, Louis. *Hasidic Prayer.* New York, 1973.

——. "Honour Thy Father: A Study of the Psychology of the Hasidic Movement." In *Hagut ivrit be'Eiropah,* edited by Menahem Zohori and Aryeh Tartakover, 136–43. Tel Aviv, 1969.

———. "Tobacco and the Hasidim." *Polin* 11 (1998): 25–30.

———. "The Uplifting of Sparks in Later Jewish Mysticism." In *Jewish Spirituality: From the Sixteenth-Century Revival to the Present*, edited by Arthur Green, 2: 99–126. New York, 1989.

Jacobson, Yoram. *Hasidic Thought*. Translated by Jonathan Chipman. Tel Aviv, 1998.

James, John Thomas. *Journal of a Tour in Germany, Sweden, Russia, Poland, during the Years 1813 and 1814*. London, 1819.

Johnston, Robert. *Travels through Part of the Russian Empire and the Country of Poland along the Southern Shores of the Baltic*. New York, 1816.

"Jüdische Kaufmannsbriefe aus den Jahren 1780 bis 1804." *Jüdische Familien-Forschung* 5, no. 4 (1929): 203.

Kaczor, Jacek. "Kahał ostrowiecki w XVII–XVIII wieku." In *Żydzi wśród Chrześcijan w dobie szlacheckiej Rzeczypospolitej*, edited by Waldemar Kowalski and Jadwiga Muszyńska, 63–68. Kielce, 1996.

Kalik, Yehudit. "Hakenesiyah hakatolit vehayehudim bemamlekhet Polin-Lita bame'ot ha17–18." Ph.D. diss., Hebrew University, Jerusalem, 1998.

———. "Hayahasim bein hakenesiyah hakatolit layehudim bemamlekhet Polin-Lita." In *Kiyum veshever*, edited by Israel Bartal and Israel Gutman, 1: 193–208. Jerusalem, 1997.

———. "Hayahas shel hashlakhta lamishar hayehudi." *Gal-Ed* 13 (1993): 43–57.

———. "Patterns of Contact between the Catholic Church and the Jews in the Polish-Lithuanian Commonwealth: The Jewish Debts." In *Studies in the History of the Jews in Old Poland in Honor of Jacob Goldberg*, Scripta Hierosolymitana, 38, edited by Adam Teller, 102–22. Jerusalem, 1998.

Kamelhar, Yekutiel. *Sefer mofet hador*. Piotrków and Warsaw, 1934.

Kamiński, Andrzej. "The Szlachta of the Polish-Lithuanian Commonwealth and Their Government." In *The Nobility in Russia and East Central Europe*, edited by Iwo Banac and Paul Bushkovitch, 17–45. New Haven, Conn., 1983.

Karkucińska, Wanda. *Anna z Sanguszków Radziwiłłowa*. Warsaw, 2000.

Karlinsky, Nahum. *Historiyah shekeneged: Igerot hahasidim me'erets-Yisra'el: Hatekst vehakontekst*. Jerusalem, 1998.

Kasabula, Tadeusz. *Ignacy Massalski biskup wileński*. Lublin, 1998.

Kasperek, Józef. *Gospodarka folwarczna ordinacji Zamojskiej w drugiej połowie XVIII wieku*. Warsaw, 1972.

Katz, Jacob. "Bein tatnu letah-tat." In *Sefer-yovel leYitshak Baer*, edited by S. Ettinger, S. Baron, B. Dinur, and I. Halpern, 318–37. Jerusalem, 1960.

———. *Tradition and Crisis: Jewish Society at the End of the Middle Ages*. Translated by Bernard Dov Cooperman. 1961. 2d ed., New York, 1993.

Katz, Moshe ben Yishayah. *Sefer berit mateh mosheh*. Berlin, 1701.

Katzenellenbogen, Pinehas. *Yesh manhilin*. Edited by Yitshak Dov Feld. Jerusalem, 1986.

Kaźmierczyk, Adam. "The Problem of Christian Servants as Reflected in the Legal Codes of the Polish-Lithuanian Commonwealth during the Second Half of the Seventeenth Century and in the Saxon Period." *Gal-Ed* 15–16 (1997): 23–40.

———. *Żydzi Polscy, 1648–1772: źródła*. Kraków, 2001.

———. *Żydzi w dobrach prywatnych w świetle sądowniczej I administracyjnej prakyki dóbr magnackich w wiekach XVI–XVIII*. Kraków, 2002.

Kelpius, Johannes. *The Diarium of Magister Johannes Kelpius*. Translated by Julius F. Sachse. Lancaster, Pa., 1917.

Kitowicz, Jędrzej. *Pamiętnik czyli Historia Polski*. Warsaw, 1971.

Klausner, Israel. *Vilna betekufat haga'on: Hamilhamah haruhanit vehahevratit bekehilat Vilna betekufat haGR'A*. Jerusalem, 1942.

———. *Vilna: Yerushalayim deLita: Dorot rishonim, 1495–1881*. Edited by Shmuel Barantchok. Tel Aviv, 1989.

Klier, John Doyle. *Russia Gathers Her Jews: The Origins of the "Jewish Question" in Russia, 1772–1825*. De Kalb, Ill., 1986.

Kłoczowski, Jerzy, ed. *Kościół w Polsce*. Kraków, 1968.

Kmita, Jan Achacy. *Talmud albo Wiara Żydowska*. Lublin, 1610, 1642.

Kobielski, Franciszek Antoni. *Światło na oświecienie narodu niewiernego to iest kazania w synagogach żydowskich miane, oraz reflexye y list odpowiadaiący na pytania synagogi brodzkiey*. Lwów, 1746.

Koidonover [Kaidanover], Tsevi Hirsch ben Aaron Samuel. *Kav hayashar*. Frankfurt a/M, 1705.

Konopczyński, Władysław. *Dyaryusze Sejmowe z wieku XVIII*. 3 vols. Warsaw, 1911–37.

Korngruen, P., ed. *Tarnopol*. Jerusalem, 1952.

Kowalska, Maria, ed. *Ukraina w połowie XVII wieku w relacji arabskiego podróżnika Pawła, syna Makarego z Aleppo*. Warsaw, 1986.

Kowalski, Waldemar. "Ludność żydowska a duchowieństwa archidiakonatu sandomierskiego w XVI–XVIII wieku." *Studia Judaica: Biuletyn Polskiego Towarzystwa Studiów Żydowskich* 1 (1998): 177–199.

———. "Pińczowski spis konwertytów XVII–XIX wieku." *Nasza Przeszłość* 73 (1990): 5–33.

———. "Stopnicki rejestr konwertytów XVII–XIX wieku." *Nasza Przeszłość* 76 (1991): 193–285.

———. "W obronie wiary: Ks. Stefan Żuchowski—między wzniosłością a okrucieństwem." In *Żydzi wśród chrześcijan w dobie szlacheckiej Rzeczypospolitej*, edited by Waldemar Kowalski and Jadwiga Muszyńska, 221–33. Kielce, 1996.

Kraushar, Alexander. *Frank i Frankiści Polscy, 1726–1816: Monografia historyczna osnuta na źródłach archiwalnych i rękopismiennych*. 2 vols. Kraków, 1895.

Kriegseisen, Wojciech. *Ewangelicy polscy i litewscy w epoce saskiej 1696–1763: Sytuacja prawna, organizacja i stosunki międzywyznaniowe*. Warsaw, 1996.

Krochmal, Jacek. "Dekret biskupa W. H. Sierakowskiego z 19 lipca 1743 roku w sprawie Żydów przemyskich." *Rocznik Przemyski* 29–30 (1993–94): 285–99.

———. "Hayahasim bein ha'ironim vehakenesiyah bePrzemysl levein hayehudim bashanim 1559–1772." *Gal-Ed* 15–16 (1997): 15–33.

Kulczykowski, Mariusz. *Kraków jako ośrodek towarowy Małopolski zachodniej w drugiej połowie XVIII wieku*. Studia z Historii Społeczno-Gospodarczej Małoposkiej, 6. Warsaw, 1963.

Kulejewska-Topolska, Zofia. *Nowe lokacje miejskie w Wielkopolsce od XVI do końca XVIII wieku.* Poznan, 1964.

Kumor, Bolesław, and Zdzisław Obertynski, eds. *Historia Kościoła w Polsce.* Poznan, 1974.

Kupfer, Efraim. "A tsushteyyer tsu der frage fun der batseyung fun kahal tsum yidishn ba'al mlokhe, meshares un oremshaft in amolikn Poyln." *Bleter far geshikhte* 2 (1949): 207–22.

Kutrzeba, Stanisław. *Zbiór aktów do historyi ustroju sądów prawa polskiego i kancelaryi sądowych województwa krakowskiego z wieku XVI–XVIII.* Kraków, 1909.

Lamm, Norman. "The Letter of the Besht to R. Gershon of Kutov." *Tradition* 14 (1974): 110–25.

———. *The Religious Thought of Hasidism: Text and Commentary.* New York, 1999.

Landau, Barukh. *Reshit limudim: Limudei hateva ushevilei ha'olam.* Berlin: Hevrat hinukh lana'ar, 1789.

Landau, Ezekiel ben Judah. *She'elot uteshuvot noda biyehudah.* Jerusalem, 1990.

Lech, Marian. "Powstanie chłopów białoruskich w starostwie krzyczewskim 1740r." *Przegląd Historyczny* 51 (1960): 314–30.

Leiman, Shneur Zalman. "Sefarim hahashudim beshabbeta'ut: Reshimato shel haga'on 'Y'abetz'." In *Sefer hazikkaron lerabbi Moshe Lifshits,* edited by R. Rozenbaum, 885–94. New York, 1996.

Leszczynski, Anatol. *Żydzi ziemi bielskiej od połowy XVII w. do 1795r.* Wrocław, 1980.

Levitats, Isaac. *The Jewish Community in Russia, 1772–1844.* New York, 1943.

Lewalski, Krzysztof. "Szkic do dziejów misji Chrześcijańskich wśród Żydów na ziemiach polskich w XVIII–XX wieku." *Studia Historyczne* 36 (1993): 185–202.

Liberman, Hayyim. "Bamerkungen." *Yivobleter* 36 (1952): 305–19.

———. *Ohel Rahel.* Vol. 2. Brooklyn, 1984.

Liebes, Yehuda. "Hadashot le'inyan haBesht veShabbetai Tsevi." *Mehkerei Yerushalayim bemahshevet yisra'el* 2 (1983): 564–69. Reprinted in id., *Sod ha'emunah hashabbeta'it,* 262–65.

———. "Hamashiah shel haZohar: Ledemuto hameshihit shel R. Shim'on bar Yohai." In *The Messianic Idea in Jewish Thought: A Study Conference in Honour of the Eightieth Birthday of Gershom Scholem,* 87–236. Jerusalem, 1982.

———. "Hatikkun hakelali shel R. Nahman miBraslav veyahaso leshabbeta'ut." *Zion* 45 (1980): 201–45. Reprinted in id., *Sod ha'emunah hashabbeta'it,* 238–61.

———. "Megamot beheker hassiduth Braslav." *Zion* 47 (1982): 224–31.

———. *Sod ha'emunah hashabbeta'it: Kovets ma'amarim.* Jerusalem, 1995.

———. *Studies in Jewish Myth and Jewish Messianism.* Translated by Batya Stein. Albany, N.Y., 1993.

Likkutei amarim. Lwów, 1811.

Litak, Stanisław. "Jezuici na tle innych zakonów męskich w Polsce XVI–XVIII wieku." In *Jezuici a kultura polska,* edited by L. Grzebień and S. Obirek, 185–98. Kraków, 1993.

Lublin, Meir ben Gedaliah. *She'elot uteshuvot.* Venice, 1618.

Lukowski, Jerzy Tadeusz. *Liberty's Folly: The Polish-Lithuanian Commonwealth in the Eighteenth Century, 1697–1795.* New York, 1991.

M.C. "Zur Geschichte des hebräischen Buchdruckes in Russland und Polen." In *Festschrift für Aron Freimann zum 60. Geburtstage,* edited by Alexander Marx and Herrmann Meyer, 91–100. Berlin, 1935.

Mahler, Raphael. *Toledot hayehudim bePolin: Kalkalah, hevrah, hamatsav hamishpati.* Translated by Avigdor Hame'iri. Merhavia, Israel, 1946.

———. "Di Yidn in amolikn Poyln." In *Di Yidn in Poyln: Fun di eltste tsaytn biz der Tsveyter Velt-milhome.* New York, 1946.

———. *Yidn in amolikn Poyln in likht fun tsifern.* 2 vols. Warsaw, 1958.

———. "Z dziejów Żydów w Nowym Sączu w XVII i XVIII w." *Biuletyn Żydowskiego Instytutu Historycznego* 55 (1965): 3–32; 56 (1965): 29–58.

———, ed. *Sefer Sants.* Tel Aviv, 1970.

Maimon, Salomon. *Salomon Maimon's Lebensgeschichte von ihm selbst geschrieben.* Edited by K. P. Moritz. 2 vols. Berlin, 1792–93.

Maimon, Salomon. *The Autobiography of Solomon Maimon.* Translated by J. Clark Murray. Oxford, 1954.

Malino, Frances. *A Jew in the French Revolution: The Life of Zalkind Hourwitz.* Cambridge, Mass., 1996.

Mandel, Arthur. *The Militant Messiah: or, The Flight from the Ghetto: The Story of Jacob Frank and the Frankist Movement.* Atlantic Highlands, N.J., 1979.

Marcus, Ivan. *Piety and Society: The Jewish Pietists of Medieval Germany.* Leiden, 1981.

———, ed. *Dat vehevrah bemishnatam shel hassidei Ashkenaz.* Jerusalem, 1986.

Margoliot, H. Z. *Dubno rabbati.* Warsaw, 1910.

Margoliot, Zelig ben Yitshak Isaac. *Sefer hibburei likutim.* Venice, 1715.

Mark, Tzvi. "Dibbuk udevekut be*Shivhei haBesht:* He'arot lefenomenologiyah shel hashiga'on bereshit hahassiduth." In *Bema'agalei hassidim: Kovets mehkarim lezikhro shel Professor Mordekhai Wilensky,* edited by Immanuel Etkes, David Assaf, Yisrael Bartal, and Elhanan Reiner, 247–86. Jerusalem, 1999.

Markgraf, Richard. *Zur Geschichte der Juden auf den Messen in Leipzig von 1664–1839.* Bischofswerda, 1894.

Markiewicz, Jerzy, Ryszard Szczygiel, and Wiesław Śladkowski. *Dzieje Biłgoraja.* Lublin, 1985.

Materiały do dziejów Sejmu Czteroletniego. 6 vols. Wrocław, 1955–69. Cited as *MDSC.* Vol. 2, edited by Janusz Woliński, Jerzy Michalski, and Emanuel Rostworowski. Wrocław, 1959. Vol. 6, edited by Jerzy Michalski, Emanuel Rostworowski, Janusz Woliński, and Artur Eisenbach. Wrocław, 1969.

Matuszewicz, Marcin. *Diariusz życia mego.* 2 vols. Edited by Bohdan Krolikowski, commentary by Zofia Zielińska. Warsaw, 1986.

Mazurkiewicz, Józef. *Jurydyki lubelskie.* Wrocław, 1956.

———. "O niektórych problemach prawno-ustrojowych miast prywatnych w dawnej Polsce." *Annales Universitatis Mariae Curie-Skłodowska,* sec. G, 11 (1964): 97–124.

Menahem Mendel of Vitebsk. *Peri ha'arets.* Kapust, 1814.

Michałowska, Anna. "Pinkas gminy żydowskiej w Bockach." *Biuletyn Żydowskiego Instytutu Historycznego* 190 (1999): 55–97.

———. "Protokol procesu o mord rytualny (fragment czarnej księgi krzemienieckiej z 1747 roku)." *Biuletyn Żydowskiego Instytutu Historycznego* 175–78 (1995–96): 108 20.

Michalski, Jerzy. *Historia Sejmu polskiego.* Vol. 1. Warsaw, 1984.

———. "Sejmowe projekty reformy położenia ludności żydowskiej w Polsce w latach 1789–1792." In *Lud żydowski w narodzie polskim: Materiały sesji naukowej w Warszwie 15–16 wrzesien 1992,* edited by Jerzy Michalski, 20–44. Warsaw, 1994.

Miller, Perry. *Errand into the Wilderness.* 1956. Cambridge, Mass., 1964.

Mondshine, Yehoshua. "Al 'Hatikkun hakelali shel R. Nahman miBraslav veyahaso leshabbeta'ut.'" *Zion* 47 (1982): 198–223.

———. "Ma'amad shene'erakh bein hamadpisim beLevov veZolkiew." In *Sefer hazikkaron lerabbi Moshe Lifshits,* edited by R. Rozenbaum, 898–916. New York, 1996.

Mordecai ben Samuel. *Sha'ar hamelekh.* Żółkiew, 1762.

Morgensztern, Janina. "Notes on the Sephardim in Zamość, 1588–1650." *Biuletyn Żydowskiego Instytutu Historycznego* 38 (1961): 69–82.

Moses Hayyim Ephraim of Sudylków. *Degel mahaneh efrayim.* Zhitomir, 1874.

Moszczeński, Adam. *Pamiętniki do historii polskiej w ostatnich latach panowania Augusta III i pierwszych Stanisława Poniatowskiego.* Poznan, 1858.

Motylewicz, Jerzy. "Ulice etniczne w miastach ziemi przemyskiej i sanockiej w XVII i XVIII wieku." *Kwartalnik Historii Kultury Materialnej* 47 (1999): 149–55.

———. "Żydzi w miastach ziemi przemyskich i sanockiej w drugiej połowie XVII I w XVIII wieku." In *Żydzi w Małopolsce: Studia z dziejów osadnictwa i życia społecznego,* edited by Feliks Kiryk, 113–35. Przemyśl, 1991.

Mrozowska, K. *Funkcjonowanie systemu szkolnego Komisji Edukacji Narodowej na terenie Korony w latach 1783–1793.* Wrocław, 1985.

Müller, Wiesław. "Jews in the *ad limina* Reports of Polish Bishops in the Seventeenth and Eighteenth Centuries." Typescript.

———. *Relacje o stanie diecezji krakowskiej 1615–1765.* Materiały do Dziejów Kościoła w Polsce, 7. Lublin, 1978.

Nadav, Mordechai. "Iyun behitrahashuyot beshalosh kehilot bePolin-Lita biyemei milhemet hatsafon ule'ahareha." *Proceedings of the Eighth World Congress of Jewish Studies,* Division B, 2 (1982): 89–96.

———. "Kehilot Pinsk-Karlin bein hassiduth lehitnaggedut." *Zion* 34 (1969): 98–108.

——— [Markiel Katzykovich], ed. *Pinkas kehal Tiktin [5]381–[5]566: Haskamot, hahelatot vetakanot kefi shehe'etikan min hapinkas hamekori she'avad basho'ah Yisra'el Halperin.* Vol. 1: *Pinkas kehal Tiktin.* Jerusalem, 1996.

———. "Toledot kehillat Pinsk: 1506–1880." In *Pinsk: Sefer edut vezikaron,* edited by W. Z. Rabinowitsch, 15–195. Tel Aviv, 1973.

Nadler, Allan Lawrence. *The Faith of the Mithnagdim: Rabbinic Responses to Hasidic Rapture.* Baltimore, 1997.

Neale, Adam. *Travels through Some Parts of Germany, Poland, Moldavia and Turkey.* London, 1818.

Neumann, R. P. "Masturbation, Madness, and Modern Concepts of Childhood and Adolescence." *Journal of Social History* 8 (1975): 1–27.

Nigal, Gedaliah. *Magic, Mysticism and Hasidism: The Supernatural in Jewish Thought.* Northvale, N.J., 1994.

———. "Makor rishoni lesifrut hasippurim hahasidit: al sefer 'keter shem tov' umekorotav." *Sinai* 79 (1976): 132–146.

———. *Torot ba'al hatoledot: Derashot R. Ya'akov Yosef mi Polenoye lefie nos'ei yesod.* Jerusalem, 1974.

Nisenbaum, S. B. *Lekorot hayehudim beLublin.* Lublin, 1920.

Opas, Tomasz. "Rynek lokalny Tarnowa w XVIII wieku." *Roczniki dziejów społecznych i gospodarczych* 36 (1975): 29–58.

———. "Sytuacja ludności żydowskiej w miastach szlacheckich województwa lubelskiego w XVIII wieku." *Biuletyn Żydowskiego Instytutu Historycznego* 67 (1968): 3–37.

———. "Upadek i odrodzenie miasta." In *Lubartów: Z dziejów miasta i regionu.* edited by S. Tworek, 25–40. Lublin, 1977.

———. "Wolność osobista mieszczań miast szlacheckich województwa lubelskiego w drugiej połowie XVII i w XVIII wieku." *Przegląd Historyczny* 61 (1970): 609–29.

Orłowski, R. *Działalność społeczno-gospodarcza Andrzeja Zamoyskiego, 1757–1792.* Lublin, 1965.

Partyka, Joanna. "Szlachecka silva rerum jako źródło do badań etnograficznych." *Etnografia Polska* 32 (1988): 67–94.

Pazdro, Zbigniew. *Organizacja i praktyka żydowskich sądów podwojewodzińskich, 1740–1772.* Lwów, 1903.

Pęckowski, Jan. *Dzieje miasta Rzeszowa do końca XVIII wieku.* Rzeszów, 1913.

Pedayah, Haviva. "Lehitpathuto shel hadegem hahevrati-dati-kalkali bahassidut: Hapidyon, hahavurah, veha'aliyah leregel." In *Dat vekalkalah: Yahasei gomlin,* edited by Menahem Ben-Sasson, 311–73. Jerusalem, 1995.

Pelenski, Jaroslav "The Cossack Insurrections in Jewish Ukrainian Relations." In *Ukrainian-Jewish Relations in Historical Perspective,* edited by Howard Aster and Peter J. Potichnyi, 31–42. Edmonton, 1988.

———. "The *Haidamak* Insurrections and the Old Regimes in Eastern Europe." In *The American and French Revolutions, 1776–1848: Sociopolitical and Ideological Aspects,* Proceedings of the Second Conference of Polish and American Historians, Iowa City, Iowa, 29 September–1 October, 1976, edited by Jaroslav Pelenski, 228–47. Iowa City, 1980.

Perets ben Moshe. *Sefer beit Perets.* Żółkiew, 1759.

Piechotkowie, Maria and Kazimierz. "Polichromie polskich bóżnic drewnianych." *Polskie Sztuka Ludowa* 43 (1989): 65–87.

Piekarz, Mendel. *Bein ideologyah limetsiut: Anavah, ayin, bitul mimetsiut udevekut bemahshavtam shel rashe hahassidut.* Jerusalem, 1994.

———. *Biyemei tsemihat hahassidut: Megamot ra'ayaniyot besifrei derush umussar.* Jerusalem, 1978. Rev. ed., Jerusalem, 5758 [1998].

———. *Hahanhagah hahassidit: Samkhut ve'emunat tsaddikim be'aspaklariyat sifrutah shel hahassidut.* Jerusalem, 1999.

———. "Hara'ayon hameshihi biyemei tsemihat hahassidut." In *The Messianic Idea in Jewish Thought: A Study Conference in Honour of the Eightieth Birthday of Gershom Scholem,* 237–53. Jerusalem, 1982.

———. "R. Elimęlekh miLezajsk umamshikhei darko." *Gal-Ed* 15–16 (1997): 43–80.

Pikulski, Gaudenty. *Złość żydowska Przeciwko Bogu y bliżnemu Prawdzie y Sumnieniu na obiasnienie Talmudystów. Na dowód ich zaślepienia, y Religii dalekiey od prawa Boskiego przez Moyżesza danego. Rozdzielona na trzy części opisana.* 1st ed. 1758, in two parts. Reprint, Lwów, 1760.

Pipes, Richard. "Catherine II and the Jews: The Origins of the Pale of Settlement." *Soviet Jewish Affairs* 5 (1975): 3–20.

Podhorizer-Sandel, E. "Judaica w Muzeum Narodowym w Warszawie." *Biuletyn Żydowskiego Instytutu Historycznego* 78 (1971): 44–48.

Podraza, Antoni. "Jews and the Village in the Polish Commonwealth." In *The Jews in Old Poland, 1000–1795,* edited by Antony Polonsky, Jakub Basista, and Andrzej Link-Lenczowski, 299–321. London, 1993.

Poliakov, Léon. *L'Épopée des Vieux-Croyants: Une Histoire de la Russie authentique.* Paris, 1991.

Poniatowski, Stanisław [King Stanisław II of Poland]. *Pamiętniki Króla Stanisława Augusta.* Edited by Władysław Konopczyński and Stanisław Ptaszycki. Vol. 1, pt. 1. Warsaw, 1915.

Przyboś, Adam, ed. *Akta radzieckie rzeszowskie.* Wrocław, 1957.

Ptaśnik, Jan. *Miasta i mieszczaństwo w dawnej Polsce.* Kraków, 1934.

Rabinowitsch, Wolf Zeev. *Lithuanian Hasidism from Its Beginnings to the Present Day.* Foreword by Simon Dubnow, translated by M. B. Dagut. London, 1970.

Radliński, J. *Prawda Chrześciańska od nieprzyiaciela swego zeznana.* Lublin, 1733.

Rakover, Nahum. *Hakehillah.* A Bibliography of Jewish History, 4. Jerusalem, 1977.

Rapoport-Albert, Ada. "Al ma'amad hanashim bashabbeta'ut." In *The Sabbatian Movement and Its Aftermath: Messianism, Sabbatianism and Frankism,* Jerusalem Studies in Jewish Thought, 17, edited by Rachel Elior, 143–327. Jerusalem, 2001.

———. "Hasidism after 1772: Structural Continuity and Change." In *Hasidism Reappraised,* edited by Ada Rapoport-Albert, 76–140. London, 1996.

———, ed. *Hasidism Reappraised.* London, 1996.

———. "Hatenu'ah hahassidit aharei shenat 1772: Retsef miveni utemurah." *Zion* 55 (1990): 183–245.

———. "On Women in Hasidism: S. A. Horodecky and the Maid of Ludmir Tradition." In *Jewish History: Essays in Honour of Chimen Abramsky,* edited by A. Rapoport-Albert and S. Zipperstein, 495–525. London, 1988.

Raynaldus, Odoricus. *Annales Ecclesiastici ab anno MCXCVIII ubi Bard. Baronius desinit.* Vol. 12. Rome, 1646.

Regesty i nadpisi; svod materialov dlia istorii evreev v Rossii (80 g.–1800 g.). 3 vols. St. Petersburg, 1899–1913.

Reiner, Elchanan. "Hon, ma'amad hevrati vetalmud torah." *Zion* 58 (1993): 287–328.

Reinhold, Josef. *Polen/Litauen auf den Leipziger Messen des 18. Jahrhunderts.* Weimar, 1971.

Riabinin, Jan. *Rada miejska lubelska.* Lublin, 1931.

Richarz, Monika. *Die Eintritt der Juden in die akademischen Berufe: Jüdische Studenten und Akademiker in Deutschland, 1678–1848.* Tübingen, 1974.

Ringelblum, Emanuel. "Johann Anton Krieger, printer of Jewish books in Nowy Dwór." *POLIN* 12 (1999): 198–211.

———. *Kapitlen geshikhte fun amolikn yidishn lebn in Poyln.* Buenos Aires, 1953.

———. *Di poylishe Yidn in oifshtand fun Koshtsyushko—1794.* Vilna, 1937. Polish trans., Warsaw, 1938.

———. "Projekty i próby przewarstwowienia Żydów w epoce stanisławowskiej." *Sprawy Narodowościowe* 1 (1934): 3–9.

———. "Shmuel Zbytkower: Askan tsiburi-kalkali bePolin bimei halukatah." *Zion* 3 (1938): 246–66; 337–55.

Rivkind, Isaac. "Verter mit yikhes." In *Judah H. Joffe Book,* edited by Yudel Mark, 257–59. New York, 1958.

Rok, Bogdan. "Stosunek polskiego Kościoła katolickiego do sprawy żydowskiej w 1. połowie XVIII wieku." In *Z historii ludności żydowskiej w Polsce i na Śląsku,* edited by Krystyn Matwijowski, 85–97. Wrocław, 1994.

———. "Z dziejów literatury antyżydowskiej w dawnej Rzeczypospolitej w XVIII w." *Prawo* (Wrocław) 251, *Studia historyczno-demograficzne,* edited by Tadeusz Jurek and Krystyna Matwijowski (1996): 55–64.

Rosman, Moshe J. "An Exploitative Regime and the Opposition to It." In *Temurot bahistoriyah hayehudit hahadashah,* edited by S. Almog et al., xi–xxx. Jerusalem, 1988.

———. *Founder of Hasidism: A Quest for the Historical Ba'al Shem Tov.* Berkeley, 1996.

———. "The Indebtedness of the Lublin Kahal in the Eighteenth Century." In *Studies in the History of the Jews in Old Poland in Honor of Jacob Goldberg,* Scripta Hierosolymitana, 38, edited by Adam Teller, 166–83. Jerusalem, 1998.

———. *The Lords' Jews: Magnate-Jewish Relations in the Polish-Lithuanian Commonwealth during the Eighteenth Century.* Cambridge, Mass., 1990.

———. "A Minority Views the Majority: Jewish Attitudes towards the Polish-Lithuanian Commonwealth and Interaction with Poles." In *From Shtetl to Socialism: Studies from POLIN,* edited by Antony Polonsky, 39–49. Washington, D.C., 1993.

———. "A Prolegomenon to the Study of Jewish Cultural History." *Jewish Studies: An Internet Journal* 1 (2002): 109–27. http://www.biu.ac.il/JS/JSIJ/1-2002/Rosman.doc.

Rostworowski, Emanuel. "Ilu było Rzeczypospolitej obywateli szlachty?" *Kwartalnik Historyczny* 94 (1987): 3–39.

———. *Maj 1791–maj 1792: Rok monarchii konstytucyjnej.* Warsaw, 1985.

———. "Miasta i mieszczanie w ustroju Trzeciego Maja." In *Sejm Czteroletni i jego tradycje,* edited by Jerzy Kowecki, 138–51. Warsaw, 1991.

———. *Ostatni król Rzeczpospolitej.* Warsaw, 1966.

Rostworowski, Marek. *Żydzi w Polsce: Obraz i słowo.* Warsaw, 1993.

Roth, Cecil. *The Ritual Murder Libel and the Jew: The Report by Cardinal Lorenzo Ganganelli (Pope Clement XIV).* London, 1935.

Rubinstein, Abraham Hayyim. "Al sheloshah sippurim besefer *Shivhei haBesht.*" *Sinai* 90 (1982): 269–79.

——. "Hakuntras *zimrat am ha'arets*." *Areshet* 3 (1961): 193–230.

——. "Igeret haBesht leR. Gershon miKutów." *Sinai* 67 (1970): 120–39.

——. *Shivhei haBesht; Mahadurah mu'eret umevu'eret.* Jerusalem, 1991.

Salmonowicz, Stanisław. "Pietyzm na Pomorzu Polskim oraz w Wielkopolsce w pierwszej połowie XVIII wieku." *Roczniki humanistyczne* 27 (1979): 95–105.

Samuel ben Eli'ezer of Kalwarija. *Darkhei no'am.* Königsberg, 1764.

Sanctissimi Domini Nostri Benedicti Papae XIV Bullarium. Venice, 1778.

Sandel, Jozef. *Yidishe motivn in der poylisher kunst.* Warsaw, 1954.

Sawicki, Jakub, ed. *Concilia Poloniae: Źródła i studia krytyczne, Synody diecezji płockiej i ich statuty.* 6 vols. Warsaw, 1949–52.

Schiper, Ignacy. *Dzieje handlu żydowskiego na ziemiach polskich.* Warsaw, 1937.

Schiper, Ignacy, A. Tartakower, and A. Hafftek, eds. *Żydzi w Polsce odrodzonej.* Warsaw, n.d.

Scholem, Gershom. *Devarim bego.* Tel Aviv, 1975.

——. *Major Trends in Jewish Mysticism.* New York, 1961.

——. *Mehkarim umekorot letoledot hashabbeta'ut vegilguleha.* Jerusalem, 1974.

——. *Mehkere shabbeta'ut.* Edited by Yehudah Liebes. Tel Aviv, 1991.

——. *The Messianic Idea in Judaism and Other Essays on Jewish Spirituality.* New York, 1971.

——. *On the Mystical Shape of the Godhead: Basic Concepts in the Kabbalah.* New York, 1991.

——. "R. Eliyahu hakohen ha'itamari vehashabbeta'ut." In *Sefer hayovel likhevod Alexander Marx,* 451–70. New York, 1950.

——. "Vehata'alumah be'einah 'omedet." *Behinot* 8 (1955): 79–95.

Schorr, Mojżesz. *Organizacya Żydów w Polsce (od najdawniejszych czasów aż do r. 1772).* Lwów, 1899.

——. *Żydzi w Przemyślu do końca XVIII wieku.* Lwów, 1903. Reprint, Jerusalem, 1991.

Serczyk, W. *Gospodarstwo magnackie w województwie podolskim w drugiej połowie XVIII wieku.* Kraków, 1965.

——. *Koliszczyzna.* Kraków, 1968.

Sefer toharot hakodesh. Amsterdam, 1733.

Sefer toledot adam. Żółkiew, 1720.

Sefer yetsirah. Kitab almabadi im perush hagaon Seadyah bar Yosef Fayumi makor vetargum. Edited by Yosef David Kafah. Jerusalem, 1972.

Shahar, Isaiah. *Bikoret hahevrah vehanhagat hatsibur besifrut hamusar vehaderush bePolin bame'ah ha18.* Jerusalem, 1992.

Shatzky, Jacob. "Alexander Kraushar and His Road to Total Assimilation." *YIVO Annual* 7 (1953): 146–74.

——. *Di geshikhte fun Yidn in Varshe.* New York, 1947–53.

——. "Sefardim in Zamoshch." *Yivo Bleter* 35 (1951): 93–120.

——. "'Sefer Heshek'—A farfaln refu'oh-bukh in yiddish fun 18tn y'h, un zayn mekhaber." *Yivo Bleter* 4 (1932): 223–35.

——. "Zalkind Hurwitz." *Der Farband,* May 1926, 12–13.

Sha'ul ben Moshe. *She'elot uteshuvot giv'at sha'ul.* Żółkiew, 1774.

Shmeruk, Chone. *Hakeriy'ah lenavi: Mehkerei historiyah vesifrut.* Edited by Israel Bartal. Jerusalem, 1999.

———. "Hasidism and the *Kehilla*," In *The Jews in Old Poland, 1000–1795,* edited by Antony Polonsky, Jakub Basista, and Andrzej Link-Lenczowski, 186–95. London, 1993.

———. "*Majufes:* A Window on Polish-Jewish Relations." *POLIN* 10 (1997): 273–86.

———. "Mashma'utah hahevratit shel hashehitah hahassidit." In id., *Hakri'ah lenavi: Mehkerei historiyah vesifrut,* edited by Israel Bartal, 33–63. Jerusalem, 1999. First published in *Zion* 20 (1955): 47–72.

———. *Sifrut Yidish bePolin.* Jerusalem, 1981.

Shmeruk, Chone, and Shmuel Ettinger. "Letoledot hayishuv hayehudi beKremenits." In *Bein Polin leRusiyah,* edited by S. Ettinger, 329–65. Jerusalem, 1994. Originally published in *Pinkas Kremenits,* edited by A. S. Stein, 9–45. Tel Aviv, 1954.

Shohet, Azriel. *Im hilufei tekufot: Reshit hahaskalah beyahadut Germaniyah.* Jerusalem, 1960.

Sinkoff, Nancy. "Benjamin Franklin in Jewish Eastern Europe: Cultural Appropriation in the Age of the Enlightenment." *Journal of the History of Ideas* 61 (2000): 133–52.

———. "Strategy and Ruse in the Haskalah of Mendel Lefin of Satanow." In *New Perspectives on the Haskalah,* edited by Shmuel Feiner and David Sorkin, 86–102. London, 2001.

Šinkūnaitė, Laima. *XVII a. Radvilų portretai.* Kaunas, 1993.

Slutsky, Yehuda. "Hatsa'ato shel hayehudi Ya'akov Hirsh lehakim beit sefer yehudi rashi beMohilev vesidur batei sefer aherim kedugmato beBelorusiyah (1783)." *He'avar* 19 (1972): 78–80.

Soloveitchik, Haym. "Piety, Pietism and German Pietism: *Sefer Hasidim I* and the Influence of *Hasidei Ashkenaz.*" *Jewish Quarterly Review* 92, nos. 3–4 (2002): 455–93.

Stampfer, Shaul. "The 1764 Census of Polish Jewry." In *Bar-Ilan: Annual of Bar-Ilan University,* Studies in Judaica and the Humanities 24–25 (1989): 41–147. Studies in the History and Culture of East European Jewry, edited by Gershon Bacon and Moshe Rosman.

———. "Lekorot mahloket hasakinim hamelutashot." In *Mehkerei hassiduth,* edited by Immanuel Etkes, David Assaf, and Yosef Dan, 197–210. Jerusalem Studies in Jewish Thought, 15. Jerusalem, 1999.

Stolberg, Michael. "Self-Pollution, Moral Reform, and the Venereal Trade: Notes on the Sources and Historical Context of *Onania* (1716)." *Journal of the History of Sexuality* 9 (2000): 37–61.

Stone, Daniel. *The Polish-Lithuanian State, 1386–1795.* Seattle, 2001.

Stone, Lawrence. *The Family, Sex and Marriage in England, 1500–1800.* London, 1979.

Stow, Kenneth R. *Catholic Thought and Papal Jewry Policy, 1555–1593.* New York, 1977.

Szulmiecki, M. "Zofiowka." *Rocznik Wolynski* 4 (1935): 137–56.

Ta-Shma, Israel M. "Children of Medieval Germany." *Studies in Medieval and Renaissance History* 12 (1991): 263–80.

———. "HaGR"A uva'al *Sha'agat aryeh,* ha*Penei yehoshu'a* vesefer *Tsiyun lenefesh hayah:* Letoledoteihem shel hazeramim hahadashim besafrut harabbanit erev tenu'at hahaskalah." *Sidra* 15 (1999): 181–91.

———. "Letoledot hayehudim bePolin bame'ot ha12–ha13." *Zion* 53 (1988): 347–69.

———. "On the History of the Jews in Twelfth–Thirteenth Century Poland." *POLIN* 10 (1997): 287–317.

———. "Yedi'ot hadashot letoledot hayehudim bePolin bame'ot ha12–ha13." *Zion* 54 (1989): 205–8.

Tazbir, Janusz. *Świat panów Pasków.* Łóź, 1986.

Teller, Adam. " 'Ha'aspaklariyah shel malkhut Polin' me'et Sebastian Miczyński— He'arot makdimot." In *Kroke—Kazimierz—Krakow: Mehkarim betoledot yehudei Krakow,* edited by Elchanan Reiner, 329–37. Tel Aviv, 2001.

———. "Hape'ilut hakalkalit shel hayehudim bePolin bemahatsit hasheniyah shel hame'ah ha17 uvame'ah ha18." In *Kiyum veshever,* edited by Israel Bartal and Israel Gutman, 209–24. Jerusalem, 1997.

———. "The Legal Status of the Jews on the Magnate Estates of Poland-Lithuania in the Eighteenth Century." *Gal-Ed* 15–16 (1997): 41–63.

———. "Masoret Sluck al reshit darko shel haBesht." In *Mehkerei hassiduth,* edited by Immanuel Etkes, David Assaf, and Yosef Dan, 15–38. Jerusalem Studies in Jewish Thought, 15. Jerusalem, 1999.

———. "Rabbis without a Function? On the Relations between the Polish Rabbinate and the Council of Four Lands." Typescript.

———. "Tafkidam hakalkali uma'amadam hahevrati shel hayehudim be'ahuzot beit Radziwiłł beLita bame'ah ha18." Ph.D. diss., Hebrew University, Jerusalem, 1997.

———. "Warunki życia i obyczajowość w żydowskiej dzielnicy Poznania w pierwszej połowie XVII wieku." In *Żydzi w Wielkopolsce na przestrzeni dziejów,* edited by J. Topolski and K. Modelski, 57–70. Poznan, 1999.

Teter, Magdalena Olimpia. "Jews in the Legislation and Teachings of the Catholic Church in Poland (1648–1772)." Ph.D. diss., Columbia University, 2000.

Tishby, Isaiah. "Hara'ayon hameshihi vehamegamot hameshihiyot bitsmihat hahassiduth." *Zion* 32 (1967): 1–45.

———. "Ikvot Rabbi Moshe Hayyim Luzzatto bemishnat hahassiduth." *Zion* 42–43 (1978): 201–34.

———. *Netivei emunah uminut: massot umehkarim besifrut hakabbalah vehashabbeta'ut.* 2d ed. Jerusalem, 1982.

———. *The Wisdom of the Zohar.* Translated by David Goldstein. 3 vols. Oxford, 1989.

Toharot hakodesh. Amsterdam, 1733.

Tollet, Daniel. *Accuser pour convertir: Du bon usage de l'accusation de crime rituel dans la Pologne catholique à l'époque moderne.* Paris, 2000.

———. "Le Goupillon, le prétoire et la plume: Stéfan Żuchowski et l'accusation de crimes rituels en Pologne à la fin du XVII siècle et au début du XVIII siècle." In *Żydzi wsród Chrześcian w dobie szlacheckiej Rzeczypospolitej*, edited by Waldemar Kowalski and Jadwiga Muszyńska, 207–20. Kielce, 1996.

Tomaszewski, Jerzy, ed. *Żydzi w obronie Rzeczypospolitej*. Warsaw, 1996.

Tomczak, A., ed. *Lustracja województw wielkopolskich i kujawskich 1789 r.* Pt. 3. Warsaw, 1977.

Topolski, Jerzy. *Gospodarka polska a europejska w XVI–XVIII wieku*. Poznan, 1977.

———. "On the Role of the Jews in the Urbanization of Poland in the Early Modern Period." In *The Jews in Poland*, edited by Andrzej K. Paluch, 45–50. Kraków, 1992.

———. "The Role of the Jews on the Polish Home Market in the Early Modern Period." Typescript.

———. "Uwagi o strukturze gospodarczo-społecznej Wielkopolski w XVIII wieku czyli dlaczego na jej terenie nie było żydowskich karczmarzy?" In *Żydzi w Wielkopolsce na przestrzeni dziejów*, edited by J. Topolski and K. Modelski, 71–82. Poznan, 1999.

———, ed. *Polska: Dzieje narodu, państwa i kultury*. Volume 2. Poznan, 1994.

Trachtenberg, Joshua. *Jewish Magic and Superstition: A Study in Folk Religion*. New York, 1939.

Trunk, Isaiah. *Shtudies in yidishe geshikhte in Poyln*. Buenos Aires, 1963.

Trzciński, Andrzej, and Marcin Wodziński. "Wystrój malarski synagogi w Pinczowie." *Studia Judaica: Biuletyn Polskiego Towarzystwa Studiów Żydowskich* 2 (1999): 87–102; 3 (2000): 91–98.

Tsfatman, Sarah. *Nissu'ei adam veshedah*. Jerusalem, 1988.

Turnau, I. "The Dress of the Polish Jews in the Seventeenth and Eighteenth Centuries." *Proceedings of the Tenth World Congress of Jewish Studies*, D2 (1990): 101–8.

Tzava'at Harivash. Edited and translated by Jacob I. Schochet. Brooklyn, 1998.

Vautrin, Hubert. *La Pologne du XVIIIe siècle vue par un précepteur français*. Edited by Maria Cholewo-Flandrin. Paris, 1966. Originally published as *L'Observateur en Pologne* (Paris, 1807).

Verete, Me'ir. "Hatsa'ot polaniyot lepitaron teritoriyali shel 'she'elat hayehudim,' 1788–1850." *Zion* 6 (1941): 148–55; 203–13.

Vidas, Elijah ben Moses de. *Reshit hokhmah*. Venice, 1593.

Vinograd, Yishayahu. *Thesaurus of the Hebrew Book*. 2 vols. Jerusalem, 1995.

Volumina legum: Przedruk zbioru praw staraniem XX. pijarów w Warszawie, od roku 1732 do roku [1793] wydanego. 10 vols. Warsaw, 1980. Cited as *VL*.

Ward, W. R. "Power and Piety: The Origins of Religious Revival in the Early Eighteenth Century." *Bulletin of the John Rylands Library of Manchester* 63 (1980): 231–52.

———. "The Relations of Enlightenment and Religious Revival in Central Europe and in the English-Speaking World." In *Reform and Reformation: England and the Continent c1500–c1750*, edited by Derek Baker, 281–305. Oxford, 1979.

Watrous, Stephen D., ed. *John Ledyard's Journey through Russia and Siberia: The Journal and Selected Letters*. Madison, Wis., 1966.

Węgrzynek, Hanna. "Deputacje Żydów polskich do Stolicy Apostolskiej w drugiej połowie XVIII wieku." *Kwartalnik historii Żydów* 3 (2001): 319–26.

Weigelt, Horst. "Interpretations of Pietism in the Research of Contemporary German Church Historians." *Church History* 39 (1970): 236–41.

Weinreich, Max. *Geshikhte fun der yidisher shprakh: Bagrifn, faktn, metodn*. 4 vols. New York, 1973.

———. *History of the Yiddish Language*. Translated by Shlomo Noble and J. Fishman. Chicago, 1980.

Weinryb, Bernard Dov. "Al yahasan shel hakehillot bePolin leva'alei-melakhah ulepo'alim." *Yedi'ot ha'arkheiyon vehamuze'on shel tenu'at ha'avodah* 3–4 (1938): 9–22.

———. *The Jews of Poland: A Social and Economic History of the Jewish Community in Poland from 1100 to 1800*. Philadelphia, 1973.

Werses, Shmu'el. "Rabbi Eliyahu Hakohen me'Izmir." *Yavneh* 2 (1940): 156–73.

Wertheim, Aaron. *Halakhot vehalikhot behassidut*. Jerusalem, 1960.

Widacka, Hanna. "Działalność Hirsza Leybowicza i innych rytowników na dworze nieświeskim Michała Kazimierza Radziwiłła 'Rybeńki' w świetle badań archiwalnych." *Biuletyn Historii Sztuki* 39 (1977): 62–72.

Wijaczka, Jacek. "Raport Ignacego Husarzewskiego o domach i placach żydowskich w Kozienicach z 1767 roku." *Studia Historyczne* 43 (2000): 503–12.

Wilensky, Mordekhai. "Hasidic-Mitnaggedic Polemics in the Jewish Communities of Eastern Europe: The Hostile Phase." In *Essential Papers on Hasidism*, edited by Gershon Hundert, 244–71. New York, 1991. Originally published in *Tolerance and Movements of Religious Dissent in Eastern Europe*, edited by Bela K. Kiraly, 89–113. Boulder, Colo., 1975.

———. *Hassidim umitnaggedim: Letoledot hapulmus beineihem*. 2 vols. 2d ed., Jerusalem, 1990.

Wirszyłło, K. S. "Stosunek duchowieństwo katolickiego na Wołyniu do Żydów XVIII wieku." *Miesięcznik Diecezjalny Łucki* 9 (1934): 18–25.

Wischnitzer, Mark. *A History of Jewish Crafts and Guilds*. New York, 1965.

Wischnitzer, Rachel. *The Architecture of the European Synagogue*. Philadelphia, 1964.

Wolfson, Elliot. *Circle in the Square: Studies in the Use of Gender in Kabbalistic Symbolism*. Albany, N.Y., 1995.

———. "Circumcision and the Divine Name: A Study in the Transmission of Esoteric Doctrine." *Jewish Quarterly Review* 78 (1987): 77–112.

———. "Hashpa'at Ha'Ari al haShelaH." In *Kabbalat ha'Ar'i*, edited by R. Elior and Y. Liebes, 428–29. Jerusalem Studies in Jewish Thought, 10. Jerusalem, 1992.

Wraxall, Nathaniel William. *Memoirs of the Courts of Berlin, Dresden, Warsaw and Vienna in the Years 1777, 1778, 1779*. 2 vols. London, 1800.

Ya'akov ben Moshe, *Minhat ya'akov solet*. Wilhermsdorf, 1731.

Ya'akov ben Yehezkel Segal. *Shem ya'akov*. Żółkiew, 1716.

Ya'akov Yisrael ben Tsevi Hirsh. *Sefer shevet miyisr'ael*. Żółkiew, 1772.

Ya'ari, Avraham. "Sereifat hatalmud beKamenets Podolsk." *Sinai* 42 (1958): 294–306.

———. "Shenei kuntrasim me'erets Yisra'el." *Kiryat sefer* 23 (1946–47): 140–59.

———. *Ta'alumat sefer: Sefer Hemdat yamim: Mi hibro umah haytah midat hashpa'ato*. Jerusalem, 1954.

Yakobson, Yoram. *Hasidic Thought.* Tel Aviv, 1998.

Yitshak ben Ben Zion. *Sefer Mikhlal yofi.* Frankfort a/O, 1775.

Yitshak Isaac ben Ya'akov. *Otsar hasefarim.* Vilna, 1877–80.

Ysander, Torsten. *Studien zum b'estschen Hasidismus in seiner religionsgeschichtlichen Sonderart.* Uppsala, 1933.

Zahorski, A. *Centralne instytucje policyjne w Polsce w dobie rozbiorów.* Warsaw, 1959.

Zamość, Israel [of]. *Netsah yisra'el.* Frankfurt a/O, 1741.

Zielińska, Teresa. "Kariera i upadek żydowskiego potentata w dobrach radziwił łowskich w XVIII wieku." *Kwartalnik Historyczny* 98 (1991): 33–49.

———. *Magnateria polska epoki saskiej.* Wrocław, 1977.

Zielińska, Zofia. *Walka "familii" o reforme Rzeczypospolitej, 1743–1752.* Warsaw, 1983.

Zienkowska, Krystyna. "Citizens or Inhabitants? The Attempt to Reform the Status of the Polish Jews during the Four Years' Sejm." *Acta Poloniae Historica* 76 (1997): 31–52.

———. "The Jews Have Killed a Tailor." *POLIN* 3 (1988): 78–101. Originally published as "Tumult w Warszawie w Maju 1790 roku," *Kwartalnik Historyczny* 95 (1988): 121–48.

———. "Reforms Relating to the Third Estate." In *Constitution and Reform in Eighteenth-Century Poland: The Constitution of 3 May 1791,* edited by Samuel Fiszman, 329–55. Bloomington, Ind., 1997.

———. *Sławetni i urodzeni: Ruch polityczny mieszczaństwa w dobie Sejmu Czteroletniego.* Warsaw, 1976.

———. "Spór o Nowa Jerozolime." *Kwartalnik Historyczny* 93 (1986): 351–76.

———. "W odpowiedzi profesorowi Arturowi Eisenbachowi." *Kwartalnik Historyczny* 95 (1988): 197–201.

Zimmer, Erich, ed. *Minhagim dek 'k Worms lerabbi Yuspa Shammes.* Jerusalem, 1988.

Zinberg, Israel. *Toledot sifrut yisra'el.* 7 vols. Tel Aviv, 1955–71.

Zuk, Anna. "A Mobile Class: The Subjective Element in the Social Perception of Jews: The Example of the Eighteenth Century." *POLIN* 2 (1987): 163–78.

Acknowledgments

An embarrassingly long time has elapsed since I first conceived of this book. During those many years I have accumulated a great many debts, and I have looked forward to thanking the people and institutions that have supported my work. My trips to Poland were made immeasurably more pleasurable by the kind hospitality of Barbara and Mikolaj Szymański, Konstanty and Małgorzata Gebert, Stanisław and Monika Krajewski, Alina Cała, Jerzy Tomaszewski, Joachim Russek and Michał Galas. I also want to thank Father Stanisław Musiał S.J., from whose courage I derive much strength.

I have shared various drafts and partial drafts with a number of very kind and wise colleagues and have benefited enormously from their advice, even when I did not necessarily follow it. I hereby acknowledge a great debt of gratitude to professors Daniel Stone, Adam Teller, Moshe Rosman, Jacob Goldberg, and Rhetta Dlin. Each of them offered profound and searching comments and questions that led to many changes in my thinking. Dr. Jaqueline Gutwirth has been extraordinarily generous in reading more than one version and subjecting each, line by line, to her incisive and limitless intelligence. None of these people is to be implicated in responsibility for my errors and mistakes.

My first reader for every draft was my wife, Ruth. Without her support, and her wise suggestions, completing this book would have been impossible.

I have had material support for my research at various stages from the Memorial Foundation for Jewish Culture, the Social Sciences and Humanities Research Council of Canada and from McGill University. Near the beginning of this project I spent a most stimulating and enjoyable period of months at the Institute for Advanced Studies in Jerusalem. I heartily thank the staff of the institute for their most cordial hospitality.

Work on this book took me to many archives and libraries and I found nothing in any of these institutions but cooperation and kindness. I should like to thank the directors and staffs of the Jewish National and Hebrew University Library and the Central Archives for the History of the Jewish People at Jerusalem. In Warsaw I found a kind reception at the Biblioteka Narodowa, the Library of Warsaw University and particularly its Department of Old Prints, at the Archiwum Główne Akt Dawnych and at the Jewish Historical Institute. I also want to acknowledge the cooperation of the National Museum of Poland in agreeing to grant permission for the reproduction of the painting that graces the cover of this book. In Kraków there was also unfailing courtesy on the part of the staffs of the State Archive, the Library of the Jagiellonian University, and the Czartoryski Library. In Kiev, I was very kindly received at the Vernadsky Library and at the Ukrainian State Archive. I should like to mention the consistent and enthusiastic help I benefited from at the library of the YIVO Institute in New York as well as at the library of my alma mater, Columbia University. The maps for this volume are based on maps drawn by Daniel Hackett of McGill University. For a year I also had the benefit of the enthusiastic assistance of a very promising graduate student in the Department of Jewish Studies at McGill, Dana Herman.

It is bittersweet to dedicate this book to the memory of my father, who taught me many things, especially the meaning of unconditional love.

Index

Text:	10/13 Galliard
Display:	Galliard
Compositor:	Integrated Composition Systems
Printer and binder:	Sheridan Books